The
Medieval
Woman

The Medieval Woman

Edith Ennen

Translated by Edmund Jephcott

Basil Blackwell

Copyright © C. H. Beck'sche Verlagsbuchhandlung
(Oscar Beck), München 1984
English translation copyright © Basil Blackwell 1989

First published 1989 by Basil Blackwell Ltd
108 Cowley Road, Oxford, OX4 1JF, UK

Basil Blackwell Inc.
3 Cambridge Center
Cambridge, Massachusetts 02142, USA

British Library Cataloguing in Publication Data
A CIP catalogue record for this book is available from the British Library.

Library of Congress Cataloging in Publication Data

Ennen, Edith.
The medieval woman.

Translation of: Frauen im Mittelalter.
Bibliography: p.
Includes index.
1. Women—History—Middle Ages, 500—1500.   2. Social
history—Medieval, 500—1500. I. Title.
HQ1143.E5513 1989   305.4'09'03   89—15072
ISBN 0—631—16166—X (U.S.)

Typeset in 11 on 12½ pt Baskerville by Setrite Typesetters Ltd, Hong Kong
Printed in Great Britain by T.J. Press (Padstow) Ltd, Padstow, Cornwall.

Contents

Introduction
The Middle Ages and Ourselves

Why do I introduce my subject by talking about ourselves? My intention is to forestall any judgement on women in the Middle Ages that is based too heavily on our present-day point of view. This is a mistake often made, distorting our picture of the past. Undoubtedly, we Europeans still have many links with the Middle Ages. Most of us live in towns founded in medieval times, and it is just those medieval features that we most admire. We are enchanted by a well-restored street in an old town in southern Germany or Lower Saxony, lined with half-timbered houses and adorned by wells. We marvel at the Arco Etrusco at Perugia in Umbria, a stone witness to an urban life extending back unbroken to Etruscan times, and gaze up in wonderment at the towers of San Gimignano in Tuscany. But none of us now is obliged to live in medieval conditions in a medieval house, and the old city centres so attractive to tourists are often deserted at nightfall. Not only would our high-rise blocks and the interior of our apartments, with their technological comforts, the convenience and speed of our transportation by land, sea and air, and our many effective remedies for pain and illness appear to a medieval person as satanic sorcery, but he or she would be helplessly confused by the contradictions of our life — the omnipresence and impotence of our state, the administrative constraints which prevent people in a town from crossing a street as they please, the looseness of customs and manners, and the predominance of science and specialization. These provide us with an abundance of practical devices and sources of light, heat and information, yet often we hardly understand their functions and are unable to repair them ourselves. Today, medieval people would feel like strangers even in the cathedrals built by their pious contemporaries, which outside the

1

hours of worship allow only a small space to those who pray, the
rest being given over to visitors whose curiosity clearly owes
nothing to the faith of pilgrims. They would feel lost in the hectic,
indifferent crowd in the streets, repelled by the unmistakable signs
of greed for power and money, envious ostentation and shallow
wordliness. They might envy and admire us — but they might
well abominate and pity us still more.

An historian cannot approach a past age with an attitude of this
kind. The historian's first aim is not to judge, but to understand.
We owe the term 'Middle Ages' to the Renaissance and the
Humanists; they coined it in relation to an identity of their own
which we do not share. To establish concretely what separates us
from the Middle Ages, and perhaps what still links us to them, we
cannot take the whole period of a thousand years between 500 and
1500 as our starting point, since far more divides us from its
archaic beginnings than from the fifteenth century, which we only
include in the Middle Ages with a question mark. We have grown
used to dividing this thousand-year period into three sections, the
early, the high and the late Middle Ages. I date the early period
500—1050, the high period 1050—1250 and the late period 1250—
1500. We must add at once that Italy had the Renaissance, but no
late Middle Ages. Time and place are the most important dimensions of history. Apart from the temporal location of a fact, an
institution or of cultural and economic conditions, their geo-
graphical connections must always be considered. We are aware
that all divisions into periods are an inadequate attempt to dissect
the unbroken stream of history restrospectively (leaving aside the
time lags, what I think of as the simultaneity of the unsimultaneous
that can be observed again and again), and that there are many
points at which the stream changes direction, accelerates or slows
its progress. There will never be complete agreement on which
watersheds between epochs are the most significant.

I

The collapse of the Roman Empire as an overarching political
order means the end of Antiquity as an historical period, but not
its destruction as a source of spiritual and intellectual impulses. In
addition, durably constructed cities, fortifications and palaces,
acquired skills and techniques, ingrained habits and customs, are

slow to be eradicated or altered. This makes it difficult to draw a temporal line between Antiquity and the early Middle Ages.[1] The historian of the sixth century, Gregory of Tours, though not himself a Frank, has given us a history of the Frankish realm which depicts the beginning of medieval history at least as regards France and Germany. The Merovingian Clovis, through energetic and ruthless policies, had made it a major kingdom and incorporated it into the Christian church by his baptism, in which he was followed by his Franks. He did not, like the first Germanic kings in the Mediterranean area, adopt the Arian faith. The German proportion of the population of Clovis's realm was greater than that of Italy, North Africa and Spain. Clovis's realm bordered the Germanic tribal area of the Saxons and Allemanni. But within it there was not only a substratum of Gallo-Roman population – increasingly broad towards the west – but also a small Gallo-Roman upper class, descended from the senatorial nobility of late-Roman Gaul. This group came from the region south of the Loire, on the Rhône and the lower Saône, an area which was to send out cultural impulses again and again to the north and east. Their common Christian faith united them with the leading members of the Franks, and marriage between Romans and Franks was permitted. Gregory of Tours was a member of the Gallic senatorial nobility; he was proud of his Roman descent and placed high value on education. But 'he considered past and present from a Christian standpoint . . . and felt at home in the Frankish realm. In him we can see how thin the threads connecting the old senatorial nobility with the Roman past had become by the end of the sixth century.[2] Thus the direct links with Antiquity slowly withered away,[3] while its spiritual and cultural heritage was preserved, often mediated by a Christianity whose adoption by the

---

[1] Naturally, I am unable to give an historical account of the Middle Ages here. I can only explain my way of dividing them into periods. My main wish is to provide the non-specialist reader with important information, concepts and literature relating to what comes later. On the early Middle Ages I recommend the *Handbuch der europäischen Geschichte*, edited by T. Schneider (1976). Other useful studies are: E. Zöllner, *Die Geschichte der Franken bis zur Mitte des 6. Jahrhunderts* (1970); J. Fleckenstein, *Grundlagen und Beginn der deutschen Geschichte* (1974); F. Prinz, *Grundlagen und Anfänge. Deutschland bis 1056*, (1985).

[2] K. F. Stroheker, *Germanentum und Spätantike* (1965), quotation in text is on p. 204.

[3] On this much-discussed issue cf. the recent study: H. von Petrikovits, *Der diachorische Aspekt der Kontinuität von der Spätantike zum frühen Mittelalter* (1982).

Franks was by our standards very superficial. What shocks us in
the Merovingians as violent and licentious can be explained by
the transitional situation in which they found themselves: they
were freed from earlier bonds, suddenly grown rich and masters of
an alien world, accustomed to relying on themselves, still un-
disciplined by state institutions and subject to a magical world-
view. In the sixth century the first monasteries in the Merovingian
realm were founded, centres of a deeper religiosity and of education.

The full breakthrough to the Middle Ages came about in the
Carolingian realm, in the eighth century. It is symptomatic that
the divine right of the Merovingian kings, and the supernatural
powers attributed to them and symbolized by their long hair, gave
way to election by the people, preceded in Pepin's case by an edict
from the pope, and anointment by the church. Anointment is the
clearest sign of the Christianization of a monarchy.

When the Frankish monarchy passed to the Carolingians the
political centre of gravity in Europe shifted to the north-west, to
the region between Maas, Moselle and Rhine. Charlemagne's
imperial status made the Frankish king the protector of Christendom.[4] His empire united present-day France, Belgium,
Luxembourg, the Netherlands, Germany as far as the Elbe,
Switzerland, upper Italy and a Spanish border march. Its great
size was also its weakness, so that only the powerful personality of
Charlemagne could it hold together. Its infrastructure − communications, economy, administrative organization − did not
match the demands of a major empire.

Equality among its members was unknown to early medieval
society. Neither in their rights nor before the law, nor in their
share of political responsibility, offices and honours, were people
equal, whether men or women. To legal inequality were added
sharp social distinctions. Admittedly, the barriers between social
strata were not insurmountable. Social mobility certainly existed,
as did changes in legal status. We must distinguish between the
legal affiliation of a person and his or her social position. Legal
questions were settled by German tribal laws, the *leges barbarorum*.[5]
We shall be concerned with them in detail. The normative element
for the *leges* is the free man, not the noble. But there were every-

---

[4]   W. Braunfels, ed., *Karl der Grosse*, vol. i; *Persönlichkeit und Geschichte*, ed. by
H. Beumann (1965).
[5]   R. Buchner, *Die Rechtsquellen* (1953); C. Schott, 'Der Stand der Leges-
Forschung' (1979).

where prominent families elevated by origin, influence and wealth; they also existed in the Merovingian kingdom alongside the senatorial nobility and the new nobility based on service to the king.[6] The most numerous class gradually came to be made up of unfree peasants. There were degrees of unfreedom; on the lowest rung were those who were the chattels of their lords, and so did not count as 'persons'. They differed only through their membership of the Christian community from the traded slaves, usually heathen prisoners of war, that we still come across in customs documents of the eleventh century. The Christian church never prohibited slavery in principle, although it recommended the liberation of slaves as a good work and its teaching contributed to the disappearance of slavery in central Europe and its replacement by the lesser form of serfdom. Bondsmen rose in the Middle Ages both as individuals — the king could bestow legal freedom on an unfree person by a symbolic legal ceremony — and as groups. This was matched, however, by the sinking of impoverished free persons into bondage, particularly unmarried women. Rise and fall were influenced by the development of property relationships.

Land was the only certain wealth, and here we should bear in mind the German concept of property. It allowed for a right of use distinct from ownership. This enabled the early medieval royal, noble and clerical owners of large demesnes, who could not fully exploit their enormous lands by themselves, to allot the right of use of small plots to some of their bondsmen. There, they and their families could support themselves while handing over part of their produce to the manor to which they were attached, and providing compulsory labour at the seasonal peaks. The great demesnes were decentralized, including a number of manors each with numeros bondsmen who, with their wives and children, had to be fed in winter when they could hardly be usefully employed. It was more economical to give some of these farmhands the chance of attaining self-sufficiency. This process was of the utmost economic importance; it brought into being a class of peasant farmers, though one in bondage.[7] How great was the share of

---

[6] F. Irsigler, *Untersuchungen zur Geschichte des frühfränkischen Adels*, 2nd ed. with supplement (1981).

[7] On questions relating to the agrarian economy cf. E. Ennen and W. Janssen, *Deutsche Agrargeschichte vom Neolithikum bis zur Schwelle des Industriezeitalters* (1979). On western Europe: G. Duby, *L'économie rurale et la vie des campagnes dans l'Occident médiéval* (1962). On the situation sketched above: A. Verhulst, 'La

labour performed by the maids at the manor and the peasants' wives will be shown in this study.

The economy of this time was predominantly seigneurial and agrarian. Ths lords owned land and people, whose labour the lord could use without compensation. The landowners strove for self-sufficiency, but could not achieve this completely. Local markets existed; rare but indispensable goods like salt, or luxury items, were obtained by long-distance trade. The landowners took part in this trade through bondsmen whom they sent on commercial journeys. There were also free merchants who travelled with their wares by land and sea under royal protection — a dangerous profession, from which women were excluded. Trade required money: Pepin and Charlemagne carried through a reform which standardized coinage (without lasting success), made silver the basis of currency (though gold coins still circulated in Italy) and finally revalued the *denar*. The *denar* (penny) was used for long-distance transactions; we are in the age of penny-currency. Among tradesmen free paid labour existed only in isolated cases; crafts were predominantly organized within demesnes. Great landlords owned factories for textile production; in them practically all the employees were women.

In considering the towns,[8] we must distinguish different regions. In Italy, despite some upheavals, urban life survived. In Gaul and the former Roman provinces on the Rhine and the Danube the old Roman towns fell more or less into decay. However, if they became bishops' sees or served secular lords they retained important functions and had a chance to flourish again. East of the Rhine and north of the Danube there were trading centres on the coast, and a wealth of pre-urban nuclear settlements at inland strongholds and markets. The early Middle Ages knew little of the state and almost nothing of bureaucracy, but the importance of house and family was correspondingly high. The realms of the age were kingdoms, the tribes had their dukes, the nobles and the clerical landowners were largely exempt from state power. Power at that time had to be exercised directly and personally. Hence the 'itinerant monarchy', the absence of a fixed royal residence, the migration from palace to palace. The king had his chancery,

---

diversité du régime domanial entre Loire et Rhin à l'époque carolingienne' (1983).
    [8] Cf. E. Ennen, *Die europäische Stadt des Mittelalters* (1987).

where clerics — for only they possessed writing skills — prepared his documents. These documents, the concern of a special historical discipline, diplomatics, were drawn up according to a strict pattern. A document always concerns a legal transaction, often a gift or grant of privilege; it sometimes results from pleas by intervenients, who also included women. With the cessation of the Carolingian capitularies, legislation grows sparse, and privileges sometimes take the place of laws. More widespread literacy survived in Italy.

The king had official representatives, the counts, who had wide powers as judges, administrators and military leaders. They were paid not in money but in land, receiving estates from which to exercise their functions and easily growing immune to central control, particularly as their offices became hereditary and gave their incumbents land and power of their own. They are not 'officials' in our sense of the word. In the Carolingian period the fief system came into being — it is a widespread and major misconception to confuse it with the manorial system, which is much older. In exchange for his service the vassal received from his lord an office (*beneficum, feudum*); lord and vassal owed each other loyalty, the lord 'grace' or 'favour' and the vassal 'counsel and succour'. Succour meant armed assistance, and the mounted armies of the Middle Ages, very small to begin with, were made up primarily of the vassals of a king or great lord. To be a vassal did not diminish one's status. 'Feudalism' in the strict sense means that the fief system had become fully established in a state, as was to happen in France but not to the same extent in Germany. The popular usage of the word today is overstretched and misleading. In the early Middle Ages vassals did not usually include women.

At that time the individual was protected by his relatives. Early legal historians spoke much of the German *Sippe* or clan, overestimating its importance. At that early stage kinship, as we see it today, held together the relatives on both the paternal and maternal sides. The relatives naturally had duties, including the duty to avenge the killing of one of their kin. In the early Middle Ages the individual operated in a self-helping manner that would be condemned today as lawless. But at that time the state monopoly of the legitimate use of violence did not exist. True, the *leges* prescribed financial compensation, the so called *weregeld*, which the perpetrator of a killing had to pay in atonement to relatives dutybound to bloody revenge, but pride often forbade 'carrying one's kin in one's purse', i.e. allowing one's revenge to be bought off. A murder could lead to protracted feuds which threw whole regions into turmoil. Gregory of Tours describes such a case very vividly (Bk VIII, ch. 47). The church, the king and his representatives, who received a share of the *weregeld*, had an interest in ensuring that it was paid. The feud, too, was a legal means by which the individual could assert his claims. It was only at the end of the Middle Ages that feuding was successfully suppressed. The state monopoly of legitimate violence is a major legal asset which benefits precisely the weaker members of the legal community, i.e. of the state. The individual's right of self-help brought much trouble and hardship on the people of the early Middle Ages.

The *Sippe* was also obliged to help its members by compurgation. This is another archaic institution that is entirely alien to us. In a medieval trial — up to the twelfth century and in some cases even later — the court was not primarily concerned with establishing facts. Evidence before the court was constituted by divine judgements (the judicial duel, trials by fire and water) and the oath of purgation. The accused person sometimes had to take this oath with 'compurgators'. They were not witnesses to deeds or innocence, but swore that the oath taken by the accused was pure and not perjured. In the view of the time, this could best be sworn by the kin. In these divine judgements the magical world view of the Germans continued to exert its influence. Only gradually did these ancient legal forms give way to trial by inquisition, aimed at clarifying the circumstances of the deed. (This has no direct connection with later church inquisitions.) These details may help to show how remote the legal system of the Middle Ages is from us.

The members of the *Sippe* were of equal rank, but within the household, which for the woman was undoubtedly the most important social entity, the master of the house held sway. The house enjoys a special peace. It is upheld by the master, who therefore exercises wide powers over its members, i.e. his wife, his sons before they come of age, his unmarried daughters and the servants. This power is called *Munt* (*mundiburdium*). As the enforcer of *Munt*, the master has to protect the members of the house, and represent them in court; he can also punish them or, in case of 'genuine need', sell them.

In the final phase of the Carolingian period Europe was threatened both by symptoms of internal decay and by external enemies: Normans, Hungarians, Saracens. The Saxon rulers expelled the

Hungarians from their realm, the French kings pacified the Normans, the Italian maritime cities — Venice, Pisa, Genoa — conquered the Saracens. The political movement towards the east carried forward by the kings and great lords began in the Carolingan period and was intensified by Otto I's policies towards the border marches and the churches of his empire. Under his grandson Poland achieved religious autonomy *vis-à-vis* the German empire, through the establishment of the archbishopric at Gniezno, and Hungary through the archbishopric at Esztergom. The Slavonic peoples now formed part of the Christian West previously dominated by Germanic and Roman elements. Otto I had restored the imperial status of the German kings. In 1033 the first Salian, Conrad II, had himself crowned king of Burgundy at Payerne, in the beautiful Romanic church of the sepulchre of Bertha, the mother of Adelheid, the second wife of Otto I. The wives of the Saxon and Salian German rulers are among the most outstanding women in history.

More enduringly than by political events, Europe's fate was shaped by a general undercurrent: the increase in population and the enlargement of the arable areas suitable for settlement. Europe's population had risen since the seventh century. A shift towards a warmer and drier climate between 750 and 1150 favoured this development. Chaunu writes:

The interaction of the Mediterranean with the barbarian border zones may have improved nutrition. The Germans had practised a migrant form of cultivation with long rotation periods; however, livestock-rearing and the additional use of fallow land probably yielded a more than minimal supply of animal protein. Moreover, at the boundary between the two cultural areas there began what has been called, perhaps too hastily, the technical revolution of the high Middle Ages.The heavy plough and deep ploughing, the saddle, the horseshoe and horse-collar, the exploitation of the horse in general — this all took place in the area between the Loire and the Rhine, starting in a few workshops at the end of the eighth century, and spreading from there throughout the Christian population, which became more and more numerous.[9]

The population increase was to continue until about 1300. According to the Domesday Book (commissioned by William the Conqueror in 1087 and containing statistical information on

[9] P. Chaunu, *Die verhütete Zukunft* (1981), quotation in text pp. 71f.

population, land ownership, livestock levels, tax revenues, etc.) the kingdom of England at that time had 1,100,000 inhabitants; in 1346 the figure was 3,700,000. The population increase was influenced by forest clearance and then by marsh drainage, by the intensification of agriculture, the introduction of cereals and technical advances.[10]

These great steps forward, due to immensely hard work by the farming population, were not enough, however, to banish hunger from Europe. Only the expansion of communications and the market economy could achieve this.

II

The positive results of the population increase and the opening-up of arable land, which could only have their full effect in the period here called the high Middle Ages (1050–1250), were the freedom of peasants to clear forests, greater prosperity among broad sections of the population, the formation of village communities, the resurgence of an urban market economy and the emergence of a middle class, a new, rising legal and social group between the rulers and the serfs. The population increase was not only enough to raise the number of rural settlements, to give rise to new market settlements and to fill the flourishing towns with migrants from the land; eventually peasant settlers from the west migrated to the more thinly populated Slavonic regions beyond the Elbe. This peasant movement towards the east began in the twelfth century, but was above all a feature of the thirteenth and fourteenth centuries. In the German empire the unfree vassals of the king and the great lords, the so called *ministeriales*, rose and attained their freedom; we find them among the urban patriciate or the landed lower nobility.

Greater freedom is therefore a prime political objective in this period. The peasants rebel against the landlords,[11] leave the demesnes and often obtain better conditions. The middle classes

---

[10]   Lynn White jr., *Medieval technology and social change* (1962).

[11]   L. Weinrich, *Quellen zur deutschen Verfassungs-, Wirtschafts- und Sozialgeschichte bis 1250* (1977), no. 19, pp. 70ff. contains capitularies against bondsmen's efforts to gain freedom.

want to free themselves from the burdens of old bondage and their subordinate position in municipal law. Their leading, wealthy groups rebel above all against the ecclesiastical urban rulers. In the twelfth century important new towns are founded: the Zähringians found Freiburg, Henry the Lion completes the foundation of Lübeck begun by the Schaumburgians. In the subsequent period foundations grow more and more frequent, and by 1300 the sites favoured by communications are occupied by towns. In Italy city states with their own territories come into being.

Women do not play any discernible active part in the struggle for better and freer conditions, but they profit from it.

This period is also filled, however, with a deep longing for peace. Peace is threatened by feuds among the nobility, the savagery of warlike vassals. The freedom movement comes into being in south-western France, where the central authority has been particularly weak and anarchy especially prevalent, in the last decades of the tenth century. It is above all a work of the bishops; it is given a new impulse by the *treuga Dei*, the peace of God, which prescribes a cessation of fighting during certain 'holy' periods, at Advent and Christmas, Lent and Easter, and from Friday to Sunday at other times. Such a peace was decreed by the archbishop of Cologne, Sigewin, in Cologne cathedral in 1083.[12] This marked the breakthrough of the movement in the German empire. The monarchy then became involved: the bishops' Peace of God became the king's Peace of the Land. In the thirteenth century the secular princes concluded peace treaties with the towns. These religious and secular treaties imposed heavy punishments, capital and corporal; murder now became a breach of the peace directed against the community and was avenged by it, not merely by the family of the victim.

Once the nobles had taken to living in castles, their feuds became protracted military operations. The towns, too, began to fortify themselves from the eleventh century on. A large fortified city like Cologne — the last extension of the city wall was carried out in 1179/80 — was practically impregnable to the contemporary armies of mounted men. Its relative security against outside attacks benefited the bourgeois economy; trade extended to northern and southern Europe, North Africa and Asia Minor; export

---

[12] Ibid., no. 36, pp. 140ff.

industries came into being while industries based on the demesnes declined, being unable to compete with the professional urban craftsmen. But internal peace did not always prevail in the cities. In Italy the nobility moved voluntarily or involuntarily to the towns, building their towers there, and families conducted their feuds within the towns from tower to tower. But the bishop of Worms, for example, also found himself constrained to impose heavy penalties for murder, since his vassals were 'almost daily' striking people dead in the most bestial way for absolutely no reason, while drunk or in exuberant spirits, the vassals of his own church alone accounting in the course of one year for 35 people[13] (so that the reference to 'almost daily' murders was somewhat exaggerated).

The church fostered peace, but also conducted a struggle for freedom no less significant than that of the bourgeoisie. The so-called 'investiture contest' (which will not be discussed in detail here) led to a severance of the spiritual office from its temporal trappings, and to reduced dominance by laymen of the church, a dominance exemplified by the appointment of bishops by the king. Latin Christendom distinguishes between church and state; the Roman church is not a state church like the Orthodox church separated from it in 1054, a distinction which has remained effective until today. The predominance of the nobility in the church, i.e. the appointment of members of the nobility to bishoprics and the prevalence of noble men and women in the monasteries and convents, begins to be eroded towards the end of this period. The life of religious orders is undergoing permanent reform:[14] Gorze, Cluny have just come into being. The religious unrest of the twelfth century, the desire, shared by many women, for a true imitation of Christ's poverty, leads to heresy and the foundation of new orders, first the Cistercians and Premonstratensians, finally the Franciscans and Dominicans. Christianity is now accepted inwardly as well. Monasteries, foundations and cathedral schools are centres of culture and learning — pre-eminently so for women. The importance of the church in the lives of all people at that

[13]   Ibid., no. 23, pp. 88ff; W. Altmann and E. Bernheim, *Ausgewählte Urkunden zur Erläuterung der Verfassungsgeschichte Deutschlands im Mittelalter* (1904), no. 74, p. 151 [30].
[14]   A short, penetrating survey: K. Elm, 'Die Stellung des Zisterzienserordens in der Geschichte des Ordenslebens' (1980).

time is scarcely imaginable today. In a purely external sense, the appearance of towns was dominated by the countless churches. The size of these buildings bore no relation to the number of inhabitants of towns, such utilitarian calculations being alien to people at that time. In an account of the city of Cologne as a work of art, a study which displays considerable historical empathy, Borger writes of the

landscape of soaring spires and towers rising emphatically above that of the emergent bourgeois houses. There can be no doubt that the churches were of primary importance for that age...It is striking that there were no buildings dedicated to pleasure or entertainment, not even a civic dance-hall, for which no need seems to have existed at that stage of the city's development. This fact indicates that the churches of the foundations and monasteries, like those of the parishes, also satisfied the desire for spectacle...festivities also being contained within the church framework.[15]

Let us picture the contrast between the urban dwellings, mostly modest wooden or half-timbered houses lit with a pine torch and equipped with simple utensils of wood or rough pottery, and the spacious interiors of the churches, illuminated by candles and fragrant with incense, with gold utensils and the shimmering gold robes of the priests! The church maintained schools, cared for the poor, the sick and aliens. It set the standards. A sinful king did not 'walk beneath the crown' if a confessor forbade it. The church kept the relics of the Lord, his mother, numerous saints and powerful interceding figures, to which the faithful made dangerous and laborious pilgrimages. We may smile at the belief in miracles of the age — it was nevertheless a reality.

Modern visitors to Rome are often surprised to see Marcus Aurelius sitting on horseback on the Capitol without stirrups, which were unknown to the Romans. The stirrup first appears in the West in archaeological finds dating from the eighth century; it is a precondition for knightly duels with heavy lances. Only stirrups could give the rider enough support to place the whole weight of man and horse behind the lance-thrust. Service on horseback was a duty of vassals. This kind of service required major expenditure; horses were costly; they needed fodder and might be killed in

[15]   H. Borger and F. G. Zehnder, *Köln. Die Stadt als Kunstwerk* (1982), quot. in text on p. 57.

action. The expensive war-horse was used only in battle, not on the march; the esquires looked after the additional horses and the baggage. The horseman needed expensive armour. The cost of the equipment was equivalent to that of 20 oxen. The elevation of the horseman to the 'knight' began in France, with its highly-developed fief system. Finally 'knight' became a general term[16] including the higher and lesser nobility and even dukes and kings. This did not, of course, mean a levelling of actual power relationships. But a normative idea of the knight had evolved which embraced them all, despite legal distinctions and social inequalities. In the emergence of this idea of the 'knight' which still persists in the meaning of the term today, the service-ethos of the vassal, the concepts of the religious order and of the *miles christianus*, played a part, as did the knight's service to women. The original savagery of these professional warriors was restrained by the peculiar knightly ethos, with honour as its central ideal, which included self-sacrifice alongside courage. This code was not without contradictions, and idea and reality often clashed. While chivalry has always appealed to lay interest, it has often been neglected by historians. But in recent years it has been more widely discussed; this has brought many controversial aspects to light, and shown that national variations of the notion of chivalry must be recognized. It has also become clear that only a narrow stratum of society enjoyed knightly status.

Chivalry included inaugural rites, knighting and tournaments. They were practised in Germany from 1127 onwards. They and the special knightly concept of love, or *Minne*, are often taken as the distinctive feature of the Hohenstaufen era.

Europe was catching up in the high Middle Ages: southern Italy and Sicily were no longer ruled by Byzantium and the Saracens but by the Normans; in 1194 the Hohenstaufen Henry VI was crowned king of the Sicilian-Norman empire in the cathedral at Palermo. In Spain the *reconquista* was advancing: in 1236 Cordoba was recaptured for the Christian West, in 1248 Seville. Pilgrimages were undertaken to distant places, to St Gilles in France, to Rome, to Santiago de Compostela and finally, as an armed crusade, to the Holy Land. The sincerity of the religious motive — in which the crusader's indulgence played a part — is not to be doubted, but there were also very worldly motives, a lust

[16] A. Borst, *Das Rittertum im Mittelalter* (1976).

for adventure and booty, a knightly class-ethos, as well as economic and social factors. Duby and Herlihy[17] have established these factors in the case of southern France and Italy: *frérèche*, the communal ownership of knightly allodial property by brothers, came into being in these areas. The community was wealthy enough to equip one or two mounted warriors, while the status of the family was preserved and the management of the estate was carried on by those who stayed behind. However, this procedure required strict discipline of the families and a fairly constant number of children, which was achieved by restricting marriages or by accommodating heirs more or less voluntarily in monasteries and charitable institutions. For example, in 1096, at the beginning of the First Crusade, the Mâconnais family of Les Hongre included five men, of whom two were monks and two went to Jerusalem and did not return. The brother who remained at home, Humbert, inherited the allodial property. In 1147 a grandson of Humbert's took part in the Second Crusade and left the inheritance to his brother. This is one of the reasons why the family was still wealthy at the start of the thirteenth century.

The consequences of the crusades have often been overestimated. The trade of Italian cities with the Orient had begun previously; the relations of Amalfi and Venice with Byzantium go back to the tenth century. However, thanks to their fleets the Italian maritime cities probably derived the chief material gain from the crusades. As regards the cultural fertilization of the Christian world by the Arabs — the use of Arabic numbers and the figure o began as late as the fifteenth century — Sicily and Spain were doubtless more important.

III

By taking 1250 as the starting point of the late Middle Ages I have placed the division rather early, using an important date in political history — the collapse of the Hohenstaufens — as the boundary-stone. There is no doubt that their end marked a caesura in the whole of European history. Some historians prefer 1350, the time of the Black Death. But the downturn in the population

---

[17] G. Duby, *La société aux XIe et XIIe siècles dans la région mâconnaise* (1953); D. Herlihy, '*The agrarian revolution in southern France and Italy*' (1958).

curve — which was indeed the epoch-making event of the late
Middle Ages — had begun earlier. Given the high death-rate in
medieval times a slight reduction in births was sufficient. As early
as 1312—17 central Europe was affected by a major epidemic,
which was connected to a famine but was not a plague. Florence
is an extreme example of the loss of population caused by the
plague: the city lost between 60.2 and 69 per cent of its population
between 1338 and 1426. Before the Black Death Florence was the
third most populous Italian city after Venice and Milan; in 1550
it was seventh. The general mortality rate during the plague is
likely to have been about 30 per cent. After the epidemics, the
gaps in the towns, which had been hardest hit by the plague, were
often filled by an increased birthrate and an influx from the
countryside. However, the country did not now send surplus
population to the town but gave up its own substance. Rural
settlements were abandoned, deserted villages becoming a European phenomenon, though with temporal and regional variations.
The high number of victims claimed by plague in the towns was a
result of the density of population inside the fortifications, and of
poor hygiene. The plague is known to have begun as a rodent
epidemic, transmitted from rats to humans by fleas. The confrontation with the violent death inflicted by the disease, and with
mass mortality in their immediate environment, affected people
deeply. They were tormented by fear of death and Hell. The art of
dying, the *ars moriendi*, became a special genre of devotional literature; dances of death became a frequent spectacle, and suffering is
depicted in religious art with harrowing realism. Religious emotion
sought the salvation offered by the church. But the threat of the
plague also aroused a love, even a lust, for life — these phenomena
will be studied in detail.

The late Middle Ages are revealed as a period of contradictions:
secularization, a trend towards luxury and hedonism — but also a
great piety which is itself contradictory: on one hand it is inclined
to mass manifestations, with the largest possible number of Mass
foundations, processions, pilgrimages and all but hysterical
emotion, and on the other it tends towards inwardness and simplicity. The urban economy is fully developed. We can now identify
at least the basic facts about urban population figures. To be sure,
we normally have only isolated data at our disposal, not coherent
statistics. Written records do not generally provide us with
numbers of inhabitants, but only lists of houses or households

drawn up for tax or similar purposes. The figures quoted in the literature are arrived at by estimating the size of households, the accuracy often being open to doubt. For central Europe we count towns with over 10,000 inhabitants as cities, and towns with less than 2,000 inhabitants as small provincial towns. In forming a judgement on urban life it is very important to bear these figures in mind. The numbers of inhabitants were higher in Italy. Milan is likely to have had about 100,000 inhabitants in 300, Naples 50,000, Palermo 44,000; in the fifteenth century Genoa had 84,000 people within its walls, twice as many as Cologne. The proportion of town dwellers in the total population was about 20 to 25 per cent, but there were densely populated areas like northern Italy or southern Holland with a much higher proportion, and other regions with a much lower one.

In the cities important export trades now develop, particularly in the textile sector. While the individual craftsman is still the normal economic unit in manufacture, the products of manufacture are brought together by distributors for export. There are already − particularly in the fifteenth century − some larger factories, in the metal industries above all, and there are entrepreneurial profits to be made in mining and foundries.[18] Large fortunes are amassed and, in general, differences of wealth increase. There is considerable expansion and unification of markets. There is competition for markets, communities based on old trades falling into poverty and new ones taking their place. The urban economy operates on money and credit. The Jews are now by no means the only money-lenders. They are forced into the pawnbroking business, and after the great persecutions of Jews in the fifteenth century they are even expelled from some cities. In monetary and banking affairs the Italians play the leading role. Italy reintroduced the systematic production of gold coinage in the thirteenth century: Genoese pounds, Venetian ducats, Florentine guilders; the latter circulate in central Europe and stimulate domestic gold coin production. The city merchant operates with bills of exchange; he has a writing-chamber in his house, keeps books, visits the great fairs, but also has agents at important trade centres. He has rationalized his business. The artisans in trades organized by guilds, and the

---

[18] On the fifteenth century and its peculiarities which anticipate the early modern period cf. E. Meuthen. *Das 15. Jahrhundert* (1980).

maids in the household are free wage-earners. The part played by women in urban economic life is large and many-sided.

Unearned income exists now only for the landed gentry. But here too entrepreneurial landowners begin to trade in natural produce. The corn trade conquers large expanses in the fifteenth century; it can compensate for bad harvests in one region and supply areas based on craft industries with grain. In the countryside the landscape is shaped by trades. The rural smallholders and cottagers cannot exist without a secondary craft. Specialized crops take on major importance: viniculture is most extensively developed in central Europe, and dye-producing plants — woad for blue and madder for red — become typical of whole regions. For the majority of people, agricultural land remains the basis of their economic existence. For the merchant land is a secure investment. Even the artisan keeps cattle in the town, where he has his garden and perhaps a field outside the walls as well. Within the city there are still plots used for agriculture.

The European agricultural landscapes drift further and further apart. The somewhat controversial thesis of a late-medieval agricultural crisis goes back to Abel.[19] He attributes a key function to prices, arguing that a price-scissors operates between the low revenues from the grain and the rising prices of manufactured goods. His methodological innovation lies in the tracing of statistically-based booms and slumps. He is aware that these processes were also influenced by other factors, above all the general state of agriculture. Pitz emphasizes the profound structural change in late medieval agriculture by which it 'took on the forms of the market-integrated individual concern.' A divergence in the development of agriculture in East and West begins to show itself. While the seigneurial system of agriculture declined in western and southern Germany, being replaced in many areas by a tenancy system and giving rise to a class of free and prosperous leaseholders in north-west Europe, in the East large new estates were formed. These, however, were not based on the system of feudal bonds between peasants and lords, the origins of which we observed in the Carolingian period, but were market-orientated businesses based on the compulsory labour of a hereditarily subjugated rural

---

[19]   Abel, W., *Geschichte der deutschen Landwirtschaft vom frühen Mittelalter bis zum 19. Jahrhundert* (1978); cf. my discussion of this subject in Ennen and Janssen, *Deutsche Agrargeschichte*, pp. 189 and 194ff.

population. Here a new servitude came into being. A factor stimulating this development was the eastern-European grain trade, in which the nobility had become increasingly involved from the late fifteenth century. However, only the first stages of this ill-omened development, which annihilated the free peasantry in Mecklenburg, for example, took place in the Middle Ages.

Very different developments can be observed in the Mediterranean area. In Tuscany the urban landowners transformed the landscape.[20] Here the *mezzadria*, the private share-tenancy, became the classical form of ownership. There was an extensive fragmentation of village settlements. The urban owners rounded off their estates and placed a new farmhouse at their centre; in it they could spend the period of summer heat and pestilence. Grain production was reduced in favour of vineyards, olive trees and other plantations requiring substantial investment. The vines climbed from olive tree to olive tree, and the wheat grew underneath. Naturally, strong sunlight was needed for this mixed crop. It also led to a favourable distribution of work throughout the year, which was important for the family businesses of the farmers – the *contadini* with whom we shall become acquainted in detail. By contrast, a highly extensive form of agriculture developed in Spain, the rearing of merino sheep, whose wool was in high demand in the textile industries of Flanders, England and Florence. Huge flocks of sheep wandered across Spain, grazing on the green plains in winter and finding good pasture in the mountains in summer. In England, too, there was a strong incentive to convert arable land into sheep pasture. In the fifteenth century the enclosures began to bring about a restructuring of property and consequent social changes, with sheep-owners rising as other groups of farmers declined.

Not surprisingly, this was a time of social unrest: peasant revolts in England at the end of the fourteenth century, in Germany in the fifteenth; disorder in the cities.[21] The real leaders of the urban uprisings are to be found in the new middle classes, who are opposed not so much to the city rulers as to the exclusiveness of

---

[20] F. Dörrenhaus, *Wo der Norden dem Süden begegnet: Südtirol. Ein geographischer Vergleich* (1959); and, *Urbanität und gentile Lebensform* (1971).
[21] M. Mollat and P. Wolff, *Ongles bleus. Jacques et Ciompi. Les révolutions populaires en Europe aux XIVe et XVe s.* (1967); W. Ehrecht, *Städtische Führungsgruppen und Gemeinde in der werdenden Neuzeit* (1980).

the patriciate. 'The late medieval social and political unrest was
not to do with class struggle or conflict between the estates. It was
always about complex social groups rising against the town councils or the system of government', writes Maschke, who has given
the most valid account of the social structure of late-medieval
German cities.[22] The women played a dependent role in these
urban social classes and groups. We shall try to provide statistical
information on their dependence where possible. We shall be
concerned with the way women lived, how they dressed − a
matter on which the town councils had their say − what kind of
houses they lived in, what implements they used.

In culture, a trend towards secularization is unmistakable. The
clergy no longer have a monopoly of education. More and more
lay people − including married burgher women, not just nuns −
can now read, write, add up; calculations are done with counters,
education covers a broader field, the density of schooling in-
creases.[23] In some places the city councils gain influence over the
Latin schools set up by the parish churches. Universities − confined to Italy, France and England before 1300 − now spread to
central Europe: Prague (1348), Heidelberg, Cologne, Erfurt,
Leipzig, Cracow. More burghers' sons go to university. More
trained lawyers are needed by the landowners and the cities.

Another basic trend is the increasing rationality of everyday
behaviour; this is characteristic of the professional make-up of the
merchant of this time, as we have pointed out.

Opposing this is mysticism, in the special form it took in the
devotio moderna, the religious revival that set in at the end of the
fourteenth century. It started in the Netherlands and took hold
particularly in north and central Germany. In terms of organizations, this 'temperate spirituality' (Meuthen) took forms such as
the association of Fraterherren, Brothers of the Common Life, or the
congregation of prebendaries under the monastery of Windesheim
near Zwolle. The Brothers gained a major influence on education,
being in charge of schools and, above all, students hostels. For
school pupils moved about in the Middle Ages; in the Brothers'

---

[22]   E. Maschke, Städte und Menschen. Beiträge zur Geschichte der Stadt, der Wirtschaft
und Gesellschaft 1959−77 (1980), quot. in text on p. 371.
[23]   W. Hess, 'Rechnung Legen auf Linien. Rechenbrett und Zahltisch in der
Verwaltungspraxis in Spätmittelalter und Neuzeit' (1977).

college at Emmerich on the Lower Rhine, for example, we find a number of sons of Cologne burghers. Also in the Lower Rhine area, as in Alsace, grammar schools are set up in the pre-Reformation period. In them, the ancient authors are read and Greek is studied.

The *devotio moderna* was a reform movement inspired partly by the obvious abuses in church life; the exploitation of church revenues, the accumulation of livings, the educational backwardness of the lower clergy and the wordliness of the clergy as a whole. The need for reform was generally recognized. As in the eleventh and twelfth centuries, it is the religious orders who set about the reforms in earnest, from the Benedictines, who create reform centres such as the Bursfeld Congregation in north Germany, through the mendicant orders who tighten their practices, to the new orders which are founded. There are also associations of lay people. The religious unrest takes a strong hold on women, as we shall see in more detail later. This late medieval period, marked by secularization, rationality, comfort, lust for life, and also by mysticism, a piety that is partly inward but partly very external — this pluralistic age is closer to us than the archaic era which preceded the turn of the tenth century.

What a German town looked like at that time — a compact silhouette bounded by walls and gate-towers, with its late Gothic hall-churches, its town hall, its timbered burgher houses — we can still see in Einbeck or Celle, Oberehnheim or Murten. And the painters of the time have left us pictures of their towns, even if they are only the background to a Nativity or an Adoration of the Magi.

But Italy had the Renaissance. This term, somewhat threadbare from over-use, is employed here to denote an epoch. The Italian Renaissance started in the fourteenth century. From the first, social development in Italy differed from that beyond the Alps by the fact that the nobility lived in the towns, which was the case throughout the Mediterranean area. In Italy, which held a mediating position between Byzantium, the Orient and Europe, the town-dwelling nobility became involved in commerce, abolishing the barrier between the rich merchant and the urban nobleman. The Italian cities built up a colonial empire extending from the Greek islands to the Black Sea. The many city republics, all constantly making war on each other, grew into large states still organized on civic principles: Venice, Milan, Genoa, Florence.

Venice remained an aristocratic republic, while other city communes were transformed into *signorie*. I subscribe to Sestan's account of how this came about.[24] Elected by the communes, the Renaissance princes (*signori*) had unlimited power, but a power unconsecrated by religion. These urban, secularized states, with their open societies, fostered an ideal of life based on individual achievement that was to shape the whole person, and an ideal of new general education based on Antiquity, which deliberately turned its back on the dark era between Antiquity and what was seen as the new epoch of the present. There was an attempt to sweep away the pressures towards a corporate kind of existence, that had been present in the Middle Ages, in favour of individual development. The Renaissance meant a new sense of life; how this manifested itself in the state and diplomacy, in art and social life, cannot be discussed in detail here. The concept of Humanism bound up with that of the Renaissance is more narrowly defined: it means, above all, a return to the classical authors and the incorporation of Greek into education at school and at the academies. Humanism only made its decisive breakthrough in central Europe in the second half of the fifteenth century. 'A very large field of enquiry is opened when we pose the question of the reception of the Italian Renaissance in Europe,' writes Meuthen. France probably took the lead.

The people of the fifteenth century sailed to new shores. The age of discovery began. Genoese, Portuguese and Spaniards opened up the New World. Antwerp on the Schelde became, about 1500, the centre of exchange for the products of south German industry with the spices, fruits, and sugar from the newly-discovered regions. Spain's and Portugal's lack of commercial infrastructure denied them the full profit from their colonies. The Spaniards still used the late-Gothic hall form for their oldest churches on the Canary Isles — in the church at Telde on Gran Canaria a carved altar from Antwerp is still to be found today. As their return freight to Madeira, which at that time supplied the whole of Europe with sugar, the Portuguese took Flemish paintings, which can still be admired in the museum in Funchal. But we should not forget technology: the beginnings of artillery, the developments in machine construction, in clockmaking — a reminder that time was now

---

[24] E. Sestan, 'Die Anfänge der städtischen Signorien: ein erschöpfend behandeltes europäisches Problem?' (1978).

becoming precious – and printing. By 1500 there were an estimated 27,000 titles of early printed books (*incunabula*) and about 260 printing centres, with 151 presses in Venice alone. There is no need to elaborate on what this invention meant for intellectual life, for information and communications.

On the method adopted in this study, I should say that while it cannot, naturally, avoid the critical assimilation of results of well-founded research on our theme, it does also go directly to the sources. Extensive quotation from sources seems unavoidable, since one cannot expect the interested non-specialist to look them up. Above all, it seems important to me to establish lines of development and not to make do with disconnected statements. And I believe it to be an indispensable methodological requirement – though one often neglected in dealing with this subject – that the evidence should be ordered and interpreted in terms of its location in time and place. This is especially important in a study of the Middle Ages. Medieval Europe has sharp cultural divisions, pronounced centres of innovation and backwardness; there is enormous legal fragmentation; economic areas often entirely fail to coincide with political domains or states, and no major city, even when allocated to a particular economic area and type, is without its individual features. Only case studies on the situation of women in a particular city, in a rural domain, etc., can give a true picture. For the specialist in the narrow sense of the term it may be enough to refer to the literature, but for the general reader a sketch has to be drawn, while avoiding unjustified generalizations. Precisely because women had less direct influence on their environment and their fate than men, it is essential to discuss their changing legal situation, their social position, their everyday economic context, in terms of temporal change and regional differences. The analysis of constitutional factors, of economic life and the social structure, is supplemented by data from personal histories and brief biographies. Only they can reflect the whole reality, which cannot be encompassed solely by a study of laws or statistical averages.

1

The Early Middle Ages 500–1050

WOMEN'S POSITION IN THE GERMANIC TRIBES

The Germans of the period of the *Völkerwanderung* who concern us in this chapter are not the Germans of Tacitus.[1] Our knowledge of the Germans of Tacitus's time, the first century AD, is very fragmentary. Where the written sources cannot be verified from archaeological evidence – on matters of law and social conditions – much is unclear and contentious. The Germans of the first centuries after Christ were organized in tribes. The smallest but most important unit was the 'whole house', ruled by its individual master. Land-ownership now begins to be the basis of government, with a small ruling class and many freemen and slaves. The agrarian economy is supplemented by trade and crafts. Apart from archaeological evidence there are accounts by ancient writers and epigraphic material.[2] The detailed account in Tacitus's *Germania*, which paints a very favourable picture of German women, must be read critically. For one thing, Tacitus wanted to hold up a mirror to the metropolitan society of Rome to show it the decay of its ancestral values; for another, his work is part of an historiographic and ethnographic tradition, which deprives his statements of a good deal of their factual value. He often reproduces a general classical typology of the barbarian without correcting it from his own observations. His poetic intuition sketches an idealized picture of the German woman, which reaches its peak in the famous sentence 'inesse quin etiam sanctum aliquid et providum putant'

---

[1] R. von Uslar, *Die Germanen vom 1. bis 4. Jahrhundert nach Christus* (1980).

[2] R. Bruder, *Die germanische Frau im Lichte der Runeninschriften und der antiken Historiographie* (1974).

(the Germans believe that women possess holy and visionary powers). In his *Historiae*, Tacitus tells of the wise prophetess Veleda. She came from the tribe of the Bructerii and played a part in the rising (AD 69) in the Lower Rhine region led by the noble Batavian Julius Civilis, which her tribe joined. The Roman leader Cerialis, a kinsman of the Emperor Vespasian, brought the collapsing rebellion to an end by diplomatic means. He negotiated with Veleda, who had prophesied a favourable outcome for her countrymen in the war against the Romans. Did he believe she could be manipulated? Undoubtedly she wielded political influence.

When, in Tacitus's *Historiae*, the Batavians declare at the end of the war that they would rather live under the Romans than suffer the dominion of women, this does not accord with the exalted picture of the prophetess Veleda painted in the *Germania*. Strabo tells us that German priestesses of an earlier time, Cimbrian women, sacrificed prisoners of war to the gods and prophesied victory for their own side from the victims' blood and entrails. It can therefore be taken as fairly certain that the Germans believed women had magic powers. German women did not take a direct part in battles; they stayed behind the barricade of wagons, from where they must have spurred the men on and in dire need helped them. As prisoners and slaves they bore their fate with dignity and honour. The German expected absolute moral purity from his wives and daughters. He left the running of the household to the women, as well as the work in the fields with the slaves. As in all Indo-Germanic peoples, the family structure was entirely patriarchal.

In the Roman Empire the legal position of women was much better. The Roman *materfamilias* had always been a respected figure. After Augustus, the woman became a completely autonomous legal person: sexual guardianship lapsed after the father's death; his rights no longer passed to another male relative. However, the senate's resolution of AD 76, the *vallejanum* that was often quoted later and survived throughout the Middle Ages, deprived women of the ability to stand security for others, which placed a limitation on their role in commercial life. The *dos* of Roman law is different to that of the Germanic *leges*. In Roman law the *dos* is the bride's dowry; the Germanic *dos* corresponds to the Roman *donatio ante nuptias* — a gift from the bridegroom to his bride before the wedding. Both laws have in common that the *dos* is a hallmark of legitimate marriage, as opposed to concubinage.

In classical Roman law the *dos* has the social function of benefiting the wife. The Justinian concept of *dos* left the husband with only a formal right over the wife's property.[3] After Justinian, the wife had the right to deny the husband access to the *dos* if he was squandering it. However, the patriarchal structure was preserved even in Rome, and the children belonged solely to the father.

It is obvious that the great migrations of peoples, the clash with Rome and the foundation of Germanic empires on former Roman territory, brought profound changes in the material life and social structure of the Germanic tribes. Social distinctions were accentuated, and the number of slaves increased considerably. In many ways the Germans proved willing pupils of the far more civilized Romans. Roman and Christian ideas found their way into the Germans' legal thinking. The Germanic tribal rights, the *leges*,[4] present many textual problems. The law embodied in them is by no means a primordial Germanic law. It is influenced by the Roman vulgar law that operated in the western Roman Empire and must be distinguished from the eastern Roman *corpus iuris* of Justinian, and by Christian ideas, although in very diverse ways. The vulgar Roman influence is especially strong in the lawmaking of the Germans who settled in those regions of the former empire which still had a large Roman element in their populations: the Goths and Burgundians, to a lesser extent the Langobards, and the Salian Franks. These *leges* are the oldest body of Germanic law, dating from the end of the fifth to the seventh century. A second group is formed by the *leges* that came into being under Frankish rule, in regions populated predominantly or solely by Germans. This includes the Ripuarian Franks in the Rhineland in the seventh and eighth centuries, the Alemannians dependent on the Franks (*Pactus Alemannorum*), and the *leges* of the Bavarians and Alemannians from the first half of the eighth century.

The *lex* of the Bavarians comes into force in 748; in it Christian notions are very prominent. Finally, the laws of the Saxons, Thuringians and Frisians were set down in the early ninth century

---

[3]   H. J. Wolff, 'Zur Stellung der Frau im klassischen römischen Dotalrecht' (1933).
[4]   This type of source is best referred to as *leges*, being written in Latin. Cf. Buchner, *Die Rechtsquellen*; K. Kroeschell, *Deutsche Rechtsgeschichte* (1972/3); Schott, 'Der Stand der Leges-Forschung'; H. Nehlsen, *Sklavenrecht zwischen Antike und Mittelalter*. (1972).

at the command of Charlemagne. These distinctions and timelags must be kept in mind.

The content of the laws includes catalogues of penalties for crimes against property and life — limits were set to self-administered justice, or blood revenge — tribal laws, marriage laws and the law of inheritance, which is particularly important in agrarian societies. In the latter, the overriding Germanic principle was that heirs were born and not chosen. A main exception was formed by gifts to the church. I can point here to the need, although I cannot fulfill it, for an exhaustive critical analysis, taking account of current research, of all the passages dealing with women in these laws.

From what I have said about the household in the early Middle Ages, it is only to be expected that the family was organized on strictly patriarchal lines. Of course, women were not entirely without rights. But they were incapable of taking legal action, they could not appear independently before a court or manage their own wealth, and they were at a disadvantage in the law of succession. Extreme chastity was demanded of girls and absolute fidelity of wives — towards men, the law was more lenient. Rape of a woman was severely punished, but there were also penalties for baring her head, pulling her hair or offending her modesty. Divorce was treated very unequally. A woman was subject to the guardianship of her father or nearest male relative — which gave the guardian the right to give her in marriage — and after marriage she was likewise subject to her husband or his kin. One of the disadvantages suffered by a woman was that in the course of her lifetime she belonged to at least two families — her parents' and husband's — although she belonged to neither as completely as a man belonged to his family of birth. The more agnatic the family structure becomes, the more keenly this is felt by women. In peasant communities the difficult position of the daughter-in-law has persisted to our day.

According to Germanic law, a marriage was agreed between the woman's guardian and her future husband. The marriage gift, the *dos*, was given by the bridegroom. This endowment was a normal part of the Germanic marriage. Although the woman was largely the object, it would be misleading to speak of a marriage by purchase. The woman is fully respected as a person; the *dos* was not a purchase price but signified a transfer of the family's legal rights over the woman.[5] Wührer, in his study of early Swedish law, stresses that in that law marriage was not a contract about objects but an agreement between two families relating to persons.[6] Nor did the Germanic form of marriage evolve from marriage by capture. The concept of wife-capture presupposes contractual marriage as the regular form which it violates. A decree by the Merovingian king Childebert II threatens such abduction with death.

In the Germanic *Muntehe*, the marriage based on the *mundium* or guardianship, two acts stand out, the betrothal (*desponsatio*) and the wedding (*traditio puellae*).[7] The betrothal took the form of a legal agreement in which the bridegroom paid at least a part of the marriage gift or *Muntschatz* in advance, and obliged the guardian to transfer to him both the girl and the right of guardianship (*Muntgewalt*). If the bridegroom withdrew from the engagement, he was liable to a penalty . The betrothal demanded fidelity from the bride toward her betrothed; a breach of fidelity by sexual intercourse with another man was a capital offence in Langobard law. The wedding, the handing over of the bride by her guardian (*Muntwalt*), took place among the kin, and was celebrated by a banquet. By a number of formal actions of knee, foot and hand, the bridegroom made manifest his acquisition of tutelage over the bride. This was followed by the leading of the bride to the husband's house in a solemn procession, and finally the entering of the marriage bed in the presence of witnesses. After the wedding night the bride received from her husband the morning gift designating her a legitimate wife. In this way the marriage contract was agreed between the guardian and the bridegroom. Apart from the full marriage, the *Muntehe* with the marriage gift, marriage by abduction was also recognized, if the abduction took place with the girl's agreement; however, this form had legal disadvantages. There was also an unendowed form of marriage, the *Friedelehe*, which did not involve the transfer of *Munt*. But whether this form ever had the same standing as the endowed *Muntehe*, or whether there was a dual standard of Germanic marriages, is doubtful.[8]

[5] R. Köstler, 'Raub-, Kauf- und Friedelehe bei den Germanen' (1943), p. 120, though with some misinterpretations; P. Mikat, *Dotierte Ehe — rechte Ehe.* (1978), contains a survey of the literature.
[6] K. Wührer, 'Zum altschwedischen Eherecht' (1957), pp. 213ff.
[7] H. Conrad, *Deutsche Rechtsgeschichte* (1962), pp. 153ff.
[8] H. Meyer, 'Ehe und Eheauffassung der Germanen' (1940); and, 'Friedelehe

The *Friedelehe* was based on the partners' free choice; here the marriage bond was formed by the groom publicly leading the bride home and entering the bed, and the *dos* was replaced by a morning gift to the wife after the wedding night, which was additional to the *dos* in the *Muntehe*. Among the nobility the unendowed form of marriage often served to prevent a wife of lower standing and her children from gaining accesss to the estate and family of her husband. The 'morganatic' marriage that still occurs in princely families in our time goes back to the *Friedelehe*, but cannot be equated with it. As an alternative to traditional marriage it was a privilege of the high nobility, but was a valid form of marriage even in the religious sense. The *Friedelehe* did not confer a common social status on the spouses. In Leon and Castile the *dos* was called the *arras* (plural), a peculiarity of Spain, with a prehistory that has been described by Ritzer among others. At the time of the Spanish *reconquista*, the *barragania* was a quasi-marital arrangement not unlike the *Friedelehe*. The marriage of the clergy, which incurred no censure in the Arian church, was tolerated only as a secret *barragania* in the Spanish *fueros*, or municipal charters.[9] West Gothic law explicitly ordained the equality of rights between daughters and sons in the event of intestate inheritance; Kroeschell suspects the influence of Roman law in this.

I should like to support these general comments on early marriage forms with quotations from tribal law. It is striking to us today that the tribal divisions — into freemen, those less free, and slaves — are always mentioned in the laws. Let us start with the laws of the Burgundians who settled in the Rhône area in the 'twilight between late Antiquity and the earliest Germanic period'.[10] These laws mostly go back to the Burgundian king Gundobad and were made before 501. Inheritance is so arranged that if there is no son the daughter becomes the heir to the father and mother. If there are one or two brothers, virgin daughters consecrated to God receive a third of the paternal inheritance, and a proportionate

und Mutterrecht' (1927); W. Ogris, article on *Friedelehe*, in HRG *I*, Cols. 1293ff; Mikat, *Dotierte Ehe — rechte Ehe*, pp. 50ff.

[9] T. Melicher, *Die germanischen Formen der Eheschliessung im westgotisch–spanischen Recht* (1940). Cf. the review by A. Schultze in *ZRG Germ.*, 1943, pp. 378ff. On the *arrha*, cf. K. Ritzer, *Formen, Riten und religiöses Brauchtum der Eheschliessung in den christlichen Kirchen des ersten Jahrtausends* (1962), pp. 223ff; H. Dillard, *Daughters of the Reconquest. Women in Castilian town society* (1984).

[10] F. Beyerle, *Gesetze der Burgunden* (1936).

part if there are four or five brothers. On the daughter's death this share passes to the next of kin (§ 14). A woman who, after the death of her husband without issue, does not remarry, owns a third of the entire possessions of her dead spouse until her death; it then passes to the legitimate heirs of her husband. She is also free to remarry, but she must then renounce her third of the property of her first husband (§ 42). If the mother wishes to take over the guardianship, the next of kin shall not be given preference to her (§ 85). Anyone who rapes a girl has to pay nine times the bridal price due to her, and a fine of 12 shillings (§ 12, section 1). A freeman who does violence to a female slave, if convicted of rape, must pay the owner of the slave 12 shillings. If a slave does the same, he is given 150 strokes of the rod (§ 30). A violent uncovering of the head or pulling of the hair of a free woman by a free man, proven by witnesses, costs 12 shillings for the woman and a 12 shilling fine, 6 shillings for a freed woman and three shillings for a slave, with a proportional fine. A slave who does the same to a free woman gets 200 strokes, 100 for a freed woman and 75 for a slave. But if the woman concerned has herself been a party to the act, an appeal can be made (§ 33). On divorce, the law ordains that if a woman parts from her legitimate husband she should be drowned in a bog. If a man casts out his wife without reason, he must pay her bridal price a second time, and a fine of 12 shillings. Proven adultery, proven witchcraft and the desecration of a grave allow a man to reject his wife; the law is then obliged to pass judgement on the offender. A husband cannot reject his wife for any other reason. 'But if he prefers, he should leave his house but leave all his goods behind. Then she must take her husband's possessions for herself and her children' (§ 34). The slave who violates a free woman, if the woman can prove the crime, is put to death. If a free girl cohabits voluntarily with a slave, both are killed. But if her kin do not want the girl punished, she forfeits her free status and becomes one of the king's slaves (§ 35). A widow whose virtue is compromised may not marry the man concerned (§ 44). Such an offence by a bride is dealt with on the precedent of a royal judgement: the widow Aunegilde had promised herself of her own free will to the king's sword-keeper Fridegisel. She had received the main part of her widow's *dos* from her bridegroom. She then tore up the bond of betrothal and turned — or ran, as the text puts it — to Baldomod. Both thereby made themselves liable to the death penalty, which was only remitted because the holy days of Easter were about to begin; both were condemned to pay *weregeld* instead (§ 52). Adulterers caught in the act, both men and women, are put to death.

In some *leges* there are whole catalogues of punishments for the exposure of a woman's body. A special case is discussed in the laws of the Langobard king Liutprand (in the year 733): We quote the passage directly:

It has been reported to us that while a woman was bathing in a river a depraved person (*aliquis homo perversus*) took all her clothes, so that she was left naked, and anyone passing the place sinfully witnessed her nakedness. For on one hand she could not stand in the river for ever, and on the other she was ashamed to walk home naked. We therefore ordain that anyone who shows such effrontery shall pay *weregeld* to the woman who is so impudently offended. We explain our pronouncement as follows: if her brother or husband or near relative had caught the offender in the act there would have been a bloody conflict; and one might easily have killed the other if he got the upper hand. It is better that the culprit should live and pay the *weregeld* than that there should be a feud between the kinsmen and a far greater penalty.[11]

Here the king's desire to limit acts of revenge is evident.

The legal position of women under the Frankish monarchy has been examined by Ganshof with his characteristic precision.[12] The *Lex Salica*,[13] the law of the Salian Franks that women have no right to inherit land, *terra* (or *terra Salica* in a different version of the text), has become widely known. *Terra Salica* should probably be understood to mean inherited land as against newly-purchased land. In the fourteenth century this principle − in a falsified form − contributed in France to women's exclusion from inheritance of the crown. Sexual tutelage is found in Frankish law only in the early Merovingian period. Saxon law, which the Thuringian and Frisian laws followed on this point, took a different course. It applied a strict form of sexual tutelage, even to a woman who is

---

[11]   F. Beyerle, *Die Gesetze der Langobarden* (1947). p. 302.
[12]   F.-L. Ganshof, 'Le statut de la femme dans la monarchie franque' (1962), part *II*.
[13]   On the dating of the *Lex Salica* cf. Mikat, *Dotierte Ehe − rechte Ehe* p. 20, n. 44. I support the dating of the 65-title text at the beginning of the sixth century. On the law of inheritance cf. K. Kroeschell, 'Söhne und Töchter im germanischen Erbrecht' (1982).

subject to neither father nor husband, that is, a widow. The son from the first marriage of her dead husband was made the widow's guardian, or the husband's brother or the male next of kin. Accordingly, her marriage was agreed between her guardian and the future husband, even if the woman was a widow. If a husband died and left only a daughter, although the daughter received the entire inheritance, it was her brother or other male next of kin who became her guardian, not her mother. If a widow with a daughter remarried and had a son, he had guardianship over the daughter; in the inverse case, the guardianship of a daughter from a second marriage did not go to the son from the first marriage, but to the brother or next of kin of the father.

Both Salian and Ripuarian law imposed a fine of 600 shillings for the killing of a woman capable of bearing children. The *Lex Ripuaria* imposed a fine of 700 shillings for killing a pregnant woman whose unborn child also died.[14] This is the second-highest fine in this catalogue of *weregeld*; only someone who slew a bishop had to pay more — 900 shillings. If a Ripuarian killed an immigrant Frank the *weregeld* was 200 shillings. Given the barter economy of that time, there was no question of paying in money or silver. The money sum served as a yardstick; the *Lex* gives equivalent values: a healthy, horned, sighted ox is worth 2 shillings, a healthy, horned, sighted cow 1 shilling, a sword with sheath 7 shillings, etc. The *weregeld* for the pregnant woman was therefore equivalent to whole herds of oxen and cattle, or the armour of a large body of men, which consisted of mail-shirt, helmet, leg armour, sword with sheath, shield and lance. Who had all that? The penalty lay in the annihilation of the offender's economic existence — if the woman's kin did not prefer to kill him. In Frisian law there is an interesting special clause. The man who strikes the hand of a woman who embroiders clothing (*fresum*) is fined four times as much as he would have been in the case of an unskilled woman. This probably reflects the importance of the textile industry, which became established very early in Frisia. The *Lex Frisionum* made similar provisions for the harp-player and the goldsmith.

Using extensive Christian arguments, the Bavarian law set out the penalties for abortion (Section 18, pp. 120ff).

According to the *Eva ad Amorem*, the law for the Franks on the

---

[14]   K. A. Eckhardt, *Die Gesetze des Karolingerreiches* (1934), §. 36.

Lower Rhine, the paternal inheritance went to the sons and the maternal inheritance to the daughters. In Alemannian, Bavarian and Saxon law the daughters inherited if there were no sons.

These laws began to be moderated at an early stage. By the sixth century in Frankish law the husband paid the *dos* to his wife, not to her guardian. The *dos* thereby lost its character of a compensation; it was a provision for widowhood. The wife was able to own wealth, but the administration of her wealth was the affair of her husband. All the same, he was not allowed to sell her estate. A special possession which the woman controlled entirely was her personal clothing and jewellery.

The Langobardic laws, which we can trace over a long period, show what Schott calls a 'clear contour of development'. According to Heinrich Brunner, they represent the outstanding creation of the *leges*. The *Edictum Rothari* promulgated in 643 gives great emphasis to the tutelage of men over women: (§ 204) 'No free woman living within the domain of our kingdom according to Langobardic law can live freely as she thinks fit. She must always remain under the tutelage of men (or the King). Nor has she authority to give away or dispose of any of her movable or fixed goods without the consent of her guardian.' But the law also states: 'If a man other than the father or brother is the guardian of a free girl or woman and wishes to give her to a husband against her will, he loses his guardianship; in that case she can either go to her other kin or entrust herself to the royal court.' But Rothari's law-book also ordains (§ 182) that a widowed, free Langobardic woman can take a freeman as her husband at her own choice. Here the widow has a privilege not enjoyed by a woman living under Saxon law. Liutprand confirmed and extended the earlier law, whereby the man who mistreats a free woman loses her *Munt* or guardianship: the guardian 'shall not marry her without her consent even to a freeman. For there is no greater mistreatment than to marry her to a man she does not want' (§ 120). A law of Prince Aregis of Benevento — Benevento had kept its independence after the conquest of the Langobard empire by Charlemagne — concedes to the woman the right to sell part of her property before a judge, if accompanied by two or three relatives and with the agreement of her guardian (§ 29). Langobardic law also provides for the unmarried daughter living in her father's house (§ 65, Liutprand thirteenth year):

He who has an unmarried daughter at home, but leaves no legitimate son, cannot pass on more than two-thirds of his possessions to anyone, no matter under what legal title, whether as a gift or for his spiritual salvation. He must leave the last third to his daughter, as King Rothari of glorious memory has ordained. If, under the old edict, someone who has made a bargain then has a daughter and breaks his bargain to provide her third, or to provide half of his property if two or more daughters are born, and if, as we read further in the edict, the bargain is a gift, it does not seem to us that a man can disinherit his daughter of her third of his estate for the sake of any gift, even if he is compensated, or of half his estate if there are two or more daughters.

In Liutprand's sixteenth year there is a decree to protect widows (§ 100, p. 265):

No one may make a woman who is under his guardianship take the veil or dress of a nun before the end of one year after her husband's death. If she decides to do so of her own free will before the end of the year, she should come to the king's palace and declare her intention. Only after careful questioning and with the king's permission may she put on the dress of the life dedicated to God. If anyone dares to force her to do so before the end of the year without the king's permission, he shall pay *weregeld* to the king. The woman's guardianship as well as her property will then fall to the palace. He who urges her to take the veil before the end of the year acts out of lust for gain and wordly craving, not from love of God or the desire to protect her soul. For after her husband's death, while the pain is still fresh, her feelings can be easily swayed. But once she has regained command of herself and then enjoys a pleasure of the flesh she is guilty of the far worse crime of unchastity: then she may not become a nun, nor can she be a lay-person ... [§ 101]: If a woman takes the veil of the life consecrated to God, or if she wishes ... to enter a convent, and if she has sons who are her guardians, or daughters, she may go into a convent with a third of her own estate. And this third shall be kept by the convent after her death. But if she has no sons or daughters she may, if she wishes, take half her property into the convent ...

Girls are of marriageable age at the end of their twelfth year.

Aistulf also shows concern for aunts; his law from the fifth year of his rule (AD 755) ordains:

We are well aware that the old law book states that if a brother dies without sons or daughters but leaves behind sisters, they should inherit from him. Yet the sisters of fathers were unable to receive the property of their nephews because the law says nothing about aunts. The sisters or next of kin inherited in their place. And while they remained at home unmarried and unprovided for, they suffered great need and even married slaves. God has therefore inspired us to make· the following resolution: if henceforth a Langobard dies and leaves behind one or more sisters unmarried at home, and one or more sons, his sons must ensure that each of his sisters can live without indigence. Depending on their wealth they shall take care that their aunt lacks neither food nor clothing nor service. If she wishes to live under strict rules in a consecrated convent, her nephews shall equip her properly for it. But if one of the said nephews dies without sons or daughters and without testate heirs, but leaves behind sisters, their aunts, if they are still unmarried and at home, shall inherit their nephew's or brother's estate in equal shares with their nieces, no matter how many there are.

Finally, the later laws castigate a multitude of abuses. Liutprand vigorously condemns pandering (§ 130):

Someone gives his wife a wicked freedom by saying to her: Go and lie down with that man. Or he says to that man: Come and sleep with my wife. If such a foul deed is performed and it is proved that the husband has caused it, we ordain that the wife...shall die. For she is not allowed either to perform this act or to keep silent about it...But her husband...shall compensate his wife's kin as if she had been killed in a fight...The other man, who committed adultery with the woman, even on her husband's advice, shall be handed over to the wife's kin.

He tells of a disturbance in the country, brought about by women (§ 141):

We have had the following report: a number of unclean and vicious fellows were afraid to break into a another village (*vicus*) or house (*casa*) by force of arms for fear of the penalty imposed by the old law-book. They therefore ordered their wives to bring together as many as they could, free and unfree alike, and send them against people less able to defend themselves (*minore virtute*). The women seized the people of this village, wounding them and doing violence more cruelly than men. When this came before us and the weaker people complained about their mistreatment, we had the following decision recorded in the law-book. If henceforth women dare to commit any such offence again, we solemnly declare that if in this act they are defamed, wounded, beaten, or even killed, those who wound or kill them in self-defence shall not need to pay any penalty to the women or their husbands or guardians. Furthermore the authority in the place where the offence is committed shall arrest the women, shave their heads and whip them to the surrounding villages (with no distinction of rank), so that in future no women will dare to commit such foul deeds. And if the women have beaten or wounded anyone in the course of their deed, their husbands shall make good the wounds or blows inflicted by them according to the law-book. We ordain this ... because such a thronging together of women (*mulierum collectionem*) cannot be equated with either the army or an uprising of country-dwellers; for such things are done by men and not by women.

Prince Aregis (after 774) is very concerned that Langobardic widows should behave honourably — which does not seem always to have been the case.

A dishonourable and illicit fashion has run riot in our day. Some wives, freed of their husband's power after his death, take unrestrained advantage of their freedom. Within the four walls of their houses they put on nuns' garments so that they need not bow to husbandly power ... And under the cover of religion they lay aside all modesty and pursue every desire of their hearts. They plunge into amusements, regale themselves with banquets, pour wine down their throats, frequent bathing houses and misuse their status to indulge in luxurious dress. When they walk through the streets they beautify their faces, powder their hands and inflame desires in those who behold them. Often they are shamelessly intent on seeking a pleasing form and being noticed for their own. To be brief: they loosen the reins of their souls to permit themselves every kind of lewd desire. And indeed, once the tinder of a licentious existence has been lit, they let it burn out with all the excitations of the senses. Indeed ... they secretly lie down not just with one but with many. And if they do not grow large, this cannot even be easily proved. Such damnable pestilence we condemn entirely and decree that if anyone is related to such a person, whether unmarried or a widow, who puts on the veil of devotion, and does not have her placed in a convent within a year at the latest, and if she is afterwards convicted of lewd vices, that man must pay *weregeld* to the palace. The prince ... may place her in a convent with this *weregeld* and her own wealth (p. 388ff).

Let us remark in conclusion that even within Germania efforts to improve the lot of women were successful. In England, the transformation of the legal position of women began before the Norman conquest; about 1030 the girl's consent became a prerequisite for a marriage contract.[15]

The high value placed on feminine honour by the law was matched in reality. But just as a noble Frank regarded it as more

[15] H. Würdinger, 'Einwirkungen des Christentums auf das angelsächsische Recht' (1935) pp. 105ff.

honourable to avenge his kin with blood than to be content with a fine, feuds arose when the innocence or reputation of a woman was called into question. I quote Gregory of Tours:

In Paris at that time − in 579 − a woman got a bad reputation, being suspected of leaving her husband and fornicating with another. The husband's kin therefore came to her father and said: 'Either prove that your daughter is innocent, or she must die, so that her adultery does not bring shame on our family.' 'I know,' said the father, 'that my daughter is completely innocent, and there is not a word of truth in the accusations of wicked people. But to prevent the accusation from being made again I shall support her innocence with an oath.' Whereupon they said: 'If she is innocent, confirm it by an oath on the grave of the blessed martyr, Saint Dionysius [St Denis].' 'That I shall do,' said the father. So they agreed and met at the church of the Holy Martyr. The father laid his hands on the altar and swore that his daughter was without guilt. But those who were of the husband's party cried out that he had committed perjury. First they exchanged words, then they drew their swords and fell on each other before the altar. However, they were of high birth (*maiores natu*) and in favour with King Chilperic. Many received sword wounds, the holy church was spattered with blood, the doors pierced by swords and lances, and the infamous missiles even reached the martyr's tomb. Peace was established only with difficulty, and the church was closed for worship until the matter came to the ears of the King. They hastened to appear before him, but instead of being pardoned they were handed over to the bishop of the city with the order that they should only be readmitted to the church community if their innocence was proved. They were received back into the church after atoning for their offence. But the woman ended her life with a rope a few days after she had been brought before the court.[16]

THE CHRISTIAN CONCEPT OF MARRIAGE AND CANON LAW

Diametrically opposed to the Germanic concept was the Christian concept of marriage. Christian marriage comes into being through the free consent of the partners; the woman's right over her person is preserved. The Christian conception of marriage was tightly bound to the principles of biblical revelation, however diversely they might be interpreted: monogamy, the indissolubility of marriage, the prohibition on incest. The prohibition on marriage between kin was taken to extremes. The indissolubility of marriage

---

[16] R. Buchner, ed., *Gregor von Tours. Zehn Bücher Geschichten* (1967), vol 1, pp. 338f.

was a quite new demand. Jesus's radical ethic of marriage over-
turned the rule going back to Moses that the wife could be
legitimately expelled by a divorce order from her husband. Paul
rejected divorce — whether by Jewish or ancient Roman law —
but he believed remarriage permissible after the dissolution of a
mixed marriage between a Christian and a non-Christian partner
(1 Cor. 7. 8—21).[17] In his Epistle to the Ephesians, the Apostle
compares the relationship of Christian spouses to the relationship
of Christ to his church. The husband is the head of the Christian
marriage as Christ is the head of the church, and he should love
his wife as Christ loves the church. For this reason a husband will
leave father and mother to be joined to his wife, and the two will
be of one flesh: 'This is a great mystery: but I speak concerning
Christ and the church' (Eph. 5. 22—33).

Naturally, the church authorities saw in woman 'the weaker
sex, sinful Eve'. But man and woman alike are, according to
Christian doctrine, created by God and redeemed by Christ:
'There is neither Jew nor Greek, there is neither bond nor free,
there is neither male nor female: for ye are all one in Jesus Christ'
(Gal. 3. 28). The equality of man and woman from the point of
view of redemption, and the personal dignity of women, are thus
recognized. The Christian church — like Judaism — has excluded
women from the priesthood until now. The early church institution
of the deaconess was not destined to survive long. 'The institution
of the deaconess,' writes Kalsbach[18] in a study based on the
Epistles of St Paul, 'is part of the missionary stage of the church.
Once this was over . . . it loses its significance . . . The history of
official church service by women in the Orient divides into two
stages clearly distinguished both by their connection and by their
differences: the viduate [ascetic widowhood] and the office of the
deaconess. . . The diaconal idea that linked widowhood with the
deaconship in the East is not to be found in the western viduate.
In other words, the precondition for the office of deaconess is
lacking.' In the second half of the fourth century the first convents
are founded in Italy, often by aristocratic women on the fringes of
the urban Christian community. They provide scope for action for
unmarried women — from the upper classes. The Catholic church

[17]   G. Dilcher, 'Ehescheidungen und Säkularisation' (1981).
[18]   A. Kalsbach, *Die altkirchliche Einrichtung der Diakonissen bis zu ihrem Erlöschen*
(1926), pp. 110f.

accepted marriage without reservation, quite unlike the heretical Antinomians, Gnostics and Manicheans. But it attached still higher value to a virginity dedicated to God. That is the core of the Augustinian doctrine.[19] The sexual act is subordinated to the primary purpose of procreation; the pursuit of pleasure for itself is rejected, as are contraceptive practices. In his two books on 'Marriage and Lust' — *De nuptiis et concupiscentia* — in which Augustine takes issue with the Pelagians' objection that marriage as such is condemned by his doctrine of original sin, and in his tract 'Against Two Pelagian Letters' — *Contra duas epistolas Pelagianorum* — the great teacher calls chastity a gift of God, and the union of man and woman for the sake of conception a 'natural blessing of marriage'. According to him, these principles are only truly valid for believing spouses. As Emile Schmitt argues in his recently published study of the Augustinian doctrine of marriage, baptism takes on fundamental importance as the source of the sanctification of the spouses. In full agreement with the passage quoted from the Epistle to the Ephesians, Augustine develops his idea of the mysterious marriage of Christ and the church and recognizes a 'sacramental statute' for spouses, based on rebirth through baptism. These are still living ideas; in the ninth century they were widely held, by Archbishop Hincmar of Rheims among others.[20] Augustine also compared the virgins consecrated to God in the early church with the Roman vestals, who were also required to lead a virginal life, and he pointed to a 'great difference' between them. For 'it is not virginity in itself that deserves to be honoured, but only a virginity dedicated to God, which is preserved in the flesh, but through the religious devotion of the spirit ... The high value placed on virginity consecrated to God, and on abstinence before marriage, is 'the unanimous conviction of the early church' (Zumkeller, p. 411). In the *libido carnalis* Augustine does not see a gift of nature but a punishment consequent on original sin. Zumkeller comments as follows:

It was not only the Pelagians who pointed out the shadow cast on Augustine's doctrine of marriage by his wrong evaluation of libido. They saw something purely natural in the libido and refused to acknowledge

[19]   Aurelius Augustinus, *Schriften gegen die Pelagianer* (1977); Emile Schmitt, *Le mariage chrétien dans l'oeuvre de Saint Augustin* (1983).
[20]   P. Toubert, 'La théorie du mariage chez les moralistes carolingiens' (1977), vol. 1, pp. 277ff.

any disturbance of the harmony between spirit and body after the Fall. In more recent times objections have been raised to Augustine's morality of marriage on the grounds that it falls foul of an unbridgeable dualism between an ideal of purely spiritual perfection on one hand and physiological human realities and the daily difficulties of marital life on the other. What can one reply to that? Even if one concedes that through his negative attitude to sexuality, Augustine arrived at a rather rigorous set of conditions for a morally permissible marital intercourse, there is no question of a dualism of the kind mentioned ... Only the flesh—spirit dualism of John and Paul is present in Augustine's doctrine of marriage, and with his personalistic conception of marriage in relation to Christ's omnipotent grace he is quite able to overcome this dualism. (pp. 415f)

The sacramental view of marriage must be seen in the context of the historical development of the doctrine of the sacraments. Augustine did not evolve a general doctrine of the sacraments. St Peter Damian (1007–72), a zealous guardian of the purity of the church who lived in the period of transition from the early to the high Middle Ages, names 12 sacraments: baptism, confirmation, the anointment of the sick, of bishops, of kings, the consecration of churches, confession, the ordination of canons, monks, nuns and hermits — and the sacrament of marriage.

The marital laws of the church developed much earlier. We find a reciprocal influence between early Christian and Roman law on marriage:

The development of the post-classical Roman law on marriage (and on the contraction of marriage) from the fourth and especially the fifth century on, was increasingly influenced by the Christian concept of marriage ... just as, in its turn, a church law of marriage in the strict sense only emerged and took on a clear judicial outline under the shaping influence of Roman matrimonial law.[21]

According to this Christian law, the basis of marriage was consent. The consent, the mutual affection of bride and bridegroom (*affectio maritalis*), was a main constituent of marriage. This is expressed most strongly in the fact that the partners themselves administer the marriage sacrament. For the woman, marriage by consent lays the foundation of her equality of rights with her husband. But the church marriage of consent did not fully establish itself until the twelfth century.

[21]   Mikat, *Dotierte Ehe — rechte Ehe*.

This does not yet tell us about the form of the marriage ceremony. The church commandments concerning the indissolubility of marriage and the impediments of consanguinity demanded a public ceremony. But up to the Council of Trent the church had never really been able to enforce this; the malaise of secret marriages persisted throughout the Middle Ages.

In converting the Germans to Christianity, the church was forced to grapple once again with the ethical and the specifically Christian implications of marriage. From 741, after the reforming alliance between Boniface and the sons of Charles Martel, church and state collaborated on questions of marriage law, giving the reforms special impetus. Admittedly, the chapters on marital law drawn up by the synods of Les Estinnes and Soissons (744) left open the contentious question of the permissible degrees of consanguinity, and the prohibition on remarriage applied only to women. Nevertheless, Mikat argues,

the principles of church matrimonial law (no matter how controversial some of their details may have been) are now given a validity transcending the inner realm of the church. The boundaries between church and secular law are blurred, the *decreta canonum* emerge more strongly as the basis of future marital law, and offences against the order it imposes are from now on subject to the episcopal court not only under church law. (p. 21)

Chapter 15 by the Synod of Ver near Senlis convoked by King Pepin in 755 and probably conducted in his presence, ordered that all marriages, whether of nobles or non-nobles, should be public. But as we have seen, the Frankish law on marriage demanded a public ceremony in any case. This applied to both the *Muntehe* and the *Friedelehe*. Mikat takes this as the starting-point of his penetrating study, which investigates the background of the decree. He points out that the term *publicae nuptiae* is already found, closely associated with the requirement of a *dos*, in a letter of 458 or 459 from Pope Leo the Great to Archbishop Rusticus of Narbonne. The pope saw in the *dos* an important feature distinguishing marriage from concubinage. Whether Pope Leo was following Roman law[22] or Judaeo-Mosaic principles need not

---

[22] R. Schröder, *Geschichte des ehelichen Güterrechts in Deutschland. 1. Teil. Die Zeit der Volksrechte* (1863), pp. 79, 112: 'The *dos* in Roman law is radically different from that of popular law, but they are the same in one respect, that they only appear in true marriage.'

concern us here. What is important is that the decree made the
validity of a marriage dependent on the giving of a *dos*, that there
were analogies between the Germanic *dos* and the bridal gift
mentioned in the Old Testament, and that the wording of the
decree could apply to quite different forms of *dos*. This papal letter
could be taken in the Germanic—Frankish area as an authoriza-
tion of the *Muntehe*, one of the characteristics of which was the gift
to the bride from the bridegroom. Mikat thus answers the previously open question, convincingly in my view, as to why the
church recognized the *Muntehe* and not the *Friedelehe* as the legitimate form of marriage in the Germanic area.The church did not
regard the two forms as genuine alternatives, since it did not
define a true marriage solely in terms of consent. What also
counted against the *Friedelehe* was its ease of dissolution, and the
fact that it could be carried on beside a *Muntehe*, infringing the
principle of monogamy. In addition, the distinction between a
Friedelehe and various forms of concubinage was more difficult to
draw in the Merovingian—Frankish period, so that the division
between *Muntehe* and *Friedelehe* was sharpened. Ewig has shown[23]
how fluid the borderline between concubines and *Friedel*-wives
had become among the Merovingian lords. How far the *Friedelehe*
also existed among the broad population in the Frankish period
cannot be ascertained; but it is likely to have been an exception
found primarily among the nobles. The normal form of marriage
— even for the rulers — was the *Muntehe*.

A church benediction of marriage in the West can be traced as
far back as the mid-fourth century. An indication that the church
was involved in the marriage ceremony among Christians is to be
found in a letter of Ignatius of Antioch to Polycarp of Smyrna. In
the Frankish period, church marriages have been demonstrated
for Ermentrude, the wife, and for Judith, the daughter of the west
Frankish king Charles the Bald, performed by Archbishop Hincmar
of Rheims. However, in this case the blessing of the marriage is
not a separate rite, but a part of the coronation ceremony, which
also has a sacramental character. In general, the deeply ingrained,
earlier marriage customs with their worldly character and festive
spirit survive intact. Bishop Rudolf of Bourges forbids his priests
to attend wedding celebrations — 'these vain, worldly festivities.'[24]

[23]   E. Ewig, 'Studien zur merowingischen Dynastie' (1974).
[24]   Toubert, 'La théorie du mariage chez les moralistes carolingiens', pp.
273ff.

For the unfree — and the great mass of the population lived in varying degrees of unfreedom in the Carolingian period — there were legal restrictions on the freedom to marry. The idea of their marriageability did not establish itself without difficulty. It had at least the theoretical support of the church, for only by recognizing sexual unions between the unfree as marriages was it possible to subjugate the diverse forms of free sexual relationship — especially common with unfree people — to the church's demand that there should be no sexual intercourse outside marriage. The laws of the west Gothic kings Chindasvinth and Reccesvint (seventh century), which guaranteed permanence to the marriages of slaves, even without the agreement of their masters, if they were kept secret for one year, were 'without parallel in the written laws of the Germanic tribes'.[25] Among the Langobards, Liutprand in 734 was the first to give effective protection to slave marriages. And as we have shown, developments within land ownership also helped to make it economically possible for unfree people to found families in the Carolingian period — an advance which especially benefited unfree women.

FROM THE WIVES OF THE MEROVINGIAN KINGS TO THE *CONSORS REGNI* OF THE OTTONIANS AND SALIANS

In the Frankish empire the monarchy was the preserve of the Merovingians. Only the male line could inherit; there was no fixed order of succession. The empire was divided, and while the sons of the dead ruler who had attained majority had the first claim, the offspring from *Friedel*-marriages and illegitimate children also had certain rights of inheritance, which had to be confirmed by the father. The dead king's brothers could also be considered as heirs to the throne. When Chlotar I died in 561 he left four sons among whom the empire was divided *aequa lancea*. Another factor to be considered was that each Merovingian heir, as a Frankish king, had to receive a share of Francia in northern Gaul. Thus Paris was allotted to Charibert, Orléans to Guntram, Rheims to Sigebert I and Soissons to Chilperich I. When Charibert died in 567 his part was divided into three and the capital, Paris, came under joint rule.

---

[25] Nehlsen, *Sklavenrecht zwischen Antike und Mittelalter*, pp. 178 and 368.

The Merovingians' wives came either from other royal houses or from the common people.[26] The marriages with kings' daughters were *Muntehen* and the royal wife could not be cast out. Although the Merovingians had many wives, they did not have more than one *Muntehe*. The queen dowager, if she stayed at the court, often played an important role. We need to be aware of this to understand the strife which broke out between Chlotar's sons, in which women played a fateful part. Gregory of Tours gives the following account (bk IV, ch. 27):

When King Sigebert saw that his brothers were choosing wives who were not worthy of them, debasing themselves so far as to take even serving-maids in marriage, he sent an envoy to Spain with rich gifts to woo Brunichilde, the daughter of King Athanagild. For she was a maiden of refined upbringing, beautiful of countenance, modest and pleasing in her manners, intelligent and charming in conversation. Her father did not hold her back, sending her to Sigebert with much treasure. The king gathered together the great ones of his realm, ordered a banquet and took her as his bride amid great rejoicing and revelry. As she was of the Arian faith, she was converted by the teaching of the bishops supported by the king himself; she believed, acknowledged the Holy Trinity and was anointed. [The anointing betokened the admission of heretics into the true church.] And to this day she has kept the Catholic faith in the name of Christ.

When King Chilperich saw this, although he already had several wives, he wooed Galsvintha, Brunichilde's sister, promising through his envoys that he would dismiss his other wives if he could wed a king's daughter who was his equal in birth. The father believed these promises and sent him his daughter with many treasures, as he had done with the first. However, Galsvintha was older than Brunichilde. When she came to King Chilperich she was received with great honour and married to him; and he honoured her with great love. For she had brought rich treasure with her. She too entered the true church and was anointed. But the king's love for Fredegund, who had been his wife earlier, caused great discord between them. Galsvintha complained to the king of the incessant insults she had to endure, claiming that she meant nothing to him. She therefore asked to be allowed to return to her homeland, although the king could keep the treasures she had brought with her. But the king artfully denied her wish, placating her with sweet words. Finally he had her throttled by a servant and found her dead in her bed ... But a few days later, after he had wept for the dead woman, the king took back Fredegund as his wife.

[26]   Ewig, 'Studien zur merowingischen Dynastie', pp. 38ff.

It must be said that such a violent removal of a queen was rare among the Merovingians. The fault lay with the king's consuming passion for Fredegund, who had been a servant to his previous wife Audovera.

The murder of Galsvintha, together with some territorial disagreements,[27] was a main cause of the violent conflict which now broke out between Sigebert and Chilperich. It ended in 575 with the murder of Sigebert at Fredegund's instigation:

When Sigebert came to the court called Vitry, near Arras, the whole army of the Franks gathered around him, raised him on his shield and set him up as their king. Then two servants whom Queen Fredegund had beguiled pushed their way towards him with large poisoned knives known as *scramasax*, as if they had a petition to make, only to pierce him on both sides. He cried out aloud, fell to the ground and soon breathed his last. (Gregory, bk IV, ch. 51)

At the time Brunichilde was in Paris with her children. Duke Gundowald, an opponent of Chilperich, rescued Sigebert's five-year-old son, Childebert II, from Paris. Brunichilde was at first imprisoned by Chilperich, but managed to escape to her son's domain in 577. Between Brunichilde and Fredegund there was pure hatred, but Brunichilde did not use hired murderers, having a political plan of her own. The former princess of the west Goths had a different attitude to power and a different political style to Fredegund, the maidservant who had been abruptly raised to queen, the 'regina pulchra et ingeniosa nimis et adultera'.[28] Brunichilde brought about an alliance with King Guntram, but was outmanoeuvred by a group of aristocrats in the Champagne region and on the Maas, headed by Archbishop Aegidius of Rheims; these lords befriended Chilperich. However, Brunichilde succeeded in causing the downfall of the alliance. In the autumn of 584 Chilperich, the 'Nero and Herod of our time' as Gregory calls him, was murdered. Among more grievous misdeeds, Gregory taxes him with composing 'lame' verses in two books he had written.

[27] On the whole political background which I have sketched to aid understanding of the drama of the two queens, cf. F. Steinbach, 'Das Frankenreich' (1967); E. Ewig, 'Das merow. Frankenreich (561−687)' (1976); Jane L. Nelson, 'Queens as Jezebels: the career of Brunhild and Balthild in Merovingian history' (1978).

[28] *MG SS rer. Merov. Tomus II* (Fredegar), p. 302: 'the beautiful, wily and adulterous queen.'

They 'cannot stand on their feet, since he has, in his ignorance, put short syllables in place of long and long in place of short.' All the same, he did have some literary interests and was probably the most adroit politician among the brothers.

Now King Guntram of 'Burgundy', as his part of the realm was later called, gained the upper hand. He took Fredegund and her three-month-old son Chlotar under his protection and laid hands on Paris. But he did not seek to become the sole ruler, respecting Childebert's reign and granting a regency to Chlotar. However, his relations with Fredegund soon deteriorated. In 585 and 586 two sons, Theudebert and Theuderich, were born to Childebert. The Treaty of Andelot of 587 settled the conflict with Childebert II. The two courts, Paris and Rheims, also agreed to distance themselves from the lords of the eastern realm, then called Austrasia, who were hostile to Guntram. This was the same group that Brunichilde also regarded with reserve or even hostility. The campaign reached its conclusion in a lawsuit against Archbishop Aegidius of Rheims. The joint victory of Guntram and Brunichilde was also a victory for the monarchic principle. The realm of the Chilperich—Franks, soon called 'Neustria', was now much reduced. Fredegund played a quite important part in this, but was herself hard pressed until she was reconciled with Guntram, with whom she had quarrelled, in 591. When Guntram died in 593, Childebert II succeeded him, but himself died in 596 at the age of 26. Now Brunichilde's era began. Her grandson Theudebert II succeeded to the throne in the eastern realm, and Theuderich II in 'Burgundy'. The opposition of the Austrasian lords increased again. In 597 her arch-foe Fredegund died, and Brunichilde's grandsons defeated Fredegund's son Chlotar II. It may have been the Austrasian opposition which caused Brunichilde to pursue her political goal, the unity of the realm and the consolidation of the monarchy, not with Theudebert, the successor to her dead husband Sigebert, but with Theuderich, who had succeeded Guntram. She made use of the senatorial nobility, appointing the neo-Latin Protadius as Theuderich's steward and then, when he was murdered, the Roman Claudius. In the war between her grandsons Theuderich triuimphed and took Theudebert prisoner. The latter was taken with his son to Chalon, where both were killed (although Bruni-childe had tried to avert the worst by interning her grandson and great-grandson in a monastery). Theuderich now prepared to wage war on Chlotar II, but died in Metz in 613 at the age of 27.

This was a heavy blow to Brunichilde. At once she had Theuderich's
11-year-old son Sigebert II declared king. In practice this meant a
long regency for the old queen, and met with unanimous opposition
from the nobles. They called on Chlotar II to join them. The
army which Brunichilde sent to meet Fredegund's son disbanded
without fighting. Brunichilde fled but was captured and handed
over to Chlotar. He had her tied to a wild horse and torn to
pieces. 'Fire was her grave, her remains were burnt.'[29] 'The death
of the queen of the west Goths,' writes Steinbach, 'who had tried
with the help of descendants of the Roman senators to create a
new central government, was the gruesome end of the efforts to
renew the empire with Burgundy as its centre. The attempt
foundered on the opposition of the Burgundian and Austrasian
nobility to monarchic rule.'[30]

Such were the fates of Merovingian queens. We note that their
influence during their husbands' lifetimes, though occasionally
decisive, had no constitutional basis. But as dowager queens,
mothers or grandmothers — that is, as as regents and guardians —
strong women could certainly make their mark.

A very different, peaceful world of prayer and good works
appears to open before us if we move to Poitiers, to the convent of
Sainte-Croix founded by St Radegunda. When Chlotar I, the
father of Charibert, Guntram, Sigebert and Chilperich, defeated
the Thuringian king Herminafrid in 531, he bore off that king's
niece Radegunda as a prisoner and made her his wife. When he
had her brother unjustly killed, she withdrew into the convent of
the Holy Cross that she had founded at Poitiers. Some 200 nuns
lived there. The convent was close to the city wall; beyond the
wall Radegunda built the church of the Virgin in which she was
buried; today it is the church of Sainte Radegonde. She installed
monks there to look after the spiritual welfare of the convent,
which was first governed by the local bishop. After differences
with him she placed it under the protection of the king. After her
death the bishop persuaded King Childebert to restore his role as
supervisor. This played a part in the conflict over the convent
which is about to be described. Radegunda, matured by the
many sorrows of her life, did not lose her interest in worldly
matters — i.e. the political events at the royal court — despite the

[29]   MG SS rer. Merov. Tomus II pp. 310f.
[30]   Steinbach, 'Das Frankenreich'.

ascetic moderation of her life. Like many pious women before her, she saw the convent as a haven of culture, bringing the poet Venantius Fortunatus to Poitiers. He came originally from Venice and had acquired the learning of the old schools of rhetoric. In 565 he arrived at Sigebert's court, where his poetry — which in many of his works seems rather mannered — was much appreciated. Where his feelings and experience were truly engaged, he was capable of creating genuine poetry. Thus he wrote a moving poetic epistle on the downfall of the Thuringian realm in Radegunda's name to her cousin in Constantinople, who was the last of the Thuringian royal line. He devoted a long poem to the lamentable Galsvintha. He also wrote a *vita* of Radegunda. She died in 587; Gregory of Tours was himself present at her funeral and recorded the miracles that occurred at that time. Here we have a glimpse of a truly different world — one bathed in the late glow of classical culture, an early flowering of Christian feeling.

Unfortunately, even this oasis was not spared the savagery of the age. After Radegunda's death, strife and dissension broke out in her convent.[31] Two Merovingian princesses, Chrodechilde, a daughter of Charibert, and Basina, a daughter of Chilperich, had entered the convent of the Holy Cross, Basina against her will. Neither was suited to the religious life, particularly Chrodechilde with her unbridled barbarian wildness and consuming pride in her Merovingian blood. After Radegunda's death she stirred up an outright rebellion against the abbess Leubowera, who came from a noble but not a royal family. She induced Basina and 40 nuns to join her; they had to swear to drive Leubowera out. Chrodechilde and her followers left the convent of Ste Croix for St Hilaire, violently resisting the admonitions of the bishop. The conflict smouldered for a long time, then came to a head. Gregory has vividly described the final stage (bk X, chs 15, 16):

The scandal in the convent at Poitiers, that had sprung from the Devil's seed, grew daily in wickedness. When Chrodechilde...had gathered murderers, poisoners, pimps, fugitives and criminals of all sorts around her and was ready to create a tumult, she ordered her people to break into the convent at night and drag off the abbess by force. But the abbess heard the approaching uproar and asked to be carried to the Ark of the

[31]　G. Scheibelreiter, 'Königstöchter im Kloster. Radegund († 587) und der Nonnenaufstand von Poitiers (589)' (1979); M. Weidemann, *Kulturgeschichte der Merowingerzeit nach den Werken Gregors von Tours* (1982), pp. 257ff.

Holy Cross — she suffered from gout — so that it might give her support and protection. When the mob broke in, they lit a candle and ran all over the convent with their weapons looking for the abbess. Arriving at the chapel, they found her lying on the ground before the casket of the Holy Cross. One who was even worse than the rest was making ready to perform the foul dead of hacking the abbess to pieces when another, as I believe inspired by divine providence, stabbed him with his sword. As the blood gushed forth and he fell to the ground, he could not carry out the intention that had formed in his infamous heart. Meanwhile the prioress Justina [she was a niece of Gregroy's, so that although his information comes directly from the convent it was not impartial] and the other sisters covered the abbess with the cloth from the altar that stood before the cross, and put out the candle. But the other side advanced with drawn swords and lances, tearing her robe, almost cutting the flesh from the nuns' hands and, as it was dark, seized the prioress instead of the abbess . . .

Finally, the mob took the abbess prisoner — releasing the prioress when they realized their mistake — and plundered the convent. The uprising spread further until the king called a conference of bishops to put an end to the misdeeds with penalties imposed by church law. Bishop Ebergisel of Cologne was one of the participants, so wide were the ramifications of the affair. The bishops demanded first of all that the king's responsible officer, Count Macco of Poitiers, should quell the uprising. Chrodechilde met the count's men holding out the cross of the Lord 'whose miraculous power she had earlier scorned,' with the words: 'I demand that you use no force against me, for I am a queen, daughter of a king and cousin of another king. Use no force, for otherwise the time may come when I take my revenge.' But the rising was brutally put down. Among other charges that she was able to rebut, the abbess was accused before the bishops' court of playing dice, banqueting with worldly people and even celebrating a betrothal in the convent. She had also had clothes for her niece made from a heavy silk altar-cloth, it was said, had cut gold leaves from the hem of the cloth, and had a gold-adorned headband made for this niece, all out of presumptuous ostentation . . . Concerning the dice, the abbess replied that she had played during holy Radegunda's lifetime, so diminishing her guilt, and that in any case neither the rules of the convent nor the laws of the church forbade the game. But at the bishops' command she promised contritely to do the penance imposed on her. As for the banquets, she said, she had not introduced a new custom into the convent but had kept up the practice of Radegunda's time. While she had given consecrated bread to people of Christian piety, the allegation that she had ever feasted with them could not be proved. Regarding the alleged betrothal, she stated that she had received the marriage gift for her niece, an orphan, in the presence of the bishop, the clergy and other respectable people. She had therefore been acting as *Muntwalt* to her niece — but declared that if this was an offence she begged forgiveness; she had arranged no revelries in the nunnery.

As for the altar-cloth ... she called on a nun of high birth to bear witness that she had given the abbess a heavy silk hanging that she had brought with her from her parents as a present, and had cut a piece for the abbess to use as she pleased. Of the remainder she had used as much as was needed to make a worthy cover for the altar, and had used the rest as a purple trimming for her niece's dress. As for the gold leaves and the headband adorned with gold, she called on the Count of Poitiers as her witness that she had received 20 gold florins through him from the niece's bridegroom, which she had used for this purpose.

For all this she received a fatherly admonition. But the bishops' court expelled Chrodechilde and Basina from the church community. Basina repented, Chrodechilde remained obdurate; at the king's request they were re-admitted to the church. Basina returned to the convent, and Chrodechilde was ordered to stay at an estate previously given to her by the king.

From the life of Radegunda and the events just recounted we learn that Merovingian queens wore purple robes and rich jewellery. How costly the dresses and jewellery were has been shown by the excavations at St Denis[32] and under Cologne cathedral[33]. In 1959, beneath the main aisle of the present church of St Denis — a building from the thirteenth century — the tomb of Queen Arnegundis was discovered. She too was a wife of Chlotar I and the mother of Chilperich. She wore a chemise of fine linen under a robe of violet silk, both garments not quite reaching to her knees; she wore linen stockings held by garters wound crosswise around her calves. Over her robe was a long tunic of reddish-brown silk that reached almost to her feet and was open all the way down at

[32] A. France-Lanord and M. Fleury, 'Das Grab der Arnegundis in St. Denis' (1962).
[33] O. Doppelfeld, 'Das fränkische Frauengrab unter dem Chor des Kölner Doms' (1960).

the front. At her hips the robe was held by a leather belt ornamented with two rows of triangular holes through which were threaded gilded strips of leather. At her neck were two golden brooches inlaid with almandine. They held together the tunic, which was open at the bottom, revealing the violet dress, the ornate garters and the trimmings of her shoes. Over her left breast a very long pin of gold and silver was fastened to her tunic. The tunic was lined with fine material; its long sleeves were adorned above the cuffs with a strip of red satin embroidered with rosettes and triangles in gold thread. Her shoes, of thin leather, were held by leather straps tied crosswise and closed by a silver-plated buckle. A satin veil covered her head and fell to her hips. A large, precious gilded buckle for her belt, probably placed under her tunic when she was buried, was sure to have been worn visibly over the tunic. Two cup-shaped earrings were also found. The dead woman's name was engraved on the gold signet-ring that she wore on her left thumb.

In 1959 Doppelfeld found a woman's grave as rich as the one just described six metres below the chancel of Cologne cathedral. Cologne was the residence of a separate Merovingian kingdom which, although Clovis had deprived it of its autonomy, continued to possess its own *aula regia* and was constantly visited by Merovingian lords. The princely burial of a high-born woman and a boy can be dated about 550. Doppelfeld surmises that the woman was Wisigarde, the bride of Theudebert, king of Austrasia, who died in 547.[34] Although the woman's robes were not found in the grave, it contained burial gifts and jewellery: the headband interwoven with gold-spun threads that free-born Frankish maidens used to tie their long hair and which was a main bridal ornament; gold earrings, rings on the woman's fingers, a bracelet of solid gold with thickened ends, jewellery, brooches, gold chains, coin-pendants, a large necklace, belt hangings including a distaff, scissors and knife, and shoe buckles with silver-plated ornaments. Glasses and coins were also buried with her.

Our knowledge of the wives of Carolingian mayors of the palace is limited.[35] However, they played a considerable part in the rise

[34] O. Doppelfeld, 'Köln von der Spätantike bis zur Karolingerzeit' (1973), p. 125.
[35] E. Hlawitschka, 'Die Vorfahren Karls des Grossen' (1965); and, 'Zur landschaftlichen Herkunft der Karolinger' (1962); and, *'Studien zur Genealogie und*

of the Carolingians because of the land they brought with them. Pepin the Middle, the first *de facto* ruler of the whole Frankish empire, showed a keen awareness of how to strengthen the Carolingian position in choosing Plectrudis as his wife. She was a daughter of the seneschal Hugobert, an outstanding figure in the history of Trier and the mid-Moselle region, and his wife Irmina, the foundress of the abbey at Echternach and, after her husband's death, abbess of the convent of Oeren at Trier. By this marriage Pepin laid the foundation for the Carolingian estates on the middle Moselle. For Plectrudis had no brothers, only sisters and thus stood to inherit much — but that was not all. She persuaded her husband, among other things, to found the convent at Kaiserswerth, which would radiate Christian influence to the east. She bore him two sons who died before their father, but both sons left children. Pepin granted Plectrudis guardianship over her grandson Theudoalt, to whom he promised the rank of mayor of the palace, as he did to the young Merovingian king Dagobert III. Plectrudis, aware that the greatest threat to her grandson came from Pepin's son by a *Friedel*-marriage, Charles (who soon earned his nickname 'Martel' — that is, 'the Hammer'), imprisoned Charles on her husband's death and seized the royal treasure. Her rule was later described as 'crueller than necessary' and 'conducted with the wiles of a woman.' She was unable to quell the insurrection which followed, and fled to Cologne. Charles Martel won power, unified the realm and finally halted the expansion of Islam. In Cologne Plectrudis founded the church of Maria im Kapitol, where a Benedictine convent was later established, probably by Archbishop Bruno.[36] A special tradition grew up around Plectrudis in Cologne. Hlawitschka explains her failure to attain the full status of a saint by the fact that there was no convent community at St Maria am Kapitol that could have built up a cult. The earliest evidence of veneration of Plectrudis is a Romanesque plaque with the inscription 'S. Plectrudis regina' made in

---

Geschichte der Merowinger und der frühen Karolinger' (1979); S. Konecny, *Die Frauen des karolingischen Königshauses. Die politische Bedeutung der Ehe und die Stellung der Frau in der fränkischen Herrscherfamilie vom 7.–10. Jahrhundert* (1980) (superseded in some respects); K. Schmid, 'Heirat, Familien folge, Geschichtsbewusstsein' (1977).

[36] E. Hlawitschka, 'Zu den klösterlichen Anfängen in St. Maria im Kapitol in Köln' (1966/7).

1150–60 and still extant. Customs relating to Plectrudis are documented for the thirteenth century: celebration of her memory on 10 August, gifts of wine and money to hebdomadaries, sextons and nuns on St Plectrudis's Day, the existence of a Plectrudis cup for the donation of wine to the nuns, etc.

Charles Martel's son Pepin, proclaimed by the Franks and anointed by the bishops – the importance of this act should be noted – married Bertrada the Younger, a daughter of Count Heribert of Laon and granddaughter of the elder Bertrada. This younger Bertrada had inherited old family possessions of the Irmina-Hugobert family. Her grandmother, the elder Bertrada, was probably a sister of Plectrudis. With her son Heribert she had founded the Eifel monastery at Prüm, which the younger Bertrada re-founded with her husband and richly endowed. Bertrada, who survived her husband (Pepin died on 24 September 768, she died on 12 June 783) played a political role as the queen dowager. She tried to act as mediator in the conflicts which soon broke out between Pepin's sons – he had given the west and north to Charles and the middle and southern lands to Carloman. In 770 she launched a peace initiative, achieving a settlement with Tassilo of Bavaria and the Langobards. She arranged the marriage between Charles and the daughter of the Langobard king Desiderius. Even the plan for the marriage met violent opposition from Pope Stephen III, who warned – in his own political interest – against a union of the Frankish royal line with a woman from the 'faithless and stinking' tribe of the Langobards. He also brought forward legal objections: both Carloman and Charles were already married. And indeed, Charles had a prior alliance with Himiltrud, the mother of his son Pepin the Hunchback. This was probably a *Friedel*-marriage, which the pope clearly regarded as legitimate. Einhard later describes Himiltrud as a concubine. But Bertrada's plan foundered, and in 771 Carloman's death ended the conflict between the brothers and with it Bertrada's political role. Although Charles married the daughter of the Langobard king, he was soon separated from her. He then married Hildegard, who was of Frankish–Alemannian descent, and she gave him three sons – Charles, Pepin and Louis – and as many daughters – Hrodtrud, Bertha and Gisela. After Hildegard's death he married the Frank Fastrada, mother of his daughters Theodrada and Hiltrud. A further daughter, Hruodheid, was by a concubine whose name is unknown. When Fastrada died, he married the Alemannian

Liutgard, from whom he had no children. After her death he lived with four concubines: Madelgarda, the mother of Rothild; Gerswind, of Saxon blood, who bore him a daughter, Adaltrud; Regina, mother of Drogo and Hugo; and Adallinde, who bore him Theoderich. Einhard distinguishes only genuine wives and concubines and acknowledges none of Charles's *Friedel*-wives, although they existed. We are in a transitional time where it is difficult to draw a sharp line between the different types of Germanic marriage because of the growing influence of the church. But the legal position of the children, particularly the sons, was important: the sons of *Friedel*-wives or concubines, Pepin the Huchback, Theoderich, Drogo, Hugo, are all sent to monasteries.

The question of the succession to power is closely connected to that of marriage. Marriage is used more and more deliberately as a means for bringing about the rise and fall of families. Advantages gained by some members of a family through the women they married could lead to factions, and the *Munt*-marriage caused a hierarchy of sons, with all its consequences. Einhard records that Charles allowed his daughters much freedom, as he was unwilling to give them in marriage either to his subjects or to outsiders, claiming that he could not live at court without their company. But was that the only reason? As the emperor grew older he clearly shrank from the consequences of dotal marriages, wishing for no more children from them. Although this denied political influence to the women at court, they added lustre to his rule and contributed to a flourishing cultural life.

Female political influence only became strong again under Charles's heirs, notably his son and successor Louis, whose later sobriquet — 'the Pious' — probably only dates from the tenth century[37] and should not influence our judgement of his personality. In his second marriage Louis married the beautiful young Judith, a Guelph and a highly educated lady; indeed, her links to the world of scholars and poets were closer than her husband's. Her prime concern was to secure the future of her son Charles, who was born in 823 and so was much younger than Louis's sons from his first marriage: Lothar, born in 795, Pepin, born about 803 and Louis, born about 806. The plans to partition the empire that gave rise to much commotion, in which Judith

---

[37]   R. Schieffer, 'Ludwig "Der Fromme". Zur Entstehung eines karolingischen Herrscherbeinamens' (1982).

was involved, need not concern us here. We shall only note[38] that in 806 Charlemagne planned to divide the realm among his sons, a plan that was unrealized only because two of them died before their father. In 817 Louis the Pious, influenced by the church, intended in the much-discussed *Ordinatio Imperii* to change the Frankish custom of the division of the empire by giving Lothar the title of emperor and his two younger brothers that of under-kings. But in 829/30, when he was again under the influence of secular lords, he reverted to the notion of partition.

Judith's concern was all for her son.[39] She first placed her hope in his godfather, Lothar. Then Bernard of Septimania became her most trusted adviser; it was she who had him summoned to the court. She came under suspicion of having a liaison with him, and of practising witchcraft. In the great rising against Louis of 830, Bernard had to flee to Barcelona while Judith was taken to the convent of Radegunda at Poitiers and put under strong pressure to induce Louis to abdicate. However, there was a change of fortunes and Judith was rehabilitated in Aachen in 831. In the joint rebellion of the sons against Louis in 833/4 she was banished to Tortona in Italy, but found ways of sending messages across the Alps. Louis got the upper hand again, but the provision for Judith's son Charles remained an open question. Pepin's death opened the way for the solution desired by Judith. Louis the Pious died before it was realized. Judith helped her son to the best of her ability in his struggle for his inheritance, bringing him an army in the decisive battle at Fontanetum (Fontenoy near Auxerre). Then there was a rift between mother and son; before the signing of the Treaty of Verdun (August 843), which divided Charlemagne's empire irreversibly between his grandsons, Judith died on 11 April 843.

Dhuoda, the wife deserted by Count Bernard of Aquitaine, wrote an erudite handbook for her two sons while she was sick, probably with leprosy, and in exile at Uzès on the lower Rhône.

---

[38] E. Hlawitschka, *Zum Werden der Unteilbarkeit des mittelalterlichen Deutschen Reiches* (1969/70).

[39] U. Gauwerky, *Frauenleben in der Karolingerzeit. Ein Beitrag zur Kulturgeschichte* (Phil. Diss. Göttingen, typescr. 1951), refers to Dhuoda and Angilberga; P. Riché, 'Les bibliothèques de trois aristocrates laïcs carolingiens' (1963), also on Dhuoda. On Angilberga: E. Hlawitschka, 'Die Widonen im Dukat von Spoleto' (1983), pp. 55ff.

The book is evidence of the cultural influence and literary pro-
ductivity of Aquitaine. She drew on a broad reading of scholarly
literature, which she simplified according to her own understanding.
The 'most distinguished' of the Carolingian women, according to
Konecny, was Angilberga. She came from one of the Frankish
noble families that were firmly rooted in Italy, probably the
Supponids of Parma, and was betrothed in 851 to Louis II — the
eldest son of Lothar I — who had been given Italy in the partition.
Louis had been crowned king of the Langobards in 844. Angilberga
had a strong sense of family, power and property. She is one of a
group of women of similar temperament: her daughter Irmgard,
wife of Boso of Vienne;[40] Liutgard, wife of Louis the Younger; and
Ageltrudis, widow of Wido of Spoleto, who shut the gates of Rome
in the face of the advancing German ruler Arnulf, defending the
eternal city and the imperial title for herself and her son Lambert
— admittedly without success. Angilberga took an active part in
politics as early as 871, while her husband was still alive and
firghting against the Saracens in southern Italy. She governed
northern Italy and held an imperial assembly at Ravenna in place
of the emperor. Angilberga is already called the *consors et adiutrix
regni*, the first medieval woman ruler. The fact that Louis II
married a second time did not weaken her position, and she
continued to exert her influence on Italian politics. She controlled
a large estate that she administered wisely and profitably. In
Piacenza she built a monastery, and supported many others; in
877, two years after Louis's death, she herself retired to a convent.

At that time, therefore, the indissolubility of marriage advocated
by the church had by no means been achieved. Then, gradually,
the church authorities increased their influence. One example is
the role of Pope Nicholas II in the conflict surrounding Lothar
II's marriages.[41] Lothar had a childless marriage to Theutberga,
whom he wished to divorce in order to marry his *Friedel*, Waldrada,
and legitimize his *Friedel* son, but Theutberga appealed to the
pope. The church concept of marriage opened new opportunities
to women who were being treated as political objects.

---

[40] W. Mohr, 'Boso von Vienne und die Nachfolgefrage nach dem Tode Karls
des Kahlen und Ludwigs des Stammlers' (1956), pp. 147ff.

[41] T. Schieffer, 'Das karolingische Ostreich (751–843)' (1976), pp. 613ff;
and, 'Eheschliessung und Ehescheidung im Hause der karolingischen Kaiser und
Könige' (1968).

Nicolas I intervened in another marriage dispute which is not quite so well known. Here, in the hard and glorious life of the Carolingian princess Judith, queen of England and countess of Flanders, we come upon the fate of a woman which mirrors the reality of the late Frankish period in its conflict between the norms and the harsh demands of politics, in the victory of faithful love between spouses and in the importance of marital links for the status of a dynasty and for the cultural flowering of a region. Heinrich Sproemberg[42] has written a scholarly biography of Judith.

She was the daughter of the west-Frankish ruler Charles the Bald and is mentioned for the first time on the occasion of her engagement to Ethelwulf, king of the Anglo-Saxons. This betrothal, in July 856, was dictated by state interests. Ethelwulf was at least 50, but obviously still vigorous, the father of a six-year-old son, and victorious against the Normans at the battle of Ockley in 851. Judith was 12 or 13, and so had just attained the canonical majority for women. An obstacle to the marriage from the first was that Ethelwulf had a large number of sons from his first marriage, the eldest of them, Ethelbald, already representing his father as regent in England. Ethelwulf's second marriage, to Judith, had a political background. The friendship and kinship with the Anglo-Saxon over-king gave Charles the Bald the welcome opportunity to enhance his standing *vis-à-vis* the neighbouring Frankish kings and his own vassals. Dissension with his brother, Louis the German, and the attacks of the Normans were making his position difficult. To put his family ruthlessly in the service of his political interests was second nature to him. For Ethelwulf, who had to defend the over-kingdom of the West Saxons, inherited from his father, against the other parts of the dismantled empire, the marriage link to the great-granddaughter of Charlemagne meant an important step up in status. The marriage was celebrated with great splendour in Verberie on the Oise, near the palace of Senlis.[43] Present at the wedding, as already mentioned, was Archbishop Hincmar of Rheims, one of the most important figures in Western Francia. At the wedding, according to Frankish custom,

---

[42] H. Sproemberg, *Beiträge zur belgisch—niederländischen Geschichte*, (1959), pp. 56ff. The essay on Judith reprinted there first appeared in 1936 in the *Revue belge de philologie et d'histoire*, 15.

[43] C. Brühl, *Palatium und Civitas. Bd. I. Gallien* (1975), p. 84.

Judith was crowned queen of the west Saxons.[44] The Latin coronation sermon by Hincmar, which has been preserved, instructed
Judith on her duties as wife and ruler. This was followed by the
handing over of the ring, the special coronation formula and the
consecration of the queen. However, this magnificent prelude was
not matched by the reception of Judith in England, where
Ethelwulf found himself confronted by a conspiracy between
Ethelbald and the great Anglo-Saxon lords, probably inspired by
a desire to strengthen the crown on the Carolingian pattern. In
his will Ethelwulf conferred on his son Ethelbald sovereignty over
the whole realm. Judith, whose queenship was acknowledged,
does not appear in this will, but she had been endowed by her
husband with important possessions in England.

Ethelwulf died in 858. Ethelbald ascended to the throne—and
married Judith. This marriage between stepmother and stepson
contravened church precepts and secular law. But the west Frankish court recognized the marriage for political reasons and the
church tolerated it; here an older Anglo-Saxon custom prevailed.
The initiative for the marriage had lain with Ethelbald. But two
and a half years later, in 860, he too died. The childless widow
Judith, after disposing of her English property, returned in honour
to France. She and her treasure were held in the fortified town of
Senlis under paternal and royal protection and in the custody of
the bishop. The only choice she had was to live there under arrest
or to take a husband of her father's choosing.

After two joyless years rescue drew near in the spring of 862:
she escaped, disguised and by night, with the knight Baldwin,
who had won her love. Baldwin's origins are a matter of dispute,
but we can probably assume that he was not of equal birth to a
Carolingian princess. However, the shortage of Germanic royal
houses had always posed a difficulty in marrying off Carolingian
princesses, so that spouses from the high aristocracy were not
always insisted upon. But this marriage of Judith's ran quite
counter to her father's political calculations. Perhaps Baldwin had
found his way to Judith in the retinue of her brother Ludwig, who
gave his blessing to the union. Judith's two young brothers, Louis

---

[44] M. G. Enright ('Charles the Bald and Aethelwulf of Wessex. The alliance
of 856 and strategies of royal succession' (1979) argues that Judith's anointment
had the magic purpose of increasing her fertility; this seems unlikely to me in
view of Hincmar's personality.

the Stammerer and Charles of Aquitaine, who despite their youth were already dignified by the title of king, also contracted marriages which their father refused to recognize. Judith's third marriage had a political background: the rebellion of the sons and barons against the despotic Charles the Bald. But this time Judith had married for love. Her royal father, probably forewarned, scattered the conspirators by a forced march on Senlis, but was not able to seize the young couple. He summoned a court tribunal which condemned Baldwin for abduction (although it was clear that Judith had followed him of her own free will) and disloyalty; Baldwin's fief was withdrawn. Charles also appealed to the church; led by Hincmar, the bishops residing at the court excommunicated Baldwin and Judith.[45] This annulled Judith's claims to the English gold deposited in Senlis. Hincmar's implacable hostility towards the young couple stemmed from his violent opposition to any form of abduction, a practice which was becoming prevalent at the time. Baldwin and Judith first fled to the court of the Lothringian ruler Lothar II, who received them willingly. They were probably married there. Charles the Bald demanded their extradition. Baldwin knew that in the long run he was not safe with his young wife at Lothar's court and played a bold stroke: he fled with Judith across the Alps to the Curia and appealed to the pope, claiming that 'he trusted more in the help of the Apostles Peter and Paul than in the protection of the kings of this Earth.'[46] The legal issue was a complex one. A condemnation of Baldwin by the church would have implied violent abduction, of which there was no question. By Frankish law Judith, as a widow, was no longer subject to her father's *Munt*.[47] From the standpoint of the church, which saw in the consent of the spouses the legal basis of marriage, this was not the decisive question, even though Judith's third marriage was not a dotal *Muntehe*. But Baldwin had violated the

---

[45] *Ann. Bert. ad a. 862*: 'Canonicam in iam dictum Balduinum et Judith, quae cum fure cucurrit et adulteri portionem se fecit, secundum edicta beati Gregorii: ut siquis viduam in uxorem furatus fuerit, et consentientes ei, anathema sint, depromi sententiam ab episcopis petiit.'

[46] *MG Epp. VI*, p. 273[25]: 'Sanctorum Apostolorum Petri ac Pauli quorum auxilium ipse Balduinus magis quam regum terrae fide devota quaesivit.' 23 November 862.

[47] *Cap. III ad legem Salicam*: 'Siquis mulier vidua post mortem mariti sui ad alterum marito se dare voluerit, prius qui eam recipere voluerit reibus secundum legem donet. Et postea mulier si de anteriore marito filios habet, parentes infantum suorum consiliare debent.'

royal protection in which Judith stood, and infringed the rights of his liege lord.

The pope proceeded very cautiously. Politically, he had to take account of his dispute with Hincmar over the limits of papal and archiepiscopal power. He accepted Baldwin's plea. His decision was affected by Judith's unreserved support for Baldwin. In a letter to Charles the Bald he stressed that Judith had told him from her own lips that she loved Baldwin above all else and had followed him of her own free will.[48] He begged the king to forgive Baldwin and receive him back with good grace, since he feared that otherwise Baldwin might ally himself to the Normans. In his letter to Judith's royal mother he stresses Baldwin's guilt and penitence. He sees himself as a mediator in a family conflict.

His understanding of the law emerges from a letter he wrote to Charles on the marriage of his younger son Charles of Aquitaine, which was also contracted without his father's permission. He censures marriage without paternal consent, but refuses to dissolve it for that reason alone.[49]. Baldwin's case was similar. The pope asked the bishops to intercede with the king on his behalf. Hincmar complied with the request, and it was through his influence that the king summoned Judith before him in 863, and even chose Verberie, where her first wedding had taken place, as the scene of the meeting. Baldwin, with papal support, demanded an immediate offical wedding, which took place in Auxerre. But three years after the wedding Baldwin had still not received any provision from the king. The pope urged the king to do his duty.[50] Although the word *dos* was not used, since forgiveness meant the restitution of Baldwin's fief, the idea of a bridal gift was probably in the protagonists' minds. At last, Baldwin's tenacity was rewarded with the endowment of Flanders.

We hear nothing more of Judith. She had found happiness. Her royal descent and her rich dowry strengthened the position of her

[48] *MG Epp. VI*, 273[17], no. 7: 'Balduinus, vassalus vester . . . qui vestram se habere indignationem eo quod Judith filiam vestram, illum prae ceteris diligentem' sine vestrae voluntatis consensu in coniugium elegerit, eamque volentem acceperit, ore proprio retulit.'

[49] Ibid.: 'Quod si nulla invenitur ex latere alia causa, quod grave pariat peccatum, non reperitur auctoritas ut eorum scindi debeat coniugium, nec nostrum est eis sine manifesti delicti culpa suae separacionis inferre preiudicium.'

[50] Ibid.: 413[33]: '. . . denuo quod deest oblatis pro eo petitionibus nostris supleri per pietatis vestrae munificentiam deprecamur.'

husband, who had a difficult assignment in this precarious outpost of the west Frankish realm, a region where water and forest were the dominant influences and a political order was lacking. It was thanks to Judith's close links with the west Frankish court that Carolingian culture gained a deep and lasting influence in these most eastward regions of *Francia occidentalis*. She bore Baldwin two sons, Baldwin II, the successor to his father, and Rudolf, Count of Cambrai. Baldwin II repulsed the Norman threat, made his castle in Bruges the centre of his dominion and secured an independent position for Flemish counts within the French state. The Flemish dynasty founded by Judith flourished until 1127. Shortly after the middle of the tenth century the priest Witger wrote down the genealogy of Judith's grandson, Arnulf the Great of Flanders. In keeping with the family sentiments of the time he gives particular importance to Judith, the ancestor with royal blood; he says she was both wise and beautiful.[51]

In the German empire — as we can call it from the time of the Ottonians — the status of the wives of rulers rose noticeably.[52] The queen was the *consors regni, particeps imperii*. Six weeks after the coronation of Otto I as emperor, the term *consors regni* enters German official use; up to then the formula, originating from late Antiquity, was confined to the 'imperial land', Italy. We came across it in connection with Angilberga. The Empress Theophanu, a Byzantine princess, was solemnly admitted to the *consortium imperii* in 972: 'in copulam legitimi matrimonii consortiumque imperii', and referred to as, 'coimperatrix augusta necnon imperii regnorumque consors'. In the East the co-imperial function had had a long tradition.[53] Adelheid, the daughter of King Rudolf II of Burgundy and Queen Bertha, whose grave was rediscovered in the abbey church at Payerne in 1818, married King Lothar of Italy, who died on 22 November 950, in her first marriage. According to Langobardic legal tradition Adelheid could have designated a successor; but on 15 December Markgrave Berengar of Ivrea had himself elected and crowned with his son Adalbert in

[51] H. Patze, 'Adel und Stifterchronik' (1964), p. 17: 'Quam Judith prudentissimam ac speciosam se sociavit Balduinus comes fortissimus in matrimonii coniugium.'

[52] T. Vogelsang, *Die Frau als Herrscherin im hohen Mittelalter. Studien zur 'consors regni'—Formel* (1954).

[53] Cf. W. Ohnesorge, '*Das Mitkaisertum in der abendländlischen Geschichte des früheren Mittelalters*' (1950).

Pavia, and had the young queen dowager imprisoned. However, Adelheid did not allow herself to be forced into an unwanted match by her imprisonment in Garda, but sought the hand of the widowed German king, Otto I, which she gained after a perilous flight in 951. She brought him an additional right of Italian kingship. It took until 2 February 962 for Otto to be crowned and anointed emperor in Rome, Adelheid becoming empress. Both husbands, Lothar and Otto, gave Adelheid rich dotal estates, which she used primarily to endow monasteries and convents. However, she had less restricted use of her estate in Italy than in Germany.[54] Even during Otto I's lifetime Adelheid played a part in government business, as is shown by her role as intervenor in royal charters. Adelheid was called the 'Mother of Kingdoms, Mother of Europe'. And indeed, her daughter from her first marriage, Emma, married the west-Frankish king Lothar in 966, and Mathilde the Carolingian, King Lothar's sister and Otto I's niece, was Adelheid's sister-in-law, the wife of her brother who was educated at Otto's court, the Burgundian king Conrad. After Otto I's death tensions arose within the royal family. Adelheid had contacts with Duchess Judith of Bavaria of which Otto II did not approve, as he rightly feared a Bavarian–Swabian power constellation. Another contentious issue, as already mentioned, was Adelheid's right to control her dotal pro erty in Germany. From 975 to 980 she spent most of her time in Burgundy and Italy. In 980 she was reconciled with her son in Pavia. In 982 she again appears as intervenor in Capua, then she stayed at the imperial court until Otto's early and unexpected death on 7 December 983.

As early as 967 Otto I had tried to marry his son and co-regent to a Byzantine princess. At first he was unsuccessful. But after a change of government in Constantinople there was a new chance to settle his relationship to Byzantium. Theophanu, a niece of the Armenian general John Tzimiskes, who had taken over as regent in Byzantium, was intended to be the wife of the successor to the German throne. In the spring of 972 the imperial legation returned to Italy with the bride. The disappointment that Theophanu was not a Byzantine princess by birth was balanced by the charm of the 16-year-old girl and by Byzantium's recognition of the Ottonian

---

[54] M. Uhlirz, 'Die rechtliche Stellung der Kaiserinwitwe Adelheid im Deutschen und im Italischen Reich' (1957).

Empire, which probably happened at the same time. For the Byzantine usurper, too, the link with the German throne was a gain. Otto's wedding with Theophanu took place on 14 April in Rome. Pope John XIII blessed the couple in St Peter's and crowned Theophanu empress beside her husband. Theophanu received important lands in Italy and Germany as her *legitima dos* according to German martrimonial law, and a few days later she acted with her mother-in-law Adelheid as intervenor for convents in Pavia in papal charters.

Concerning the wedding of the German emperor to his Byzantine bride, and his dotal gift to her, we are informed by a fine contemporary scroll of purple parchment[55] with a golden border at each side, with blue and white leaf-motifs at the bottom and delicate miniatures at the top. The writing surface imitates Byzantine purple cloth with a pattern of circles and semicircles framed by a double string of beads and showing symbolic fights between animals. Against this animated purple background the golden script shines with a calm clarity. The model for the document was the dotal deed that Empress Adelheid had received from her first husband Lothar, the wording of which went back to the *libelli dotis* of private law. The *arenga* of the document − the general rhetorical preamble − reveals something of the ruler's Christian conception of marriage. It declares:

God took a rib from the man and of it made a helpmate for him, and in his wonderful providence ordained that both should be one flesh, should leave father and mother and cleave to their spouses ... The Lord Jesus Christ, taking on human form from the womb of the immaculate Virgin and betrothing himself to the church like a bridegroom, that he might show how good and holy was a marriage legitimately celebrated, turned the water to wine ... And he said in the Gospel: What God has joined, let no man put asunder.

In the dispositive part of the document we read:

---

[55]   H. Goetting and H. Kühn, 'Die sog. Heiratsurkunde der Kaiserin Theophanu (DO *II*, 21), ihre Untersuchung und Konservierung' (1968); W. Deeters, 'Zur Heiratsurkunde der Kaiserin Theophanu' (1973); W. Ohnesorge, 'Die Heirat Kaiser Ottos II mit der Byzantinerin Theophanu (972)' (1973). We cannot here take sides on the divergent views advanced by Goetting and Deeters on one hand and Ohnesorge on the other; the essay by Goetting referred to above includes parts of the documents in a fine facsimile print.

Thus have I, Otto, decided, on the advice of my father, the Emperor, in the great city of Rome and with the blessing of Pope John, to betroth myself to and take as my wife the faithful Theophanu, the celebrated niece of Emperor John of Constantinople, as my co-empress in the bond of lawful marriage, under the guidance and protection of Christ. I therefore make it known ... that I have granted to my beloved bride as a legitimate dowry *(dote legitima)* and as her eternal right, according to the custom of my ancestors, properties within the Italian borders and within my realms beyond the Alps.

In the early summer of 980 — after two daughters, Adelheid and Sophie — the couple's first son was born; he was to become Emperor Otto III. The male successor to the throne was three years old when his father died. During his minority three women, the dowager empresses Adelheid and Theophanu, and Abbess Mathilde von Quedlinburg, Adelheid's daughter, helped to bear responsibility for the fate of the great empire.[56] There were no firm rules for a regency. The Ottonian party turned first to Adelheid, who was staying with her daughter Mathilde and her daughter-in-law Theophanu at the imperial palace at Pavia, asking her to come to Germany. But soon after the handing over of the royal child by the duke of Bavaria, Theophanu took control as mother and *coimperatrix*. She was admirably suited to the task, and tenaciously, astutely and wisely achieved her aim of preserving the realm and the Ottonian crown for her son. She has been accused of ambitiously outmanoeuvring and insulting the ageing Empress Adelheid. The main source of these charges is Adelheid's biographer, Abbot Odilo of Cluny, and they are doubtless somewhat exaggerated. Mathilde Uhlirz sees the primary cause of the unquestionably intense rivalry between the two empresses in their opposed views on the proper use of Adelheid's dotal estate, which Theophanu saw as imperial property. She stresses that Mathilde, an intelligent and very devout woman, took the side of Theophanu rather than of her mother.

How muted by culture and Christian values the two women's struggle for supremacy appears, if we think back to the Merovingian age. Naturally, Theophanu did not govern without helpers and advisers; her co-regents were the arch-chancellor and archbishop of Mainz, Willigis, and Chancellor Hildebald. At that time the

[56] M. Uhlirz, *Die Jahrbücher des Deutschen Reiches unter Otto II. und Otto III* (1954); H. Zimmermann, *Das dunkle Jahrhundert* (1971).

chancellorship was the only continuous office; its incumbent was not replaced. Even during Otto III's minority (984–95), the documents of government, the royal charters, were issued in the name of the child king. They differed from the diplomas of his adult predecessors only in that they almost always named intervenors, usually the arch-chancellor and chancellor apart from the two empresses. Only twice did Theophanu issue a document on her own account, on the journey she made to Rome towards the end her life in late autumn, 989.[57] In Rome Theophanu wrote *divina gratia imperatrix augusta* under a confirmation of the property rights of the monastery of S. Vincenzo on the Volturno. In April of the same year, in Ravenna, which was not part of imperial Italy, she issued a document in favour of the abbot of the abbey of Farfa, this time using the masculine form of her title: *Theophanius gratia divina imperator augustus.* The cause of her Roman journey is unknown. Zimmermann has tried to unravel its purpose. She granted the release of the sons of the princes of Salerno and Amalfi, who had been handed over as hostages to Otto II in 981. There was no question of pursuing an expansionist imperial policy in southern Italy at that time, and Byzantine Thoephanu would probably not have agreed to it in any case. It has been surmised that she took up contacts with Russia via Byzantium while in Rome. The Kiev prince Vladimir had been converted to Christianity on his marriage to a Byzantine princess, which meant the acceptance of Greek-Orthodox Christendom by the Russian empire. Rome was still attempting to win over both the prince and Russia to Catholicism. Envoys were sent to Russia, one of them while the empress was in Rome. It has been suggested that she was the real instigator, and was sending gifts to Vladimir's Byzantine wife, Princess Anna, whom her father-in-law had earlier wooed on behalf of her dead husband. Perhaps she was involved in the discussions about the mission to the East.

At the same time as Theophanu, the bishop of Prague, St Adalbert, was also staying in Rome, and is said to have been received by her in secret. Adalbert's flight from his episcopal office to the monastic life incurred the displeasure of Archbishop Willigis, whose ecclesiastical province included Prague. Hence the secret meeting with the empress – assuming the report is correct. It is

[57] *MG DD reg. et imp. II*, p. 876, nos. 1, and 2, and cf. Uhlirz, *Die Jahrbücher des Deutschen Reiches*, p. 121.

not impossible that she also met Archbishop Sigerich of Canterbury, who was staying in Rome in 990. During her Rome journey tensions began to arise between the Curia and France, triggered by the transfer of the monarchy to the Capetians. In this transition, following the extinction of the direct descendants of the west-Frankish Carolingians, Charles, duke of Lower Lorraine and vassal to the empress, had been passed over. When the new king, Hugo Capet, forbade the archbishop he had nominated, Arnulf of Rheims, to travel to Rome to receive the *pallium*, the reason may well have been his fear that the archbishop might conspire with the liege-lady of Charles of Lorraine. There was in fact a connection between Arnulf and Theophanu. Arnulf was himself an illegitimate offspring of the west-Frankish Carolingians. Unfortunately, the sources do not permit us to go beyond these informed hypotheses; that the empress was confronted in Rome by a large number of political problems with worldwide implications has been shown convincingly by Zimmermann.

Theophanu revealed to her son the treasures of her culture, and did not allow him to become estranged from his Saxon origins. She was filled with a proud consciousness of authority and distinguished by a strong sense of right. She died on 15 June 991 at the imperial palace at Nimwegen, about 35 years old. She found her last resting-place in St Pantaleon in Cologne, where Otto I's brother, Bruno, archbishop of Cologne, was buried.

When Otto III left for Italy in 996 he appointed his aunt Mathilde, as *matricia*, governor of Germany. Despite her wisdom, admirable in a woman,[58] she was not equal to the great task, but died on 6 February 999. Adelheid suffered the sad fate of surviving her children. In 999 she once again visited the grave of her mother in Payerne, the abbey of which was under the authority of Cluny. In the Benedictine abbey of Selz, founded by her and consecrated in 995 in her presence and Otto's, she found her grave;[59] she died on 16 December 999.

A connoisseur of ecclesiastical and secular writers was the Empress Kunigunde, wife of Henry II, the successor of Otto III, from a Luxembourg line. She corresponded with the archbishop of Mainz, Aribo. Ademar of Chabannes dedicated his treatise on St

[58]   *MG SS III 91, Ann. Hild*: 'in qua ultra sexum mira prudentia enituit.'
[59]   J. Wollasch, 'Das Grabkloster der Kaiserin Adelheid in Selz am Rhein' (1968).

Martialis to her among others; she is venerated as a saint. Her husband Henry II, also canonized, had established the bishopric of Bamberg in 1007. The monument to Kunigunde by Tilmann Riemenschneider, completed in 1513, found its place in the cathedral at Bamberg.

Gisela, wife of the first ruler from the house of Salis, Conrad II, is called an 'outstanding personalty' by Gerd Wunder, her most recent biographer.[60] She posed more than one riddle to historians; the contradictory information on her age and the sequence of her marriages that has come down to us has given rise to much mental exertion. She was probably born about 990 and was a daughter of Duke Hermann II of Swabia and Gerberge, daughter of King Conrad of Burgundy, the brother of Empress Adelheid. Gisela was born in Swabia, assuming that her mother Gerberga only married Count Hermann of Werl in Westphalia in her second marriage. In that case she would have spent her childhood in Swabia and her youth in Werl, and was first married to Count Bruno of Brunswick, who was murdered about 1010. After the death of her brother, Hermann II, she was married to the young Ernst of Babenberg, to whom she brought the Duchy of Swabia. This marriage accorded with Henry II's policy towards the German dukes. In May 1015 Ernst had a fatal accident while hunting; as he died he asked his knights to beg his wife to 'preserve her honour and not forget him'. But Gisela made her third marriage of her own choice, and against the will of Henry II: had Ernst suspected such a development? In 1016 she married the future German king, Conrad II. To this marriage there was an impediment of too close kinship, according to the strict church precepts of the time. Given the intermarrying of aristocratic families, such impediments led again and again to difficulties and sometimes to tragedies. Among Conrad's ancestors was Otto I, and among Gisela's, Otto I's sister Gerberga, so that they had a common ancestor in Henry I. Otto I was a great-grandfather of Conrad, Gerberga a great-grandmother of Gisela, who was Conrad's niece; perhaps, too, her paternal grandmother was a daughter of Duke Liudolf, who died in 957, and whose sister Liutgard was Conrad I's great-grandmother. Their parents were

---

[60] G. Wunder, 'Gisela von Schwaben. Gemahlin Kaiser Konrads II., gestorben 1043' (1980); E. Hlawitschka, 'Beiträge und Berichte zur Bleitafelin-schrift aus dem Grab der Kaiserin Gisela' (1978).

also interrelated, which counted as another blemish in the eyes of the church. Henry II was against the marriage for political reasons. But it took place, and in 1017 Gisela brought her son, the later German ruler Henry III, into the world. She also bore Conrad two daughters, who died very young. With the death of Emperor Henry II in 1024 the ruling house of Saxony became extinct. Next in line to the throne were Gisela's husband and his younger cousin of the same name. On 4 September 1024 the decision went in favour of Gisela's husband; on the eighth of that month he was crowned king by Archbishop Aribo of Mainz — but Aribo refused to crown Gisela, either because of the taint on her birth or because of her consanguinity with her husband. However, Archbishop Pilgrim of Cologne proved willing: on 21 September he crowned Gisela in Colonge. She then appeared frequently with Conrad as intervenor in royal documents, and when her young son was chosen as king, succeeding his father Conrad, in Aachen in 1028, Pilgrim of Cologne again performed the coronation. This was an important legal fact for the empire, since it founded the Cologne archbishop's right to crown. After her husband's elevation to the throne of Charlemagne in Aachen, she went with him on the royal ride from Aachen via Liège to Paderborn, Merseburg and Fulda, then to Regensburg, Constance, Basle, Strasbourg and Speyer as far as Tribur — then, to honour Lorraine, back to Aachen and Trier.

Gisela had a decisive influence on government; she shared the labour of the 'itinerant monarchy'. Documents show the royal couple to have been eight times in Paderborn, five times in Goslar, Nimwegen, Tribur, Worms, Strasbourg and Regensburg, four times in Magdeburg, Merseburg, Bamberg, Augsburg, Basle and Limburg on the Haardt. The preferential treatment given to Paderborn is bound up with their good relations with Bishop Meinwerk — with whose mother we shall become acquainted. The great hall of the royal palace in Paderborn beside the cathedral has been rebuilt today. Here Gisela often celebrated the feasts of Christmas, Easter and the Ascension. In spring 1026 she accompanied the army that the king was leading over the Alps to Verona, to make his dominion secure again. When there was fighting, she stayed in a fortified palace nearby. It was only a year later that Conrad and Gisela were able to receive the imperial crown in Rome, on Easter Sunday, 1027:

Two kings added lustre to the celebrations and accompanied the imperial couple from the church to their quarters: Gisela's uncle, the old king of Burgundy, and the seafaring King Knut of Denmark and England. This was probably the high point of the empress's renown. She mediated in the negotiations with the king of Burgundy (about the succession of her childless uncle), and about the same time the betrothal of her son Heinrich (III) to Gunhild, daughter of Knut the Great, was agreed. (Wunder)

Duke Ernst II of Swabia, Gisela's son from her second marriage, had joined the opposition to Conrad once before. But Gisela brought about a reconciliation. In 1027 Ernst again rebelled, was outlawed and died ingloriously. His royal stepfather glossed his heirless death with the words: 'Vicious dogs seldom have young.' What may Gisela have felt? 'Even Empress Gisela forsook her ill-advised son,' writes Wipo, the poet and biographer of Conrad II, 'a sad but praiseworthy act'.

In 1033 Conrad was crowned king of Burgundy in Payerne — without Gisela. He based his claim not on the relatively weak right of inheritance of Gisela — her mighty rival was Odo II of Blois — but by imperial law as the legitimate successor to Henry II.

Once more, in 1036, Gisela accompanied the king to Italy. At Whitsun 1039 Conrad died at Utrecht. With her son Gisela accompanied the dead emperor up the Rhine to the new tomb at Speyer, the power centre of the house of Salis. To begin with she appears as intervenor in the charters of Henry II, but differences arose between them. Gisela withdrew to Goslar, where she died on 14 February 1043 beside the Ruhr.

The emperor's *necessaria comes*, his indispensable companion, Wipo, calls this *consors imperii*. She was an ambitious woman with a strong sense of power, a born ruler. She was literate, and more educated than her royal spouse. She was generous, skilful and believed in discipline, but also enjoyed feminine pursuits. And she was beautiful. In her grave at Speyer her abundant golden hair was found.

At the court of Conrad II was educated his niece Beatrix,[61] daughter of the dead Duke Frederick of Upper Lorraine, whom he

---

[61] W. Goez, *Gestalten des Hochmittelalters. Personengeschichtliche Essays im all-gemeinhistorischen Kontext* (1983).

married to his trusted follower, the violent Boniface of Tuscia from the house of Canossa. Boniface's power extended from the southern border of the Alps to the gates of Rome; Beatrix brought him a considerable estate in Lorraine. She was much taken with the ideas of the church reform movement and had some influence on her husband in this direction — but Boniface was murdered in 1052 and Beatrix had to fight for her children's inheritance. She won the widowed Duke Geoffrey the Bearded, of Lower Lorraine, as her ally and second husband. It was not only political motives but genuine affection that united them: Geoffrey ordered a signet ring for Beatrix from a goldsmith — the earliest known woman's signet from the high Middle Ages. The stone shows the margravine seated with a book in her hand. The inscription surrounding it runs: 'Thou shalt be always happy, Beatrix beloved of God.' Contrary to the practice at Italian chancelleries, Beatrix continued to use the ring to seal her own documents after Geoffrey's death.

In Duke Geoffrey's wars with the German ruler she was brought as a prisoner to Germany. Two of her children from her first marriage died there. For her daughter Matilda, the only child left to her, Germany meant a hostile foreign land. She was betrothed to her mother's stepson, Duke Geoffrey the Hunchback, for whom she felt only revulsion.

We owe to Werner Goez the first biography of this woman who played such a significant role in the great conflict between pope and emperor, between church reform and the secular thirst for power. Henry III's early death gave Duke Geoffrey the Bearded great political responsibility in the Empire; Beatrix represented him beyond the Alps with all his rights and duties. Goez compares her political role to that of Angilberga. After the death of Geoffrey the Bearded in 1069, Matilda's wedding to Geoffrey the Hunchback was finally celebrated. She was unhappy from the start, and her first child, a boy, died soon after his difficult birth. Beatrix had at the time donated 12 villages to a monastery in the Apennines, 'for the health and the life of my child Matilda'. At the end of 1071 Matilda left her husband and fled to her mother in Italy. They resisted all Geoffrey's attempts to revive the marriage.

Church reform had been close to the hearts of both princesses from the first. It was the basis of their close relations to the reformist Pope Gregory VII — relations which were misinterpreted. When the long-smouldering dispute between the reformer-pope on one hand and the German king and the majority of the

German episcopate on the other escalated at the Diet of Worms, the pope was accused of 'wanting to rule the whole of Christendom with a senate of women and filling the church with a stink of scandal, since he shares his table with a foreign woman and shelters her more intimately than necessary.' The allusion to Matilda was unmistakable. The trust between the pope and the margravine was not troubled by this, but their correspondence grew sparser and its diction more 'official'. Their political collaboration was intensified. When Matilda considered entering a nunnery after the murder of Geoffrey the Hunchback, the pope would not allow it. She was needed in the world, he declared, and so she took control of the whole inheritance, the estates and fiefs. But she seems to have lacked her mother's self-confidence, and needed male advisers. While Beatrix signed her documents 'by the grace of God, which I am', Matilda signed, 'by the grace of God, if I have it at all'.

The struggle between king and pope was moving towards the 'Canossa incident'.[62] It is not our task to interpret the incident here; Matilda's part in it is what concerns us. She was a cousin of the king, that is, their grandparents were siblings. The king had come as a penitent to the pope, seeking release from the excommunication which made it impossible for him to rule. When the negotiations threatened to founder and the king was already thinking of his departure, he is said to have fallen to his knees at Matilda's feet to gain her intercession, saying 'Consobrina valens, fac me benedicere, vade!' (Mighty cousin, get me his blessing.) Matilda's biographer Donizio illustrated Henry's life (he died after the countess)with miniatures; one of them shows this incident. Matilda is enthroned beneath an arch supported by columns, wearing a sumptuous gown, a gold band adorning her brow; next to her Abbot Hugo of Cluny, sitting on a folding seat, points to her as mediator. The king has gone down on his left knee facing the Countess; Matilda signals to him to rise with her open right hand, the index finger of her left raised in admonition. *Rex rogat abbatem, Mathildim supplicat atque* (The king asks the abbot and begs Matilda) is written below. Henry is portrayed in royal costume with the crown and the imperial orb. How far the statement in the picture can be taken literally is a matter for conjecture, but Matilda's mediating role is beyond doubt. The king got his release

[62] H. Zimmermann, *Der Canossagang von 1077. Wirkungen und Wirklichkeit* (1975).

from excommunication, and the struggle went on. Matilda secretly made over all her possessions to the Apostolic See at that time, and repeated the bequest in 1102.

She did much to advance the papal cause, even intervening in the conflict with her own troops. She met growing resistance; in 1081 she was stripped of her fief by the German king and outlawed from the realm. In Tuscany only Count Guido remained loyal to her. When Gregory VII died in 1084 in his Salerno exile, Matilda continued to fight for reform and even influenced the papal elections. The elevation of Cardinal Bishop Otto of Ostia, a Frenchman who had been a monk and prior at Cluny, saved the reforms: Urban II combined Gregory's reformist severity with diplomatic skill. He included Matilda's estates and Matilda herself in his calculations, supporting the marriage of Matilda, now 42, to the 17-year-old Welf, half-Italian like her; his grandfather was Azzo II, margrave of Este. The marriage — for appearances only, it was agreed — was intended to strengthen the opposition of the German princes. In reality Welf first put up successful resistance to Henry in Matilda's favour, then left her. Again in full possession of her domains, Matilda now adopted Guido Guerra, the son of her loyal vassal Count Guido, but this bond also loosened. Her relationship to Paschalis, Urban II's successor, was not close. Her advisers now were two cardinals who were also heads of the episcopal churches at Reggio and Parma. For the rest, Matilda ruled autocratically, not shrinking from investing a Milan archbishop with ring and staff in contradiction to her reformist principles, and appointing bishops. She no longer intervened in the conflict between the Curia and Henry V, and even granted the king the succession to her estates that she had long since made over to the Apostolic See. Had she lost her grasp of the situation in her old age? At her request Henry had freed the cardinals who advised her. Her strength was clearly failing. At last she was unable to leave her castle at Bondeno, between Mantua and Modena. She died on 24 June 1115, aged 69, with the spiritual support of the bishop of Reggio.

Beside Margravine Matilda the Salian women pale: Agnes of Poitou, Henry IV's mother, was a devout and very cultured woman. She corresponded with Petrus Damiani, with Jean de Fécamp and promoted literary studies. But she was not equal to the regency that fell to her on Henry III's death. When the archbishop of Cologne seized the young king in Kaiserswerth in

1062, Agnes, who had already taken the veil in 1061, withdrew to Italy. Henry IV's union with Bertha of Turin was supposed to strengthen the German king's position in Italy; in 1069 Henry, striving to dissolve the marriage, took Bertha with him on the arduous journey to Canossa. After her death he married Eupraxia, a daughter of the grand duke of Kiev. In the difficult year of 1093 she abandoned him and fled to Matilda, complaining that the emperor had induced her to commit adultery. Whether the accusation was true is very doubtful.

How did the queens stand in neighbouring France? On 3 July 987 Hugo Capet, the great adversary of the western Frankish Carolingians, was elected king of France — as we can now call the west Frankish realm — and on 30 July his son Robert was crowned in Orléans; the succession was secure. The Capetians governed France until 1328, a continuity of monarchic rule that was denied to Germany. Nevertheless the king's power did not at first amount to much. Compared with the German rulers, who kept their large dominion in check despite much opposition from princes, the Capetians' realm was small. They had real control only over the crown domains, the narrow but strategically important area including Orléans, Paris, Senlis; added to that was control of the archbishops' churches of Rheims, Sens, Tours and Bourges. Their territory was smaller than that of their proud and independent vassals. There were no regencies in France in the tenth and eleventh centuries. The German queens and empresses had a far more illustrious role than the wives of these 'new' kings.

Like a true upstart, Hugo Capet aimed high when choosing a wife for his successor:[63] she was to be a Byzantine princess. Letters to this effect were sent to the emperors Basileios and Constantine. They went unanswered, but then a more promising political opportunity arose. Rozala-Susanna, a daughter of the same Italian king Berengar who had held Adelheid prisoner, was married to Count Arnulf II of Flanders — we know his distant ancestor Judith. Rozala-Susanna was widowed at a convenient moment, though she was 10 or 15 years older than Robert. The union brought Flanders into the ranks of the principalities which recognized Hugo and Robert. The marriage was severed in 992, probably unconsummated. Next came Berta, widow of Count Odo of Blois, another powerful opponent of the Capetians. Berta

---

[63]   J. Dhondt, 'Sept femmes et un trio de rois' (1964/5).

virtually seduced the young King Robert, who let it happen despite his father's wrath. Compliant bishops blessed the union, which was canonically inadmissible on grounds of physical and spiritual propinquity, Berta being a daughter of Adelheid's brother Conrad of Burgundy and having a common forbear with Robert in Henry I; moreover, Robert was godfather to one of Berta's sons. Robert separated from Berta when no heirs arrived, but was unable to give her up entirely, deceiving with her his third wife Constance, a daughter of the count of Provence. The domestic dissension split the court into two hostile parties, and Constance tried to take revenge. She stirred up her younger sons against their father. She survived her husband, and when her son Henry I succeeded to the throne in 1031, she incited a great uprising against him. A full-scale war between mother and son ensued. But Constance − Amazonidis as she was called − was forced to recognize in her son a terrible foe. Finally she threw herself weeping at his feet to beg his mercy. She was, says Dhondt, one of those 'black' women 'who occur not infrequently in the eleventh century.' By the end she was no more than poison and gall, detesting her husband, hating her children, living only to do evil and no doubt hating herself. In her the lust for power seems to have taken the place of love.

Henry I had two wives, a colourless Matilda from their imperial kin in Germany, who did not provide a successor, and then Anna, daughter of the Christian Grand Duke Jaroslav of Kiev, who had himself married a Swedish princess and clearly sought ties with the West. His wife held an important place at the court in Kiev. He had three daughters, one married to King Sven II of Denmark, and one to King Andreas I of Hungary. He would have liked to marry the third, Anna, to the ruler of the German empire. But Henry III, at that time wooing Agnes of Poitou and hoping to win the French king's consent, drew that monarch's attention − so Dhondt surmises − to the opportunity in Kiev, though with the necessary discretion, as Henry was still married. In 1044 the French king was widowed; after meeting Henry III in Ivois in 1048 he sent an envoy to Kiev (doubtless not by coincidence) and received Anna. It is clear that Henry I deliberately avoided choosing a wife from the families of the native French princes at that time; he was also determined to contract a marriage that satisfied all the canonical precepts, since the church reform had triumphed in Rome and the king did not want to be on the wrong side of the pope. But in central Europe it was difficult to avoid his own kin. Anna bore him three sons, one of whom died young. During Henry's lifetime she exerted no political influence. Very soon after his death (1060) she formed a second marriage, to Raoul of Valois, who had rejected his own wife — allegedly for adultery — in her favour. The marriage caused a major scandal in France, but that died down. After the death of her second husband Anna returned to her Russian homeland.

To sum up: a long succession of women has passed through these pages. All of them — whether mentioned briefly (for I wished to escape the charge of talking only of the great ones of the earth) or delineated in more detail — were raised above the toil of a life of 'servile' work. They were shielded from hunger — to have enough to eat was a luxury in the early Middle Ages — and from cold; they were respected and admired. They had servants, were exquisitely dressed and wore much jewellery; they were resplendent at court festivals, poets and scholars revered them, and they were themselves versed in languages, interested in literature, and generally cultured. They knew something of Antiquity (though only a shallow encyclopaedic version), they enjoyed their possessions and their dotal property, and almost all of them loved power. They were pious, as high-born women were at that time; they went to church, founded and endowed monasteries and convents. But they were often taken as young girls to foreign lands far from their own kin, where an alien husband awaited them. They were lucky if once in their lives they could marry the man of their choice, as Judith married the knight Baldwin, or if they could be sheltered by a strong partner as Adelheid was by Otto, Gisela by Conrad. Often they were unable to feel at home in their new country, and returned as widows to their old homelands. They were brave, did not easily give up. (It is true that Galsvintha, who had come laden with treasure to the court of the Frankish king, wanted to return home dispossessed and poor, seeking only to escape pernicious Fredegund.) Many fought: for their sons and grandsons who were still minors, against hostile nobles for the monarchy, as Brunichilde did to the bitter end. They dealt with bishops and popes, contended with guile and diplomacy against men accustomed to drawing their swords, and they had the instinct for power, the pride of the ruler: *Theophanius imperator*. They paid for their position not only by political marriages, they became embroiled in the inner tensions of the royal family, where son stood against father, where brothers fought for crown and inheritance. Their personal feelings — who thought about them in the struggle for power and possessions? They were not always rewarded with gratitude from the children whom they so eagerly helped. Widowhood often brought them large opportunities for regency, in which they wore themselves out as they had done in their husbands' lifetimes, by the ardours of peripatetic rule, the travel from palace to palace, the long journey from Germany to Italy and Burgundy. They died young, like Theophanu and Gisela, or retreated in resignation to a nunnery. It is striking that the title of *consors regni* is first encountered in Italy, that it was there that the two margravines of Tuscia had conspicuous political effect, no doubt based on their lands, where they wielded feudal power.

WOMEN OF THE HIGH NOBILITY IN THE WORLD AND IN THE RELIGIOUS FOUNDATION

The queens were almost all related to the families of the high nobility, for whose unmarried daughters convents and other foundations waited. These were power centres endowed with extensive land. In the convents there was rather more asceticism and stricter obligations. Radegunda had turned to Arles in southern France to obtain the rules for her convent of Ste Croix in Poitiers from Caesarius and Casaria, demonstrating the influence of the old Gallic monasticism.[64] The convents founded by Brunichilde at Autun also followed the Caesarian rules.

About the turn of the sixth century the Irish monk Columban and his companions gave a new impulse to religious life. Despite Columban's personal failure (d. 615), the influx of Irish monks to France continued. His rules were taken over by the new monasteries of the seventh century, and by convents such as Nivelles. I shall pick out the folk saint, Gertrude of Nivelles, as an example of Irish–Frankish monastic culture, as her cult expanded to fill northern and central Europe.[65] In addition, her life and work are

[64]   F. Prinz, *Frühes Mönchtum im Frankenreich. Kultur und Gesellschaft in Gallien, den Rheinlanden und Bayern am Beispiel der monastischen Entwicklung* (1965), pp. 77f.
[65]   M. Zender, *Räume und Schichten mittelalterlicher Heiligenverehrung in ihrer Bedeutung für die Volkskunde,* 2nd enlarged ed. (1973). Cf. Zender's comments on Gertrude of Nivelles, pp. 89ff. A. Angenendt, *Die irische Peregrinatio und ihre Auswirkungen auf dem Kontinent* (1982), and H. J. Vogt, 'Zur Spiritualität des frühen irischen Mönchtums' (1982).

securely documented. Her *vita* was written as early as 20 years after her death. She was a daughter of the Austrasian mayor of the palace to the Merovingians, Pepin of Landen, and entered the convent of Nivelles founded by her mother Itta. As abbess she summoned to Nivelles Irish monks whom she and her sisters instructed in singing. She founded a hospital for the Irish *peregrini*, to take care of these wandering missionaries — it was part of their strict asceticism to sever themselves from homeland and family. Apart from her own convent she endowed the monastery of Fosses, founded by the two Irish monks Foillan and Ultan. She had books and relics sent from Rome to her foundations, no simple undertaking in those days, and one needing wealth and connections. But she had the power of the rising Carolingians behind her. She asked the Irish monk Ultan to say when she was going to die. He named 17 March, the feast-day of St Patrick, the Irish national saint. And so it happened: she died on 17 March 659, aged 32. Her first biography tells of the miraculous rescue of seafarers from her convent by her intercession. Her later veneration in the church and among the common people is based, as Zender shows, on five facts reported in the first biography: her origin among the Pepinids, which means she was related to Charlemagne; the property owned by the convent of Nivelles; her friendship with the Irish missionaries; her help for seafarers in distress and her care for strangers; and her fine death on St Patrick's day. A few decades after her death she was venerated as a saint, at first only in the direct vicinity of Nivelles, but by the eighth century her cult had started to spread. Before the year 1000 principal centres of the cult begin to emerge: the Rhine—Flanders—Wallonia area, the mid-Main region and scattered parts of southern Germany. Her patronage of travellers becomes an important factor in the spread of her cult in northern Germany and Scandinavia in the later Middle Ages. She becomes the patron saint of cemetery chapels and hospices for foreigners. Zender has assembled, interpreted and mapped the evidence with his usual precision.

Women from his Anglo-Saxon homeland played a decisive part in the missionary work of St Boniface[66] among the Germanic tribes on the right bank of the Rhine. The devotional help and the

---

[66] W. Levison, *England and the continent in the eighth century* (1946), pp. 70ff; T. Schieffer, *Winfried-Bonifatius und die christliche Grundlegung Europas* (1954), esp. pp. 162ff; R. Rau, arr., *Briefe des Bonifatius. Willibalds Leben des Bonifatius* (1968).

books given by Abbess Eadburg of the Convent of the Virgin on the Island of Thanet comfort 'the stranger in Germania with spiritual light,' as he writes to her about 735. A number of women came to Germany to support him: Lioba and Walburg, both his kinswomen, Tecla and Cynehild. Cynehild was an aunt of Lul, bishop of Mainz, who, thanks to her scholarly education, later worked as a teacher in Thuringia with her daughter Berhtgit. Tecla became abbess at Kitzingen and Ochsenfurt. Lioba was originally a nun at the convent of Wimborne. In a letter from England she reminds Boniface of his friendship with her father, his kinship with her mother: 'I am my parents' only daughter, and although I do not deserve it I should like you to be my brother, as there is no other among my kin in whom I hope and trust as much as in you.' When Boniface began setting up convents in the Main valley around Würzburg,[67] Lioba joined him, bringing many other women with her; she was made abbess of the convent of Tauberbischofsheim, which had a number of subsidiary convents also under her charge. She was also fond of teaching young girls. Her biographer, Rudolph of Fulda, praises her knowledge of the Bible, of the writings of the Church Fathers and of canon law, as well as her eagerness to read whatever she could. The Frankish kings Pepin, Carloman and Charlemagne honoured Lioba; Charlemagne's wife Hildegard loved her. Her character and conduct were shaped by the Benedictine principle of moderation. Walburg, the sister of the Anglo-Saxon brothers Willibald, bishop of Eichstätt, and Wunibald, was first sent to her; then in 752 Wunibald founded the convent of Heidenheim, the only German monastery for both monks and nuns in the eighth century, and he called Walburg there. After his death in 761[68] she took charge of the monastery, bringing the convent side increasingly to the fore. Walburg died in 779 and her remains were moved to the church of St Walburg in Eichstätt (Walburg is a patron saint of the bishopric). An English nun at Heidenheim, Hugburc,[69] wrote a biography of Walburg and her brothers.

[67] Before Lioba's arrival there were convents in Säckingen, Lauterbach in the Black Forest, Baumerlenbach in Hohenlohe and on an island in the Federsee; Boniface wanted to bring them under the Benedictine rules; cf. E. Blessing, 'Frauenkloster nach der Regel Benedikts in Baden-Württemberg (735—1981)' (1982).

[68] Levison, *England and the continent in the eighth century*, p. 81.

[69] W. Levison and H. Löwe, *Deutschlands Geschichtsquellen im Mittelalter. Vorzeit*

To Wolfhard of Herrieden, who moved to the Eichstätt seminary in 893, we owe reliable reports, written in 894–9, of the veneration of Walburgis in the convent of Monheim, which also had relics of the saint.[70] Wolfhard, a great admirer of Walburg, is none the less a conscientious chronicler (within the context of an age that believed in miracles) who passes on only what he has seen himself or heard from eye-witnesses or the nuns who looked after the pilgrims. Cures, particularly of the lame and blind, are attributed to Walburg. In a dream vision she commanded one of the wives of Ingelswindis, who had a shin fracture from a riding fall that would not heal, to go to a doctor who was to cut open the leg and remove the splinters of bone. The operation was successful, and in gratitude Ingelswindis made a pilgrimage on foot to Monheim, offering a piece of the bone, which the abbess had mounted in silver and hung in the cathedral, and taking the rest home as a relic. If something was lost or stolen, Walburg helped to recover it. A woman who had come to Monheim with her husband on a pilgrimage lost a pin she used to fasten her headscarf at the first inn on the way back. She confessed the loss to her husband who (although she is described as a good wife) reprimanded her for losing the pin like a thoughtless child. The woman hurried back to the holy place – and found her pin. Two citizens of Regensburg who had brought gifts to the convent on behalf of their city and who lay down to sleep nearby, had their horses stolen. Next morning, the thieves discovered with terror that they had ridden in a circle all night and were still close to the convent; they left the horses and fled on foot.

Even when the missionary stage was over, life at a convent offered noblewomen good opportunities for exerting influence. Apart from the convents, there were *Damenstifte* – religious foundations for ladies of rank.[71] In a foundation for noblewomen the inmates did not need to take the oath of poverty and lifelong celibacy. The foundation, like the convent, gave them the

und Karolinger. II Heft (1953), p. 178.

[70] A. Bauch, *Quellen zur Geschichte der Diözese Eichstätt. Band. 2: Ein bayerisches Mirakelbuch aus der Karolingerzeit. Die Monheimer Walpurgis-Wunder des Priesters Wolfhard* (1979).

[71] *Untersuchungen zu Kloster und Stift* (1980); R. Kottje, 'Claustra sine armario? Zum Unterschied von Kloster und Stift im Mittelalter' (1982); K. H. Schäfer, *Die Kanonissenstifter im deutschen Mittelalter* (1907).

opportunity to lead a fulfilled life in regular prayer for the living and dead members of the founder's family, in charitable works and in the education of girls. They could devote themselves to poetry, writing history, philosophy and book-illustration, they could commission artists and prove their worth as administrators of large estates. One could name many pious women, later venerated as saints, who performed major feats, even in the worldly sense. In those days religious foundations were the only welfare institutions, the only hospitals, hostels for foreigners, and schools. To that extent the founding of a convent and its economic support were a charitable and cultural service. The 'saints' of the early Middle Ages were not measured by the strict standards of the modern canonization process.[72] We do not share that age's belief in miracles, and are repelled by the medieval veneration of relics. These are matters of religious style, not basic questions of faith. But the medieval cult of saints has passed down to us some extremely valuable historical documents. Of course, the 'Lives' of the saints contain many standard formulations, eulogies written according to a fixed pattern that say little about the individual case. But there are also some typical individual histories, and interesting descriptions of milieux. Such is the case with Adelheid of Vilich, the abbess of the foundation on the right bank of the Rhine at Bonn. Adelheid had Carolingian forbears on her mother's side.[73] Her parents, Count Megingoz and Gerberga, founded the Stift Vilich, and summoned their daughter, who was canoness of St Ursula's in Cologne, to be its mother superior. Adelheid's biography was written by the nun Bertha shortly after 1056 – Adelheid died after 1009 – so that she was able to draw her information directly from the convent. Adelheid first persuaded her parents to entrust the foundation to the emperor, who gave it special freedoms. Although the foundation did not become directly dependent on the empire, it was an autonomous sub-dominion within the electorate of Cologne. However, its discipline was not strict enough for Adelheid. She had long worn a rough woollen

---

[72] Good general surveys are to be found in J. Torsy, *Lexikon der deutschen Heiligen* (1959); P. Manns, *Die Heiligen. Alle Biographien zum Regionalkalender für das deutsche Sprachgebiet* (1975); D. H. Farmer, *The Oxford Dictionary of Saints* (1978).

[73] S. Corsten, 'Die Grafen von Jülich unter den Ottonen und Saliern' (1977); F. W. Oediger, *Das Bistum Köln von den Anfängen bis zum Ende des 12. Jahrhunderts* (1972), pp. 282, 401f.

chemise under the white robe of the *Stiftsdame*: then, after her mother's death, she summoned her sisters and the prioresses from St Maria im Kapitol in Cologne and placed herself under their direction, to learn convent customs. It distressed her that not all the members of her community agreed with this course. Then, about 1000, she had to take charge of Maria im Kapitol as well, a heavy burden. What makes Adelheid so appealing are the expressions of maternal concern which Bertha records: how Adelheid visited her young pupils at night after matins to rub their feet warm, and tended sick sisters herself; how, during the great famine, she did not have the usual soup cooked, but something specially suited to those weakened by hunger; how she produced a sweet from her pocket to reward those schoolgirls who had learned their Latin grammar well (Oediger).

By no means all mother superiors and abbesses resembled Adelheid of Vilich, who is still revered today. The ladies of the high nobility were often deficient in humility and obedience. Otto II's daughter Sophie, for example, wished to receive the veil only from a wearer of the *pallium*, and therefore demanded that her convent at Gandersheim should be placed under the jurisdiction of the archbishop of Mainz, not the bishop of Hildesheim. She denied Bishop Bernward of Hildesheim entry to the convent by force of arms. Assembling a body of armed men from the archbishop's retainers and her own men, she set up fortifications around the church, as if it had to be defended against a barbarian attack.[74] We know from other cases that the church's troops were under the command of the abbess or her bailiff.

Despite such incidents, convents were of special importance as centres of learning. Women's contribution to intellectual life in the early Middle Ages was very significant — more so, on occasions, than that of men. Among the strikingly numerous convents and women's foundations, or *Frauenstifte*, in Ottonian Saxony, the royal foundations at Quedlinburg and Gandersheim were outstanding both culturally and politically. The second wife of the first Saxon monarch, Matilda, daughter of a count descended from Widukind, had been educated at the foundation of Herford; she was the foundress of Quedlinburg. Here the regent Matilda, whom we have already met, was abbess from 966 to 999. Most important of

[74] *MGSS.IV*, 772, 32; K. J. Leyser, *Rule and conflict in an early medieval society. Ottonian Saxony* (1979).

all was Gandersheim.[75] Otto I obtained papal protection for Gandersheim, restricting the influence of the head of the diocese, the bishop of Hildesheim. For years Gandersheim filled the role of a palace, the court sojourning there frequently. It was there that Empress Theophanu gave birth to her third daughter, Matilda, who later married the Rhenish prince Ezzo; she had her private archive kept there. Under Abbess Gerberga, a daughter of Henry of Bavaria and niece of Otto I, the first German poetess, Hrotsvit (Roswitha) lived there. Born about 935, Roswitha entered Gandersheim at an early age, and spent her whole life in the foundation. Her works are characterized by deep classical learning and formal accomplishment. In Gandersheim she had access to an important library.[76] Her first poems deal with legends; six dramas were intended to supplant the frivolous comedies of Terence. In one heroic poem she celebrated Emperor Otto — not without a sidelong glance at the court. A second historical poem is about the founding of Gandersheim. However, Roswitha's level of poetic achievement was not attained again at Gandersheim.

In 979 Sophie, the four-year-old daughter of Otto II, was handed over to Abbess Gerberga. At her investiture (probably in 987) a quarrel over the ecclesiastical responsibility for the foundation that was to last for years broke out between Archbishop Willigis of Mainz and the bishops of Hildesheim. A compromise was reached: Archbishop Willigis celebrated mass at the high altar; he and Bishop Osdag of Hildesheim performed the investiture ceremony while the other maidens received the veil from Bishop Osdag alone. In 995 Sophie's younger sister Adelheid took the veil at Quedlinburg. Sophie vehemently upheld the claims of her family and played a certain role in imperial politics.[77] This can be shown by royal charters on which she appears as intervernor. She took a period of leave from the foundation to accompany her brother Otto III on his first visit to Rome. In 997 there was a change in the relationship between the siblings when Archbishop Willigis lost his influence with the emperor to Bernward of Hildesheim. Now, as was mentioned earlier, his aunt Matilda

---

[75] H. Goetting, *Das Bistum Hildesheim 1, Das reichsunmittelbare Kanonissenstift Gandersheim* (1973).

[76] M. Schütze-Pflugk, *Herrscher- und Märtyrerauffassung bei Hrotsvit von Gandersheim* (1972).

[77] O. Perst, 'Die Kaiserstochter Sophie, Äbtissin von Gandersheim und Essen (975–1039)' (1957).

represented him. When Otto returned from his second visit to Italy at the beginning of the year 1000, both his sisters, Sophie and Adelheid, who, after Matilda's death had succeeded her as abbess of Quedlinburg, rushed to meet him; but Otto now inclined towards Adelheid. Sophie represented Gerberga during her last illness. The conflict over Gandersheim came into the open when the new foundation church was consecrated, and above all when Bernward tried to assert judicial rights in Gandersheim. Sophie violently opposed him, having armed a band of men and put up fortifications around the church. On 13 November 1001 she became abbess; her imperial brother died on 21 January 1002. Adelheid and Sophie at once took sides with the Ottonian party, that is, with Henry II, in opposition to Bernward. The Gandersheim quarrel was only finally laid to rest in 1031. In the meantime Sophie had also become abbess of Essen, another foundation of the Saxon ruling house. There she battled with Archbishop Pilgrim of Cologne over the ownership of tithes between the Rhine and the Ruhr, which Pilgrim succeeded in settling amicably. She died in 1038. Sophie probably went too far against Bernward, but otherwise one must admire her steadfastness, her courage and her wise management of her possessions. The royal policy of using imperial abbeys as bulwarks against episcopal power found in her an admirable exponent. We should also see Sophie's conduct against the background of the sacred status of the monarchy – which at that time was unshaken. For Roswitha, Otto I was the *potestas a Deo ordinata*, the power ordained by God. The ruler's sacred attributes extended to the whole family, and this was the basis of Sophie's self-confidence.

The women living outside the convents also tended to be more highly educated than their husbands, who were overburdened with the demands of government and war. Gerberga's sister Hadwig was not sent to a convent.[78] She was betrothed at an early age to the Greek prince Constantine of Byzantium, hence her Greek education. But when a Greek painter asked to paint her portrait, so that it could be sent to her betrothed, she pulled a face so 'full of hatred for the marriage' that both the painting and the marriage came to nothing. So, at least, we read in the chronicle of Saint-Gall. Hadwig has become known through Scheffel's novel

---

[78] O. Feger, 'Herzogin Hadwig von Schwaben in Dichtung und Wirklichkeit' (1957), pp. 144ff.

Ekkehard; the modern historian Otto Feger has unravelled the historical truth. At 15 she married the Swabian Purchard, who became duke in 955 and died in 973, after 18 years of marriage. He lived on the Hohentwiel, where he founded a small monastery with his wife. It is not true that after her husband's death Hadwig became the ruler of the duchy and administrator of the empire in Swabia; we know the male successors, who were dukes of Swabia during Hadwig's lifetime. In any case, the ruler needed to be a man, who could mount a horse and lead his people personally into battle. But Hadwig was, even as a widow, a rich and important woman who controlled extensive territory, numerous villages and farms and a great many servants. Ekkehard was already head of the monastery school of Saint-Gall, a strict and highly respected scholar, when he came to Hohentwiel. By then Hadwig was a mature woman of 35 or 40, who is described as austere, tough and self-confident. Although a romance between them cannot be ruled out, it is not very likely. But Hadwig was certainly a woman who was seriously concerned about scholarship, and who wished to gather a circle of learned men around her.

By that time the nobility lived in castles. Soon the lords began to append the name of their castle to their first name as a kind of surname, which was then inherited by the male line. The women took the name of their husbands. The concept of the family grew more agnatic. On the Lower Rhine this shift can be observed about 1000. The time we are discussing is still the age of the single name.

The Hamaland had been ruled by the Wichmann family since the Carolingian period, when this region, originally the land of the Chamavi, was incorporated more solidly into the empire.[79] Count Wichmann, who died shortly after 973, had married Liutgard, a daughter of Count Arnulf of Flanders and Adèle of Vermandois. This increased the importance of his family, which now had an influx of Carolingian blood. The centre of his domain was the castle of Elten; the Elten mountain rises high above the lower

[79]   On this account of Adela cf. J. Düffel, 'Gräfin Adela von Hamaland und ihr Kampf um das Stift Hochelten' (1978) (the essay first appeared in 1953); F. W. Oediger, *Vom Leben am Niederrhein* (1973) (the essay 'Adelas Kampf um Elten 996–1002' first appeared in 1954); G. Binding, 'Spätkarolingisch-ottonische Pfalzen und Burgen am Niederrhein' (1972); Anna Wirtz née Henningsen, 'Die Geschichte des Hamalandes' (1971); J. M. van Winter, 'Die Hamaländer Grafen. Angehörige der Reich saristokratie im 10. Jhd' (1980).

Rhenish plane. Elten was evidently the residence of the Wichmanns as early as 944, for at that time King Otto visited Count Wichmann, who would have needed to accommodate the king and his retinue. In 962 Wichmann's wife died, and was followed by his only son, probably before 968. These deaths were a heavy blow to the old count, so that he founded a *Damenstift* on the Eltenberg, his eldest daughter Liutgard becoming its abbess. He obtained immunity for the foundation and had the king confirm the rich estates that he made over to it. The noble maidens, who did not need to take an oath, did not lead an ascetic life — although, of course, they lived unmarried at the foundation. Liutgard was downcast when she had no visitors. For her the *Stift*, 'in the midst of ramparts that surrounded the church like a wall', was a continuation of a noble household, with servants, knightly retainers and guests.

Count Wichmann had used a large part of his fortune to equip the *Stift* and Liutgard endowed it with her whole inheritance. After Wichmann's death her younger sister Adela demanded that part of the estate should be returned, claiming that her father had not obtained the *secundum legem Saxonicam*, the agreement of the heirs required by Saxon law. On these grounds she contested the entire endowment. And in fact we always find the heirs' consent mentioned in deeds of gifts, e.g. in bequests to the church at Paderborn made in the days of Bishop Meinwerk (1009–36). Meinwerk was a son of Adela's first marriage to Count Immed, who died before 996. Otto II tried in vain to bring the dispute between the sisters to an end. It was Liutgard who had possession, and allies. Her kinsman Godizo, originally one of Adela's followers, set fire to Adela's castle one night with Balderich. Adela escaped. Then Liutgard died of poisoning. Rumour had it that Adela was the instigator. While everyone was mourning Liutgard, Adela stormed in and took possession of everything her sister had given to the church, but was herself dispossessed, in disgrace, on the orders of Emperor Otto III. Now Adela (who during her widowhood had 'denied herself to no one'), after consulting with her people, married that same Balderich who had once smoked her out of her castle. It was not a marriage of equals, but it provided Adela with a guardian who could represent her before the princely court, and gave Balderich the prospect of some handsome property. The affair was settled at the Imperial Diet at Nimwegen in 996. In his name and his wife's Balderich conceded the protection of the foundation to the emperor — this was done by throwing a blade of straw, the symbolic gesture signifying the renunciation of land — and returned all the property to it. What was not stated explicitly, but can be inferred from a comparison of the property lists at the time of foundation in 970 and of the verdict in 996, is that Adela had succeeded in dividing the paternal inheritance and had recovered her share. She was also accused of various crimes — murdering her own son Dietrich and inciting others to murder Wichmann of Vreden in Westphalia. Each accusation seems to have been slanderous. She had a highly developed sense of property, and knew how to get her way in a legal dispute. Similar characteristics show themselves in her son Meinwerk, except that he enriched the church rather than himself. His long residence at court — he was attached to the court chapel before being made bishop — had made him more subtle and thoughtful. Adela's marriage to Balderich was childless, with the result that they made large religious endowments. After Balderich's death she sought sanctuary on church property and died in Cologne. She is said to have been buried in front of the cathedral. Another rumour, 'that during a terrible storm that threatened to submerge the whole town her body was dug up and thrown into the Rhine, which tossed and seethed for days as if publicly protesting that it would not harbour the body of this accursed woman — all that is just another of the punishments that legend is quick to dispense' (Oediger). Be that as it may, her name is entered in the books of the dead of Cologne and of the convent of Abdinghof in Paderborn. A daughter from her first marriage was a nun at Elten.

Women did not have an easy life. High birth in no way guaranteed a comfortable existence. Women of the high nobility had to be ready at all times to stand in for their husbands when they were away or unable to perform their duties. Emperor Henry V, besieging the barbarian stronghold of Mousson in Lorraine and enraged by its long resistance, threatened to execute Count von Bar, whom he had captured, unless the fortress capitulated. Countess von Bar, who was at an advanced stage of pregnancy, asked for a period of 24 hours to reflect. During this time she gave birth to a son, made the occupants of the fort take an oath of allegiance to the new-born child, and rejected the next demand for surrender, since the defenders now had a new lord — 'novum dominum, quem illa nocte uxor eius sibi peperisset, haberent'.[80]

But courage and energy were not always enough to help a woman in an age when a small class of arms-bearing magnates, *potentes*, who were ready to defend their rights and their families by force of arms if need be, stood opposed to the broad mass of *inermes pauperes*, the unarmed populace, and when the state kept the peace very imperfectly. What use was legal freedom to a woman who was alone and unprotected? She did better to renounce her freedom and accept the protection of the church, of a land-owning clergy, so gaining the *liberior servitus*, the 'free servitude' of a tribute-payer. Bosl has drawn attention to the problem of this form of dependence with reference to Regensburg sources.[81] He shows a drawing together of the citizens and populace of Regensburg, drawn from the different legal circles of the king, the bishop, the monastery and the nobility, and mentions a certain Wizala who purchased her freedom from her *dominus*, i.e. her feudal lord Pezaman, and then made him give her to St Emmeram, paying a tribute as a dependent. K. Schulz has recently dealt with this institution of tribute-paying dependence in detail.[82]

These dependent people (*Zensualen*), who appear in documents as *censuales, tributarii* or *cerocensuales* (payers of wax-duty), were either free people who dedicated themselves to a saint of the church, or unfree people who were released from bondage by their lords and then donated to the church. The *censuales* paid a yearly tax of between two and five pence; in the Lower Rhine area, especially, they were allowed to pay the tax in the form of wax for the candles on the altar. They also had to pay a death duty, either in money or, for women, in the form of their best dress, and a marriage duty. They received in exchange the monastery's protection for themselves and their possessions, exemptions from duties and services to government officials or other lords, and freedom from expropriation when there was a transfer of fiefs or land. Unlike the *servi*, or bondsmen, they enjoyed a certain freedom of movement. The transition to this form of protection can be observed

---

[80] F.-J. Schmale, *Bischof Otto von Freising und Rahewin. Die Taten Friedrichs, oder richtiger: Cronica* (1965), p. 150.

[81] K. Bosl, *Die Sozialstruktur der mittelalterlichen Residenz- und Fernhandelsstadt Regensburg* (1966), pp. 33f.

[82] K. Schulz, 'Zensualität und Stadtentwicklung im 11./12. Jahrhundert' (1982), which lists the earlier literature.

in Flanders from the tenth century on. A striking fact revealed by the documents is the large number of women who placed themselves among the *censuales*. Thus Bavin, whose mother Engelwara, born of free parents, had been incurably ill for years, donated herself to the abbey of St Peter in Ghent. On 1 October each year she paid 2 denars, for which she could live in total freedom (*plena ingenuitate secura*) under the protection of the monastery.[83] The notion of freedom is ambiguous here, as a completely free person paid no tribute. In 989 Godelinda, and in 993/4 Folcrada, give themselves to the same abbey;[84] although free, they make themselves liable to tribute (*libera cum esset, tributarium se constituit*). For the period around 1000, five other cases of women handing themselves over to St Peter's are reported.[85] It would be easy to find further examples, for, as the abbot and chronicler Rudolf, of the monastery at St Trond, pointed out: 'Whenever there was feuding in the land or strife in the empire, anyone who could claim to be the servant or maid of St Trudo dwelt safely on his land.'[86]

Otherwise, the great ladies lived in their castles. In times of peace they were responsible for the domestic economy, the management of the great household. They also did fine textile work. Our energetic Adela owned many chambermaids skilled in every kind of needlework, and she herself surpassed almost all the women of the Lower Rhine in the making of precious garments. Similar skills are attributed to Mathilde, the sister of Bishop Burchard of Worms, and other women of high rank.[87]

What did the women wear, what did they eat and drink? The author of the biography of Bishop Meinwerk, Adela's son, describes a number of annuities intended for benefactors of the church, who gave their lands.[88] Much fur was worn; there was a large fur trade by 1000. Even then, fur was a status symbol and sable was the most sought-after, while marten and grey squirrel were also

[83]   M. Gysseling, A. C. F. Koch, eds., *Diplomata Belgica ante annum millesimum centesimum scripta* (1950), no. 61, pp. 157f. Claimed as original.

[84]   Ibid., nos 73, 78, pp. 179, 184.

[85]   Ibid., also nos 91 (claimed as original), 83, 84 (claimed original), 85 (claimed original), 86, pp. 188ff.

[86]   J. L. Charles, *La ville de St. Trond au Moyen-Age* (1965), p. 122, n. 19.

[87]   J. Barchewitz, *Beiträge zur Wirtschaftstätigkeit der Frau. Untersuchungen von der vorgeschichtlichen Zeit bis in das Hochmittelalter, auf dem Boden des Karolingerreiches* (1937), pp. 98ff.

[88]   F. Tenckhoff, *Vita Meinwerci Episcopi Patherbrunnensis* (1921) and the discussion of it in F. Irsigler, 'Divites und pauperes in der Vita Meinwerci' (1970).

highly valued. The noble widow Fretherun, who had given three farms with their equipment and 38 freed persons to the Paderborn church, was to receive every Easter a blanket of fox fur and a coat and robe of squirrel fur. The items which the nun Atta stipulated for herself included a blanket of fox pelts, and a cloak and fur garment of marten skin. Such costly clothes almost counted as everyday dress. In exchange for her inheritance, the nun Liudburg received an annuity which included two vests, a woollen over-garment, the tanned hide of a ram — probably for shoes — each year, and a more costly garment every two years. For agreeing to present her son Tiedi, a mother received a full-length garment, a vest, and every four years a costly fur garment, as well as vegetables. The sisters Bosan, Christina and Ebbikan, who made over their joint property in eight villages, received in return a marten skin (*martherinum pelliceum*) and a sable fur (*zebellinam tunicam*), each worth six talents. Sable, marten and grey squirrel furs could only be obtained by trade, which made them even more expensive; fox pelts and sheepskins were an indigenous product. Fretherun not only dressed expensively, she also ate and drank well. To begin with, she received each year, apart from money and the fur clothing already mentioned, 12 hams, 20 measures of wheat and 30 urns of wine; a second contract provided the following annuity: 6 hams with offal and 6 without, 20 measures of wheat, 20 measures of other grain, 5 barrels of beer, a *carrada* of wine, 10 sheep with lambs and 5 without, 5 pigs, and money. The elevated pretensions of this lady are expressed in the fact that she ate white bread and drank wine. We can assume that it was Rhine wine which, in the Paderborn area, could be easily obtained from Cologne. The nun Atta's annuity included 90 cheeses and 3 jugs of honey. Up to the sixteenth century, honey was the most im-portant sweetener in the kitchen, as sugar beet was not yet culti-vated (it was introduced by Napoleon) and cane sugar from the Orient was very expensive. Fish is not mentioned in annuity agreements, but fishing rights do appear in the gifts to the church as appurtenances of estates. At that time all secular and church landowners had fishponds, and the clear rivers and streams still contained plentiful fish. But by the eleventh century herring was also traded, as we know from customs documents. In the medieval economy it had far more importance than it has today. Herring was an important part of the popular diet, both as food during fasts and as a source of protein. From excavations of the stronghold of Haus Meer[89] north of Neuss, inhabited from the tenth to the thirteenth century, we know the animal and vegetable diet of the residents. The following cultivated varieties of plants have been identified: sweet cherries, plums, damsons, peaches, sloes, apples, walnuts, hazelnuts, vines, black elder, blackberries, sweet chestnuts, medlars, pears. The following cereals were eaten: seed oats, millet, yellow millet, wheat, oats, rye. Strawberries, sloes, raspberries, rosehips and cranberries were gathered, as was the medicinal herb dwarf elder (*Sambucus ebulus*). Also cultivated were: amaranth (a salad plant), dill, celery, hemp, carrots, flax, peas, corn salad. The most commonly found bones were those of the domestic pig, followed by cattle, sheep or goats. There was also wild or domestic duck, greylag or domestic geese and domestic chickens, and the following wild animals: rabbit, hare, red deer, wild boar.

After this glimpse into the kitchen, a point of constitutional law. In this period we find the first evidence of women becoming capable of holding a fief; it occurs in the innovating areas of north-west Europe, in an agreement between the Bishop of Liège and the Count of Namur.[90] But these were only the beginnings. The fief-holding by women spread from the west eastwards, and was quickly established in the south: The *libri feudorum* of the end of the eleventh century in Bologna mention subsidiary rights of female succession, the so-called *feudum femineum*.[91]

MAIDSERVANTS AND THE WIVES OF SERFS

For a long time there were legal restrictions on the right of unfree people to marry. Indeed, the idea of a natural right to marry first had to be established for these people. It was far from existing in the early Frankish period.[92] According to the *Lex Salica*, it was for the master to decide whether or not to allow a slave of either sex to marry. If a male slave married someone else's female slave

[89] W. Janssen, 'Essen und Trinken im frühen und hohen Mittelalter aus archäologischer Sicht' (1981).
[90] J.-L. Kupper, 'Une "conventio" inédite entre l'évêque de Liège Théoduin et le comte Albert II. de Namur (1056–64)' (1979).
[91] S. Bovet, 'Die Stellung der Frau im deutschen und langobardischen Lehnsrecht' (1926–8), p. 47.
[92] H. Nehlsen, *Sklavenrecht zwischen Antike und Mittelalter*, pp. 271f.

without her master's agreement, he was soundly beaten. The unfree evidently tried to get protection for their marriages from the church. The matter was discussed at the Council of Orléans in 541, but the clergy were forbidden to protect such unions; they were instructed to return the couple to their masters in exchange for an assurance that they would not be punished; but the masters had the right to separate them. Gregory of Tours tells of a vindictive contemporary whose behaviour shows what could happen if a priest even took sides with an unfree couple who wished to marry (bk V, ch. 3): 'The man in question is a certain Rauching, who treated his subordinates as if there were not a trace of humanity in him.' Rauching must have been something of a sadist, for the following is told about him:

There were among his people a man and a girl who, as often happens, were in love with each other. When their relationship had gone on for two years or longer, they married and took refuge in a church. When Rauching found out, he went to the village priest and demanded that his people should be handed over to him at once, for he had forgiven their offence. The priest said to him: 'You know the respect that must be shown to God's church; they will not be returned unless you give your word that you will allow their union to continue, and promise that you will administer no corporal punishment.' First the man kept silent for a long time, uncertain in his mind; then he placed his hands on the altar and swore: 'Never shall they be parted by me, and I shall take good care that they stay together, for although I was displeased that they married without my consent, I am glad that my slave (*servus*) did not marry another man's slave (*ancilla*) and that she did not marry another man's slave.' The unsuspecting priest believed this artful promise and handed the slaves over on the condition they would not be punished. When he had them, Rauching thanked the priest and returned home. At once he had a tree felled and the branches cut off, the trunk split with an axe and hollowed out. Then he had a pit dug three or four feet deep and the box lowered into it. Then he had the girl laid into the trunk with the slave on top of her, closed the lid and refilled the pit with earth, and so he buried them alive. 'I have not broken my oath,' he declared, 'since I promised that they should be united for eternity.' When this was reported to the priest, he hurried to the place. Rebuking the man, he succeeded with much trouble in having the couple dug out. Although the man was pulled out alive, the girl had already suffocated.

Nor do the Frankish sources forbid a master to violate a marriage that he has permitted between his slaves by intercourse with the female slave concerned. In the eighth century the Langobard king

Liutprand issued a prohibition on such acts: it was not pleasing to God, he decreed, that any man should fornicate with the wife of another (*cum uxorem aliena*).[93] The *Decretum Vermeriense* (about 750), probably drafted by a capitulary, confirms the right to separate the marriages of slaves when they are sold. 'Late-Roman law,' Nehlsen comments, 'which made considerable attempts to protect the slave family, clearly had no influence here.'

Two factors improved the situation of the the unfree: firstly the church, although, as we have seen, it had difficulty in enforcing its demands in practice.[94] Secondly, the developments within land-ownership (described in the Introduction to this book) played a part: the change from patriarchal slavery within the household to an unfreedom tied to a piece of land, the removal of unfree people from the manor house to become *servi casati*, bondsmen living in houses. It was now in the master's interest to allow families to be founded, both between the unfree, and between the half-free and the unfree.[95] The monarchy and the clergy pushed this development forward. But there were constant difficulties when people belonging to different domains wanted to marry. Which landlord was to forgo the service of the spouse and the children from such a marriage? Should they follow the mother or the 'worse hand', i.e. the partner with lower status in tribal law? Special agreements were often needed between landowners. It is here that the real problems of unfree women lay — not in the law of the 'first night' which is given disproportionate attention, and for which little actual evidence exists.

From earliest times there had been a sex-specific division of labour regarding the work women were to do in their everyday lives. This generally allotted work within the household to women. In a peasant family this would have meant the following: the wife prepares the bath, grinds the corn in a hand-mill, brews the beer, cooks and cleans, and also helps in the landlord's vineyard, with the picking of berries in the forest and with the corn harvest. The *Admonitio generalis* of 789 connected with the observation of the sabbath gives detailed information on the *opera servilia* (menial

[93]   Ibid., p. 368.
[94]   G. M. Müller-Lindenlauf, *Germanische und spätrömisch-christliche Eheauffassung in fränkischen Volksrechten und Kapitularien* (1969). Cf. p. 48.
[95]   L. Kuchenbuch, *Bäuerliche Gesellschaft und Klosterherrschaft im 9. Jhd. Studien zur Sozialstruktur der Familia der Abtei Prüm* (1978).

labour) forbidden on Sundays. The men are not to work in the vineyard, or to plough or harvest, or to mow grass, make fences, clear the forest, build houses or work in the garden. The women are to perform no *opera textrilia* — which included all work from harvesting thread-producing plants or sheep-shearing, to making the finished garment. On Sundays they are not to cut out clothes, to sew or to pick wool, to beat flax, to wash in a public building or to shear sheep. Whereas garden work is here allocated to men, Bishop Meinwerc makes the wife of one of his estate officials (*uxor villici*) responsible for the untended state of her garden, which has become full of nettles and weeds (cap. 148). Now the sewing done by peasant wives was by no means limited to the clothing needed for their own families. The working of the plant and animal fibres (flax, hemp and wool) produced by the socage farm is exclusively the affair of women, according to the property list of the Eifel monastery of Prüm in the ninth century. They have to make linen sheets, shirts and trousers. This was done, according to the Prüm register, in the peasants' houses.

On secular domains, and in the socage farms of church estates, there were also cloth factories in which only women worked. These factories had been introduced by the state in late Antiquity and were taken over by the Merovingian kings. According to Gregory of Tours (bk IX, ch. 38) such a factory, or *genitium*, existed in Marlenheim in Alsace. A certain Septimia, who had intrigued aginst Queen Brunichilde and King Childebert, was punished by being sent to the royal court at Marlenheim, where she turned the mills to supply the maids in the workhouse with their daily requirement of flour. The women in these textile factories were provided with shelter, food and clothing by the landowner, but are unlikely to have been paid a wage.[96] Up to 40 women worked in some *genitia*. A woman of higher status was in charge. According to the regulations of the royal domains, the famous *Capitulare de villis*, raw materials and implements were supplied by the landowner: flax, wool, woad (the medieval dye-plant for blue), scarlet dye, madder for red, wool combs, teasel, soap, oil, vessels, etc. The dyeing of textiles was therefore carried out in the *genitium*. The women worked in solidly-built houses with rooms and sheds

Cf. Barchewitz, *Beiträge zur Wirtschaftstätigkeit der Frau*; and especially the detailed information in Irsigler, 'Divites und pauperes in der Vita Meinwerci', pp. 482ff.

that could be heated, or in houses recessed in the ground. The seven women at a *genitium* owned by the abbey of Werden on the Ruhr, at an estate at Leer in Westphalia, received yearly for their subsistence 104 bushels of rye, 80 bushels of barley, 148 bushels of oats, 222 bushels of other grain, 10 bushels of beans, and money. The excavations at the Ottonian palace of Tilleda have yielded precise archaeological information on the nature of this institution: there were two cloth-making shops, both dug into the front rampart of the palace, where the other utility buildings were also located. One shop was 29 metres long and 6 metres wide, the other about 15.5 metres long and 4.5 metres wide. Inside both buildings there were long pits in which groups of large, round, weaving weights point to the use of standing looms. P. Grimm,[97] who carried out the excavations, estimates that there were 22 to 24 women to each shop. The lives of workers in such factories were certainly not easy, and their status was low. These cloth workshops existed up to the twelfth century, when the dissolution of the socage farm and the development of an urban textile industry with professional workers and a superior product, put an end to them.

Compared with the large family communities of the nobility, the peasant family was small. However, tenant farmers (*servi casati*) in their turn owned slaves, servants and maids who were at the very bottom of the social ladder. Scholars have only recently begun a statistical analysis of the information available from property lists and documents. So far we have only scattered conclusions on the early period. Kuchenbuch has established for Prüm that a married couple had three to four children on average. Nuclear familes are predominant, sometimes as many as four families living together on a hide of land (*mansus*); extended families are rare. In these peasant families the wife takes the husband's place on his death, but often relinquishes it to one of her sons, who keeps his mother and siblings with him until he founds his own family. The single or widowed woman is uncommon as an occupant of a *mansus*, though men in the same situation are often to be found. In the *Polyptichon Irminonis* of the abbey of St Germain-des-Prés (about 829), 63 widowed women appear as occupants of a *mansus* and 42 unmarried women. Only in one case had a married man his mother, two brothers and a sister at his house as

[97] P. Grimm, 'Zwei bemerkenswerte Gebäude in der Pfalz Tilleda. Eine zweite Tuchmacherei' (1963).

well as his wife and child; he owned a relatively large *mansus*. The *servus* as husband of a *colona* or *ingenua* is always the head of the family and the owner of the *mansus*. The wife nearly always moves to the husband's house. The predominant position of the husband is unmistakable.[98] By means of a deed of gift of 820 for the monastery of Engelbrechtsmünster in Bavaria,[99] the following information has been gathered about the mansion in present-day Oberlauterbach: the socage farm included its own church, i.e. a church built by the landlord to which he could apppoint the priests, and 94 persons, including 47 unhoused slaves and 46 serfs on 11 smallholdings. The smith's house was very large. In what is now Niederlauterbach there were 80 *manentes*, housed peasants, on 20 smallholdings belonging to a manor house of the monastery of St Emmeram; 14 were run by one married couple each, three by two married couples each, one by two brothers, one by a widow and one by a widow with three children. On three of the farms the peasants had slaves.

The gulf between the property, income, influence and style of life of the upper class, the *potentes*, and the *pauperes* or serfs, was so wide for three main reasons: because there was not yet an intermediate burgher class; because the upper class was so small and the lower so large; and because the inequality was not merely social but legal. Of course, there were gradations within the upper and lower classes. But to rise from one to the other there was always a double barrier to overcome.

The possibility of rising nevertheless existed, and even took several forms. Not only freemen became *censuales* to gain the church's protection, but slaves did so as well. It showed a lack of delicacy to make God and his saints a gift of the unfree, so that slaves were first freed and then given to the church, where they became liable to duties — sometimes the wax duty, which helped to supply churches with the large quantity of wax needed for candles. For example, between 996 and 1029 Erkenrad and her children give the abbey of St Peter in Ghent her slave Alfgard, with her children Everbold, Eremfrid, Herlinde and Gertrud, for the salvation of her husband, herself and her children. She frees them from all

[98] F. Schwind, 'Beobachtungen zur inneren Struktur des Dorfes in karolingischer Zeit' (1977).
[99] M. Heinzelmann, 'Beobachtungen zur Bevölkerungsstruktur einiger grundherrschaftlicher Siedlungen im karolingischen Bayern' 1977/8.

bonds of servitude, so that they are, and will remain, as free as if they were born of free parents. They are to enjoy the protection of the monastery and pay an annual tax of two denars, and six denars on marriage; on their deaths the sum of 12 denars shall be paid to the monastery from their wealth.[100] This is one example of many such gifts.

The increase in markets in the eleventh century gives the peasants the chance to earn money. They want the tithes they pay to landowners in produce to be converted into money duties, and sometimes achieve it by confrontation. This allows them to profit from the creeping devaluation of money, although the conversion was never completely achieved. In the eleventh century their right to use the land leased to them by the landlord became a hereditary right of ownership, and the tithes were no longer imposed on persons but were reified, being levied on the farm and remaining the same even if the farm were divided. The peasants are not afraid to improve their lot by tax-strikes, and sometimes they simply run away from the landlord, taking their wives and children with them. After all, they can make a new life in the nearest town.[101] This brings us to a great historical turning-point, and to the beginning of a new chapter.

[100]   Gysseling and Koch, *Diplomata Belgica, no.* 82, p. 188.
[101]   E. Ennen, 'Die Grundherrschaft St Maximin und die Bauern von Wasserbillig' (1977), pp. 472ff.

2

The High Middle Ages 1050–1250

WHAT URBAN LIFE AND THE DEVELOPMENT OF FAMILY LAW MEANT FOR WOMEN

How did the emergence of an urban burgher class, with a uniform law, a free civic society and an urban economy based on trade and crafts, affect the position of women?

Medieval towns depended on migration from the land to maintain themselves; they did not grow solely from their own resources. The town always attracted people, with its many opportunities for gain and work, the greater security within its walls, the amusement and conviviality it offered, the splendid processions to welcome great lords, the pomp of its churches, the displays, dances and festivities. Finally, the towns were almost the only places where people of lowly status could attain the right to personal freedom in the Middles Ages. Admittedly, this right was not given at the outset. In a protracted process, the old German settlements that were distinguished by a bishop's see, a palace or a dynastic stronghold, etc., became towns with their own jurisdiction and a special civic law. The *servus casatus* who left his plot of land and the oppressive drudgery that went with it, probably taking his wife, risked having his lord demand his return. The following tale is recorded in Rheims about the end of the twelfth century:[1] a young man of the lesser nobility claimed that a citizen of Rheims was his bondsman; the other denied it. The young man followed him, tracked him down, met him in the market square at Rheims and killed him. This caused an uproar in the whole town, and the

---

[1] F. Vercauteren, *Etude sur les civitates de la Belgique seconde* (1934), p. 105, n. 2; *MG SS t. XXV*, p. 154.

murderer was pursued. He, however, was the son-in-law of a porter in the town, Baldwin, whose house was close to the market-place. The young man fled to the house and hid there until the unrest had died down. His kinsman led him out by night, and so the offender made his escape. Not every landlord struck his absconding bondsman dead if he caught up with him. There were ecclesiastical landlords who won back bondsmen by reducing the taxes imposed on them, but there are sure to have been some lords who recovered their serfs by threats and punishment.

The residents of the quasi-urban communities of the early Middle Ages were legally and socially mixed. There were the dependants of the town ruler, including many slaves and serfs, and there were professional merchants travelling the country under royal protection, *ministeriales*, that is, higher servants of the town ruler and of monasteries and other religious foundations in the town, or dependent on it. Added to these were many people still subject to the burdens and ties of rural existence. The frictions resulting from this juxtaposition were particularly sharply felt in the confined space of the town. Towns offered new opportunities of livelihood and gain, but only to those who had freedom of movement and were exempt from the old feudal obligations. In the country the limits of personal freedom imposed on the bondsmen had a certain justification, since the bondsmen had received land and protection from the landlord. In the town this basis for hereditary taxes largely ceased to apply, and the taxes absorbed profits and revenue from trading and crafts that would otherwise have circulated in the urban economy. The marriage restrictions which, in the country, were the legal outcome of marriages between social unequals, had a devastating effect in towns. A 'villainous, useless custom' − thus the citizens of Speyer[2] designated the *Buteil*, a duty imposed on socially mixed marriages, or the marriages of widowed serfs to partners outside the estate. This *Buteil*, as Knut Schulz[3] has convincingly shown from other sources, should be clearly distinguished from normal death duties. It was imposed only on 'mixed' marriages, and when it was levied two-thirds of the husband's property went to the lord, who could even annul such marriages under certain circumstances. In the

[2] F. Keutgen, *Urkunden zur städtischen Verfassungsgeschichte* (1899), nos 21, 14.
[3] Schulz, 'Zensualität und Stadtentwicklung im 11./12. Jahrhundert', pp. 81ff.

towns, which were growing through the migration from the country, such mixed marriages were common. The privilege of freedom from the *Buteil* granted by Henry V to all inhabitants of the town of Speyer in 1111, is interpreted by Barbarossa in 1182 to mean that the inhabitants of Speyer should also be exempt from the *Houbetreht*, the normal death duty.

We have good knowledge of the population structure of Worms[4] from the town-wall regulations of that time; as often happened in medieval towns, these regulations assigned the defence of a particular section of wall to a particular group of citizens. The Frisians are the first self-contained group to be mentioned — Frisian merchants who carried on the Rhine trade and had settled here, as also in Mainz, for example. They were installed in the north of the medieval town. Next to them we find the *familia S. Leodegari*, the smallholders on the estate of the Alsatian abbey of Murbach. Their numbers were such that they were put in charge of a gate on the Rhine side of the wall. The last group to be named, most numerous of all since they have to defend the longest section of wall, are the *urbani*, the townspeople, probably de-pendents of the bishop or the king. Now supposing a girl from the *familia S. Leodegari* wanted to marry a Frisian merchant, or a townsman a Frisian merchant's daughter. These were unequal marriages and were simply dissolved by the landlord's bailiff. The treatment their marriages brought down on them incensed the citizens of Worms.[5] One of the most important achievements of medieval town-dwellers was the abolition of these feudal restrictions and disadvantages. It fundamentally affected the lives of towns-people — including women. Emperor Henry V's privileges granted to Speyer in 1111 and to Worms in 1114, and their interpretation and confirmation by Barbarossa in 1182 and 1184, guaranteed free choice of a marriage partner and free rights of property and inheritance to both the male and female lines. And this applied to the whole town population, decisively advancing its legal unifica-tion. The emperor ordained:

that any man, whoever he be and from wherever he may come, whether he has taken his wife from his own community or from a different *familia*

[4]   H. Büttner, 'Zur Stadtentwicklung von Worms im Früh- und Hochmittel-alter' (1960).

[5]   B. Diestelkamp, 'Quellensammlung zur Frühgeschichte der deutschen Stadt (bis 1250)' (1967), no. 51, pp. 79f, no. 91, pp. 150ff.

or has come here from another place as a married man, they shall all without distinction have this one and equal right for ever, that no bailiff shall put asunder their marriage by force of oath [this refers particularly to the immigrant who had to declare his legal status under oath], and that no power (*potestas*) may demand a part of their estate as its right on the death of the husband or the wife, and that the matter shall be arranged as we decree below. If the husband dies before the wife, his wife and her offspring from this husband shall retain without contradiction the property left by her husband, and the same rule applies if the wife dies first.[6]

Derived from this Worms decree is an appendix to Freiburg municipal law: 'omnis mulier viro parificabitur et econtra et vir mulieris erit heres et econtra', which naturally does not anticipate Article 3, Section 2 of the Bonn constitution. It stems from the text of the civic law of 1293: 'A wife is her husband's consort and a husband his wife's; a husband inherits from his wife and a wife from her husband.' Here too the equality of the marriage partners in terms of status and hereditary rights is established; the lower-born partner — whether husband or wife — has the same legal status as the other free partner in relation to civic freedom.[7] In the town, marriage makes one free! This principle becomes established in the cities of central Europe. For the citizens of Laon in northern France, a privilege of 1128 determines that they can marry women of any status (*cuiuscumque generis*).[8] It takes some time for this right to extend to all towns. It is not until 1232 that the daughters of citizens of the royal cities of Frankfurt, Wetzlar, Friedberg and Gelnhausen are exempted from compulsory marriage to members of the royal socage farm.[9]

These decrees made it more attractive to found new towns. The foundation articles of the town of Geerardsbergen/Grammont[10]

---

[6]   Ibid., no. 51.

[7]   W. Ebel, 'Uber die rechtsschöpferische Leistung des mittelalterlichen deutschen Bürgertums' (1966) esp. pp. 249f.

[8]   Charter of Louis VI of 26 August 1128, section 10: 'homines pacis, exceptis familiis ecclesiarum vel procerum que de pace sunt, cuiuscumque generis potuerint uxores accipere; de familiis autem ecclesiarum, quae sunt extra terminos pacis, vel procerum qui de pace sunt, nisi voluntate dominorum uxores accipere non licebit.'

[9]   Keutgen, *Urkunden zur städtischen Verfassungsgschichte*, no. 349, p. 448.

[10]   M. Martens, 'Recueil de textes d'histoire urbaine belge' (1967), no. 12, p. 302, §§ 6 and 7.

state that on the death of the father or mother in a fertile marriage without inheritance, the plot of land on which the house is built, the ownership of which was the basis of civic freedom, passes to the surviving partner, together with the movable possessions. Sons and daughters inherit in the same manner. The primary issue is no longer the rebuttal of feudal demands on the estate — which is taken for granted — but the equality of rights of inheritance between husband and wife, son and daughter. How different this was to the situation in the country is shown by a communication of 1270 from the jurors' court at Aachen to Otto, provost of the imperial churches at Aachen and Maastricht.[11] On the provost's estates, we read, there is a legal custom whereby sisters are passed over in favour of brothers when hereditary goods (here called allodial goods) are divided up. Because the custom has been observed for so long, the letter continues, it can only be changed by the king. King Richard confirms the practice: sisters continue to be disregarded. There are, however, general improvements to the law of inheritance in the towns.

In this way women gain a share of civic freedom. In many civic legal codes, e.g. that of Bremen dating from 1186 and of Stade from 1209, the husband and wife are both explicitly mentioned in the important article which states that any person who lives in the town under municipal law for a reasonable period is free. Women swear the civic oath and are entered in the register of citizens. The wife's share of the civic rights of her husband continues in full after his death. By marrying a widow or daughter of a citizen, a newcomer to a town usually finds it easier to obtain civic rights.[12] However, the sources do not indicate that women played any part in the gaining of these freedoms, and those who fought for them were not concerned with the emancipation of women in the modern sense. The medieval concept is not based on the notion of a personal sphere of freedom; it is seen in corporate terms, and it is the freedom of the citizenry as a whole, the town community, that is pursued.

The abolition of feudal restrictions on urban marriages did not

---

[11] W. Mummenhoff, arr., *Regesten der Reichsstadt Aachen* (1961), no. 243, pp. 127, 245, 127f.

[12] G. Dilcher, 'Zum Bürgerbegriff im späteren Mittelalter. Versuch einer Typologie am Beispiel von Frankfurt am Main' (1980).

mean, of course, that matches were now made purely for love. In the towns, too, it was family politics that decided whom daughters were to marry, no doubt often against their wills, and even with legal enforcement. As in the country, women remained a means for a family to rise socially and, conversely, unequal marriages brought social decline.

This special development in the towns must be seen in the context of the general evolution of family and marital law. Marriage by consent had established itself in central Europe by the twelfth century. In outlying areas, e.g. northern Europe, older customs survived. The Norwegian *Birkinselrecht*[13] − or market law − still requires a *Mund* payment to be made by the bridegroom to obtain legal guardianship of his wife. A marriage concluded on this basis is full marriage: 'No man shall have two wives bought with a dotal gift (*mundr*), states chapter I. Here the extended family still exists; II, 9 decrees: 'There are seven women on whose account one may kill a man who is caught fornicating with them: first a man's wife, second his daughter, third his sister, fourth his mother, fifth his son's wife, sixth his brother's bride, seventh his stepmother.' The later civic law of King Magnus Hakonarson of 1276 relating to Bergen no longer requires a *mundr*. On women's marriages it states: 'If the father and mother are alive, they shall decide on the marriages of daughters. If they are absent, the paternal and maternal next of kin shall decide.' The involvement of the maternal kin is not required by law. 'The guardian shall decide the dowry and the contribution (*tilgiof*) for his kin, as he and the groom agree between them.' The contribution referred to here originally meant the bridegroom's contribution of one-third of the dotal gift, but after the disappearance of the word *mundr*, *tilgiof* came to mean the bridegroom's contribution as such.

If a woman marries without the agreement of her father or her brother or mother, or of the person who is her marriage guardian, she forfeits all the inheritance that would be due to her from then on, and this legacy falls to the nearest heir, as if the woman were not born to it; except if her guardian seeks to refuse her an equal marriage, in which case she can marry with the agreement of sensible relations ... A widow may marry whomever she will, with the agreement of any one of her kin ... No girl

---

[13] R. Meissner, *Stadtrecht des Königs Magnus Hakonarson für Bergen, Bruchstücke des Birkinselrechtes* ... (1950). On the concept of *mundr* cf. A. Schultze, *Zum altnordischen Eherecht* (1939), pp. 32ff.

shall have control of her wealth before she is 20, even if it has fallen due to her, unless she be married with the agreement of her kin, in which case the man who marries her has control of her and her wealth.

It is also ordained that all negotiations on a marriage shall be recorded in a document, 'and if one cannot obtain a seal one should make a chirograph'. The document is then cut through with a jagged line, so that the fit of the pieces guarantees authenticity. These elaborate laws on inheritance put daughters at a disadvantage, excluding them from inheriting *odel* land. The land designated as *odel* must remain the property of the family.

In the large area of Slavdom which remains open to Byzantine influences, the situation is complex.[14] Christianity has tried to introduce monogamy where it does not already exist, among the great lords. When Duke Mieszko I of Poland married a Christian princess, he first had to dismiss his seven heathen wives. In Bohemia Bishop Adalbert fought against the principle of *plures uxores unius viri* (several wives of one man), and in Pomerania, as late as the beginning of the twelfth century, Bishop Otto preached against polygamy. From the eleventh to the thirteenth century there is evidence of informal marriages in Poland and Russia that were tolerated by the church as a form of marriage by consent. The contractual marriage — Gieysztor speaks of a marriage by purchase — is described by Ibrahim Ibn Jakub, an Arab traveller, as follows: the prince must give in marriage the children of his vassals; when he marries the young men, he has to make a gift to the bride's father; when he marries a vassal's daughter he must make a gift to her father, so that fathers grew rich from their daughters. However, this travel report should not be taken too literally. In the twelfth century marriage by consent was making inroads in this area too. Prohibitions on divorce were promulgated from the ninth century, but were not always respected.

In the twelfth century there was a dispute between the law schools of Bologna and Paris on whether the consent of the bride and groom was sufficient to make a marriage fully valid, or whether the consummation of the union (*copula carnis*) was also

[14] A. Gieysztor, 'La femme dans les civilisations des X^c-XIII^c s. La femme en Europe orientale', in: *Actes du Colloque tenu à Poitiers les 23—25 septembre 1976, Poitiers 1977*; and, '*Le tradizioni locali e le influenze ecclesiastiche nel matrimonio in Polonia nei secoli X—XIII*' (1977); S. Vilfan, 'Le tradizioni locali e le influenze eccleisastiche nel matrimonio in Slovenia e nelle regioni vicine' (1977).

needed. The argument was won by the view that the consent of the partners, if effective and referring to the present, was the foundation of marriage. Thus Pope Alexander II (1159–81) decreed: 'solus consensus facit nuptias'. However, the question of consummation remained important, as church law declared only the *consummated* sacramental marriage indivisible, and sometimes allowed a separation of bed and board if the marriage had come about by consent but had not been consummated. A divorce followed by a new marriage was not possible under canon law, but a marriage could be declared null and void on grounds of impediments, particularly consanguinity of the spouses. Such annulments occurred again and again in the European ruling houses and among the high nobility. Consanguinity was often only a pretext. Given the intermarriage of the ruling houses and the high nobility it was nearly always present. Barbarossa and Henry the Lion divorced their first wives in this way. The case was different with Philip I of France.[15] He rejected his wife, Bertha, daughter of the count of Holland, and married Bertrada, the wife of Fulco of Anjou. No grounds for annulling the marriage to Bertha, who had borne him a son, existed; that she was 'too fat' for him, as one chronicler asserted – even if the anecdote was true – was of no account. On the other hand, he was actually related to the adultress Bertrada. Despite all this the bishop of Senlis blessed the marriage in the presence of the crown bishops, and Bertrada was recognized in France, where she had influence, particularly in the matter of appointing bishops. The pope and the great reformer Ivo of Chartres condemned the scandalous relationship, but Philip persisted with it. It is true that when he had grown old, in 1105, he did penance with Bertrada and promised to improve, but he resumed the liaison all the same. After Philip's death (1108) Bertrada retired to the reformist convent of Fontevrault. Philip Augustus of France also had a protracted dispute with the curia over marriage questions.[16]

The consequences of too close kinship could be tragic if a couple were unwilling to separate when the spiritual and worldly authorities demanded it. This was the situation with Otto of

---

[15] Dhondt, 'Sept femmes et un trio de rois'; G. Duby, 'Les mariages du roi Philippe', in: *Le chevalier, la femme et le prêtre* (1981). English ed.: *The Knight, the Lady and the Priest: the making of modern marriage in medieval France* (1985).

[16] Ibid., pp. 214ff.

Hammerstein and Irmgard. Otto was a count of Engersgau, his residence the castle of Hammerstein, situated on a mighty cliff on the right bank of the Rhine, between Leutesdorf and Rheinbrohl. The opposition to the marriage had a political background: the ruling German emperor, Henry II, was an enemy of the Conradians, the family to which Otto belonged. Otto gave him a pretext for intervening when he made a rash attack on the archbishop of Mainz, who wanted the marriage dissolved. In 1020, after a three-month siege of Burg Hammerstein, the emperor forced Otto to submit, he and Irmgard barely escaping with their lives. When the couple continued to live together, Archbishop Aribo of Mainz had them excommunicated. Otto submitted; Irmgard went to Rome, where Benedict VIII responded to her appeal. This led to a conflict between pope and archbishop. Otto and Irmgard continued their marriage. Otto became a count in Wetterau, Hammerstein remaining the property of the empire.

The church continued to try to influence the outer forms of marriage, particularly the public nature of the marriage ceremony. The fourth Lateran Council of 1215 made it obligatory for a formal marriage to be blessed and witnessed by a priest. The marriage had to be made *in facie ecclesie*, 'before the face of the church'. The wedding itself was to take place before the church door, the 'bridal gate', in the presence of lay witnesses and a priest. In many cases this actually happened, often in conjunction with a celebration at home, where old customs survived and where the marriage contract was concluded. One sometimes reads that the sacrament of marriage was founded in 1215. That is a misunderstanding. Historically, it is correct to say that the concept of the sacrament remained unclear until the twelfth century. The clarification of this concept made it possible about the middle of the century to enumerate the seven sacraments, as is still done by the Catholic church today. Despite its great difference to the other sacraments, marriage was counted as one of the seven. The Lateran Council of 1215 moderated the impediment of kinship. The church had extended the prohibition on marriage between blood relations to the seventh degree of kinship, as calculated by the church. The Lateran Council's reform limited the impediment of consanguinity in the lateral line to the fourth degree, so removing the obstacle to marriage between in-laws. But the church's demand for public marriage still failed to find acceptance. The problem of secret marriages (*clandestina matrimonia*) persisted. An order prohibiting secret marriages was only issued by the Council of Trent in the sixteenth century.

To bring the chapter on secret marriages to a close we shall mention the sensational case of Joan Plantagenet (the 'Fair Maid of Kent'), although it actually happened in the fourteenth century. Joan was the daughter of Edmund, duke of Kent, a son of Edward I of England from his second marriage to Margaret, daughter of Philip III of France. She finally married Prince Edward of England and became the mother of Richard II, but had been twice married secretly before that.[17] Joan was born in 1328. Her father was executed for his involvement in a conspiracy against Edward III. The young Queen Philippa, daughter of Count William III of Hennegau, adopted Joan, who grew up at the royal court under the guidance of Sir William and Lady Elizabeth Montague. In 1337 Sir William became duke of Salisbury, and his son William Montague was regarded as Joan's future husband. But in 1340 Thomas Holland, son of Sir Robert Holland, began to woo Joan. In the spring of 1340, aged 12, she decided to marry him. She already promised to be very beautiful. The marriage was performed in secret, not *in facie ecclesie*, before only lay witnesses. About that time Edward III began his struggle over the French succession. Thomas Holland took part in the naval battle of Sluys, in which England was victorious, in the landing in France and the siege of Tournai. When an armistice was declared, he went to Prussia to support the knights of the Teutonic orders against the Tartars, like many other English and French knights. Holland's interest in Joan had not escaped her foster parents. Wishing to take advantage of his absence to marry her well, they chose as her husband the above-mentioned William Montague, who was the same age as Joan and the son and heir of the Duke of Salisbury. Was it fear that made Joan keep quiet about her marriage to Holland? Or was she persuaded the marriage was invalid, since her agreement had only been given under pressure from him? At all events, she was ceremonially married to Montague in the winter of 1340, the loveliest and most charming lady in England, as *Froissart* writes.

In 1341/42 Holland returned from Prussia and pressed his claim to Joan. When his pleas with her fell on deaf ears, he appealed to the pope at Avignon — but not at once. Lacking the

---

[17]   K. P. Wentersdorf, 'The clandestine marriage of the Fair Maid of Kent' (1979), pp. 203ff.

considerable sums of money needed for this task he planned first to distinguish himself in war service to the English king, earn money in so doing and then approach the curia. By 1347 he had completed this stage; he appointed Master Robert Siglethorne Beverley, a doctor in both laws, to represent him at the curia. How the situation had changed through litigation and commercialization since Baldwin and Judith sought the pope's protection for their marriage! Holland's party attempted to have Joan's marriage to Salisbury annulled. He knew well that Edward III and Queen Philippa had favoured his wife's marriage to Salisbury. But relations between Pope Clement VI and the English king were tense, and it was unlikely that the pope would pay special regard to the king's wishes in this affair, even disregarding the anglophobia of his cardinals. The pope declared that the case was not necessarily the curia's business and appointed Cardinal Adhémar Robert as judge. From the beginning of the trial Joan was kept in strict seclusion. Holland informed the curia that she was being given no opportunity, either in person or through a lawyer of her choice, to present her side of the case to the cardinal's tribunal without hindrance or fear of the consequences. At this, in May 1348, Clement VI appointed the archbishop of Canterbury and the bishops of Norwich and London to see to it that Joan could put forward her own interests. The opposing party — Salisbury — tried to drag the trial out. At last the pope passed the matter to the much-feared cardinal of Albi, the cardinal bishop of Porto, a man highly respected for his piety and wisdom. He concluded that Joan's union with Sir Thomas Holland was a legally valid marriage and that she should be returned to Holland forthwith, that their marriage should be publicly consecrated and that the *de facto* marriage to the duke of Salisbury was null and void. A papal bull of 13 November 1349, addressed to the papal nuncio in England and the bishops of Norwich and London, made Albi's judgement known and instructed the bishops to ensure that the secret marriage was now publicly consecrated 'solempnizandum huius matrimonium cum dicto Thoma contractum in facie ecclesie'. All this was done. Thomas rose to new heights in his military career and in 1359 was made captain-general of all the English possessions in France and Normandy. He died in 1360, as the duke of Kent. Joan had borne him three sons and three daughters.

At that time Prince Edward of Wales was 30 and unmarried.

Edward III wanted to marry him to the rich heiress Margaret of Flanders, but he was in love with his widowed kinswoman, Joan, and in 1361 Joan contracted her second secret marriage. This one, however, was invalid from the first through consanguinity and spiritual affinity, both bride and groom being descended from Edward I. He was the great-grandfather of the prince of Wales and Joan's grandfather, and apart from this the prince was godfather to Joan's eldest son. Edward informed the pope, now Innocent VI, asking for a dispensation which would allow the couple to marry publicly. The pope complied, and imposed the penance that the couple should build and endow two chapels. But in a private letter of the same date he asked the archbishop of Canterbury to find out if Joan's marriage to Salisbury had been correctly annulled. Salisbury was still living, and was married to another woman. The question as to the annulment of Joan's marriage to Salisbury was answered in the affirmative, her second secret marriage was formally annulled, and she and Edward were given dispensation from the impediments to marriage, made to promise that they would indulge in no more secret marriages, and would donate the two chapels. This opened the way to a public wedding, which took place four days later at Windsor Castle. In 1362 Edward became prince of Aquitaine, residing at Bordeaux, with Joan, who bore him two sons. He died in 1376, Joan in 1365. In her will she had asked to be buried beside her first husband, Thomas Holland.

Undoubtedly, secret marriages were to be deplored but, as this story proves, they were genuine marriages. Blessing by a priest and the publication of banns, ordained since 1215, were an obligation on Christians intending to marry, but not a precondition of validity.

The patriarchal family structure survived, because it accorded with the Christian notion of revelation and the scholastic doctrine of the imperfection of women, based on Aristotle. The church which, for all its eulogies of a virginity dedicated to God, approved of marriage, nevertheless demanded wedded chastity of the spouses.[18] Payer has discussed some aspects of this with extensive support from literature and the sources. Penitential manuals and

---

[18]   P. J. Payer, 'Early medieval regulations concerning marital sexual relations' (1980).

the *Decretum* of Bishop Burchard of Worms,[19] give an idea of what was permitted and what was regarded as sinful. Whereas in our century we may still have 'closed' periods when 'quiet' weddings, or no weddings at all, are preferred, at that time the church demanded abstinence in marriage at certain holy times and on certain days. It desired abstinence from sexual intercourse on the first or the first three nights after a wedding. Advent and Lent were long periods of abstinence, as well as two weeks before and one after Whitsun, Fridays and Wednesdays, generally regarded as days of penance, and the nights before Sundays and major feast-days. The restrictions on marital intercourse vary, and are reduced in the later Middle Ages. They express a certain depreciation of sexual pleasure which, as Ziegler argues,[20] has its origin in 'Gnostic dualism, the Old Testament precepts on purity, Augustinian theology on original sin and the reification and demonization of the sexual instinct...In the thirteenth century ... this embarrassed attitude towards sexuality is discarded.' In the handbooks on pastoral care a matter-of-fact, Aristotelian, scientific attitude begins to emerge. Albertus Magnus, Bonaventure and Duns Scotus found in the doctrine of marriage the Christian way of forming the personalities of the spouses through the marriage community. The prescribed abstinence, where it was observed, may have shielded women from over-frequent pregnancies. Birth control and abortion were, naturally, forbidden, but equally naturally occurred, though probably not on a large scale.[21] The early age of marriage, at puberty,[22] was a characteristic of the early and high Middle Ages. Children were still welcome at that time. In the upper classes the succession had to be secured in face of the high rate of infant mortality. The possibility of filling important church posts with further sons or unmarried daughters was an important factor, particularly before the investiture controversy. In the peasant family, children were a useful source of labour. Only a high birthrate supported the growth needed by the economy.

In conjunction with the reform movement, celibacy spread to

[19] G. Theuerkauf, 'Burchard von Worms und die Rechtskunde seiner Zeit' (1968); Duby, *The Knight, the Lady and the Priest*, pp. 65ff.
[20] J. G. Ziegler, *Die Ehelehre der Poenitentialsummen von 1200–1350* (1956).
[21] Shahar, *The Fourth Estate*.
[22] Chaunu, *Die verhütete Zukunft*, p. 81.

the whole of the clergy from the eleventh century on. This led to a defamation of the children of priests.[23]

The legal aspect of the relationship between spouses was governed by two main principles: tutelage of the husband on the one hand and the marriage community on the other.[24] The mixture between them varied. The medieval development in matrimonial property law tended towards a community of property. It meant that the entire wealth of a couple, or certain parts of it, were combined into a total wealth shared jointly by the two partners. For the wife this was a considerable improvement on the situation in the Frankish period. Especially in towns, the community of property became the most important aspect of marital property law, though with a multitude of variations. Extreme fragmentation of the law in this area is characteristic of the Middle Ages. We shall look at the arrangements in the region of North Rhine—Westphalia, which became the models for those in important coastal cities.[25]

Dortmund law[26] made man and wife equal as regards inheritance. The case was similar in the old law of Münster, while Soest gave preference to the male line. In Dortmund and Münster the communal estate existed from the first day of a marriage, but in Soest only after the birth of the first child and as long as this child lived. In Dortmund, and originally in Münster as well, husband and wife held equal rights to those of the children on the dissolution or separation of a marriage. The surviving spouse of an infertile marriage, that is, a marriage in which no child has been born, was granted half of the entire estate by Dortmund law; in fertile marriages which had no heir through the death of the child, the surviving spouse inherited everything; when there was an heir and the surviving spouse remarried, the estate was shared by halves with the child or children. The same rules applied in Münster and Bielefeld at the beginning of the thirteenth century: 'Si vir moritur subito, uxor habebit medietatem hereditatis sue et

---

[23]   B. Schimmelpfennig, 'Zölibat und Lage der "Priestersöhne" vom 11.—14. Jahrhundert' (1978); J. Gaudemet, 'Le célibat ecclésiastique. Le droit et la pratique du XIᶜ au XIIIᶜ siècle' (1982).
[24]   Schröder, *Geschichte des ehelichen Güterrechts in Deutschland*. Part 2, section 3 (1874), p. 295.
[25]   W. Ebel, 'Das Soester Recht. Wesen, Herkunft, Bedeutung' (1959); K. Deissner, *Zum Güter- und Erbrecht im ältesten Schleswiger Stadtrecht* (1966).
[26]   L. von Winterfeld, 'Die stadtrechtlichen Verflechtungen in Westfalen' (1955), pp. 189ff.

pueri medietatem. Quilibet puerorum accipiet hereditatem alterius, et matri cedet hereditas puerorum.' (The mother inherits half on the sudden death of her husband and the children the other half; if a child receives the inheritance of another, she, the mother, also has a corresponding share of the estate.)[27] Münster later dropped the distinction between fertile and infertile marriages, so that in all marriages without heirs that had been concluded according to the city law, the surviving partner was the sole heir. Then, in the first half of the fourteenth century, Münster − though without being followed by its dependent towns − abandoned the half-share law in favour of the Soest system, so that the widower always received half of the total estate, but the widow only did so when there was more than one child; when there was a single child she had to be content with a third. In Soest there was a quota system for the surviving spouse which varied according to gender. Dortmund, through its commercial links, was influenced by the Lower Rhine and Flanders. The earliest Dortmund records, the Latin Statutes, date from soon after 1250. In Wesel, which was subject to the Dortmund court, the privilege of the count of Kleve of 1241[28] confirmed the following ruling:

When a citizen dies in [the city], the husband shall freely receive the estate of his wife and the wife the estate of her husband [i.e. without taxes being paid to the ruler]; if both die, the children inherit, and if there are no children, the next of kin ... Those living in the city who are liable to wax duty must pay to their ecclesiastical landlord the best part of the estate as *Kurmede* [tribute].

The count of Kleve, whose lands lay primarily on the left bank of the Rhine, gained an important trading centre on Wesel's right bank; to extract the full value from it he had to make it attractive to merchants and craftsmen. He therefore confirmed Dortmund's position as the upper court and the citizen's customs regarding inheritance. He also had to pay heed to the church landowners and their ancient rights. Thus a pluralistic local law of inheritance came into being for citizens and those who paid wax duty. A

---

[27] Keutgen, *Urkunden zur städtischen Verfassungsgeschichte*, (1899), including: 'Münster: Mitteilung des Stadtrechtes an Bielefeld' [*c.* 1221], pp. 153f, §§ 58 and 59.

[28] C. van de Kieft and J. F. Niermeyer, *Elenchus fontium historiae urbanae quem edendum curaverunt* (1967), no. 165, p. 256, §§ 4, 5, 6 and 24.

century later another count of Kleve was to decide in Kleve itself, where he had free jurisdiction, in favour of a different law on inheritance for the town. The Dortmund–Münster type of community of property created exceptionally clear relationships regarding marital wealth and inheritance.

This old Westphalian, Rhenish, Flemish communal estate generally fitted the needs of a simple population of merchants and artisans who had severed themselves from the bonds of rural law and moved to the towns. The communal estate that originated with marriage and continued unchanged provided the citizens with credit ... The object of this simple marital law, which for centuries was only valid in the towns of Westphalia and not in the country, lay less in the accumulation of large amounts of wealth for citizens in the male line, than in an attempt to secure the wealth newly acquired in the towns from passing to relatives outside, and to promote the development of large, prosperous, intermarrying merchant families by the equal inheritance of husband and wife. (von Winterfeld)

This property law could be modified by individual marriage contracts and further developed by statutes.

The Dortmund law established itself in Schleswig in strict opposition to the indigenous Jutlandic law, as Deissner has convincingly shown. Lübeck adopted the Soest law.

Another characteristic of urban law is the amalgamation of special portions of wealth held separately by the spouses, the *Heergewäte* or *Herwede* of the husband and the *Gerade* of the wife. Dortmund ordains that men or women living in Dortmund and owning their own houses may neither give or receive *Herwede* or *Gerade*. When Prince Heinrich Borwin of Rostock issued a deed of civic law to the newly-founded town of Parchim in 1225/6,[29] he expressly ruled that gifts of *Herwede* or *Wiberade* should not be made, and that the estate should be divided into equal halves. Sons and daughters were to inherit in equal parts and if there were no sons the father's estate was to go to the daughters and not to his own kin. The law of Münster decided differently in a communication to the city of Bielefeld in 1209–14:

Of the *Heergeräte* (*Heergewäte*) and the *Gerade*, six denars shall be used for the burial of the deceased if there is no other wealth. If the wife dies

[29]   Ibid., no. 133, p. 209, §§ 9, 10 and 11.

and has daughters, the elder shall share and the younger choose. The women's portion [*Frauenrathe*] goes equally to the daughters if there is no estate and if they are of the same class. The women's portion comprises: the best bed, the second best being kept by the husband, pillows, cushions, table-cloths and linen, although the husband keeps the second-best of each; gold, but not gold coins, all ready-cut clothing, all flax; but not woven cloth or yarn, nor chest or cupboard.[30]

According to the civic law communicated to the town of Neumarkt in Silesia by the lay assessors of Halle, the *Gerade* comprises: all women's clothes, all women's jewellery made of gold and silver, all bedclothes, table-cloths, towels, linen, carpets, curtains, tapestries, candelabras, dishes, chests with feet, horses, sheep, everything pertaining to brewing apart from the large vat, geese, hens, kitchen utensils and all swine.[31] The woman who receives the *Gerade* has to provide the heir's bed, table and chair, with everything belonging to them. The fact that all the utensils needed for brewing except the large vat were part of the women's portion in Neumarkt, shows that the wife was responsible for home brewing. This takes us to the question of how the town economy of commerce and crafts affected the division of labour between husband and wife, and how far women played a part in this economy. These questions can be answered fully only in chapter 3. What can be said here is that the trade in groceries that came into being at an early stage in towns may have reduced some of the burden on the town housewife, but certainly not all of it. The urban household was not as dependent on home produce as the peasant or feudal household in the country, but far more so than a modern one.

A story about a woman baker in Mainz proves that free paid labour existed in the groceries trade as early as the ninth century. On the feast-day of St Laurence, when everyone else had gone devoutly to church, this woman stayed at home baking rolls for sale. She took no notice of the censorious comments of her neighbours, but soon received her punishment: the fine white rolls were burnt to a cinder.[32] The possibility of buying special pastries did not, however, relieve the wife of the merchant or artisan of the

[30] Ibid., no. 111, p. 179.
[31] Ibid., no. 159, p. 253.
[32] E. Ennen, 'Das Gewerbe auf dem europäischen zisalpinen Kontinent vom 6. bis 11. Jahrhundert in verfassungsgeschichtlicher Sicht' (1975), pp. 9f.

daily toil of baking, brewing and slaughtering. She probably also had the main share of work in the garden of the town house, or the orchard or vineyard, and looked after the pigs and fowl, which were also part of the urban household. Like the Mainz baker-woman, she also took advantage of the opportunity to earn money by practising a craft. Crafts were, however, primarily the preserve of men. Paid work as house-maids was open to women; many maids were needed in these labour-intensive households for the extensive chores, the autumn feasts of fresh pork and home-made sausages and pickles, for brewing beer, mending and making clothes and bed-linen, spinning and sewing, and supervising the many children. Also attached to the craftsman's household, especially in this period, were the unmarried assistants and apprentices, just as carters, etc., were a part of the merchant's household.

From 1100 crafts begin to be organized in guilds. Often, the medieval craftsman did not work in the direct service of his customer. He used his own raw materials to produce for the free market; he was his own merchant. It was only in the late Middle Ages that the production of many small craft workshops was brought together by rich guild-masters or merchants who acted as distributors. Thus craft workshops were small businesses, and the guild rules did everything to keep them small. The work process was not broken up by a horizontal division of labour, as often happens today, but was split vertically, a trade being broken up into many distinct branches. Thus leather-work was divided into shoemakers, saddlers, harness-makers, belt-makers, handbag-makers, purse-makers and craftsmen who made collars for draught-horses; and of course, shoemakers specialized in boots, women's shoes and slippers, while shoemenders were not to be so presumptuous as to make new shoes. The guilds had the function of cartels; they excluded non-members, particularly village craftsmen. But they also had religious and social goals. Religious brotherhoods are sometimes the point of contact or the framework for a new guild. However, the complex motives behind the formation of guilds cannot be unravelled here, any more than the other questions relating to this manner of organizing crafts.

From the first, alongside the craft character of the guild, there is the communal honouring of the dead and the communal feast. In these latter aspects women, the 'sisters', are as much involved as the masters, the 'brothers'. This is clear from the very early regulations of the Cologne guild of turners (1178–82).[33] It is called a *fraternitas*, a brotherhood. The turners pay an entrance fee of 12 solidi (shillings); anyone who is not a turner but wishes to belong to the brotherhood pays 24 denars, that is, 2 solidi, i.e. very much less. This wider circle of members includes women; generally they will be the wives of the masters. If a member of the guild dies, whether man or woman, four pounds of wax are donated and six men keep the death-watch; all the men and the women must attend the funeral. Anyone who does not come to the funeral must pay a fine of two denars. But the members did not only meet for the funeral of a member, but for sociable drinking and dances – although fines were not usually imposed for non-attendance, and perhaps for this reason only the obligatory attendance at funerals is mentioned in our document. Cohesion in a craft was very high. Although the guilds were not as closed at the early stage as in the late Middle Ages, it was common for a son to take over his father's firm or a young master to marry the widow of a guild-master – whereby his entrance fee was reduced. The statutes of the weavers' guild at Stendal (1223)[34] lay down that a weaver coming from outside must pay 23 solidi to the guild after attaining citizenship, but a master's son or the husband of a master's widow need only pay 3 solidi.

In the medieval town, almost everyone found his place in a tightly-knit group – in a craft guild, the merchants' guild or the patrician's community. For the latter, however, no entrance fee or acquired skill was enough, not even wealth; the newly rich man had to marry into it. Origin and wealth make the patrician. Another important group is the neighbourhood, the parish community. Larger cities can be divided into quarters, districts and parishes. The individual is sheltered within the group, but he also has duties towards it. The gradual achievement of legal equality by citizens in no way means an equalization of political rights or social status. Differences of wealth are large. Social class and group do not coincide. This is particularly obvious in the guilds: in one and the same guild there can be rich masters who earn more than enough to live on, but also poor craftsmen. But even

[33] Keutgen, *Urkunden zur städtischen Verfassungsgechichte*, no. 256.
[34] This is documented for the weavers' guild of Stendal by Keutgen, ibid., no. 264, p. 358.

the rich weaver attends the poor weaver's funeral. The guild form of organization only becomes generally established about 1250.

In the period before 1250 craftsmen play scarcely any part in town government. The large, old cities, the bishops' sees and the imperial towns, are generally ruled by the partriciate. The group of about 40 Cologne families who combined to form the *Richerzeche* ruled until far into the fourteenth century. The Cologne patriciate assimilated *ministeriales*, the higher servants of the bishops and of the religious foundations, no less than rich merchants. The wealth of this group was based on trading profits, property and land ownership and the leasing of revenue-earning rights, e.g. the tolls of the archbishop.

The urban upper-class families intermarry: Heinrich of Zudendorp, whose name appears about 1173—80 on the Cologne guild list, married a daughter of the merchant Siegfried of Neuss, who brought several houses in the market district into the marriage.[35] Reiner of Basle and his brother-in-law Hermann married two sisters from the Cologne family of Mühlengassen, and at once became owners of property near the market and in the draper's quarter. Drapers are retail cloth merchants; they have the right to sell cloth by the ell, i.e. to cut it from the bale. Reiner's daughter Hodierna also married someone from Basle. The patrician family of Jude, perhaps of Jewish origin, had three members among the Cologne ruling class by 1151 and invested its profits in land and vineyards outside the city at Remagen. Its family home in Cologne was a large complex with orchards, bakery and taverns in the Rheingasse. In the fifth generation Daniel Jude, who died in 1284, surpassed his prosperous kinsmen and most other citizens in wealth; he pursued an adroit policy of land acquisition. He made three advantageous marriages. The large dowry from his first wife Ida, from the Lintgasse, is seen in her will; she died in 1252. She donated the most expensive of her show dresses, of fur-bordered gold brocade, for altar-robes and set aside an annuity of 20 marks for masses to be said for her. His second wife came from a property-owning merchant's family from Neuss; the third, Beatrix, may have been a noblewoman. He married two of his daughters to members of the high nobility and a third to a knight from the rural nobility.

---

[35]   Cf. L. Von Winterfeld, *Handel, Kapital und Patriziat in Köln bis 1400* (1925).

In the city patriciate of Cologne in the twelfth century we find several cases of intermarried Jewish families. The Jews were probably always something of a foreign body in medieval cities, and this must have been felt especially by Jewish women. But their legal position gave them a degree of security in the early and high Middle Ages. Privileges going back to the Carolingian age place the Jews, like the other travelling merchants, under royal protection. In the eleventh century the Rhine cities of Cologne, Mainz, Worms and Speyer had respected Jewish communities. The Jews were still allowed to acquire land in the cities — as we know in detail for Cologne — and in the country, and to have it tilled by Christian day-labourers. A change begins to make itself felt at the end of the eleventh century, the first signs being the serious attacks on Rhenish Jews in connection with the First Crusade.

Information of practices within the Jewish communities can be found in the study by Thérèse and Mendel Metzger,[36] which is based largely on iconographic sources. It was the men, above all, who were bound by strict cult rules. During prayers in the synagogue the sexes were segregated. For women there were only three obligations: monthly purification in the ritual bath, the removal and burning of a small portion of dough when baking — which every Jewish baker had to do — and the lighting of lamps on the sabbath and feast-days. Women played an important part in domestic cult practices. The ritual bath was a very important communal institution, which involved not merely cleansing but immersion. These baths were roofed in. A well-preserved example is the Jewish bath at Speyer; steps lead far down to the groundwater level of the Rhine, as the ritual bath must be fed with the living water. Within the household the wife had just as much importance as her husband. The wedding ceremony, which was preceded by negotiations and agreements, had two stages: at the betrothal the *ketuba*, the marriage contract, was handed over to the bride and rings were exchanged before two witnesses. At the second stage the officiant pronounced seven blessings with a chalice in his hand, from which the bride and bridegroom then drank while standing under a symbolic tent. This ceremony of the blessings and the drinking from the chalice was repeated at the wedding feast and after saying grace on the seven following days. Divorce

---

[36] T. and M. Metzger, *Jüdisches Leben im Mittelalter nach illuminierten hebräischen Handschriften vom 13. bis ins 16. Jhd.* (1983).

was possible under Jewish law. If a wife was widowed before becoming a mother, the law imposed the levirate on one of the dead husband's brothers: he had to marry the widow. To evade this obligation was to meet with heavy opprobrium. Thus motherhood was, in the Jewish view, the destiny of women. The Jewish way of life was characterized by a strict observance of law and general literacy, which included women.

Such was the nature of life in the cities. We cannot deny that woman played a largely passive part in the great expansion of cities in the twelfth and thirteenth centuries, as the companion and helper of her husband. She does not belong to the jurors' committees in the cities of northern France, she does not sit on the town councils which develop as civic organs in German towns in the thirteenth century. She shares the adventure of the bondsman, the little man who moves to the town and begins a new life with the money from the sale of his land or with nothing more than his labour-power. She shares in his social rise, as when a town merchant's profits allow her to wear expensive clothes, to keep maids, to run a large, well-furnished house. She has probably worked at a town trade. But of this we know little before 1250. In our discussion so far we have been thinking primarily of the area between the Seine and the Rhine. It is a region where the medieval town underwent early and important development.

A second major centre of medieval urban development is northern Italy. The contrast between the central European and the Italian city is a large one. A striking, common feature of Mediterranean cities is the fact that the nobles resided in them, as mentioned in the Introduction to this book. The urban population of Italy included an element of large and small landowners; like the merchants and craftsmen, the nobles owned land outside the city gates. The Italian cities dominated the countryside politically and economically.[37] The urban environment of Italian women differed fundamentally to that of the knights' wives and burgher women north of the Alps. Although they also lived in a fortified structure and were exposed to the trials of war, they enjoyed all the excitement and animation of rich trading and manufacturing cities and could exchange the haste and bustle of town life for the seclusion

[37] E. Ennen, 'Zur Typologie des Stadt-Land-Verhältnisses im Mittelalter' (1977), p. 181f; H. Keller, 'Der Übergang zur Kommune: Zur Entwicklung der italienischen Stadtverfassung im 11. Jhd.' (1982).

and good air of their country houses and the regular rhythm of the seasons.

But we should not forget the darker sides. In many places in the Mediterranean area slavery persisted in the full sense of the word, particularly in harbour towns. We cannot discuss this important phenomenon in its full scope here, and will take Genoa as a typical case. As Haverkamp's[38] study shows, the registers of the Genoese notariate contain an abundance of evidence and permit some quantification of conditions in the twelfth century. For the period from 1154 to 1200, about 4,500 notarial documents are published. Some difficulties are presented by the terminology; the term *sclavi* or *sclavae* can only be traced back to the beginning of the thirteenth century; from the 1180s slaves are referred to by the term *sardus* or *sarda*, which originally only denoted their origin in Sardinia, but *sarracenus* or *sarracena* do not always signify slaves when used in legal documents concerning the sale of such persons or in wills or deeds of emancipation. The terms *servi* and *ancillae* in documents of sale and emancipation are unequivocal evidence of slave status. The foundation of slavery in Genoa was laid by the struggle of the maritime city against the Saracens and the importation of slaves from Spain, where Mohammedans were enslaved as a result of the *reconquista*. There were also imports from Sardinia, Sicily and North Africa, hence the negro slaves. Of the 4,500-plus notarial documents, 79 are concerned with slaves, and in these, 92 slaves, male and female, are mentioned. For the 25 male and 21 female slaves for whom sale agreements were concluded in 43 of the documents, just under 60 individuals are identified as sellers. However, this ratio is changed by a 'very striking' exception: on 17 June 1191, 15 part-owners sell their varying shares in the *sarda* Justa and her daughter Vereta to the other part-owner Raimundus Baltigarius, a member of an upper-class family aged about 20 who found himself in financial difficulties, with only money for small transactions; the many shareholders in these slaves were small craftsmen and traders. Some of the part-owners had probably imported the slaves from Sardinia to Genoa. Such importation can be proved with certainty for a *sarda nomine Maria Pagano*. Non-Genoese traders sell to the Genoese, in Genoa, slaves from an area extending from Narbonne in the west to Lucca in the

[38] A. Haverkamp, 'Zur Sklaverei in Genua während des 12. Jahrhunderts' (1974).

east, along the northwestern coast of the Mediterranean. Other importers of slaves to Genoa come from places within its direct sphere of influence on the Ligurian coast: Albenga, Noli, Savona, Rapallo. While the market for male slaves is clearly based on importation, a different picture emerges for the female slaves: only 13 of the 22 female slaves are referred to as *sarracenae*; only three *sarracenae* and four *sardae* are slaves imported to Genoa by traders from outside the city. Most of the sellers of female slaves are Genoese, e.g. Simon Botarius, who in 1190 sells the *sarda* Maria to Simon Gattus, who is involved in long-distance trade, particularly with Sicily. Simon Botarius was a trading partner of the de Volta family, which belonged to the urban nobility; he took large sums of money from them on a trading trip to Tunis, from where individual slaves were also imported to Genoa. His son-in-law Ingo de Cartagenia was a nephew of Ogerius and Bonusvasallus de Cartagenia, known to be slave traders, and had close links to Fulco de Castello, a member of a politically influential Genoese family who owned slaves. Ownership of and trading in slaves can also be assumed for Rubaldus de Molo and Gandulfus Figal, who sold the *sarracena* Maimona for 3 pounds to Amicus Macellarius, probably a butcher. Wuilielmus Culcanus engaged in long-distance trade with Salerno; he sold the *ancilla* Agnese for 8 pounds to the rich finacier Wuilielmus Filiardus. The *sarracena blanca* Mocal was sold for 7 pounds and 11 shillings. The *sarda* Maria was resold by Simon Gattus to a Genoese noble two weeks after he had bought her from Simon Botarius. Female slaves were often sold by women. In divorce cases there are disputes over ownership of a female slave; they were also part of the dotal gifts of city noblewomen. Thus property exchange within the city was a more important factor than imports, in the female slave market in Genoa. Both importers and buyers would own several male slaves at one time, but not more than one female. The demand for male slaves was confined to a narrower section of the population than that for females but this section needed larger numbers per buyer. The female slaves were clearly required, economically and socially, in the sphere of the Genoese woman, the household. A substantial proportion of the male slaves imported to Genoa were used as ship or galley slaves, while others were bought by small traders or craftsmen. It was different with the female slaves; the most expensive of them, costing 8—9 pounds — were bought for the households or rich upper-class families, cheaper ones for labour in commerce or crafts. In general, female slaves were bound far more closely to the family life of the owners than males. The differing economic and social situation of male and female slaves is confirmed by the emancipation documents. It is primarily the members of the consular, aristocratic upper class of Genoa who emancipate slaves. For them it was not financial considerations that were decisive, but the personal relationship that grew up between owner and slave. Sometimes religious motives played a part; thus, Sibilia left her husband 10 pounds in her will so that he would emancipate her slave Gacella and have her baptized before the next Whitsun. The rich merchant Wuilielmus Scarsaria ordered that his *ancilla* Melese should be freed after serving his sons for 15 years and after being baptized, and should receive four pounds at that time. The slaves clearly had the possibility of earning a *pecunium*, i.e. property that legally remained the possession of their owner. The owner could either release the *pecunium* on emancipation, or partially release it or retain it, so producing a sum with which slaves could buy themselves free. This passed to the heirs of slaves whose emancipation was ordered by will. Childless testators were more generous. The childless Ansalmus Buxonus granted his slave Vitoria freedom in the event of his death and left her her *vestes* (clothes) without mentioning the *pecunium*. The trader Safran de Clavica, who was well-off but not rich, ordered the liberation of his *sarda* Vera; but this was only to be put into effect when Vera, with the agreement of his wife and sons, had found a husband who would provide for her. As the personal relationships between owners and female slaves were further developed than between owners and male slaves, the female slave's social position was more variable, depending on the economic situation of her owners. Members of the upper class who used their slaves mainly for housework and personal service were better able to afford the unconditional emancipation of their slaves than members of the lower classes. Female slaves had better prospects of an improvement in their legal and social position through the personal favour of their owners than male slaves. On the other hand, male slaves had a better chance of improving their position by their own work in the crafts and trades, and of earning their own *pecunium*. Female slaves had a special wealth-value in that they could bear children who would become part of the owner's property.

THE WOMEN'S DEVOTIONAL MOVEMENT

There was no freedom movement pursuing political goals among burgher women in the medieval towns. But in the high Middle Ages we can observe a broad and powerful religious movement among women.[39] It has all the features of a 'movement'. It is emotional and *engagé*, often no more than a fitful search for an 'apostolic' life for the 'followers of the poor and naked Christ'. It often moves exaltedly between heresy, the religious order and the free religious community. It comes to the fore at a time when church reform was taking on sometimes revolutionary traits, a time characterized by a dangerous proximity between heresy and a 'saintliness' that was still contained within church forms, a time in which the Cathari build up a counter-church. Reform as such is inseparable from life in religious orders, and always exists. But in the eleventh century it takes hold of the church as a whole. At that time there were too few convents; and those few were open only to ladies of the high nobility. When Archbishop Frederick I of Cologne founded the convent later called Nonnenwerth on the Rhine island of Ruleicheswerd opposite the Siebengebirge with the support of the abbot of Siegburg and a number of lay people, on 1 August 1126,[40] he was full of blame for himself: through his 'sinful guilt and negligence' there was 'hardly a single convent in our whole realm to which a woman who has taken the vow of abstinence can flee.' This is why he founded the Benedictine convent here, giving it a free choice of prioress but otherwise putting it under the jurisdiction of the abbey of Siegburg. Even in the twelfth century some famous women from religious orders still held to the principle of nobility — an example of the time-lags characteristic of the epoch, the simultaneity of the non-simultaneous. For women from broad sections of the population are by now seeking entry to the convents, the wives of ministerials and urban patricians, as well as members of the burgher classes. They first strive to be near the men's institutions. Dual monasteries for men and women had always existed, as had the opposition to them. A

[39] H. Grundmann, *Religiöse Bewegungen im Mittelalter*, with appendix, (1970); K. Elm, 'Die Stellung der Frau im Ordenswesen. Semireligiosentum und Häresie zur Zeit der heiligen Elisabeth' (1981), which lists further literature.

[40] *Reg. Eb. Köln II*, no. 228.

monk is committed to an ascetic life without women; he resists their proximity. In the first reformist zeal, the urge of women to achieve a life dedicated to God was frequently accommodated in a monastery for both sexes. But as the institutions took on more permanent form, the dual-gender principle was often abandoned.

The first impetus for the canonical reform at Springiersbach in the Moselle region[41] was given by Benigna, the widow of a ministerial serving the count's palace. Here a group of previously unfree servants was beginning to assert itself. About 1100 Benigna retired with her children and probably some of her relatives to a life of prayer and penance. She used her widow's estate to found a community of priests who would live by the rules of St Augustine. From this grew Springiersbach, from which Benigna's son Richard exerted an influence that went far beyond the borders of the Trier bishopric. At Springiersbach there was from the first, beside the canon's monastery, a women's convent that had grown up from Benigna's community. Richard rejected this dual form of monastery and set up special women's convents. A strong representation of *ministeriales* among founders and inmates is also to be found in the Cistercian convents of southern Swabia in the thirteenth century.[42] The Premonstratensian convent at Schillingskapellen near Bonn was founded in 1197 by the knight William, called Schilling, and the one at Niederehe in the Eifel by the von Kerpen brothers, who were probably ministerials of the empire.[43] To the hermitage founded by canon Ailbert of Antoing at Klosterrath near Aachen in 1104, came Embricio, a servant of the count of Saffenberg, with his wife Aleidis and his two children, a son and a daughter, and all his possessions. The settlement grew, but Ailbert would not tolerate brothers and sisters living together. The sisters had to be housed elsewhere, and their number was finally limited to eight women who lived in strict seclusion. In 1140, 37 sisters were moved to Marienthal on the Ahr, but remained under the guidance of Klosterrath. But by 1141 a number of sisters were again admitted to Klosterrath, to make clothes for all the members and because the church could not do without the services of

[41] F. Pauly, 'Anfänge und Bedeutung der Chorherrenreform von Springiersbach' (1961).

[42] M. Kuhn-Rehfus, 'Die soziale Zusammensetzung der Konvente in den oberschwäbischen Frauenzisterzen' (1982); and, 'Zisterzienserinnen in Deutschland' (1980).

[43] *Reg. Eb. Köln* II., nos 1522, 1523 and 1524.

women, an argument buttressed by the fact that the scriptures
state that people of both sexes had been among the followers
of the apostles. As Oediger writes,[44] 'One sees the concern caused
to religious authorities by the influx of pious women. They are
needed as weavers and seamstresses, but are not wanted near the
men.' Norbert of Xanten accommodated some of the women
attracted by his preaching in his monastery, founded at Prémontré.
Their living quarters were separate from the brothers', but they
attended mass with them and worked for them. They were under
the charge of a prioress, but an abbot or prior had overall charge.
But as early as 1140 the Premonstratensians, in institutions that
had been originally founded as dual monasteries, moved the women
into separate convents which were under the care of the monastery.
The attitude of the Cistercians is not quite clear or consistent. A
refusal to admit women in principle is partly contradicted by
decisions to admit them in practice.[45] At any rate, about 1200 the
Cistercian order abandoned its rejection of convents. Kuhn-Rehfus
tells us that about 1250 there were 33 female Cistercians in the
archbishopric of Mainz, 25 in the archbishopric of Cologne, 11 in
the archbishopric Trier, 15 in the bishopric of Constance and 9 in
the bishopric of Würzburg. Apart from the nuns there were lay
sisters, as well as converses, paying guests and oblates. The average
size of convents in Germany was 20—30 nuns and 10 sisters. At
the time of foundation the nuns almost all came from the nobility
and the lesser nobility, but later some convents admitted the
middle classes. The nuns knew Latin, copied and illuminated
manuscripts, produced medicaments, practised handicrafts and
ran schools. Incidentally, the oldest surviving pair of spectacles —
from about 1320 — was found in the convent of Weinhausen near
Celle; it is a riveted pair, 11.5 cm long when unfolded and 6 cm
wide.[46]

The reformist French convent of Fontevrault — we shall hear of
one of its famous inmates, Eleanor of Poitou, and we have already
met another, Bertrada — was a dual monastery with the abbess as
its head. The founder and itinerant preacher Robert of Abrissel
had insisted on this arrangement. He saw it as his life's task to
care for religious women. However, the fact that a woman was in

[44]   Oediger, *Das Bistum Köln*, pp. 402ff.
[45]   B. Degler-Spengler, 'Zisterzienserorden und Frauenklöster' (1982).
[46]   Elm, *Die Zisterzienser*, cat. D 28, p. 497.

charge attracted notice and mistrust. The same arrangement was adopted by an English convent, founded by Gilbert of Sempringham in Lincolnshire in 1131. The regime at Abelard's convent of the Paraclete at Quincey, near Nogent-sur-Seine, was not imitated. Its abbess and head was his beloved Héloïse, and the brothers were instructed to protect the weaker sex in a spirit of charity and care. About 1200 Fontevrault and its dependent convents also entered a crisis. It continued to be the practice that young girls, children by our standards, were put into a convent aged 8 to 12, and spent their lives in an order as a matter of course. The high-born women in the old foundations and Benedictine convents were less affected by the poverty movement.

A number of factors caused the secular and spiritual movements to become interwined. The fundamental social change brought about by the bourgeois freedom movement and the growth of towns influenced the church movement. Monasteries open to middle-class circles became urgently needed, as did spiritual care for the towns and their problems. There was an unmistakable increase in the search for ways of living devoutly in the world, not isolated from it as in a monastery, and solutions were found. Economic factors, the desire for social and economic security, for independence outside marriage, also played a part. At heart the movement was religious in nature, and the question of shelter and social security in the monastery or convent only came to prominence in the fourteenth century. The strength of the movement is reflected in the numerical growth of the institutions. In Germany alone the number of convents rose from about 70 in 900, to 150 about 1100, and to around 500 in 1250, so that by that time there must have been about 25,000–30,000 nuns and canonesses. In 1300 there were already 74 Dominican convents, in the fifteenth century the Benedictines had 115 institutions for women and the Cistercians 220; about 1600 the Franciscans had about 900 female communities. A characteristic of religious feeling in the twelfth and thirteenth centuries is the growing cult of the Virgin.

We find it difficult today to understand the religious motivation which caused so many women to seek refuge in convents or to lead a life of monastic abstinence in the world. Our value system differs fundamentally from that of the high Middle Ages.

Asceticism with a religious motivation is ranked higher than life in the world. Even in the early Christian hierarchy, the virgin dedicated to God was given a higher place than widows or married women. We find this valuation in Cyprian and Augustine as well as in Thomas of Aquinas and Bonaventure. There is a well-known parable of the hundred-fold, sixty-fold and thirty-fold fruit brought forth by virgins, widows and wives. The proportions are taken from the parable of the sower, Mark 4. 1–20 and Matthew 13. 1–23.

The emphasis on virginity does not mean a rejection of marriage, merely a lower valuation, as Bernards[47] argues in his analysis of the *Virgin's Mirror*, a widely disseminated work that originated in the mid-Rhine area about 1100. A rejection of marriage is to be found in the Manichaen heresies. The *Virgin's Mirror* warns against the view that virginity as such constitutes a higher state: 'God seeks the spirit of that state, rather than the garment', and 'the humble widow ranks higher than the proud virgin'. Many women sought to meet the high standards demanded by the *Mirror*; not all succeeded. The *Speculum virginum* considers the fall of a virgin dedicated to God as adultery towards the church. The normal punishment was withdrawal of the sacraments.

A fallen convent virgin is sure to have had a difficult time in her convent. It is told of Archbishop Anno of Cologne[48] that on one of his nightly rounds at the convent of St Ursula he witnessed the repentance and despair of a sister who was expecting a child. He noted her place at matins next morning, sent for her afterwards, persuaded her to confess and put her in the charge of one of his Westphalian *ministeriales* for the birth, with the express demand that the matter should be kept secret and mother and child returned to him. The child was brought up elsewhere, and the mother returned to her place in the convent. A lady from St Maria im Kapitol had been unfaithful to her vow of chastity but had escaped pregnancy and had tried to atone by 11 years of strict penitence; beginning to feel pride oppressing her again, she confessed to the Archbishop. He instructed her to remain humble and to live in exactly the same way as her sisters. The great achievements of many nuns show that they were able to lead fulfilled lives in convent or foundation, that asceticism does not wither the human being but liberates spiritual forces.

[47] M. Bernards, *Speculum virginum. Geistigkeit und Seelenleben der Frau im Hochmittelalter* (1955).

[48] *Reg. Eb. Köln I*, no. 1093, ad annum 1065–1075.

Let us return to the *Speculum virginum*. The question of a person's suitability for the life of a nun was hardly posed, the 'vocation' was not a problem but an assumption. As I said, people entered convents as children, and women who believed they had completed their wordly task decided to enter as widows. The root of monastic virtues is humility; it is the mother of love. Humility is bound to love and chastity in an ethical triad. Hence the primary vice is pride; it robs virginity of its value. The *Speculum* demands of the virginal life (1) an untainted body and mind and the will to serve God ; (2) voluntary renunciation of the world and the resolve to despise worldly things; (3)inward and outward obedience, friendly demeanour, humility and chastity on the model of the mother of God and as required by St Paul; (4) an attitude wholeheartedly devoted to the divine word and striving for spiritual peace, to preserve the words of life and sit at the feet of the Lord like the two Marys; and finally(5) awareness of the uncertainty of the long race, and a desire to endure, since each receives their reward according to their labour (Bernards, p. 86). This impressive image of virginity is the high point of the teaching given by the *Speculum*. It is made clear that, apart from the intactness of the chaste body, God sees the virtous intention of the heart; the traditional distinction of a double virginity is emphasized. The *Virgin's Mirror* shows that the education of women played a part in the spiritualization of the high Middle Ages. From the eleventh century more and more importance is attached to the individual conscience; the image of the battle is often used, and an easy life cannot be the reason for entering a convent. The spiritual striving enjoined by the *Virgin's Mirror* is marked by moderation. Life in the community must be one of concord. Noble birth should not be a source of arrogance in a convent. The *Mirror* distinguishes between true and false nobility: true nobility depends on inner disposition rather than on the honour of the parents. Here a main concern of the reformists is addressed: the breaking down of noble privileges. Cluny, Hirsau and later Cîteaux abolished the advantages of birth. However, Bernards sees no close connection between the *Mirror* and the reform of monasteries at the time: the *Mirror* hardly touches on the question of poverty. Asceticism is not presented as a burden. The virgins of the *Speculum* live unquestioningly in a clearly defined world without mystical excesses. Summing up his perceptive analysis Bernards writes:

The subjective, experiental piety of German mysticism is the exact opposite of the objective, intellectual spirituality of the Romance age and the *Virgin's Mirror*. Health of mind and body characterized the women addressed by the *Mirror*. Illness does not interest them, death strikes no fear. Serious character faults are unknown. The magic word 'freedom' has cast its spell over these true children of their time. If the church and the monasteries are fighting for freedom under the banner of the great reforms, freedom is an alluring goal for them too. The fact that freedom from the drudgery of marriage is seen only as a freedom to serve God makes clear the religious orientation and spiritual strength of these women. As contemporaries of the knights of the crusades and participants in a bellicose age, they like to see themselves as combatants in God's wars. They are all marked by the masculine trait that has been discerned in the face of Hildegard of Bingen. (p. 210)

Here Bernards mentions the name of probably the most important nun of the twelfth century.[49] She was born of noble stock in Bermersheim near Alzey in 1098 and at the age of eight was put into the care of Countess Jutta of Sponheim, who had taken up residence in the women's hermitage on the Disibodenberg. Hildegard, who shows a number of 'modern' tendencies, adhered to tradition on one point: she defended noble privilege. When the mistress of Andernach, Tengswich, expressed surprise that she admitted only noble nuns to her first convent at Rupertsberg, Hildegard replied that distinctions should be respected in convents too; just as cattle, asses, sheep and goats were not kept in the same stable, members of different classes should not be brought together in a single herd. Otherwise pride and shame, but above all strife, would be the consequence. God drew distinctions between people, she maintained.

In the hermitage she was instructed by the monk Volmar of Disibodenberg, who later worked with her as her 'secretary'. She made her vows between 1112 and 1115. After Jutta's death Hildegard became mistress of the hermitage, which had now grown into a small convent. In 1141 she had a mystical experience there, which inspired her great work *Scivias* — know the way. She worked at it for 10 years. In 1147 the first sections of the work were submitted to Pope Eugene III during his stay at Trier, parts being read out in the presence of Bernard of Clairvaux and prelates, and much admired. *Scivias* presents a comprehensive

[49]   *Hildegard von Bingen. 1179–1979*. Festschrift ed. by A. P. Brück (1979).

picture of the world in 26 visions; man's need for redemption, his way to Christ through struggle and suffering and the story of salvation in its irresistible growth are the great themes of the work. Her second great visionary work, *Liber vitae meritorum*, the 'Book of Life's Recompense' — or, translated more freely, 'Man and Responsibility' — was written in 1158–61, and the *Liber divinorum operum*, freely translated as 'The World and Man', in 1163–74. Each of these three works consists of a chain of visionary images; the description of the vision is followed by its interpretation. It is understandable that illustrated manuscripts of *Scivias* and *Liber operorum* were produced quite soon after the works were written. Apart from the visionary books, Hildegard wrote treatises on natural history and medicine. Her musical gifts are shown by her compositions.

A more modern trait in the life of this remarkable woman is her public activity as a preacher. The demand of a lay right to preach was put forward again and again in the twelfth century. Hildegard made three major preaching trips. On her Rhine journey of 1161–3 she preached against the heretics in Cologne. In the twelfth century the Cathari built up their antichurch and were quite widespread in the Rhineland. Heretics were burnt in Cologne in 1143 and again in 1163.[50] In her sermon Hildegard also took the clergy to task, arguing that their worldly life gave succour to heresy. She opposed the Cathari's hostility to the flesh and their contempt for the world, manifested particularly in their attitude to women. In 1163 Ekbert, a monk at Schönau, also dedicated his *Sermones adversus Catharorum errores et haereses* to the archbishop of Cologne. Her sister Elizabeth of Schönau shared Hildegard's convictions and probably knew her. She wrote visions of her own in her *Liber viarum Dei*.

When the monastery at Disibodenberg became too small, Hildegard left it with her nuns in 1151, moving to Rupertsberg near Bingen. A second convent was founded at Eibingen near Rüdesheim, and Hildegard was head of both convents. She died, aged 81, on 17 September 1179.

Hildegard had had good reason to warn women in particular against the heretics. The heretical sects were at first glad to admit women, and women played a special part in them. In 1028 we hear of a group of false believers near Turin, including men and women and led by a woman, the countess of Monteforte. The Cathari admitted women not only as as sympathizers, *credentes*, but as initiates, *perfecti*. There were also women's communities among the Albigensians. About 1200 countess Esclarmonde of Foix, after her husband's death, became a follower of the heretic Guillabert de Castres, who administered the *consolamentum*, spiritual baptism, to her and other devout women in 1204. In 1207, in the presence of numerous secular and clerical notables, the countess of Foix intervened in the debate between the Waldensians and the Cathari on one hand and the bishops of Toulouse and Couseran on the other. A monk is said to have rebuked her: 'Go back to your distaff, Mistress, it is not for you to speak at this assembly.' Women also belonged to the Waldensians in Metz in 1199. Apart from the very different motives that caused women to join the heretics there was, as Elm remarks, one generally valid reason, 'the opportunity to lead an unconventional, active life in close company with ... men who travelled about the country, and to do what the church had always denied to lay people and particularly to women: to preach publicly and to administer the sacraments.' But as the sects became institutionalized, this initial openness towards women faded away. We should stress that many of these women came from the high nobility, but at the other extreme the heretics at first showed a readiness to admit women of very doubtful reputation. At his first appearance at Le Mans in 1116, the heretic Henry was accused of allowing his followers to marry prostitutes as a means of converting them. Robert of Arbrissel admitted harlots to Fontevrault − along with the high-born women. This aspect of the women's question had two sources: the reformer's condemnation of priests who lived with women, and the desire of women from all social groups to take an active part in religious life. Innocent III gave the directive that such prostitutes should be married, or that they were to be admitted by the penitential orders or the order of Magdalen. An influential attempt to guide female piety into ordered channels was originated by James of Vitry.[51] He obtained papal permission for the pious women in the bishopric of Liège and in the whole of France and Germany to live together in communal houses and to help each other in right living by mutual admonition. In concrete

---

[51] Grundmann, *Religiöse Bewegungen im Mittelalter*, p. 170.

terms, this meant the permission to form convent-like women's communities, unaffiliated to existing orders and without adopting the approved convent rules, and to give edifying sermons in these communities. Pope Honorius seems to have given only verbal permission, without adding any other instructions; it is known only from James of Vitry's letters. The fourth Lateran Council had prohibited the formation of new orders, and the building of communal houses (*domus religiosae*) unless they accepted the approved rules. James of Vitry had lived as an Agustinian canon close to Maria of Oignies, who was at the centre of the religious women's groups in Wallonie, and who had once wanted to go to the south of France 'to honour God where he has been deserted by many.' She was married at 14, living in an unconsummated marriage with her husband and tending the poor and lepers with him, until she joined a circle of like-minded women at St Nicholas in Oignies. After her death, in 1213, James of Vitry wrote her biography to hold up to the French heretics – as Bishop Fulco of Toulouse had wished – an image of a *modern* saint ('si contra hereticos provincie tue ea que Deus in sanctis modernis in diebus nostris operatur, in publicum posses praedicare'). On his journey to Rome James had direct experience of the women's religious movement in Italy. Grundmann surmises that he also met St Francis of Assisi and played some part in mediating between the movements on both sides of the Alps. From these circles the Beguine order developed. *Béguine* was originally a name for a heretic. Before James of Vitry's sympathetic intervention the religous women's movement in the bishopric of Liège had been placed under suspicion of heresy by the clergy of the diocese; hence they were called Beguines, which is probably a truncated form of the word 'Albigenses'. 'Reform' within the church was always in danger of leading out of the church. The beginnings of Beguinism fall within our period; in chapter 3 we shall be concerned with it as a phenomenon of the late Middle Ages.

James of Vitry was far from being the only one who helped to give the religious women's movement a more definite form. The knight Philip of Montmirail, who founded many Cistercian convents and Beguinages, knew many men and women who were leading a religious life, i.e. a life specially dedicated to God, in Greece, Lombardy, Burgundy, Provence, Gaul, Flanders and Brabant.

Beguinism became the 'basis of early female mysticism in the vernacular'.[52] An early centre of this mysticism, that was much influenced by Bernard of Clairvaux's sermons on the Song of Songs and by his emphasis on the passion of Christ, was the southern Netherlands. Hadewich (b. 1180–90), the head of a Beguine community in Nivelles, came from an eminent Antwerp family. She was highly educated, familiar with the songs of the troubadours and versed in theology; she knew Bernard's writings. Her *Brieven* — epistles to real or fictitious recipients — were aimed especially at her own Beguine community. Her 'visions' are usually centred on a face. In a vision she is entranced, swept away by *orewoet* — the storm-winds of the spirit. Hildegard had a more objective stance towards her visions. Ruh calls Hadewich's poems 'the high point of the spiritual and secular medieval lyric in the Netherlands.' Of her prose he writes that she 'put everything into words, the tenderest and boldest of her experiences, the sublimest cosmic and prophetic images, with a vigour and precision unequalled in the whole literature of the Netherlands. No less astonishing are her intellectual gifts, the confidence of her theological speculations, her awareness of her own extraordinariness'. It can be no accident that this woman came from the intellectually innovative region of the southern Netherlands.

The first Beguines in Germany are recorded in Cologne in 1223.[53] They come from patrician families, the old *Damenstifte* in Cologne being reserved for the daughters of the rural nobility. A. Schulte's observation that no Cologne woman, no matter how high her status, had ever headed the three Cologne women's foundations of St Ursula, St Cecilia and St Maria im Kapitol, remains true for the period after 1250. F. M. Stein, in his careful and well-documented study, which does, however, underestimate the strength of class barriers, has pointed out three exceptions at Maria im Kapitol for the period around 1200: two members of the Cologne patrician family of Mummersloch and one from the Jude family, which was related to the high nobility. Moreover, Maria im Kapitol was originally a Benedictine convent, only being turned

---

[52] K. Ruh, 'Beginenmystik. Hadewijch, Mechtild von Magdeburg, Marguerite Porète' (1977).

[53] A. Schulte, *Der hohe Adel im Leben des mittelalterlichen Köln* (1919); E. Ennen, 'Kölner Wirtschaft im Früh- und Hochmittelalter' (1975), pp. 165f; F. M. Stein, *The Religious Women of Cologne: 1200–1320* (1977); G. M. Löhr, 'Das Necrologium des Dominikanerinnenklosters St Gertrud in Köln' (1927); J. Prieur, *Das Kölner Dominikanerinnenkloster St Gertrud am Neumarkt* (1983).

into a *Stift* in the twelfth century. Whereas women from patrician families had access to the old Cologne convents, the middle classes lacked opportunities to lead a *vita religiosa* in the way they wished. By no means all Beguines were 'frustrated nuns'. The movement offered a more flexible and more open form of religious life than the convents, particularly the older ones.

The view that the basis of the religious movement is to be found in the nobility and the urban patriciate is not uncontested. When Hildegard of Bingen preached against the heretics in Cologne and was asked where they were to be found, she replied: 'in speluncis terrae, domos vocans subterraneas, in quibus textores et pellifices operantur' — in caves, subterranean houses, where weavers and furriers work. Was there perhaps a connection between weavers and heretics after all? Grundmann has shown, convincingly in my opinion, how such a link may have come about. It was a part of the apostolic life the heretics sought to lead that they should work with their hands, and weaving was a convenient form. 'Weavers did not become heretics, but heretics became weavers', as Grundmann neatly puts it. There may, of course, have been exceptions.[54] We have come across high-born women among the heretics in southern France, and anyone who has climbed to the old Cathari strongholds at Peyrepertuse and Queribus can see that lords were at work here. The new orders and the Beguine communities integrated into the church were only the other side of the heretic coin. They all desired the inner renewal of the church; I would stress the important part played by the towns and broad middle sections of the population — not only the high nobility, but not yet the lower classes — in this religious movement.

The Cologne convent of St Gertrude on the Neumarkt developed from a women's community living without rules; it was recognized as a Dominican convent in 1263—83. Before the end of the thirteenth century, daughters from 18 patrician families were represented among the nuns.

How far, we may ask, did the new orders of the Franciscans and Dominicans satisfy the needs of the women's movement? Even they were resisted. Grundmann and Elm have demonstrated in detail how attempts to meet the women's demands were evolved in a detemined struggle between the reluctant orders and the

[54] In *Frauenfrage und Ketzertum im Mittelalter* (1962), G. Koch does not refute Grundmann.

papacy. Let us try to show the part played by the women themselves. The starting points of the Dominicans and Franciscans
were very different. St. Dominic had begun by winning back
women with strong but uncertain religious feelings for the true
faith by preaching. When he was preaching at Fanjeaux near
Prouille, nine *matronae*, elderly women, approached him, saying
they had believed those he was preaching against and thought
them good men. The preaching of Dominic and his assistants was
needed to convince them that these men were heretics. The
foundation of the convent at Prouille was thus connected with the
fight against heresy in southern France. It was the first convent
belonging to the Dominican order, from which Dominic and his
companions launched their missions against the heretics in the
following years. On a journey to Spain in 1281 Dominic laid the
foundation for a convent in Madrid, and in 1221, in the newly
established convent of S. Sisto in Rome, which was a gift of the
pope, the Benedictine sisters who were transferred there from S.
Maria in Trastevere were reformed on the principles of Prouille.
The start in Bologna was more difficult. Here the preaching
brothers found a hearing among the wives of the city aristocracy
as well as the university teachers and students. Diana of Andalò,
aged about 18, and other women of the Bolognese nobility,
changed the whole conduct of their lives; in 1219 Diana took her
vows before St Dominic and asked him to establish a convent on
the model of Prouille. The plan met with opposition. In 1221
Diana entered a Benedictine convent in Bologna. When she took
up her plan again after St Dominic's death, the new head of the
order, Jordanis of Saxony, at first gave her strong support. Diana
and four other sisters took up residence in the new convent of S.
Agnes in 1223, but it was only after strong papal pressure that the
new order took S. Agnes in Bologna under its protection, administration and spiritual care. The chapter's decision of 1228, forbidding the preaching order to take on further convents or to take
vows from women, was not directed against S. Agnes, as emerges
from two letters from Jordanis to Diana of Andalò. The reasons
given are the condition of the order in other provinces, particularly
Germany. There the brothers were alleged to have unhesitatingly
taken vows from young women and harlots who wished to repent
and pledge themselves to chastity; the order was intended to put a
stop to this. In Germany, Grundmann comments, 'the waves of
mendicant orders coming from the south met the women's religious

movement from northern countries.The result was an enormous influx of pious women into the new orders'. Thus the first sermon given by Heinrich, the first Dominican prior at Cologne, was a great success with young women, widows and penitents, and the women of Cologne wept at his death. The Cologne clergy at first kept their distance from the Dominicans, as Minorites. The flood of women to the new orders was more than the orders themselves wished for. Many women's communities already existed before they were made Dominican convents.

We have already mentioned the example of Cologne, The case of Nuremberg is very revealing. In 1211 the young Elizabeth of Hungary passed through Nuremberg on her way to her betrothal to the son of the count of Thuringia. One of her women attendants, the harpist Alheit, stayed in the town and was converted there to a life of penitence and devotion to God. A Beguine community established soon afterwards asked Alheit to be its head. These *sorores Rotharinne* as they were called, after their mistress the *Rotherin* (harpist), became widely known, receiving gifts and endowments, including gifts from Queen Kunigunde of Bohemia. When Nuremberg was under the interdict in 1239, the women appealed to the *ministerialis* of the empire, Ulrich von Königstein, who donated the necessary land for the foundation of the convent at Engelthal. In this way the women's community developed into a convent. There was an attempt by Cistercians — despite the order's prohibition on the admission of convents — to win over the convent. But the women decided to join the Dominicans. When Bishop Frederick of Eichstätt took the convent under his protection in 1244, he made the sisters accept the Augustinian rules and the statues of S. Sisto in Rome. In 1248 the women gained admission to the Dominican order through papal mediation.

The attraction exerted on pious women by Dominican preaching is demonstrated by Grundmann, using the example of Jolande, daughter of the count of Vianden in Luxembourg. Her desire for the convent life seemed almost 'cured' and, to the relief of her family, she had the prospect of a brilliant marriage. Then the Dominicans entered her life and, against the resistance of all her relatives, she entered a wretchedly indigent women's community — one of hundreds. The daughters of wealthy Zurich families lived on bread, water and scraps in a bleak , dilapidated house. This convent of Otenbach near Zurich had no founders, but it finally grew rich from the dotal property of the sisters and from alms. But before its admission to the Dominican order in 1245, the community lived 'in great poverty and infirmity, in dire want of worldly goods, but rich in divine love and true humility'. A model for many Dominican convents was the convent of St Mark in Strasbourg, the constitution of which generally coincided with that of S. Sisto in Rome. In this way there arose in Germany a close collaboration between 'religious' women and Dominicans. The local bishops, and the order as a whole, were not entirely pleased about this, unlike the curia. The French convent at Montargis on the Loing provided the occasion for counter-measures by Pope Innocent IV. A convent for 50 women had been founded there by the widowed Countess Amicie de Joigny, daughter of Count Simon de Montfort who was a friend of St Dominic. The order refused to incorporate it. While the curia was staying in Lyons, Amicie negotiated personally with Innocent IV, with the result that the admission of the convent at Montargis to the Dominican order was ordered by a bull of 8 April 1245. At this the floodgates opened.

In 1211/12 Francis of Assisi had won over Clara Sciffis as a very young girl 'like a noble prey from the pernicious world'. A women's community with her as its head came into being next to the church of St Damian before the gates of Assisi, adopting St Francis's directives on poverty, simplicity and strict fasting. St Francis had commended St Damian's to the love and care of his brothers, but the *Regula Bullata* of 1223 forbade the admission of convents without the special permission of the pope. Here again Innocent IV intervened decisively. On 2 June 1246 he affiliated 14 convents in Italy, France and Spain to the Franciscan order in one day. Clara introduced the strict principle of poverty and the Franciscans' spiritual care at St Damian's to the full extent envisaged by St Francis. After her death the order of St Damian was officially called Ordo S. Clarae. 'About 1300,' Grundmann concludes his discussion of the relation of the Franciscans and Dominicans to the convents, 'a state had finally been reached, which bore in its diversity the traces of protracted controversy, particularly in the order of St Clarissa. The independent strivings of the religous women had been largely contained within the fixed forms of the church orders.' But not all the wishes of the women's movement were satisfied. Many women sought refuge in the free community of the Beguines, or, within the convent, made the inward journey towards mysticism. The multiplicity of spiritual life among women had increased constantly and around the abbeys, foundations and convents — as Elm has pointed out[55] — were grouped large circles of people: converses, lay sisters, paid servants and women who had obtained by donations the right to receive their sustenance and spiritual care from the nuns and their spiritual guides. The economy of the convents could not be sustained by the nuns alone. The work in the house, kitchen and garden, the care of the sick and guests, were the task of the lay sisters.[56]

It is against the background of this diverse and energetic religious movement among women that Elizabeth of Thuringia is to be understood.[57] Elm emphasizes her spiritual affinity to Francis of Assisi, of whom she knew at an early age. Both finally decided on a life divided between the monastery and the world. Hence the difficulty historians have in pigeonholing Elizabeth. Was she more strongly influenced by the Cistercians or the Franciscans? Did she belong to an order or did she remain a laywoman; can she be described as a penitent, a hospital sister or a Beguine? What drove her was a desire for the absolute imitation of Christ in poverty, renunciation, mortification and obedience.

WOMEN IN THE WORLD OF CHIVALRY

The great majority of the population of central and western Europe still lived in the country, not in the towns. The countryside had its own political ruling class in the castle-dwelling nobility. From the king, through the dukes, counts and nobles, the pyramid spread down to the horseman, the 'knight'. Chivalry is a phenomenon often misunderstood by the layman; the knight is sometimes idealized as the champion of Christianity, the troubadour devoted to courtly love or *Minne*, and sometimes vilified as the 'robber knight'. The historian is concerned with the sober reality. I quote Arno Borst's[58] apt description:

[55] K. Elm, *Ordensstudien I: Berträge zur Geschichte der Konversen im Mittelalter* (1980).
[56] M. Toepfer, 'Die Konversen der Zisterzienserinnen von Himmelspforten bei Würzburg' (1980).
[57] *St Elisabeth. Fürstin, Dienerin, Heilige*, (1981).
[58] See Borst's article 'Das Rittertum im Hochmittelalter. Idee und Wirklichkeit', in *Das Rittertum*, pp. 219f.

The lesser nobility in France were a horde of ambitious ruffians who respected nothing but success and the rule of force. In league with death and the Devil, they set on all those weaker than themselves. Consideration for others was cowardice, and the bravest opponent was mercilessly cut down without a trace of chivalry. After war and rapine, the favourite pastime of these open-air fanatics was deer hunting ... What they had gained by hunting or pillage they prodigally handed out; in their view, only weaklings who worked were tight-fisted. Chastity or abstinence they also considered miserly traits, and the cramped wooden towers they inhabited were crawling with illegitimate children, of whom no-one was ashamed. Life in the tower was passed in noisy disorder. People sat tightly packed on long benches and took meat from the dishes with their fingers. What was left over was snapped up by the dogs, or fell into the straw that covered the cold floor. These lords could seldom read or write. At the most, they had someone read to them of mighty warriors who were as they wanted to be, muscular, daring and with an insatiable appetite. They were superstitious rather than pious, and women were treated with little respect and often beaten.

Things did not remain as bad as that. Nevertheless, after reading this it is easier to understand why so many women sought admission to convents. Kings and princes disciplined and pacified the knights and the church reform movement outlawed the abuses. Borst continues:

Because this lesser nobility was not based on ancient traditions or on inheritance it was receptive to anything new and grandiose. Without a revolution, it was willingly drawn into grand schemes and ideas, God and church, king and state, morality and women. Still open to anyone of ability and valour, not entirely carried away by any of the new ideals yet fascinated by all of them, the new class developed its collective consciousness in the eleventh century, giving its members, first of all in France, a new name, *chevalier, riddere, ritter,* knight. The name became necessary because this class clearly did not fit into the older categories of nobles and *ministeriales.* It stood between them, between the ruling nobles and the serving horsemen...And now, from 1100, the form first shaped in France spread across the whole of Europe.

It was also in France that the chivalrous lyric first joined the old heroic song. It glorified the court woman and the knight's love for his mistress, who was married to another.[59] 'We shall never know,' writes Sidney Painter,[60] 'whether the woman or the troubadour created the lyric poetry of the south, but while the masculine mind gave it the form which now survives, feminine beauty provided its inspiration'.

Eleanor of Poitou was a queen of the troubadours.[61] In 1137 this rich heiress of Aquitaine, aged between 13 and 15, was married to Louis VII of France, then 16 years old. The first child, a girl, Marie, was not born until 1145, and a second daughter arrived after the return from the unsuccessful second crusade, on which Louis had taken his wife. In Antioch Eleanor met her uncle Raimund, the prince of this crusaders' state in which her native tongue, the *langue d'oc* was spoken. Here she felt at home. Raimund's political aims differed from Louis's plans for the crusade, which led to a serious quarrel between Eleanor and her husband. Personal factors were also involved. Did Louis suspect his wife of having too close a relationship with Raimund? Was he right? On this point Eleanor does not enjoy an overly good reputation among historians of the time. Was this beautiful, intelligent woman dissatisfied with her monkish husband? (Louis had originally been intended for the clergy.) The pope reconciled the couple in Italy on their way back from the crusade. He calmed Eleanor's doubts about the legitimacy of her marriage to the Capetian; she feared their kinship was too close. Naturally, the birth of a second daughter was a great disappointment to Louis, who needed a male heir for his house and for Aquitaine. In Paris, in 1151, the dissatisfied queen formed an alliance with Louis's vassal, Geoffrey Plantagenet, count of Anjou, and his son Henry, duke of Normandy, who had claims to the throne of England. Was this relationship treasonable? It strengthened Eleanor's desire to be separated from Louis, who also wanted the marriage annulled. Thus, in 1152 in Beaugency, came about the assembly of archbishops, bishops, lords and barons of France, who declared Louis's marriage to Eleanor void on grounds of consanguinity. Eleanor kept her hereditary lands, and she and Louis were granted the right to make legitimate second marriages. She moved to her fortress at Poitiers, where she was visited by the young Duke Henry, who had now inherited Anjou and Maine as well, following

[60] Sidney Painter, 'Die Ideen des Rittertums', in: *Das Rittertum* p. 41.
[61] R. Pernoud, *Eleonore von Aquitanien* (1966); Duby, *The Knight, the Lady and the Priest*, pp. 201ff.

the early and sudden death of Geoffrey Plantagenet. About eight weeks after her divorce from Louis, Eleanor became Henry's wife and duchess of Normandy. Her favourite residence came to be Angers. Poets came to her court, the troubadour Bernard de Ventadour chose her as his 'mistress'. In 1154 we find her at Rouen. On 25 October King Stephen of England died; on the Sunday before Christmas 1154, Henry and Eleanor were crowned in Westminster Abbey. As queen, Eleanor found complete fulfilment. She bore her English husband eight children including five sons, although the first son died in infancy. On many occasions Eleanor and Henry shared the government of the different parts of their realm. The queen stays in England when Henry is called to Normandy, or she resides in Anjou, Poitiers or Bordeaux while Henry inspects his possessions on the island. Although her rights as duchess of Aquitaine passed to her husband, her agreement was needed for every decree. As queen of England she has control of her dotal lands, and as queen consort she can issue charters in her own name.[62] At the ceremonial court banquets, held in a different city of the realm each year, she sits beside the king. She renders accounts, for example for the market at Oxford, for the tin mines on which the king levies a tax or for a mill which she owns. The first accounts in which the queen is explicitly mentioned concerned the purchase of oil for her lamps, which she preferred to tallow or wax candles, and purchases of wine, which the daughter of Aquitaine preferred to English beer. She buys linen for table-cloths, copper kettles, cushions and curtains, gold for the gilding of her dishes and cutlery, spices for the kitchen, incense for the services in the palace chapel. And she did more: she played a part in uniting the courtly poetry of southern France with the Celtic legends.

In 1167 her last child, John (later King John of England), was born in England. About this time there was an irremediable breach with her husband, on account of 'fair Rosemond', the daughter of a Norman knight. Eleanor withdrew in mortification to Poitiers. There her court was the centre of courtly and chivalrous life, although she was not always present, between 1168 and her return to England as a prisoner in 1174. Her

[62] H. G. Richardson, 'The letters and charters of Eleanor of Aquitaine' (1959); E. Ennen, 'Zur Städtepolitik der Eleonore von Aquitanien' (1984).

daughters from her first marriage often stayed there: Alix of Blois, who later entered Fontevrault, and Marie of Champagne. The private discord between the royal spouses was overshadowed by a larger event; the conflict over the relationship of church and state between Henry II and Thomas à Becket, archbishop of Canterbury, who was murdered in his cathedral in 1170. This caused a major upheaval in Henry's realm with the rising of his sons, which Eleanor supported. In the summer of 1174 Henry had her seized and imprisoned in England.

She regained her freedom step by step. In 1185–6 she stayed in Normandy and again issued deeds in favour of Fontevrault. In 1183 her second son Henry, already crowned king, died. From 1186 to the death of her husband she lived in England, but without regaining her earlier position. After her husband's death and up to the arrival of Richard in England she enjoyed great authority, though she was probably not regent. Outwardly Ranulf de Glanvill, the head of the judiciary, was in charge, but a number of edicts were issued *per preceptum regine*, or *per reginam*. What is certain is that she saw to it that those languishing in royal gaol were released or brought before a court, and that she did everything to prepare for Richard's coronation. Richard was almost unknown in England. His first appearance was celebrated with all imaginable pomp: the robes of the queen and her retinue cost over seven pounds, her cloak, made of five-and-a-half ells of silk bordered with squirrel and sable, cost just under five pounds. Ten ells of scarlet material, two sables, and one squirrel coat were needed for other garments. After his coronation Richard armed himself, like Barbarossa and Philip Augustus of France, for the Third Crusade. Eleanor arranged Richard's betrothal to Berengaria, daughter of the King of Navarre, whom she brought to meet him at Messina. In 1192 she again set foot on English soil. When the bad news of Richard's imprisonment by Leopold of Austria reached her, she did everything in her power to help her favourite son secure his freedom. She appealed to the pope, she collected ransom money from her vassals. Even now she was not formally appointed regent and had no chancery or administration of her own. She herself took the ransoms money to the empire. In the city of Cologne, which now harboured the bodies of the Three Magi, she celebrated the feast of the Epiphany with Archbishop Adolf I. On the feast of Candlemas in 1194, the archbishops of Mainz and Cologne handed Richard over in Mainz.[63] They travelled to Antwerp via Cologne, where the archbishop held a great feast in their honour, and landed in England in March. In May Richard left again for Normandy, which was being claimed by the French king Philip Augustus, accompanied by Eleanor who — now over 70 — often withdrew to Fontevrault. She was violently roused from her monastic peace by the news that Richard had been mortally wounded in a feud; he died in her arms. Of her five sons, only John, a feckless, unreliable, underhand character who was to lose Normandy to the king of France, was left alive. Eleanor still displayed astonishing energy; the charters she now issued were mainly for the freedom of towns in Poitou. She had clearly sensed the importance of the new forms of economic life and the military significance of the flourishing towns, as well as opportunities they presented to the crown. When over 80 she crossed the Pyrenees to visit her youngest daughter Eleanor, married since 1170 to Alfonso III of Castile. From there she took her granddaughter, Blanca, as a bride for the heir to the French throne. This was her own idea, and proved a happy one; Blanca was to be an energetic regent when her son, Louis the Pious, was away at the crusades. Eleanor of Aquitaine died on 31 March 1204, and is buried at Fontevrault. Her monument shows her swathed in the folds of her dress and cloak. Her face is framed by veil and chinband and she is reading a book: a fitting portrait of this highly-educated queen whose intellect remained alert until her last moment, who had inspired troubadours and *Minnesänger*. Her daughter from her first marriage, Mary, was a zealous champion of courtly love. She was married to Count Henry of Champagne, to whom the markets of the region brought great wealth. She was filled with the ideas of the troubadours, and gave Chrétien de Troyes the material for the story of Lancelot and Guinevere.

Eleanor's eldest daughter from her second marriage, Matilda, married the great Guelph, Henry the Lion, duke of Saxony from 1142 and duke of Bavaria as well from 1154.[64] Henry the Lion's grandmother, Richenza, was the last important *consors regni* in Germany. Her rich inheritance made Emperor Lothar III the most powerful man in Saxony. After his death, and the death of

[63] *Reg. Eb. Köln II*, nos 1466–71.
[64] K. Jordan, *Heinrich der Löwe* (1979).

her son-in-law Henry the Proud, she had become leader of the Guelph cause; she died in 1141. Henry's marriage to Matilda was a political union; it was connected to a German–English alliance agreed by Chancellor Rainald of Dassel in 1165, which was to be cemented by marriages. Thus the nine-year-old Matilda was betrothed to the 35-year-old duke. Henry the Lion was fully in favour of this marriage to a king's daughter, which enhanced his standing. In the winter of 1167–8 he took advantage of the truce usual at this season to hold the wedding. He sent a legation led by Prior Baldwin of Utrecht, from the house of the count of Holland, to bring the princess of Saxony from the English court. Two counts and other English lords accompanied her; she brought with her a large quantity of gold and silver and a rich dowry. On 1 February 1168 the marriage was blessed in the cathedral at Minden. The secular wedding celebrations took place in the castle of Brunswick. Between 1172 and 1184 Matilda bore the duke five children, including the later German king, Otto IV. In the 1170s the Guelph court at Brunswick was a centre of much culture, Duke Henry being a patron of the arts who adorned his residential city with important buildings, and had the figure of a lion cast and set up in the open in front of his castle. He gave a strong impetus to book illumination and the goldsmith's art. His wife Matilda introduced the new chivalric poetry at the Guelph court. Two works were produced by members of the duke's entourage which are among the earliest courtly epics to appear in Germany: the *Song of Roland* by the priest Conrad, and the *Tristan* of Eilhart von Oberg, a Guelph ministerial. In the epilogue to the *Song of Roland* the author, the 'parson Conrad' as he calls himself, records that a Duke Henry, at the request of his noble wife, the daughter of a mighty king, had obtained the book, which had been written in France, so that it could be translated into German. The identification of this duke with Henry the Lion is fairly certain, and the years 1168–72 can be taken as the period when the work was written. It is not possible to date the composition of *Tristan* with any certainty. Eilhart's model was the great French epic of Tristan and Iseult, now lost. Duchess Matilda may have passed on knowledge of this poem. This is one example among many of how important the interrelationships of the ruling houses and of the nobility were in the development of European culture. For Matilda, the years of splendour were followed by years of care and exile. In the period 1176–80 came the dramatic conflict between Barbarossa and Henry the Lion, which resulted in Henry's being stripped of his two dukedoms and forced to leave Germany for three years. His wife, his only daughter and his two sons accompanied him into exile. In the autumn of 1182 he made a pilgrimage to Santiago de Compostela, but spent Christmas back with his family and the court of King Henry at Caen. During his absence Matilda stayed at the royal court at Argentan in Normandy. Through her brother, Richard the Lionheart, she met the troubadour Bertrand de Born, who dedicated two of his finest love songs to her. Bertrand extolled the charm of the princess, then 26, comparing her to Helen of Troy. In the spring of 1164 Matilda followed her father to England and gave birth to her last son, William, at Winchester; he was to be the ancestor of all later Guelphs. In the spring of 1185 Henry and Matilda were able to return to Brunswick. But when Barbarossa left on a crusade in 1188, he again compelled Henry the Lion to go to England for three years. Matilda stayed in Brunswick to protect his interests, and died there on 28 June 1189, aged only 32 or 33.

'The German chivalrous lyric, the spring of *Minnesang,* flowered in the Hohenstaufen lands close to France after 1170'.[65] The chivalrous form of life took on a clearer shape at the meeting of spiritual and temporal dignitaries at Mainz in 1184, the *curia celebris* [66] at the knighting of the emperor's two sons, King Henry and Duke Frederick. The festival, for which a special city of tents had been erected on the plain between the Rhine and the Main, began on Whit Sunday with the ceremonial coronation of Barbarossa, his wife Beatrix and his son Henry. The knighting took place on Whit Monday after the early mass, giving the feast a chivalrous stamp. The *novi milites,* the new knights, displayed suitable largesse with rich gifts, and were emulated by the princes and lords. There followed a friendly trial of arms, though probably not yet a tournament in the French style,[67] but it had to be broken off on the Tuesday after Whitsun because of a storm which demolished the wooden chapel and several tents. Politics now claimed their due, and the important political act was the elevation of Count Baldwin of Hennegau to the status of imperial prince.

[65] Borst, *Das Rittertum,* pp. 236ff.
[66] J. Fleckenstein, 'Friedrich Barbarossa und das Rittertum. Zur Bedeutung der grossen Mainzer Hoftage von 1184 und 1188' (1976), pp. 392ff.
[67] H. Thomas, 'Zur Datierung, zum Verfasser und zur Interpretation des Moritz von Craûn' (1984), pp. 362ff.

Some saw the havoc caused by the weather as divine retribution for the sumptuous and over-worldly festivities. Such criticism was not levelled at the second great Mainz meeting of 1188, the *curia Jesu Christi*. The theme of this meeting was the great task of the Christian knights, the reconquest of Jerusalem, and it was decided to launch a new crusade (from which Barbarossa was not to return). At both the meetings the emperor's adherence to the code of chivalry was shown in the fact that all lay members of the court, from the simple vassal to the king, were regarded as knights, however much they were otherwise divided by class boundaries and their places in the social hierarchy. Even the emperor's sons submitted to the ritual of being knighted, and the emperor himself joined in the tournaments. 'The world of chivalry was thus given a focal point at the imperial court', as Fleckenstein puts it. Honour, fame, dignity and generosity are here seen as courtly and knightly virtues. Outward splendour, the heraldic embellishment of tents, are a part of the chivalrous life — coats of arms being important for recognition at tournaments. An element of play in fighting, as in love, is a basic feature of chivalry.

However, the Mainz celebrations also offered nobler pleasures: Guiot de Provins and Heinrich von Veldecke were the best poets present, if not the only ones. Guiot expressly names the emperor as his patron; perhaps Empress Beatrix was behind this. It is appropriate that Fleckenstein, looking for the first signs of a link between the imperial throne and the chivalry which made such a brilliant show at Mainz, settles on the meeting of 1157 in Besançon, made famous by a clash between Cardinal Roland and Chancellor Rainald of Dassel. Emperor Frederick had gone there with Beatrix, after they had been married for a year, to receive the homage of Burgundy. Now the whole country outdid itself in glorifying the ruler with 'new' honours and eulogies. These new forms of celebration may well have been chivalrous ones, as Fleckenstein suggests, and Beatrix could then be seen as their inspiration. Barbarossa and Beatrix were a handsome couple. Acerbus Morena[68] says of Beatrix: 'She was of medium build with hair shining like gold and a very beautiful face, her teeth white and well formed. She had an upright bearing, a very small mouth, a modest gaze, bright eyes, and a chaste and gentle manner of speech. She had very beautiful hands and a graceful body.' He

---

[68] 'De rebus Laudensibus', *MGSS 18*, p. 640.

also praises her literary knowledge. Gautier of Arras dedicated his epic romance *Ille et Galeron* to her, and the annals of Cambrai stress the active part she played in intellectual life. [69] In education Barbarossa was her inferior. Their wedding — she was Barbarossa's second wife — took place in 1156 in Würzburg. Afterwards Beatrix accompanied the emperor on his travels. She bore him eight sons and three, perhaps four, daughters[70] and died long before him, aged only 40, in November 1184

With one exception, the Hohenstaufen women did not pursue independent policies of their own. They were primarily the objects of a marital politics aimed at enlarging territories; this is true of Beatrix as it is of Constance of Sicily, the wife of Henry VI, and the many wives and even some of the concubines of Frederick II — not for nothing was he mocked as the 'Sultan of Lucera'. His first wife Constance, daughter of King Alfonso II of Aragon, is buried beside the emperor in the cathedral of Palermo. 'I was Sicily's queen and empress, Constantia. Here I live now, Frederick, your wife', the grave inscription runs. Her marriage to the young Hohenstaufen was arranged by the pope; Frederick hoped to enlist the help of the Catalan knights to win back the dominion of Sicily which was in revolt. She was at least 10 years older than the emperor. In 1211 she bore him an heir, Henry. When Frederick was summoned to Germany by the Hohenstaufen party in 1212 to receive the crown, he made her regent for their little son who had been crowned king of Sicily, a proof of great confidence in view of the difficult situation there. She witnessed the imperial coronation in Rome on 22 November 1220, and died on 23 June 1222 in Catania.

The capacity of women to hold fiefs, spreading from the west, was now becoming more firmly established. Following the Concordat of Worms of 1122 the bishops, abbots and abbesses of the empire counted as holders of fiefs for the empire, exercising this power without regard to religious status or sex.

The statutes of the duchy of Austria of 1156 state[71] that the children, whether sons or daughters (*indifferenter filii sive filie*), shall inherit and own the duchy, which is held in fief by Duke Henry and Theodora. This striking event did not lead, however,

---

[69]   *MGSS 16*, p. 541. Cf. J. Mühlberger, *Lebensweg und Schicksale der staufischen Frauen* (1977).

[70]   H. Decker-Hauff, 'Das Staufische Haus' (1977), vol. 3, essays, p. 352.

[71]   *MG. Const. I*, nos 159, 222, c. 4.

to a recognition in principle of women's rights to sucession in feudal matters. Such rights still had to be granted as a privilege. An edict of the empire promulgated in 1299 answered the question of whether a daughter could succeed to a fief through the right of inheritance, by stating that no daughter or wife could do so unless she had the full agreement of the feudal lord.[72] Mitteis also shows[73] that the right of succession cut both ways for women: for the liege lord the ability of daughters to succeed to a fief meant that fiefs reverted less often to the lord to be retained or redistributed. The lords countered this disadvantage by exerting greater influence over the marriages of heiresses to fiefs. This was first manifested in the form of compulsory marriages, a throwback to the old idea of the *Munt*. It became a part of the vassal's service to his lord to allow his daughters to be married by the lord. The English kings enforced such marriages with brutal ruthlessness. William II sold marriage licences, an abuse which Henry I promised to end in 1100. He married fief-heiresses, with their land, as his barons advised, and widows only with the barons' agreement. In the treaty between Emperor Henry VI and Duke Leopold of Austria on the release of Richard Lionheart, one of the conditions imposed was that an English princess should marry a son of the duke yet to be specified. This niece of the English king was to be presented to one of the duke's sons at Michaelmas. In Germany and France the feudal lord's right to impose marriages was weakened to become only a requirement for his consent.

---

[72]   Ibid., IV, 1, nos 59, 47.
[73]   H. Mitteis, *Lehnrecht und Staatsgewalt* (1933), pp. 653ff.

3

The Late Middle Ages 1250—1500

THE GENERAL AND LEGAL FRAMEWORK

To begin this chapter we should recall the fall in population discussed in the Introduction. Chaunu estimates that Latin Christendom fell from over 60 million in 1300 and at least 65 million in 1340 to about 40 million in 1420[1]. He also notes a change in the system of marriage, a considerable number of women now remaining unmarried throughout their lives and the age of marriage rising for women. That this new model was a late-medieval phenomenon can be shown in England from poll tax records, the per capita tax lists of 1377. It can be calculated that only 67 per cent of the female population over the age of 14 were married. Chaunu takes a very positive view of this:

late marriage allowed individual choice of partner instead of one dictated by family, and favoured ... a marriage based on gentle mutual affection rather than marriage on impulse or to serve the partners' interests. By shifting the age of fatherhood or motherhood to 32—5, it replaced education by grandparents with education by the parental generation. The raising of the age of marriage thus, paradoxically, made for younger educators; the decisive task of passing on the cultural heritage was entrusted to adults of about 45, who were in full possession of their mental and material powers. The delay in paternity and maternity compensated for the loss of potential and theoretical fertility by the improved health of the mothers. (p. 84)

This optimistic interpretation of developments has only limited validity for the late Middle Ages; such a model only really estab-

---

[1] Chaunu, *Die verhütete Zukunft*, p. 87.

lishes itself in the modern age. Compulsory marriage continued to exist in the late Middle Ages, and very late motherhood has its risks.

An important problem of the late Middle Ages is the relation of the extended family to the nuclear family, in town and country, the tension between the wide consciousness of kin in the earlier structure and the restricted one typical of the town, i.e. a married couple forming a household with their children. For the towns, we can use the word family in our modern sense. The question of a possible surplus of women in towns is a matter of debate. What is unquestioned is the lasting importance of kinship and family interests in the composition of councils, merchant bodies and guilds. Erich Maschke has addressed this question in his recent major work.[2] He works with exemplary cases, and we shall follow his method, avoiding general conclusions from local data in the Middle Ages; a limited number of trends can be discerned. Guardianship persisted in matters of marriage. Thus we read in the Frankfurt *aculus iudicii* (number 34): 'For [the husband] is the wife's guardian, but she is not his guardian'. In the towns women were given a certain right − within very narrow limits − to control the marital wealth. Minor household expenses may be met by the wife: in Freiburg, Lübeck [to which we shall return] and Hildesheim she can spend 2½ pfennig on her own initiative, in Schleswig, Apenrade and Flensburg 12 denars. Should the husband be ill or absent without making provisions, she is entitled to spend any sum. In Cologne, in 1218, a man who was leaving on a pilgrimage to the Holy Land drew up the following legal agreement with his wife: 'quicquid cum domo et area ... absque marito suo Renardo agere voluerit, ipsi licebit, et tamquam Renardo presente et per manum eius factum fuerit, ratum erit.[3] (Whatever she may decide without her husband Renardus, regarding the house and land, shall be as valid as if it had been done in her husband's presence and by his hand.)

In contrast to this, the women traders who were to be found in medieval cities had extensive opportunities to make financial commitments, to testify before the law and to run their own

[2]   E. Maschke, *Die Familie in der deutschen Stadt des späten Mittelalters* (1980).

[3]   E. Ennen and G. Eckertz, *Quellen zur Geschichte der Stadt Köln*, (1863) vol 2, p. 74.

affairs. Schröder has assembled plentiful evidence.[4] The Augsburg municipal law states: 'If she buys and sells in public or makes other regular transactions without her husband, what she does in such cases has legal force.' Women 'who sit and sell at the market' can also appear independently before a court. A Memmingen statute likewise states that women buying and selling at a market 'must compensate and suffer the law like a man'. The Bavarian municipal law of 1347 ordains that a woman working at a market has the same right as her husband, but may not sell her inheritance or property. Schröder gives examples demonstrating wide legal powers of trading women in Herzogenbusch, Oppenheim, Nuremberg and Freiburg/Uechtland. Prague is an example of the opposite situation: if women who sell daily at a market are accused in court they must be represented by their husbands.

The town women could also learn and practise a craft and join a guild. At that time only guild members were allowed to engage in the crafts organized by guilds. There were even guilds reserved for women — of which more later. The guilds were concerned that the wives of their members should be 'worthy of the office', 'office' (*Amt*) being a synonym for guild (*Zunft*). 'Nor shall anyone take a wife unless she be worthy of the guild', the statutes of the Lüneburg tanners ordained in 1476; and the statutes of the shopkeepers (1350), linen weavers (1430), furriers (1456), and wool weavers (1432) contain similar precepts. The cobblers' charter of 1389 even states:

If one of our guild-brothers wishes to marry an honourable maiden or dame, he should present her to the guild at the first morn-speech after the wedding. And she should leave both guild and trade and have nothing more to do with us.

Anyone who makes a bad marriage thus loses his guild and his craft. A master's widow was subject to fixed rules which varied between guilds and towns.[5] What is generally true is that the widow or daughter of a master facilitated, (i.e. made cheaper) a journeyman's entry to a guild, if he married her. A master's

---

[4] Schröder, *Geschichte des ehelichen Güterrechts in Deutschland*, part 2, pp. 100f and part 2, sect. 2, p. 10.

[5] P. P. Krebs, *Die Stellung der Handwerkerswitwe in der Zunft vom Spätmittelalter bis zum 18. Jahrhunder* (1974); E. Bodemann, arr., *Die älteren Zunfturkunden der Stadt Lüneburg* (1883).

widow could continue her husband's business, even if she were not herself a master-craftswoman, in a number of ways: as a lifelong widow's right, as a right to continue on account of children and as a right to continue for a limited period on condition that she remarries within a certain period. In Lüneburg the following regulations were adopted: if a butcher dies and leaves behind a son who is still a minor, the next of kin, with the knowledge and consent of the guildmaster, shall have the business administered by a pious and hardworking journeyman; the widow is not considered. The widow of a shopkeeper may keep guild membership; if she remarries, the guild must agree to it. If a furrier dies without a son, the widow can only work up the furs that are already tanned and in stock; if there is a son she shall retain guild membership until he is 20, and if the son wishes to stay in the guild, he shall be admitted at the first hearing. A shoemaker's widow may make shoes for one year after her husband's death; at the end of that time, if she has a son who wishes to stay in the guild, he takes over the membership. If she only has daughters or no children at all she must sell the workshop. If a wool-weaver leaves a widow and children, including sons, she remains a member, but if she has daughters or no children, she keeps membership for a year only. If she marries she loses her membership. Thus some provision was generally made for the widow, through not always the right to continue the business for life. The limited continuation rights were intended to prevent overmanning of the craft concerned.

These arrangements favourable to women in the area of urban trade are counterbalanced by archaic, unfavourable ones where the military effectiveness of a fortified town was at stake, e.g. in Kleve. Male guardianship is very pronounced in the municipal laws of this town and the women of Kleve are also disadvantaged by the law on inheritance. A deed of urban law issued by Count Johann in 1348 ordains[6] that on the death of a citizen, the next of his blood line (rather than his wife) shall inherit ('proximus sibi linea consanguinitatis hereditatem ipsius libere percipiat'). If the deceased has left behind a horse or horses and weapons, the best horse and the weapons shall remain at his house ('loco mansonis dicti defuncti'). If no legitimate heir presents himself within a year

[6] R. Scholten, *Die Stadt Kleve. Beiträge zur Geschichte derselben aus archivalischen Quellen* (1879), Sources supplement no. 65, p. XC.

and six weeks, the estate goes to the landlord. The German confirmation of the privilege of 1368[7] maintains this rule and refers explicitly to the *Heergewede* of the deceased, which shall remain at the disposal of the count and the town. We recall the regulation of 1241 in Wesel, which had just come under Kleve's administration, whereby the law on marital property was designed to serve merchant family interests on the Dortmund model. There man and wife inherited from each other and there was no question of a *Heergewäte*. In the fortified town of Kleve it is the interests of the lord, who needs well-armed vassals, that are paramount. The municipal law, probably dating from the fifteenth century, stresses the rights of the husband. 'Guardianship is a male office and not a female one', it states. The mother can become a child's guardian only if this is stated in the will and if there is no legal guardian, and the duke's permission is needed as well (p. 44 recto). The article 'On the Wife's Guardianship' states that the husband is the guardian of his wife and she is the companion of her husband, and that the guardianship of the husband is of a different kind to that based on kinship or ordered by a court, since it cannot be revoked. Changes are only possible if the estate is misused (p. 46 verso). The husband's legal position regarding marriage (p. 47 verso) is justified in the following terms: 'A husband is the head of his wife and she must live according to his will; a wife is not responsible for herself but must be subject to her husband's power'. Only if the estate is misused can judges, mayor, jurors and council intervene on the request of the wife or children.

The use of seals by women began later in Germany than in Italy — in the second half of the twelfth century, according to a study of documents in Würzburg.[8] Jenks has counted 224 women using seals in Würzburg documents from the fourteenth century — 117 noblewomen, 78 burgher women and 29 of unknown origin.

The dignity which undoubtedly attached to the position of housewife was called into question by the husband's right to chastise. It is true that some preachers now demand that the punishment is not administered in public. Adultery by a man is

[7]   I am much indebted to Dr K. Flink for making available copies of the town charter of 1368 and the municipal laws of Kleve (the latter in the Stadtarchiv Kleve Hs. 1).

[8]   S. Jenks, 'Frauensiegel in den Würzburger Urkunden des 14. Jahrhunderts' (1982).

referred to as such, as we shall see in more detail in the discussion of the situation in Cologne. But infidelity by women is still taken far more seriously. The ecclesiastical and secular atonements for adultery by women did not everywhere cancel the husband's right to revenge, as Koebner shows.[9] The capital court judgement by Johannes von Schwarzenberg at Bamberg in 1507 finds that the murder of an adultress caught *in flagranti* by her husband should not incur a heavy punishement; it assumes that the deed was done in an emotionally disturbed state. Among south German peasants adultresses had their hair cut off. However, there are also indications that public opinion can sometimes look indulgently on loose women — like Agneta Willeken, whom we shall meet later. Philippe Wolff[10] has discovered revealing individual examples among the notaries' records from the Toulouse region. A farmer, Ramundus de la Casa, who wished to change his residence, was deserted by his wife; she was unwilling to go with him and retired to a convent. There was a settlement between the spouses: they were to take up residence together in Toulouse. Ramundus was to support his wife as a good man should, and was not to treat her badly or beat her *ultra modum maritale* (more than was customary in marriage!) (1440). Adultery by Guilherma, wife of Geraldus de Labeyria, is atoned by an increased dowry to be paid to Geraldus by his wife's parents and a guarantee in case of further infidelity (1414). In another case the husband forgives his wife, who has been accused of adultery, and makes her a substantial gift in the event of his death (1448). About 1450 a legal document deals with the concubinage of Jean Sudre with Clara who, it emerges, has been married before. There is no further mention of the husband. The archbishop's court does, it is true, order Sudre to dismiss Clara and send her back to her father. But it also orders Sudre to give Clara a shop not far from his home (!) and pay her an annuity of corn, wine and money. Such — at least in the Toulousain — was the actual way such matters were dealt with, which can always be better understood from notarial documents than from general decrees. By now the widow has attained considerable legal independence; she can choose her own guardian and only in isolated cases does she need a guardian appointed *ad hoc* to represent

[9] R. Koebner, 'Die Eheauffassung des ausgehenden Mittelalters' (1911).
[10] P. Wolff, 'Famille et mariage en Toulousain aux XIV^c et XV^c siècles' (1978).

her in court. The widow exercises parental powers; Flossman[11] quotes the jurors' records at Prüm: widows have charge of sons and property as long as their widowhood lasts.

Parental permission is still needed for a daughter's marriage. Although it is not a condition of a legitimate marriage in church law, it poses an important problem in secular law. Its absence can lead to disinheritance. Jurisdiction over marriage lies primarily with the church. It decides on the legality of a marriage, on declarations of nullity, and in cases of separation.[12]

RELIGIOUS WOMEN

In the second half of the thirteenth century the Cistercian convent of Helfta, headed since 1259 by Abbess Gertrude of Hackeborn, a woman of noble birth and the sister of the mystic Mechthild, became a school of mysticism.

The nuns of Helfta had a classical education, a liturgical standpoint and extensive biblical and academic learning. The abbess encouraged their studies and was indefatigable in acquiring books by purchase or copying. Gertrude the Great was a member of the convent; Mechthild of Hackeborn was the head of the convent school. Both wrote in Latin. Mechthild concealed her miraculous inner life until her fiftieth year. Written records, later confirmed by Mechthild, were kept by Gertrude and other sisters. The starting point of both nuns' spiritual experiences is the church prayer, the *offizium*.

Mechthild of Magedburg found refuge at Helfta, where she had lived as a Beguine, from people hostile to her. She had first received the *Gruoz*, the sign of celestial grace, at the age of 12. She was trained in theology by the Dominican Heinrich of Halle. Her 'streaming light of the Godhead' — Ruh calls it the 'lyrical confession of a spiritual love' — follows the three rising stages of ecstatic contemplation: at the third stage she attains an 'indescribably blissful place. There she forgets entirely about the

---

[11] U. Flossmann, 'Die Gleichberechtigung der Geschlechter in der Privatrechtsgeschichte' (1977), p. 140, n. 20.

[12] R. Weigand, 'Zur mittelalterlichen Kirchlichen Ehegerichtsbarkeit, an Hand von Augsburger, Regensburger, englischen und französischen Beispielen' (1981).

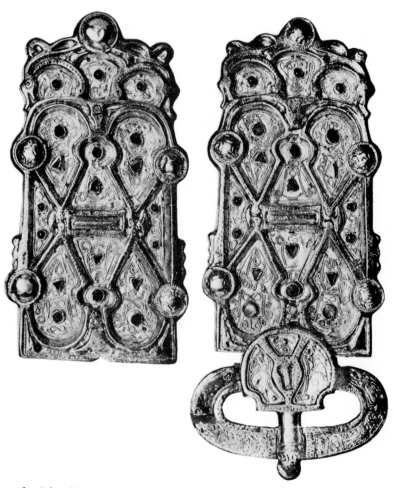

1. A buckle belonging to the Merovingian Queen Arnegundis

REX ROGAT ABBATEM. MATHILDIM SUPPLICAT ATQ; ;

2. King Henry IV kneeling in penance before Margravine Matilda

3. Adelheid, abbess of Vilich. A pilgrim's pamphlet with 12 scenes showing her miraculous powers of healing

4. The three stations of life according to the 'Speculum
virginum': married women,
widows and maidens

5. St Bernard of Clairvaux with a Cistercian nun

6. Elizabeth of Thuringia nursing and feeding the poor

7. Beguinage in Bruges

8. A young noblewoman with ornamental head-dress

9. Women dancing at a banquet

10. Tomb effigy of Eleanor of Poitou in Fontevrault

11. From a dance of death: the townswoman

12. A townsman and his wife: the engraver Israhel van
Meckenem and his wife Ida

13. Looking after children

14. The living room of a townsman's house with the family: the
father is doing the accounts, the son is learning his letters and the
wife and daughter are spinning

15. An upper-storey window of the 'Overstolzenhaus', a patrician house at 8 Rheingasse, Cologne

16. Section of a view of Cologne after Anton Woensam, 1531

17. Women working silk: collecting the cocoons and weaving the silk

18. The 'Runtingerhaus' in Regensburg

19. A shopkeeper in her office

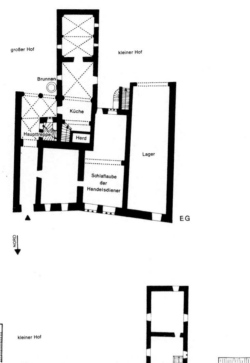

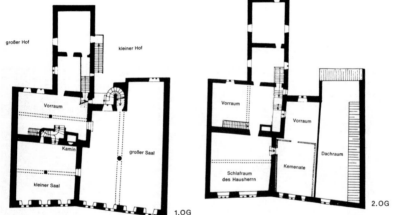

20. A plan of the 'Runtingerhaus'

21. Burg Rheinfels, once the residence of the counts von Katzenelnbogen

22. Joan of Arc with a banner. The scroll reads: here comes the maiden, sent by God, to the Dauphin in his country

23. Seal of Countess Loretta von Sponheim (on a document
dated 28 July 1330)

24. Living room of a canoness of the Fraumünster in Zurich

miracle and knows not that she was ever on earth.'[13] For Mechthild as for Hadwich, the union with God has the character of transitory grace.

This was not the case for Marguerite of Porète. In her the French-speaking world finds its tongue. She comes from Valenciennes on the medieval border between Germany and France; in 1292 Valenciennes seceded from the empire.

Marguerite is part of the same cultural sphere as Hadwich. The state which she describes in the *Miroir des simples âmes* — i.e. a mirror, in the sense of a text-book, for simple souls — a state in which the soul is annihilated and therefore freed, needs none of the church's grace. This concept of freedom was condemned by the church as heretical. The bishop of Cambrai had the *Miroir* burned; Marguerite stood by what she had written, was brought before a court in Paris and was burned to death at the Place de Grève in Paris on 31 May 1310. But even during the Middle Ages the *Miroir* was translated into Latin, Italian and English.

The spirituality of the Dominican order was the formative influence on many female mystics in Dominican convents, particularly in the south-west of the empire. Franciscan mysticism had its origin in the everyday experience of the order's founder, his mystical love of poverty and the cross. It was influential in the Netherlands, as at the convent of Helfta, and especially in Italy. Women's mysticism spread throughout Europe, if to varying degrees, and in the fourteenth century to Scandinavia — an example is Birgitta of Sweden — and the land of the Teutonic orders. Dorothea[14] grew up a peasant's daughter in the village of Gross-Montau near Marienburg, married a wealthy Danzig craftsman and bore him nine children, eight of which were carried off by the plague; she had mystical experiences while still a child and her first vision known to us when a young woman. She subjected herself, without revealing it to others, to a strict ascetism, had a great love for the eucharist and perceived with her natural acuity (for she had not been to school) the abuses existing within the order and the vices of the church. On long pilgrimages — to

---

[13]   Ruh, 'Beginenmystik'; and, *Vorbemerkungen zu einer neuen Geschichte der abendländischen Mystik im Mittelalter* (1982); and, *Kleine Schriften, Bd. II Scholastik und Mystik im Spätmittelalter* (1984); M. Schmidt, 'Elemente der Schau bei Mechtild von Magdeburg u. Mechtild von Hackeborn. Zur Bedeutung der geistlichen Sinne' (1985).
[14]   R. Stachnik and A. Triller, *Dorothea von Montau* (1976).

Aachen, Ensiedeln, Rome — she got to know the world. In the cathedral dean Johannes Marienwerder, who had studied in Prague, she found a spiritual adviser who wrote down her revelations and prayers. She spent the last 14 months of her life as a recluse in a cell in the cathedral of Marienwerder. Among her ideas there are 'religious images and concepts from three main sources: the piety of the German order, Birgittine spirituality and doctrines and tendencies coming from Prague' (A. Triller).

This outline of the history and some of the exponents of women's mysticism must be enough here. My object was to show that women's contribution to medieval mysticism, both in its devotional forms and in its literary achievement, particularly in the vernacular, was considerable, that all social strata including the peasant wife of a craftsman were affected by it, and that the women mystics found in their very personal forms of the religious life a fulfilment and a joy that surpasses rational understanding.

Mystical experience, ecstasy and passion are one aspect of life in the late-medieval convent, the béguinage and the hermit's cell.

In the religious sphere a tendency towards worldliness and shallowness appears, and then, towards the end of our period, a new inwardness. The old institutions and convents had been relatively little affected by the religious women's movement in the twelfth century. Repeated 'reformations and corrections' by the authorities, often after a report by a commission, show where the weaknesses lay in the late Middle Ages. Instead of the nun's habit worldly clothes are worn — we hear of pointed shoes, silk dresses, fur-lined hoods, etc. — and dances and feasts are more popular than the mass. Indiscipline towards the abbess, arguments in the chapter-room, scorn, anger and slander spoil the atmosphere in convents. The financial administration is in a bad state. The inmates of convents are suspected of immorality. Even the reformist order of the Cistercian nuns is not exempt from such tendencies in the fourteenth century. In south-German Cistercian orders the *vita communis* often no longer exists. The canonesses run their own households with maids and cooks, and take in younger nuns, usually related to them, so that they will have company and someone to look after them in old age and sickness. Enclosure no longer exists: nuns travel about the country, go to market, visit their families and friends, participate in parish fairs and Shrovetide carnivals. They act as godmothers, appear in person before a court to settle legal matters, entertain male and female guests and hold banquets in the convent. The religious timetable and the fasting rules are neglected. All the same, violations of the vow of chastity are the exception. The Beguine convents continue to grow significantly in the fourteenth and fifteenth centuries. Two styles of living emerge in the order: in western Germany, Wallonia and northern France communal living persists. In the Netherlands proper, particularly the south, the predominant form consists of small, adjoining houses grouped around a church and administered by a clergyman. Sometimes there are small houses for rich Beguines and communal dwellings for poorer ones.[15] Again and again the Beguines were suspected of heresy.[16] Outwardly similar to the Netherlandish Beguine convents, but to be distinguished from them, are the free dwellings or *hofjes* which came into being in the fourteeth century as a means of caring for the poor; they were more like the hospices for prebendaries who held a fixed benefice.

At the end of the fourteenth century, starting from the Netherlands and embracing northern and middle Germany especially, there began a movement of religious renewal that has become known as the *devotio moderna*. Its form of organization was based on the *Fraterherren*, the 'Brothers of the Common Life', and the congregation of Augustinian canons governed by the monastery of Windersheim. Huizinga writes:

In the Fraters' houses and the monasteries of the Windesheim Congregation the glow of a religious inwardness forever kept in consciousness is spread over the quiet work of daily life. Tempestous lyricism and unbridled striving are renounced, and the danger of heresy thereby banished; the brothers and sisters are entirely orthodox and conservative in their beliefs. This was mysticism in small doses; one had received the merest flicker, a tiny spark, and now felt a muted rapture in the narrow, silent and modest sphere of familiar spiritual routine, in correspondence and meditation. The life of the feelings and the spirit was nurtured like a hothouse plant. Here was much narrow puritanism, ecclesiastical dressage, the suppression of laughter and healthy instincts, much pietistic simple-mindedness.[17]

---

[15] O. Nübel, *Mittelalterliche Beginen- und Sozialsiedlungen in den Niederlanden. Ein Beitrag zur Vorgeschichte der Fuggerei* (1970).

[16] M. Wehrli-Johns, *Geschichte des Zürcher Predigerkonvents (1230–1524)* (1980).

[17] J. Huizinga, *The Waning of the Middle Ages* (1955).

Geert Groot, a patrician's son from Deventer, experienced a decisive religious conversion under the influence of the Carthusian monk Heinrich von Kalkar in 1374. He gave over the major part of his house at Deventer to the poor. In 1396 this was reorganized into a community with statutes for the women living there. The Geertshuis became the model for many new houses of the Sisters of the Communal Life. The sisters differed from the Beguines by having a truly communal form of life with refectory, dormitory, common possessions and common income. They were recognized by the Council of Constance.

The sisters were obliged to work with their hands. Craftwork, particularly in textiles, and sometimes agricultural labour, were the rule. But the work did not only serve to provide the means of material life. The prizing of work 'as activity in the vineyard of the Lord' is expressed, for example, in the sisters' biographies from Emmerich, which have been rediscovered. The intrinsic value of work must be recognized and affirmed — this too is an important contribution by the convents to human culture.[18]

The new piety permeated the whole of convent life. It also reached the Benedictine monasteries, which joined with other monasteries to form reformed congregations in Italy and south Germany. Bursfeld to the west of Göttingen was the starting point of the Bursfeld Congregation. In the Rhineland Johann II, archbishop of Trier, encouraged both the Windesheim and the Bursfeld reforms. Humanism too made its way into some monasteries. Johannes Butzbach, a native of Deventer who entered the monastery of Laach, dedicated his book on famous painters to the artist-nun Gertrude of Büchel, who became abbess of Rolandswerth in 1507. He also included in his dedication Adelheid Raiscop, who came from Goch in the Netherlands and had become known through her seven homilies on St Paul and her correspondence with Butzbach, Siberti, Cardinal-Legate Raymund and Prior Benedict. Benedict dedicated a tract to her, and Butzbach included a laudatory entry on her in his dictionary of writers. I expressly draw attention to this almost unknown woman humanist; of course, she is not as important as Caritas Pirckheimer, the patrician's daughter and abbess of the Nuremberg convent of St Clare. But

[18]   G. Rehm, *Die Schwestern vom gemeinsamen Leben im nordwestlichen Deutschland* (1985).

Caritas's fate belongs to the early modern period, the epoch of *Christianitas afflicta*.[19]

Lay piety is characterized by emotional exaltation and an uncontrollable urge to go on pilgrimages; new saints come into prominence and new places of pilgrimage exert an almost inexplicable attraction — like Wilsnack in Priegnitz, where three bloody hosts were venerated. This site was a source of controversy in the church. Nicholas of Cues and the archbishop of Magdeburg took a critical view, while the elector of Brandenburg favoured it.

Nothing unusual had taken place there, no new miracle had occurred, when suddenly, in the mid-1470s, people all over middle Germany were seized by the urge to set off towards the Holy Blood, with young people and children in the lead. They crossed the fields with crosses and flags in their hundreds, their numbers swelling constantly. Peasants joined them, ploughmen left their animals in the fields, housewives deserted their houses and children[20]

It was a time of contradictions, of inner disharmony and turmoil.

WOMEN IN MEDIEVAL URBAN SOCIETY

We now have detailed information on the activities of women in the medieval urban economy and on their social position in towns. Their position varies greatly with the kind of town, whether it is a large city or a medium or small town, whether it is north or south of the Alps and, if a city, whether it is primarily a trading city or one which has significant export industries as well. We are generally better provided with sources on the larger and medium towns than on small ones, and the information is unevenly distributed over the social classes, being better for the patriciate and artisans than for the lower orders. Apart from the economic framework we need to know the legal regulations in each particular case. The numerical relationship of the sexes affected the professional activities of women: was there a surplus of men or of women?

As indicated earlier, this question is very difficult to answer

---

[19] K. Kossert, *Aleydis Raiscop. Die Humanistin von Nonnenwerth* (1985); G. Krabbel, *Caritas Pirckheimer. Ein Lebensbild aus der Zeit der Reformation* (1940).

[20] W. Andreas, *Deutschland vor der Reformation. Eine Zeitenwende* (1959), p. 181.

reliably. The Middle Ages knew nothing of statistics for their own sake. The figures that have come down to us served concrete practical purposes: taxation, military resources, supplies in time of war, etc. Particular figures have survived, not series of statistics over time. We are working with snapshots — does the figure available to us apply to a normal year, or to one with an epidemic, a siege or suchlike? Does it embrace the whole population of a town, a region, or only part of it? These are questions that have to be allowed for in our conclusions. The taxation lists that are now used both to calculate population figures and to discover family and wealth structures, pose all manner of problems.[21] These lists were drawn up to show which citizens were liable to tax and how much they owed. This means that by no means all the inhabitants of a town are listed: the nobility, the clergy of both sexes, university professors, students, crafts journeymen, maidservants, paid labourers, as well as beggars and prostitutes are not usually included, nor are households automatically listed.

It is quite possible for a wife and her children to be mentioned but not her husband, since he owned no taxable wealth. Schematic analyses therefore show this woman as a widow or a single woman. As the tax lists only included the people liable to tax, they must be used in conjunction with other sources when investigating family and household structures. (Schulen, p. 168)

Moreover, each list is based on specific tax laws, which in extreme cases may even lead to several different lists for the same town. And if it is problematic simply to calculate the population of a medieval town, it is far more hazardous to try to assess the sex ratio. Where the lists are based on numbers of fireplaces, one is left with the problem of the size of households, when trying to establish the overall number of inhabitants. A medieval household may under certain circumstances include the servants and craftsmen in addition to the nuclear family. House and household do not always coincide in the town. The part reserved for parents at the back of a house is sometimes shown as a separate household, and there were already lodgers in the Middle Ages — houses themselves were often let.

[21] P. J. Schuler, 'Die Bevölkerungsstruktur der Stadt Freiburg im Breisgau im Spätmittelalter. Möglichkeiten und Grenzen einer quantitativen Quellenanalyse' (1979).

Earlier scholarship accepted a surplus of women for many medieval towns. In his study of the population structure of the city of Freiburg/Breisgau already mentioned (one of the best works on the subject, though unfortunately not free of misprints in the statistics), Schuler makes use of the registers of the 'common penny', the Turk-tax of 1496—9. He calculates an average population of 6,300 persons and notes a surplus of men. Freiburg was a medium-sized town with a craft economy and at the time of the penny-lists it had a university. After subtracting the clergy and the members of the university there were at the end of the fifteenth century 1,703 (49.3 per cent) men as against 1,653 (47.8 per cent) women, with 99 (2.9 per cent) unknown. If we take into account the whole population of the town including the clergy and the university people, the male surplus is considerable. We then find 52.6 per cent men as compared to 44.7 per cent women. Using the penny-lists, Schuler also calculates a surplus of men for Bruchsal, where there were 616 men to 609 women, and for the villages of Ober— and Niedergrombach, Neibsheim and Büchig, in which there were 279 men and 252 women.[22] In Landau and Lauterburg he records a surplus of women, there being 756 and 252 men to 791 and 261 women respectively. Including the clerical and university households, there were in Freiburg 114 female and 241 male single-person households. Schuler considers that an average of at most four persons per household can be assumed. This agrees with a result achieved by Hektor Ammann for Basle; he calculated 3.5—4 persons per household. Urban historians generally reckon on 4—5 persons per household in late-medieval towns.[23] The thesis of a late-medieval surplus of women was based partly on a census carried out by the city of Nuremberg in 1449, when there was a threat of siege in the Margraves' War, so that a survey of the number of people in the city and the stocks of grain it held was needed. It showed a ratio of 100 men to 117 women, and if menial servants and maids were included the proportion rose to 100 male citizens and servants to 121 female citizens and maids. A recent critical study by Kurt Wesoly has examined

[22] P. J. Schuler 'Die Erhebungslisten des Gemeinen Pfennigs von 1496—1499. Eine demographische, wirtschafts- und sozialgeschichtliche Untersuchung' (1978).
[23] H. Ammann, 'Die Bevölkerung von Stadt und Landschaft Basel am Ausgang des Mittelalters' (1950), p. 38.

these findings.[24] He takes account of the exceptional circumstances at the time of the census, and by considering other material shows it to be likely that the effect of the war had increased the ratio of maidservants to labourers. Moreover, he found the ratio of 100 male to 117 female citizens unaffected by his study. The male servants, probably mostly crafts journeymen, were undoubtedly a fluctuating element in the urban population which could easily distort statistics.

In the light of current research, therefore, we cannot presuppose that there was a substantial surplus of women in the German towns of the late Middle Ages, nor can we assume the opposite to have been generally the case. In addition, we should not exaggerate the size of urban families and must reckon with a fairly high number of single-person households. We shall come back to these statistical questions when discussing the cadastral survey of 1427 for Florence. Of course, the authors also raise the question of the reasons for the ratio between the sexes. The higher mortality rate for male infants, which is sure to have been still more pronounced then than it is today, was in some circumstances counterbalanced by a reverse tendency in later years. According to some English studies, a man's life expectancy was longer than a woman's. A table of deaths based on English data shows that more men died between the ages of 40 and 60 than between 20 and 40, whereas the opposite was the case for women.[25] The many births and the heavy work in the fields weakened women and made them more prone to illness. Fossier surmises that in the eleventh and twelfth centuries there were 110 men to 90 women, but stresses the provisional nature of such figures and points out, no doubt rightly, that we should expect differences between the women of the upper classes — better midwifery, etc. — and the lower. D. Herlihy tries to show that while male life expectancy was greater in the early Middle Ages, the situation was reversed in the later Middle Ages, when female life expectancy exceeded that of men. But in reaching

[24] K. Wesoly, 'Der weibliche Bevölkerungsanteil in spätmittelalterlichen und frühneuzeitlichen Städten und die Betätigung von Frauen im zünftigen Handwerk (insbesondere am Mittel- und Oberrhein)' (1980). The Nuremberg population count is readily accessible in: G. Möncke, *Quellen zur Wirtschafts- und Sozialgeschichte mittel- und oberdeutscher Städte im Spätmittelalter* (1982), no. 100, pp. 137ff.

[25] C. M. Cipolla and K. Borchardt, *Bevölkerungsgeschichte Europas* (1971), pp. 30 and 44ff.

this conclusion — influenced by earlier German studies — he posits a considerable surplus of women in late-medieval towns. The question is in a state of flux at present. The great progress made by historical demography in recent decades is likely to yield better results in due course, which may allow us to observe regional differences and to project the figures now available, mainly derived from the fifteenth century, back on to the fourteenth century. The average life expectancy of women was probably barely 30 years; but we all know how little such averages mean for an individual life.

After these introductory statistics, let us take a walk around German towns, starting with **Lübeck**. In his *Slawenchronik*, Helmold von Bosau tells the following about the year 1143:

Then Count Adolf [von Schauenburg] came to a place named Buskow where he found the rampart of an abandoned castle, which had been built by Kruto [a Slav prince], the enemy of God, and a very large peninsula skirted by two rivers. On one side flowed the Trave, on the other the Wakenitz, both having marshy banks difficult to cross. But where the ground is firm there is a rather narrow hill, rising to the castle rampart. When this circumspect man saw how suitable the place was and how excellent the harbour, he began to build a town (*civitas*) there and called it Lübeck, because it was not far from the old harbour and town (*civitate*) that Prince Henry [of the Abodrites] had founded.[26]

There are not many towns whose beginnings have been described so graphically, yet which have posed so many riddles for historians. To write on Lübeck has become *de rigueur* for almost every urban historian. Archaeologists are currently at work in Lübeck under the aegis of G. P. Fehring.[27] Some time ago they brought to light the old Slavonic Lübeck on a spit of land where the Schwartau flows into the Trave, and they are now successfully uncovering the Slavonic settlement on the Lübeck hill. They consider it probable that the 'so called German founders' coming from the Rhineland and Westphalia 'enlarged on the not inconsiderable Slavonic roots

[26] H. Stoob, *Helmold von Bosau. Slawenchronik* (1963). Although Stoob translates *civitas*, referring to old Lübeck, as *Hauptort*, meaning a smaller entity than a town, a merchants' colony has been shown to exist in old Lübeck.

[27] G. P. Fehring, 'Zur archäologischen Erforschung topographischer, wirtschaftlicher und sozialer Strukturen der Hansestadt Lübeck' (1980); and, 'Alt-Lübeck und Lübeck. Zur Topographie und Besiedlung zweier Seehandelszentren im Wandel vom 12. zum 13. Jhd: (1982).

under the protection of the feudal castle to produce a market and
trading centre which had an early urban character' (Fehring).The
ceramics imported from the coastal countries of the North Sea
give way more and more in the late thirteenth and fourteenth
centuries to Rhenish stoneware. The population of this town had
a wide radius of immigration. Whether the newcomers arrived
alone or with wives and children our sources do not tell us. One is
inclined to assume that many of them were unmarried younger
sons coming from distant places. Long-distance trade remains
characteristic of Lübeck, although export industries are not entirely
lacking. It becomes the headquarters of the German Hansa, the
association of merchants which opened up and dominated the
Baltic area. It had a trading post in Novgorod giving access to the
rich fur market in northern Russia, and another in Bergen, Norway
(there was a society in Lübeck for traders on the Bergen route),
where they bought dried cod and stockfish. The Lübeck traders
took Lüneburg salt to the herring-fishing areas around Schonen,
at that time Danish. It was said that the prosperity of the Hansa
was built on herring barrels. Finally, from the thirteenth century
on, the Hanseatic traders pushed out across the North Sea to
England, though their competitors from Cologne were already
established there, and to the southern Netherlands, where a trading
post was established in Bruges. They travelled a great deal, and to
very distant places, these German Hanseatic merchants, and there
is nothing to indicate that women went with them. Those who
traded with Bergen were usually bachelors. According to the wills
that have survived, of 187 Bergen traders 82 were married and
only 43 had legitimate offspring.[28] The wives stayed at home with
the children and servants.

The women of Lübeck in the twelfth century are likely to have
led the life of frontier pioneers. The town was the cause of a
conflict between the count of Schauenburg and Duke Henry the
Lion. The duke forbade the holding of a market in Lübeck. In
1257 the town was burnt down and the duke built a rival town
which failed to prosper. However, he finally induced Count Adolf
to cede Lübeck to him, and then promoted the town vigorously.
After his fall the Hohenstaufens took Lübeck into the empire. A
high point in the town's history was the Hansa's successful struggle

---

[28]   F. Bruns, *Die Lübecker Bergenfahrer und ihre Chronistik* (1900); Maschke, *Die
Familie in der deutschen Stadt des späten Mittelalters*.

with the Danish king, Valdemar, and subsequent Treaty of Stralsund.[29] At that time Lübeck had about 22,000 inhabitants.[30] But only 3,200 people had civic rights; these generally did not include women, or crafts journeymen, wage labourers, clerics or the poor. A. von Brandt has characterized Lübeck in the fourteenth century as a 'success-orientated society with horizontal and vertical mobility'. It was in the fifteenth century that barriers to mobility began to form. Within the commercial upper class, which was open to merchants rising from below, the families forming the town council made up the leading group, about a fifth. Immigration from the west was heavy, but there were also many who moved on into the whole Baltic area, to Wismar, Rostock, Kolberg, Elbing, Wisby, Stockholm, Riga, Reval. The terrible losses in the plagues — the epidemics of 1349/50, 1358, 1367, 1376, 1388 and 1396 — were quickly made up. Behind the enormous contributions to pious foundations lay the fear of death. About the turn of the century, from 1384, there were uprisings and social unrest. Craftsmen continued to be excluded from the council. And the women? There was much intermarrying in the upper class, and kinsfolk maintained strong links over long distances. The wives' dowries were an important factor for merchants.

Fritz Rörig has edited and annotated a very old merchants' ledger kept by Hermann Warendorp and Johann Clingenberg.[31] At the beginning of the fourteenth century there were several Warendorp families in Lübeck, three of which provided council members. The ledger dates back to Hermann junior, who died of plague in 1350, and whose first wife was a daughter of Johann Clingenberg. His business enterprises stretched as far as Riga (he was probably related to the Warendorps in Riga), Flanders and England; he was also active in shipping. In 1335 he was admitted to the municipal council. As a younger son he had received only a modest share of the paternal estate: the site at 16 Fleischhauer-strasse where he first lived but sold in 1333. With his brother-in-law, Wedekin Clingenberg, he put up a new building at 12

[29] Cf. 'Zum 600. Jahrestag des Stralsunder Friedens', in: *Hans. Geschbll.* 88, 1, 1970, pp. 83ff.

[30] A. von Brandt, 'Lübeck und die Lübecker vor 600 Jahren' (1978); and, 'Die gesellschaftliche Struktur des spätmittelalterlichen Lübeck' (1966).

[31] F. Rörig, 'Das älteste erhaltene deutsche Kaufmannsbüchlein', in: *Hansische Beiträge zur deutschen Wirtschaftsgeschichte* (1928). We now know that still older account books exist.

Mengstrasse; a third of the land came from his wife's dowry. In 1346 Warendorp became the sole owner of this house. It stood opposite the bread stalls near the church of St Maria, had a terrace in front with steps leading down to the street, glass windows and a cellar well fitted-out for business, with easy access to the street. In 1333 Warendorp acquired other sites and in 1339 he bought a large corner complex on the Lower Trave, these sites being in great demand for warehouses. The acquisition is an indication of his business success; he probably used money from the dowry of his second wife, Mechthild, to buy the property. When Hermann went on his travels, the ledger shows that he left his wife money for major purchases of rye, beer, bread and herrings. His son Hinrich also brought in a considerable increase in wealth through his marriage to Kunigunde, daughter of the mayor, Wickede: 1,000 Lübeck marks in bond capital alone, excluding cash and silver. In his second will of 1380 Hinrich set aside 800 marks in bonds for his wife, as well as her beds and the gold and silver jewellery that had been part of her dowry. However, the engagement ring was to be kept by the children. They were also to receive the house with all utensils and the gilded and silver vessels – probably drinking goblets. His widow was only to have a lifelong right to live in the house.

Bertram Morneweg[32] had the typical career of a 'rising' merchant. Beginning without any land of his own, he acquired great wealth and was admitted to the council. His wealth can be traced from sources at the time of his death in 1286, when the money from his enterprises flowed back to Lübeck to be administered by his widow Gertrud Morneweg, a shrewd and energetic businesswoman. The Lübeck bond market was flooded by capital from Morneweg's enterprises, so that values actually fell. At that time Lübeck had overstretched itself in buying the River Wakenitz; its water was needed for the mills that ground the flour for export to Norway and Sweden. Widow Morneweg made large credits available to the town, and also financed a number of respected old families who owned valuable properties that were used as security for the credit. Some quickly repaid the debt, but others sank into a financial dependence which led to the loss of their properties. By 1301 Gertrud Morneweg had invested about 14,500 Lübeck marks

---

[32] F. Rörig, *Hansische Beiträge zur deutschen Wirtschaftsgeschichte* (1928), pp. 132f.

in bonds, a sum worth millions of marks in modern purchasing power.

How much control did the husband have of the wealth brought into a marriage by his wife? A judgement of 1482 by the Lübeck council states: 'Dowry goes before debts'.[33] Dowry (*Brautschatz*) here means all the money, bonds or land which the wife brings into the marriage apart from the clothes, jewellery and linen (*Ingedömte*) making up the dowry or trousseau in the narrower sense. A typically urban difficulty would arise if the *Brautschatz* included negative assets, i.e. if the husband had married a widow or businesswoman who had incurred debts. These debts were to be deducted from the *Brautschatz*. If the husband died intestate, the wife could withdraw all the wealth she had brought into the marriage from the estate before the rest was shared out with the other heirs. A value was assigned to the *Brautschatz*, since in a long marriage it would clearly not remain in its original state. The husband might have invested part of it in a trading company, for example. The wife could demand the return of the *Brautschatz* in cases other than her husband's death – for example, if the husband had fled from creditors or incurred excessive debts, or even if his extravagance could be shown to endanger the *Brautschatz*. Thus the wife's contribution did not stand as security for her husband's debts. Her claim was a debt on the estate. Even in the revised municipal law of Lübeck dating from 1586, the claims of the *Brautschatz* are included in the category of privileged debts. This leads to the question of the woman who conducts independent business, even if married. An exhaustive answer to this question is still lacking for Lübeck.[34] Most professional women were probably in commerce; as we have indicated, this had legal repercussions.

In Lübeck law, guardianship over the wife survived up to 1869, by which time it was understood mainly as a protection for women. The underlying statute, which dates back to the thirteenth century and was carried over into the revised law of 1586, is as follows: 'Nulla mulier potest bona sua impignorare, vendere vel dare sine procuratore, nec aliqua mulier potest carius fideiubere

---

[33] W. Ebel, *Forschungen zur Geschichte des lübischen Rechts* (1950), cf. chs 8: 'Die Brautschatzfreiung' and 9: 'Zur Rechtstellung der Kauffrau'.
[34] J. Hartwig, 'Die Frauenfrage im mittelalterlichen Lübeck' (1908), pp. 35ff; H. D. Loose, 'Erwerbstätigkeit der Frau im Spiegel Lübecker und Hamburger Testamente des 14. Jahrhunderts' (1980).

quam pro duobus nummis et dimidio sine mundeburdio suo id est vormunde.' (No woman may mortgage, sell or give away her goods (*bona sua*) without a representative, and and no woman can pledge more than 2 1/2 pfennig without her guardian.) By *bona sua* buildings as well as movable assets are understood. The sum of 2 1/2 pfennig, which the woman was able to pledge, was later increased to keep pace with the purchasing power of money; by the eighteenth century it was one reichstaler. A wife was also allowed to buy linen and flax for household needs on her husband's account. These were the rules for the woman who was only a housewife. In the case of a woman who bought and sold by way of trade, her commercial rights went beyond those of the housewife in a manner which was both to her advantage and to her disadvantage.[35] 'The commercial woman, the female counterpart to the merchant, is dealt with in the Latin manuscripts of Lübeck law − a sign that as early as the first half of the thirteenth century she was a noteworthy figure in Lübeck commercial life, of whom the law should take account' (Ebel,1950). The promises, security and so on, given by merchant women were absolutely binding. Because of this capacity to give pledges, the female merchant was capable of incurring debts and going bankrupt. But even a merchant woman could not make a will disposing of her 'well-earned wealth' without the consent of her heirs and guardian. If she was married, there was the question of who was responsible for her debts. As we have said, a wife without inheritance can withdraw her dowry from her husband's estate before other debts are paid. If she inherits, the total estate is security for her husband's debts. In the case of a merchant woman, however, the revised municipal law of 1586 stipulated that even if the wife did not inherit she could not withdraw her dowry. The same applied conversely to the wife's debts, for which the husband's estate was security. The joint wealth of a married businesswoman and her husband was accountable for all liabilities, regardless of the size of the dowry or any other separate property of the wife, and regardless of whether or not there was mutual inheritance. The merchant woman was

---

[35]   The statute quoted earlier in the text continues: 'exceptis illis que habent kopschat et solent emere et vendere, quicquid permittit, de iure solvere tenetur, si de promissi convinci poterit.' (Except those who have *kopschat*, [i.e.] who are accustomed to buy and sell; what she promises she must pay, if she can be proved to have promised.)

an extreme victim of a phenomenon which those revising the Lübeck law considered one of its fundamental provisions:

Because this city of Lübeck is a mercantile city devoted to trade, it must be based on faith and trust. Thus, to ensure trust, the first and ancient *conditores statutorum* hold it far better that private persons, and particularly women, should suffer some loss to their own estate and *patrimonio* than that confidence in the trading of this town should be weakened or destroyed, which would bring the ruin and downfall of the town. (Ebel, 1950)

In a morn-speech 18 December 1406,[36] the municipal council of Cologne dealt with the mutual liability of spouses in matters of debt. Interestingly, this was the result of an initiative taken by women. Many wives had refused to pay their husbands' debts, and had appealed to the ecclesiastical courts, above all the *Offizial*. This naturally infuriated the council. The women were accused of demanding the withdrawal of their *Brautschatz*. The council therefore resorted to the time-honoured custom: both spouses were declared equally liable, and the liability continued after the death of one partner and included the *Hillichsgut* or dowry. The women lacked neither understanding of their interests nor the desire to defend them but they were seriously handicapped by their lack of equal political rights and by not being members of the council. The ancient ruling was reaffirmed by a council decision of 1457.[37]

How successful were the women merchants? Loose gives some indications for Lübeck. It is certain that it was more difficult for a woman to amass a large fortune by trade than it was for a man. There are records of Lübeck women with liabilities in Sweden, so their dealings must have covered a wide radius. Women chartered vessels and were members of companies. Many women engaged in shopkeeping and huckstering, in which they sometimes had a female partner or *socia*. Street-trading was convenient as a second job, or could be carried on alongside the household. This was not true of long-distance trading, which needed long absences even

---

[36] W. Stein, *Akten zur Geschichte der Verfassung und Verwaltung der Stadt Köln im 14. und 15. Jahrhundert* (1893), vol. 1, no. 86, pp. 236ff; cf. J. Brück, *Die Grundzüge des in der Stadt Köln bis zur Einführung des französischen Rechts geltenden Ehelichen Güterrechts* (1900), pp. 68ff.

[37] B. Kuske, *Quellen zur Geschichte des Kölner Handels und Verkehrs im Mittelalter* (1917–34), vol. 2, no. 188.

when the merchants began to employ commercial personnel and agents, doing much of their work at home in the counting-house.

Hartwig names many women who were involved in commerce in Lübeck, in a variety of trades. They were mostly widows. As we saw earlier, guild regulations almost everywhere included the 'widow's right' to operate the craft business of her deceased husband for a fixed or unlimited period, usually with the help of a senior journeyman.

According to the oldest municipal laws, women who betrothed themselves without the agreement and advice of their kinsmen forfeited all their possessions, down to the clothes they had made themselves. In 1380 councillor Johann Schepenstede instructed the executors of his will, in view of his increased wealth, to marry his daughter Margarete to an equally wealthy man ('viro sibi similem secundum quod bona mea se augmentaverint'). The convents of Lübeck drew their members primarily from the upper class. Some Lübeck women entered convents in other places; in Rhena there were 40 or 50 nuns from Lübeck. The number of beguinages in Lübeck is strikingly small: only five, with about 100 Beguines in all. Altogether, the religious institutions for single women could provide for about 600 persons.

When Lübeck was ravaged by fire for the third time, in 1276, the council instructed all citizens to build their houses of stone; only small dwellings could still be of timber. All 'better' people had to pay for the luxury of brick, if only for the sake of prestige. (Lübeck was spared further fires until 1942.) Life became altogether more luxurious at this time.[38] The brick houses had glass windows, gilded or silver utensils; there was more furniture, more expensively made. Luxurious items such as painted tables are mentioned in wills in Brunswick, Lübeck and Vienna. In a Lübeck will of 1386 a table of this kind is described in more detail: it is painted with the Apocalypse and the battle of the people of Holstein against the Saxons. The houses have a special living room which can be heated, and the rooms are sometimes decorated by painting. Hasse concludes his survey based on wills by saying that in the sphere of

[38] M. Hasse, 'Neues Hausgerät, neue Häuser, neue Kleider. Eine Betrachtung der städtischen Kultur im 13. und 14. Jahrhundert, sowie ein Katalog der metallenen Hausgeräte' (1979); W. Erdmann, 'Die Entwicklung des Lübecker Bürgerhauses im 13. und 14. Jhd. unter dem Einfluss von Profanarchitektur des Ostseeraums' (1982).

domestic life the townspeople of Europe reached a standard of living roughly equal to that of Antiquity. Unfortunately, that does not apply to the hygienic and sanitary arrangements or to drinking-water, which was often lacking, or to sewerage and drainage. The very high standard attained in Antiquity in these areas was not equalled, even though recent research[39] shows that satisfactory facilities were not entirely absent in towns.

For **Hamburg**, Loose identified 76 women engaged in crafts (very few), in the accounts of the city treasury for 1350–1450. Most of the trading women were involved in huckstering geese, and in wool and linen-weaving. Loose also found some in brewing, Hamburg's most important export trade, as Reincke[40] has shown. This is hardly surprising, as we know that home brewing was regarded as women's work. Reincke not only took a quantifying approach to historical demography at a time when there was little demand for it — he supplemented the dry statistics with colourful details and accounts of human destinies. We owe to him the life story of Agneta Willeken[41] who lived in the sixteenth century in Wullenwever's time, but can be taken as a representative of urban conditions generally in the late Middle Ages. I follow his account, which is based on the records of the supreme court of the empire. At that time the sharp social differences which existed in towns manifested themselves in discriminatory rights of admission to dances and festivities, which could be enforced legally. In 1544, the 'honourable and virtuous' widow Agneta Willeken appealed to the supreme court in Speyer, in her own name and that of her daughters, who were minors, against their exclusion from a feast.[42] Her case had a highly political background. In the spring of 1538 the Hamburg municipal council had held a feast for King Christian of Denmark, who was staying in Hamburg with his court and knights. Nobles and commoners were invited. The two daughters of the plaintiff, Anna and Margareta, who were learning ladylike manners at the convent of Uetersen, looked on at the tournament and the dance under the protection of two aunts. As they stood thus in 'a fitting and orderly manner', an attendant appeared and

---

[39] U. Dirlmeier, 'Die kommunalpolitischen Zuständigkeiten und Leistungen süddeutscher Städte im Spätmittelalter' (1981).

[40] H. Reincke, 'Bevölkerungsprobleme der Hansestädte' (1951), pp. 20ff.

[41] H. Reincke, *Agneta Willeken. Ein Lebensbild aus Wullenwevers Tagen* (1928).

[42] Ibid., p. 4.

ordered one of the aunts to dismiss the girls forthwith. No reason was given but reprisals were threatened, so that Zillie von der Broke, one of Agneta's sisters, found herself constrained to lead the girls away from the dance 'in a wholly undeserved manner', which exposed them to shame, ridicule and damage. As compensation for the impaired marriage prospects of her daughters, their mother demanded from the court a sum of 24,000 guilders — which corresponded roughly to the average annual income of a household in Hamburg at that time. What lay behind this curious occurrence? Agneta Willeken, the mother of the girls, was born in 1497 to a respected family of the prosperous Hamburg middle class, and married the seaman Hans Willeken, who traded with Iceland. After his death — while her two daughters were learning decorum at the convent — she became the mistress of Marx Meyer, the notorious confederate of Jürgen Wullenwever. Wullenwever had become burgomaster of Lübeck at the head of the party with democratic and Lutheran sympathies which opposed the aristocratic, Catholic senate. In 1533, when a new king succeeded to the Danish throne, Wullenwever saw a chance to bring Denmark, the Hansa's old enemy, under Lübeck's influence by force. His commander was this same Marx Meyer, a blacksmith from Hamburg, who had had a military career, married the very rich widow of a Lübeck burgomaster, been imprisoned by the English following attacks on merchant shipping by privateers, but had been knighted by Henry VIII and presented with a heavy gold chain and an annual pension. This was the man Agneta had won. 'Who is that before my door?', she was wont to call out when he knocked; 'Hammer and tongs, you may be sure! he would reply. She promenaded about the city with Henry VIII's gold chain of honour around her neck. When Marx Meyer moved to Lübeck, he did not break off his liaison with Agneta. Indeed, it was said that just as Wullenwever listened to Meyer more than to any other, so Meyer did nothing without Frau Agneta's advice. It was claimed that she had been the brains behind the war against Duke Christian of Schleswig-Holstein, next in line to the Danish throne. 'For,' as a contemporary observed, 'women are mighty ... and can make a man do many things.' In the course of the war Meyer was captured and taken to the clifftop castle of Warberg on the Kattegat. He escaped with the help of the castle commander's wife, became master of the castle in which he had been held, and wrote to Agneta about his adventures. Her reply is dated 23 August 1535. 'Herr Marcus Meyer, my dear friend,' she begins, 'I wish I could cut out my heart and send it to you, so that you could see my grief inside.' It had gone hard with her, she wrote, for people had thought he had cut her from his coat-tails. 'My dearest friend, ... now I know: though you may sing in other chapels, I should be your main church all the same.' This letter fell into the hands of the Holstein commander, Johann Rantzau, who passed it on to King Christian. From then on Frau Agneta was popularly known as 'Main Church' in Denmark. Marx Meyer could not hold out, capitulated on ambiguous terms and was executed.

And what of Agneta? Hardly was her first grief behind her when she turned the head of Joachim Wullenwever, the brother of the deposed burgomaster of Lübeck, a man of 50 who even promised her marriage and kept her as if she were his wife. And she naturally wore Henry VIII's gold chain when she accompanied him on sledging parties. This cost Joachim Wullenwever his seat on the senate, and to prevent Agneta from causing further mischief her epistle to Marx Meyer was read out to the citizens, assembled piously before the town hall. From then on 'Main Church' lived on the Mönkedamm near the city wall, in a remote neighbourhood of low repute which had cast its gloom over more than one wife of the town. Now King Christian arrived in Hamburg, in May 1538, and Agneta sent her daughters, in the festive attire of which Marx Meyer had once relieved the Rantzaus, with her sisters to the dance. The townsfolk's daughters edged away from the offspring of 'Main Church', but some young noblemen found them captivating. Less captivated was the stern monarch, when he saw the animated group on entering the ballroom, and in the banqueting room it was whispered into burgomasterly ears that 'Main Church' was in the ballroom. At this moment Marshall Melchior von Rantzau rushed in and begged the burgomaster: 'Main Church is here with her daughters. Have her thrown out at once, or something terrible will happen.' We need only add that the trial dragged on until 1590, when Agneta and her daughters were no longer alive. The Hamburg senate was ordered to pay 1,000 Rhenish guilders as well as costs.

Cologne 'Coellen, the crown of all cities, has five names that should be explained to everyone,' begins a treatise on the municipal law and civic freedoms of Cologne from the mid-fifteenth century,[43] 'the first is the name of a holy city, because of the dear saints whose shrines and remains are in Cologne.' This is a reference to the relics of St Ursula and the Magi, whose removal from Milan to Cologne by Barbarossa's chancellor Rainald von Dassel had made Cologne an important place of pilgrimage. 'The second is the name of an imperial city.' Cologne's official recognition as an imperial city only came after the war with Neuss of 1475, but *de facto* Cologne was already free of archiepiscopal rule. 'The third is the name of a constitutional city in which the law protects everyone. The fourth is the name of a free city, so that no one may trouble or afflict others except with good reason. The fifth name means that Cologne is called a city of good customs which follow the law, both spiritual and worldly.' These are not empty phrases. The great skill of the citizens of Cologne in framing laws has been noted by historians — their fundamental innovations in land registration, for example. What particularly interests us is that important personal freedoms extended to include women citizens and residents. For example, one order declares the inviolability of the dwelling of each inhabitant of Cologne: 'It is a right granted by the state that a proper citizen and his wife should be free in their houses ... It is also a citizen's right that no one shall be apprehended in childbed, when the house and all its contents are free.' The protection of a house with childbed — before the birth — is also found in Mainz. The law which refuses to allow citizens of Cologne to be summoned before outside courts also applies to women and residents — they too are answerable only to the city court. Moreover, citizens, women and residents who own a house but have only poor, mean furniture in it, cannot be summoned to court even if they owe more than 1,000 guilders. This exemption from 'trouble' for people who have inherited property was defined more precisely in 1437. What interests us is its inclusion of women. Women in Cologne possessed civic rights, either automatically as the wives or widows of Cologne citizens, or as new residents if, like men, they had paid for admission and

[43] Stein, *Akten zur Geschichte* vol. 1, no. 335, quot. in text pp. 717f. On the conditions in Cologne in the late Middle Ages, cf. F. Irsigler, 'Kölner Wirtschaft im Spätmittelalter' (1975), pp. 217ff; and *Die wirtschaftliche Stellung der Stadt Köln im 14. und 15. Jahrhundert. Strukturanalyse einer spätmittelalterlichen Exportgewerbe- und Fernhandelsstadt* (1979); W. Herborn, *Die politische Führungsschicht der Stadt Köln im Spätmittelalter* (1977).

sworn the oath of citizenship. The lists of new citizens of Cologne are available from 1356 on; but the proportion of women is very low and falls further in the sixteenth century. A frequent reason for women to obtain citizenship was their desire to take up a certain profession, for example, the wish to gain the right to sell cloth retail.[44]

The principle of marriage by consent has established itself here, as is shown by a marriage contract formula from about 1435[45] which runs as follows:

Whoever joins two together in matrimony shall speak these words: first he shall ask the man: 'Wilt thou take Beylgine — or whatever her name may be — as thy wife and bedfellow?' Then the bridegroom shall say: 'Yes, I will.' Then he shall ask the bride by her name: 'Wilt thou take Heinrich — or whatever the bridegroom may be called — as thy guardian and bedfellow?' etc. Then she shall say: 'Yes, I will.' Then the bridegroom shall take the ring and put it on the bride's finger next to her smallest finger. Then the man who is joining them in marriage shall take the silk cloth in which 12 coins are bound and say: 'I join you on Frankish soil with gold and jewels, silver and gold according to Frankish custom and law, that you may not part from each other whether for the flesh or for grief or for anything God may visit on you'. Then he who is joining them shall give the cloth with the coins to someone who keeps it for the bride. She shall give the money in God's name to poor folk. Then the groom shall pour for the bride to drink from a chalice, and the bridegroom shall drink first and then pour some for the bride.

Even in the marriage by consent, therefore, the husband is the guardian of his wife, and the marriage bond has an element of domination. Certain offences such as bigamy were easier to put into practice than they are now, when there is uniform registration of all citizens within a state. The imperial city of Cologne had only a small rural area under its jurisdiction. It was easy to remove oneself from this area to escape the city's jurisdiction. On the other hand, the punishment of expulsion from the city was available, and solved many problems for which there are no such easy legal solutions today. The *Statuta civitatis* of 1437[46] which in

---

[44] The authoritative work on all questions relating to women in Cologne is: M. Wensky, *Die Stellung der Frau in der stadtkölnischen Wirtschaft im Spätmittelalter* (1980).
[45] Stein, *Akten zur Geschichte*, vol. 1, pp. 766f.
[46] Ibid., no. 331, pp. 631ff.

part codify existing law, concern the punishment for bigamy. It often happens, this document states, that married couples move to other towns where they separate and remarry. If a man who has a lawful wife whom he has wed in church and should keep according to the law of the church — if such a man deserts this wife and takes another to the altar, and then takes up residence in Cologne and continues such behaviour there, then those convicted of such offences, whether man or woman, shall be publicly put in the pillory and whipped out of town. If a man, whether a native of the city or a foreigner, abducts the wife of a citizen or resident with her goods, he shall be executed by the sword, and the woman shall be placed in the pillory and her cheeks branded, and then whipped with rods from the town. If she returns to Cologne she shall be buried alive. A man who betrothes himself to two women or maidens, if convicted by a court, shall suffer three months' imprisonment in the tower; the same punishment befalls a women who does the same. From the fifteenth century an adulterer could not be elected to the council or hold a council office. By an order of 1330[47] arising from a case at that time, sons or daughters who marry against their parents' will lose all their rights, although the statutes of 1437 restrict these consequences to young people aged under 20. Children who mistreat their parents by hitting, throwing or pushing, or by insults, are punished with six months in the tower on bread and water. He who abducts the son or daughter of a citizen of Cologne by force shall, if apprehended, be executed by the sword, unless he be under church jurisdiction. Whereas elsewhere women received milder punishments than men, in Cologne the same law applied to all: 'Let him be who he be, priest, student, layman, woman or man,' is a recurrent formula.[48] Women were subject to imprisonment in the tower, were often pilloried, as we have seen, and murderesses met with capital punishment: they were buried alive or drowned in the Rhine. The *Koelhoffsche Chronik* of 1487 tells how a murderess was buried alive with her daughter, who was convicted of complicity: 'And lying together they were together buried, so that it was lamentable to behold.'

Before a court the testimony of a woman was equal to that of a man. In commercial matters her statement under oath was fully recognized. That was not the case everywhere. Wensky draws our attention to a revealing case. When in 1498 the Cologne trader Johann Liblar sued a citizen of Antwerp over a defective consignment of silk, the witnesses who confirmed the poor quality were four female silk-weavers and three female silk-spinners. In its accompanying letter, the city expressly asked the people of Antwerp to recognize the women's testimony. Cologne had heard, they wrote, that it was not the custom in Antwerp to take testimony or oaths from women, but in Cologne silk manufacture was carried on almost exclusively by women, 'who had been long in trade and commerce and were highly experienced.' In 1397 the city of Metz was unwilling to recognize that the Cologne woman Katharina von Siegen could make a valid agreement, and required the city of Cologne to confirm that it was possible. The legal powers of women in Cologne were unusually extensive.

The Cologne law on inheritance[49] treats movable and immovable goods differently. Although the surviving parent receives all the movable estate in case of a marriage with heirs, the immovables go to the children; they were the actual heirs. They have the right to divide property with the surviving parent. Goods that could be divided were 'all inherited goods and annuities and movables.' If the father survives, he receives two-thirds and the children one-third of the whole estate; if the mother survives, she receives one-third and the children two-thirds. If there are no children the whole estate goes to the surviving spouse, who has control of half of it, and it is only divided after his or her death. But in view of testamentary freedom this law had only subsidiary validity in Cologne, i.e. if there was no will, bequest, or marriage certificate, etc. In late-medieval Cologne there was generally a mutual bequest that could be made either as a marriage contract or later as a joint will. The statutes of 1437 contain detailed precepts on wills.[50] With regard to will-making no significant differences between the sexes can be observed; the number of wills made by women is slightly higher. Nuns and Beguines also made wills. We can regard it as a peculiarity of Cologne law that

---

[49] G. Aders, *Das Testamentrecht der Stadt Köln im Mittelalter* (1932), A review of this book by A. Schultze is to be found in *ZRG Germ.* sect. 154, 1934.

[50] Stein, *Akten zur Geschichte*, vol. 1, pp. 640ff.

women could be executors of wills. They could also be guardians, of their own or other people's children, often jointly with other persons but sometimes on their own.

It is not only in this respect that Cologne seems an unusual city. In the first half of the fourteenth century its population grew to almost 40,000, which considerably surpassed Lübeck and the other northern and eastern German cities of the time. If we look west, however, to Flanders and Brabant, Cologne's size no longer seems so exceptional, Ghent having about 60,000 inhabitants in the fourteenth century, Bruges about 50,000 and Louvain about 45,000. These high figures were strongly influenced, though not entirely caused, by the development of large export trades which needed many workers. Another unusual feature of Cologne was that its exports were in various sectors of the textile, metal and leather trades, and did not depend solely on textiles, like cities in Flanders and Brabant. And in Cologne the weavers did not fall into such oppressive dependence on the loom owners as in the southern Netherlands. The urban society of Cologne was more closed than that of Lübeck, but more open than those of Nuremberg or Schwäbisch-Hall, for example. Cologne did not have an urban nobility but – as we said in the previous chapter – it had a patriciate. The *Richerzeche*, a powerful league of leading families in the twelfth and thirteenth centuries, had declined to a community of prebendaries by the fourteenth century and was dissolved in 1370. But the right to appoint jurors and burgomaster, and to distribute council offices, remained the almost exclusive preserve of a leading group of about 40 patrician families until well into the second half of the fourteenth century. From the turn of the century (it is clearly documented in 1321) an enlarged senate with 82 members joined that of the families. Although the new council was at first largely made up of patricians, they were joined by increasing numbers of people from the rising commercial class, who no longer had access to the more and more hermetic patrician group and sought to exert a political influence of their own. In Cologne as elsewhere the second half of the fourteenth century was a period of unrest – particularly of conflicts between the leading families, which split up into factions. The tensions were discharged in the so-called 'weavers' rising' of 1370 – we should bear in mind that the political leaders of the rich wool trade were more often cloth dealers and cloth distributors than craftsmen. It would be wrong to regard these turmoils as struggles between the guilds.

In 1388 the Cologne upper class successfully founded the university. The internal struggles which broke out again in 1391 reached a compromise in the *Verbundbrief* of 1396. This remained the primary constitutional document of the city up to the French Revolution, and was supplemented by the *Transfixbrief* of 1513 after a further outbreak of unrest. In 1396 the senate made itself the sole organ of the constitution.

A typical feature of the leading families of Cologne was their ability to survive. The old families were not completely eliminated by the events of 1396 and continued to control the college of lay assessors, or jurors, until this too underwent a change that might be said to have an early-modern character. The office of lay assessor lost its links to a particular estate and became an academic profession open only to lawyers. Irsigler,[51] elaborating a distinction suggested by Maschke, divided the Cologne middle class into an upper stratum made up primarily of merchants and a lower stratum drawn mainly from the crafts and guilds. There are broad areas of overlap and in the fifteenth century these extend to the upper class. There were rich and poor guilds, with sharp social differentiation within the individual institutions, although this may have been somewhat reduced by group cohesiveness. The broad lower stratum of the middle class included shopkeepers, second-hand dealers, trade and transport workers, excise collectors, middlemen, messengers, etc. The main groups of the lower class were made up of craftsmen's assistants, wage labourers, servants and maid-servants. Right at the bottom were the poor, beggars, prostitutes, musicians and travellers. About 1,400 destitutes were counted in Cologne in 1403.

Such, briefly sketched, was the society within which the women of Cologne achieved astonishing prominence in the commercial sphere. But it was only in the economic sphere, for in the revolutions, uprisings, wars and political conflicts they took no traceable part. Nor did they make the really large fortunes. Wensky has investigated the extensive material in the city archive using modern methods, and has given a reliable account of the position of women in the field of trade and crafts in Cologne.[52] The wide legal powers held by women was a main reason why they were able to rise to master craftswoman's status in the guilds. There

---

[51] Irsigler, *Kölner Wirtschaft*, pp. 229ff.
[52] Cf. Wensky, *Die Stellung der Frau.*

were few branches of the economy in which they were not to be found. Only the tailors, harness-makers and drapers placed working restrictions on women, and then only at certain times, or partially. Women were dominant in yarn-making, gold-spinning and silk-making.

'Coelsch garn, fil de Cologne' was a proprietary article of Cologne, a linen thread, usually dyed blue, which was popular for its finish and its pure colour. In Cologne the manufacture of the linen yarn was done by women yarn-makers, who formed a guild which probably came into being before 1397. A regulation which was a forerunner of the guild charter fixes the hours of working: work was not to start before daybreak, nor to stop later than eight o'clock in the evening, so that the quality of the work did not suffer through bad lighting. The guild charter confirmed in 1397 fixed the period of apprenticeship at four years; the teacher could be changed once, and each new teacher had to be registered with the yarn guild and entered in the apprentice's logbook within a week. Once the apprentice had finished her learning, the guild-masters had to inspect her work, to see 'whether it be merchant's goods or not.' If it was approved, the apprentice could set up a workshop in her own house on payment of a fee of 2 guilders. The daughters of yarn-makers paid half the entrance fee. Each teacher could, however, only help one daughter to become an independent yarn-maker, and then only with financial support and never with yarn. The guild was to remain open. Other regulations were designed to preserve competition between firms, and to prevent a distributor-system from emerging. The women yarn-makers developed a widower's law, whereby a widower was allowed to continue the craft as long as he did not join up with another woman who did not belong to the guild. The guildmasters and guildmistresses had to swear an oath of service after election. Supervision was performed by 'lords to the yarn-makers' appointed by the council. The yarn-making women were frequently involved in tariff disputes with the yarn-twisters, who wound the yarn on to wheels or spinning mills for wages. This had happened since 1373, when the spinning mills, which had previously been privately owned, were taken over by the city and leased out for 10 years at a time. Among the first eight people of Cologne who leased 12 mills between them, there was one woman. Of the 14 yarn-mill leaseholders of the first half of the fifteenth century, five were women. In 1498 the senate forbade the driving of the mills night and day by horses; these must have been large, capstan-driven machines with several spindles. The senate was opposed to such progress, insisting on the traditional method, perhaps to maintain employment. As with other textile crafts in Cologne, the husbands were often responsible for selling the yarn, for the women involved in yarn-making were often married. One woman yarn-maker contributed 50 guilders to the city loan of 1418. Greater wealth was not generally to be earned in this trade.

The spinning of gold was women's work in Cologne from the outset. The gold-spinners had formed a guild with a section of the gold-beaters. Gold and silver leaf was used by Cologne artists in painting and in the furniture, leather and bookbinding trades, and the thread was used for brocade, church robes and embroidery.

Silk embroidery too was at first an exclusively female occupation. In the guild of escutcheon embroiderers men and women had had equal rights since 1397. Cologne braid has survived on church garments to this day. The silk-makers received their first guild charter in 1437. It was issued at their express wish, as they felt their existence to be threatened by new ideas − perhaps technical innovations. Between then and 1506 there were three further charters and two *Transfixbriefe*. Here, too, apprenticeship usually lasted four years. The mistress or teacher could be changed once with the guild's agreement. Legitimacy was not a prerequisite for admission to the guild. The chief silk-maker, or *Heuftvrauwe*, had her workshop in her home, where she trained her own daughters, and other girls who also lived at her house and shared her table. Each *Heuftvrauwe* could keep four apprentices, not counting her own children. Membership of a guild was not, in theory, compulsory, but probably was so in practice. Each year the chief silk-makers elected two women as guildmistresses and two men as guildmasters. Married couples could not serve at the same time, and a precondition of eligibility was legitimate birth. The governing body of the guild met once a fortnight at the house of one of the guildmasters or mistresses, as there was no separate headquarters. Everyone present received an attendance fee, and refreshments − bread, wine, an apple − were provided. The committee could punish infringements of the guild rules with fines. The silk-makers were predominantly married women, and it was often their husbands who took care of sales. Some of the silk-makers were themselves distributors. Between 1437 and 1504, 116 women ran their own firms. On average, one or two women attained the status of master-craftswoman and about 12 girls were taken on as apprentices each year. The silk-makers worked at their trade for 17 years on average. According to the frequency of admissions of apprentices, Wensky divides the silk-making firms into several categories: large and small businesses, and those which operated irregularly. Of the silk-makers who took on at least one new apprentice each year, i.e. who always had at least four apprentices working for them, some were especially capable and successful, e.g. Grietgen van Berchem, Tryngen Louback and Fygen Lutzenkirchen. Grietgen van Berchem was a silk-maker from 1469 to 1476 and trained 10 apprentices. She was married to Jakob van Berchem, who belonged to a Cologne family involved in the wine trade among others. He also appeared as a raw silk importer and held the right to work as a draper. Grietgen was elected to the guild committee in 1474 and her husband in 1478. Tryngen Louback came from a silk-weaving family; her mother was the silk-maker Niesgin Wyerdt (from Solingen), who had learned her trade in Cologne and was married to Mertyn Neven, a successful Cologne merchant, silk-trader and councillor. Tryngen's husband, Conrad Louback, was also a raw silk importer. Fygen Lutzenkirchen became a chief silk-maker in 1474 and took on 25 apprentices in all up to 1497. Her husband, Peter Lutzenkirchen, was an important Cologne merchant; he was a member of the wool guild, an agent for several north German trading houses including the Ravensburger Handelsgesellschaft and the Vöhlin-Welser-Gesellschaft. From the Ravensburg company he obtained silk from Valencia, supplying Cologne gold yarn destined finally for Genoa and Venice in return. He was elected several times to the senate. Fygen was often on the guild committee. With a few interruptions, the couple alternated on the committee for a period of 18 years. Peter Lutzenkirchen visited the Brabant fairs at Bergen op Zoom and Antwerp, and the Frankfurt fair. His wife seems to have been involved in her husband's business; she also engaged in the wine trade. On her husband's death she appears to have closed her workshop, or perhaps she left the silk mill to her daughter Lysbeth, who was approved as a chief silkmaker in 1496. Fygen and Peter Lutzenkirchen must have been a very wealthy couple; they owned several houses. As we can see, silk-guild families intermarried, and the husband's trade and the wife's craft were complementary.

In the fifteenth and sixteenth centuries the apprentice girls came from the same social stratum as the guildmistresses. Ten per cent of the registered apprentices were children of members of the silk guild, and there was a large proportion of merchants' daughters. Raw silk importers also apprenticed their daughters to the guild, and girls from outside were admitted; their places of origin mirror Cologne's trading links. The silk-spinners formed a separate guild, as Wensky has now shown beyond doubt. Silk-spinning suffered from competition with the monasteries and convents and was under pressure from the much richer silk-makers, who owned the expensive raw materials. As a sign of the conflict of interests, the council repeatedly prohibited payment by the truck system.

There were important female merchants in Cologne, who were mainly married women trading on a basis of independent gain and loss. In 1460–8 women held a share of the spice import trade in Cologne varying between 1.2 and 19.6 per cent. They also had a significant share in the trade in metal and metal goods. Among the brass traders, five women made up 14 per cent of importers and accounted for 19.2 per cent of brass imports on which excise was levied in 1452–80. For the period from 1452 to 1459 the women's share was 30.3 per cent. The steel imports of Cathringen Broelmann (1497–1501, 1506–9) were, at 19.8 per cent, only slightly less than those of the largest steel importer, Gerhard Betgin, who had 22 per cent. Craftsmen's wives who obtained raw materials for their husbands often had a big share in the imports of metals and metal goods. There is thus a division of labour in the sense that in metalwork, where the women had little opportunity of practical work, they took over the commercial responsibilities which in other trades (yarn-making, gold-spinning, silk crafts) were borne by the men, while the women practised the craft. Women had a considerable share in the drapery trade. Of the seven women who paid excise for more than 100 bales, five were successors to their husbands. Stina van Waveren carried on her husband Wilhelm's cloth-trading business at its full extent for over 20 years; her average share of the Cologne drapery trade was 19.2 per cent per annum, and she was also active in the wine trade. We often find people holding two jobs (as we do generally in the Middle Ages). A large proportion of the women wine traders – up to 40 per cent – were members of senatorial families. A survey of the ways women organized their trading shows them often taking an active role in companies and trade journeys, though within a narrower horizon than men–and they are men's equals in keeping trading and household accounts. Grietgen van der Burg, a merchant in a wide variety of goods, owned 13 houses in the expensive St Alban quarter, in about 1487–92.

The extent of the independence and business success of Cologne women in trade and crafts must have been almost without equal. The only parallels elsewhere were in individual crafts, such as gold-spinning in Nuremberg. Nuremberg's patrician constitution knew no guilds, only attested crafts; in 1597 the women goldspinners attained that status.[53] A number of towns offer parallels in silk-making. There is a guild of women silk-weavers in Zurich.[54] They work not only for distributors — the Zurich silk crafts were heavily dependent on patrician merchants — but on their own account. In Zurich the auxilliary crafts of the winders, tackers and warpers were dependent on the silk-weavers. In London too, women were predominant in the silk crafts.[55] They took on apprentices and issued indentures. These silkwomen and throwsters appealed to the crown against foreign competition, particularly from Lombardy. in 1368 and 1455. They came from good families. But no guild of silk-weavers seems to have existed.

Paris is a counterpart to Cologne. In his undated *Livre des métiers*,[56] produced after 1252 and before 1271, Etienne de Boileau describes the dominant position of women in silk-making. Höppner was able to identify six solely female guilds in Paris, all in silk-making: the spinners with large distaffs, those with small distaffs, the weavers, the makers of silk bonnets and caps for ladies, the milliners who make silk hats with gold embroidery for ladies and the pursue-makers who produce small silk purses for ladies. In the silk-spinners' guild two men, probably the husbands of master-craftswomen, acted as jurors who supervised the craft, though without judicial competence. Each guildmistress could keep two or three female apprentices, and the apprenticeship lasted seven years. Some spinners with substantial capital of their own worked up their own raw silk into thread, in which they themselves

[53]   G. Schmitz, *Die Berufstätigkeit der Frau in der Reichstadt Nürnberg bis zum Ende des 16. Jahrhunderts* (1950).

[54]   H. Wachendorf, *Die wirtschaftliche Stellung der Frau in den deutschen Städten des späteren Mittelalters* (1934), pp. 48ff.

[55]   Power, *Medieval Women*.

[56]   R. Lespinasse and F. Bonnardot, eds., *Etienne Boileau. Le livre des métiers. Les métiers et corporations de la ville de Paris* (1877); M. Höppner, *Die Frauenarbeit in Paris im Mittelalter* (1922).

traded. Many worked for distributors; in Paris, unlike Cologne, these were haberdashers (*merciers*). They supplied the raw silk and took in the finished thread. The spinners were often accused of cheating; they were the worst off of all the women employed in silk-making. The guild of silk-weavers collpased in 1450, and a new one was formed, in which men and women had equal rights. The other women's silk guilds involved highly fashionable occupations. In the guild of the makers of small caps and bonnets, the offices of the three jurors were filled only by women. This was an exception; otherwise the jurors were men, or both men and women. The cap-makers were allowed to take on one female apprentice and to train one family member as well, apprenticeship lasting either seven years or eight years without fees. Here the men took care of sales; the women cap-makers were generally independent, but not rich. Their earnings were about the same as those of craftsmen. With the milliners, the husbands bought materials, sold the finished goods and supplied the capital. This craft flourished in the period about 1300; in the fourteenth century the guild came to an end. The purse-makers produced alms purses and small money pouches. In 1299, 124 women from this craft, mostly married, presented and registered their first statutes. The apprenticeship was for 10 years, but could be reduced to six by payments. The independent master-craftswomen working for themselves also employed women homeworkers outside the city. After the prescribed period the apprentices became full members of the guild without a qualifying examination or entrance fee. Women were full members of many other guilds, such as the guild of braid-makers, ribbon-makers, embroiderers and haberdashers. In the silk-cloth makers' guild they had only widow's rights. But they had full rights in the guilds of flax and hemp traders, yarn-spinners, linen-weavers, makers of short linen breeches, felt-hat makers, hat-liners and traders in bric-à-brac. In the guilds of wool-weavers, fullers, dyers, tailors and stocking embroiderers, however, they had only limited rights as widows. They were forbidden to make Arabian carpets. Some professions were open to them in the leather, metal and victuals trades, but butchery and grain-measuring were forbidden to them. They had full rights as surgeons or barbers, and limited rights to trade in medicaments. Women are not mentioned among the tanners, cobblers, saddlers, joiners, carpenters, roofers, goldsmiths and gold-beaters, sculptors, millers, corn dealers, fishmongers and smiths. Höppner emphasizes that among women working in trades, married women were as widely represented as single women. There was a good reason why women were allowed to work independently in their own workshops in the silk trade — the towns mentioned are the most important centres of silk-making north of the Alps, Italy being the chief area in which this craft was practised. This reason lay in the dexterity of women's fingers; rough male hands were less suited to the work.

What is interesting, however, is that women are not only found working as assistants in firms run by men, but often have their own workshops. And the special aptitude for silk-working does not, of course, apply to women who worked as merchants. Many Cologne wives who had full-time work were married — did they need to earn money? This raises the important question of the economic situation of the middle classes. It can be taken as certain that single women often had to work as hucksters, washer-women, maids etc., to earn the basic minimum to stay alive, and so must be counted among the lower classes. The study of income levels and cost of living in south German cities in the late Middle Ages,[57] recently presented by Ulf Dirlmeier, contains evidence that the standard of living was very modest, even in the lower-middle class, that is, among craftsmen. Dirlmeier also points to the importance of joint working and of the incomes of family members other than the main earner. In Cologne, working wives were clearly not confined to the lower and lower-middle classes. The situation there suggests rather that the wife who worked independently as a master-craftswoman or merchant played a significant part in providing the high standard of living of middle-class families in the late Middle Ages. Markets in cities like Cologne offered an attractive range of goods for the kitchen, the clothes and linen cupboards, and for the wife's jewellery box, as well as a variety of utensils and furniture for the home; and Cologne as an exporting city offered women plentiful opportunities of employment. Was it the wife's work and the double income that made possible a political career for more and more husbands in the middle classes? Offices on the council were honorary, which made it difficult for a craftsman, for example, to enter the council

---

[57]   U. Dirlmeier, *Untersuchungen zu Einkommensverhältnissen und Lebenshaltung-skosten in oberdeutschen Städten des Spätmittelalters* (1978).

even if it was actually allowed in his town. Maschke has repeatedly considered this question of lack of opportunity.[58] If our supposition is correct, there would be a close parallel with the modern situation, where many male careers are financed by the wife's work, as is the high standard of living of a large section of the population. This does not apply, now or then, to the very rich, the very high earners, but it is true for the 'upwardly mobile'. If we remember that in the Middle Ages Cologne levied hardly any direct taxes but balanced its budget with indirect taxes, so that wives' earnings were tax-free, we can understand their importance all the more easily.

We have no quantifying analysis of the social stratification of the population of Cologne, and we cannot apply Dirlmeier's conclusions directly to that city. We can merely raise these questions for discussion. At all events, we should not underestimate the desire of people to have their share of luxury. To achieve this even today, enormous sacrifices are made in the German middle classes, particularly by women.

The living standards of the high bourgeoisie of Cologne, and of the lower stratum of the upper class and the upper stratum of the middle class as well, were high. Still standing in Cologne today − and used as a museum − is No. 8 Rheingasse, the so-called Overstolzenhaus. Vogts[59] calls it 'the most elegant and opulent example of bourgeois Romanesque secular architecture in Gemany.' It was built about 1250. The building, on five axes, is divided into two main living floors and four storage floors under the massive stepped gable. The double windows on the upper floor are linked by a cloverleaf arch with round fanlights above them. 'The old fenestrated walls had slender columns in blue-grey slate at their corners and centre, giving the facade a colourful effect; further evidences of this are the traces of colour and gilding on the ornamental parts, and tinted paint of the exterior stucco may also have contributed.' The windows were not yet glazed; this came with the Gothic style. We also know how the house was divided up internally. It was constructed in two naves, with a massive wall perpendicular to the road which divided the house from the foundations to the rafters into two sections of unequal width. This

---

[58] Maschke, *Städte und Menschen*, pp. 30f.
[59] H. Vogts, *Das Kölner Wohnhaus bis zur Mitte des 19. Jahrhunderts* (1966).

is especially clear in the cellar, where the wall is broken up into a
series of round arches. Some houses of the Cologne ruling class
had guard towers. Staircase towers were built not only on to large
houses but on to the courtyard side of upper-class terraced houses.
A feature of some courtyards were vaulted, covered sections re-
calling the medieval halls of houses in Mainz and Trier; the Jude
family owned such a hall. We have fairly exact knowledge of the
internal layout of the Rinkenhof,[60] from an inventory of 1600. It
was made up of three buildings and was the residence of the
Junker Anton Rink and his sisters. The complex, described in
detail by Vogts,[61] is very intricate; there are several large
chambers, rooms of various sizes, a counting house, a library,
small rooms for the maids, a bathroom, a kitchen, a press-house,
small stables and a garden. The cellars in Cologne burghers'
houses sometimes contain the well, though it is more often found
in the courtyard. Chapels are found in large numbers of Cologne
houses; the oldest known chapel in a private house is a late
Romanesque structure in the courtyard of Gobelinus de
Merzenich, 51–53 Schildergasse. Apart from large rooms, halls
and chapels, the houses often had workshops and utility rooms
attached to them, washrooms, stables, etc. Bathrooms are often
found, the walls covered in wood, with a masonry fireplace built
into the wall or a tiled stove. The household offices – privies,
latrines – are sometimes situated in the courtyard or outhouses,
sometimes in the front part of the building, in the cellar, even in
the roof, and often in the bathroom or kitchen! Some privies had
several seats; others none at all. The floors on the upper storeys
were of boards, those at the front of the house of heavy stone
slabs; in simpler houses there were plaster floors. One elegant
kind of floor was of square earthenware slabs with figures cut into
them; they have been found in Metz, Mainz, Constance, Zürich,
Basle, and in France, and can be expected to have existed in
Cologne, to judge from pictures in the Cologne Malerschule.
Other floor coverings were of small, glazed stones or coloured
tiles. The wooden beams of the ceilings were painted, the wall
paintings being matched to the ceiling motifs. As late as the
fifteenth century there were houses which had no chimneys, the

---

[60] On the Rincks, cf. F. Irsigler, 'Peter Rinck (gest. 8. Februar 1501)' (1975).
[61] Vogts, *Das Kölner Wohnhaus*, pp. 46f.

smoke escaping through doors and windows, or through special
outlets in the walls. Open fireplaces have been preserved from the
fifteenth century, and there is evidence that they existed earlier.
In the sixteenth century the corbels and cornices of fireplaces are
of high-quality sculpture.

In such houses lived the rich ladies of Cologne. Heavy gold and
silver cutlery was bought as a capital investment. In 1420 a
Cologne merchant promises an heir a goblet worth at least 50
guilders.[62] Candlesticks and pots are often of pewter. A very
exact inventory, from 1511, from a Cologne house the owner of
which had died in Antwerp and whose children, some of them
minors, had to divide the estate, records a considerable quantity
of pewter. In one room there is a 'pewter hand-vessel'. This is a
washing bowl that was either mounted in a niche in the wall or in
part of a cupboard shaped like a niche. It consists of a container
with a tap, and a bowl below it. In the same room there was a
'*Trysoer* on which stand two pewter cans with spouts'. A *Trysoer* is
a piece of furniture which from the early fifteenth century was one
of the most important items in an elegant room. On it expensive
utensils were often displayed, here pewter. In one cupboard the
executors of the will found 18 'pewter vegetable dishes, large and
small, item another pewter saltcellar and a dozen square pewter
plates' as well as two dozen round plates and six pewter spoons.
Haedeke[63] surmises that the large and small vegetable dishes were
similar to the dish on which the lamb lies in pictures of the Last
Supper. The number of 18 plates is considerable. The round
plates will have been the discs typical of the late Gothic style.
They were used when putting down the meat that was eaten
mainly with the hands, with occasional assistance from a knife.
Forks were not usual until the seventeenth century. Spoons were
important for mash; only very wealthy people had pewter spoons,
simpler folk being content with wooden ones.

In these well-furnished houses the food was copious, varied and
strongly spiced. F. Irsigler[64] has analysed the housekeeping book

[62]   Hasse, 'Neues Hausgerät, neue Häuser, neue Kleider', p. 63.
[63]   H. U. Haedeke, 'Eisen Zinn, Bronze' 2nd ed. (1970); cf. the information in
Dirlmeier, *Untersuchungen zu Einkommensverhältnissen und Lebenshaltungskosten*, pp.
303ff.
[64]   F. Irsigler, 'Ein grossbürgerlicher Kölner Haushalt am Ende des 14.
Jahrhunderts' vol. 2, pp. 635ff; and 'Hermann von Goch (gest. 7.5.1398)' (1980).

of Hermann Goch, which records what was spent each day on food, drink, clothing and household goods for the period from 23 January 1391 to 31 October 1394. It is not our task here to describe in full the interesting personality, activities and fate of Hermann Goch, one of the richest financiers in Cologne in the second half of the fourteenth century. He was originally a prebendary in a foundation at Kaiserswerth, distinguished himself by his financial service to the court and alternated between clerical and secular status. He became one of Cologne's richest property owners, with 45 houses in the city, some of them mansions. As his own residence he chose a property made up of two nobles' houses joined together called 'Zur Kemenate' in the Glockengasse. He also owned land outside the city walls and a country estate, where he used to spend the summer months with his family and servants. His quasi-marital relationship with Irmgard von der Kemenate produced four sons and five daughters. With the help of his son-in-law, Goswin von der Kemenate, who had taken service at the papal court between 1378 and 1394, he had his children legitimized. Irmgard, of whom we unfortunately know little, apparently came from a social group equal to his own. He married his daughter Stine to the Lombard Antonius Vlegati from Asti, who obtained the civic rights of Cologne in 1387. From 1392 the young couple lived in his household, where they kept a servant at the father's expense. He married his daughter Lysato to the gold-beater and merchant Reimar Glesch, who sat on the new council from 1399 to 1408 as representative of the goldsmiths' guild, and his daughter Bela to a Cologne winemerchant, Johann von Holenter. In 1392 Irmgard and Agnes entered the genteel convent of St Clare in Cologne. He provided his sons with a good and expensive education: the eldest, Hermann, became a canon at St Severin, Johann studied at the universities of Cologne and Vienna, and Wilhelm and Heinrich, at the time of his expense-book, were still living in the parental home. Goch had become a citizen of Cologne in 1385. With his diverse activities he became embroiled in the political troubles of those years: in 1398, with his son-in-law, he was beheaded in Cologne for high treason. We owe the survival of his housekeeping book to this trial.

Goch's household was unusually large. The number of people in it varied, but must have been between 24 and 36. Goch had his own steward and a large staff. For a period of almost 27 months the total expenditure was 4,644 marks. This comprised:

for food and drink	2,530 marks
for clothing	465 marks
for household goods	131 marks
for services etc.	77 marks
for study costs	1,441 marks

We should note at once that the enormous cost of study restricted the number of burghers' sons who could afford to go to university, and that to spend such sums on a daughter was unthinkable, the more so as she needed a dowry which would go to another family, and in any case could not make use of (legal) learning. Fish accounts for a surprisingly large proportion of the entry for food and drink; this was connected with the strict observance of fasting rules: from Ash Wednesday to Easter no meat was put on the table, nor on Fridays and often not on Wednesday. Fish was also eaten as a delicacy. Almost all the bread was of wheat, and in the meatless period and on feast-days cakes were an important item: aniseed cakes, *Striezel* (white loaves), doughnuts, honey-cakes, flat cakes, pretzels, wafers and rolls. Pastries were produced at home or bought from the baker, or the public bakery was used. Much rice was eaten with the meal. The meat consumed included a high proportion of beef, and more than a quarter of it was game. Capons, pigeons, partridges, snipe and pheasants were favoured, but there was no venison. The fish eaten was extraordinarily rich and diverse. A quarter of the total outlay on fish was for herring. Of freshwater species, pike was the most popular, followed at a distance by salmon and carp; eel and trout were delicacies. The rather broad concept of 'spices' is broken up by Irsigler. He distinguishes between imported spices: ginger, saffron, pepper, cinnamon, almonds, cloves, mace, etc.; mustard and the garden spices: caraway seed, onion, dill, parsley, leek; and salt and sweeteners: sugar, molasses, honey. The most popular seasoning was mustard. Refined cane sugar could only be afforded by the rich. Cabbage, peas and small turnips were the main vegetables. The following fruit varieties are recorded: grapes (raisins), figs, apples, pears, cherries, strawberries, bilberies, nuts, chestnuts and plums. Expenditure for milk and dairy produce was low, since much of it was home-produced. The chief drink was wine, though beer was already popular. Hermann Goch and Irmgard von der Kemenate, with their children and servants, kept a luxurious table. The menu was varied: on meat days during the week there were

usually two varieties of meat and on high feast-days even three —
mutton, beef and chicken, for example. Four different kinds of fish
were not unusual, and for one Friday Irsigler notes six varieties:
sturgeon, salmon, flatfish, plaice, crab and trout. Few burgher
families could afford such a princely spread.

However, refined palates were also to be found elsewhere. An
Austrian study of late-medieval urban life tells of a meal which
took place in 1486 in Villach, at the house of the burgher Kaspar
Merendech, and was prepared by his wife. The meal consisted of
ten courses, of which the Italian who gives the account of the meal
describes only the first three:(1) three 'artificial' fish moulded of
milk, eggs and almonds and sprinkled in the pan with peeled
almonds, raisins and sugared aniseed, (2) a dish of crushed and
strained fowl (clearly a pâté) mixed with cinnamon and ginger;
(3) fattened thrushes (?) and a dish of chicken and other meat.
Thanks to its preparation, declared the Italian witness, the meal,
of which 'each course was better than the last', was just as if it
had been delivered 'straight from Florence'. Admittedly, it was a
banquet with which the housewife had taken special trouble and
spared no expense.[65]

From the thirteenth century on the council of Cologne felt itself
obliged to pass laws restraining luxury. They were concerned
primarily with the expense incurred at family celebrations,
baptisms, weddings, the admission of a child to a monastery or
convent, *primices* and, especially, funerals.[66] The restrictions
imposed — largely in vain — frequently do not apply to the next of
kin. They set fines. Maximum amounts are fixed for gifts by
godparents and wedding guests, the number of women who can
attend a baptism is limited, banquets at weddings and funerals
may only have six courses and apart from the next of kin no one
shall wear 'mourning clothes' when someone dies; on days when
the eating of meat is allowed, no fish dishes shall be offered. This
last measure was probably designed to help keep down the price
of fish. From 1439 it was also an offence to place shrouds or
candles on graves, except on All Saints' Day, All Soul's Day and
the anniversary of a death. In 1327, a certain Domina de Kusino,

---

[65] H. Hundsbichler, 'Stadtbegriff, Stadtbild und Stadtleben des 15.
Jahrhunderts nach ausländischen Berichterstattern über Österreich', (1977).
[66] W. Stein, *Akten zur Geschichte*, vol. 1, pp. 106ff (*c.* 1396); p. 389 (*c.* 1460);
vol. 2, pp. 287ff (1439).

from one of the great patrician families, was fined 10 marks for using a silk shroud at her husband's funeral.[67] In 1439 'dragging dresses', i.e. dresses with trains, were prohibited. As long as the husband paid the fine — no less than 6 Rhenish guilders — the practice might be tolerated. Mirrors became popular at that time, and in the towns there was what we now call fashion. People were far too sensuously inclined to do without luxury.

But the burghers no longer confined their celebrations to their own houses. The tower of the town hall next to the church steeple characterized the silhouette of a town, and there were now municipal halls and buildings available for festivities. From the middle of the fourteenth century there was in the Cologne town hall a long chamber for receptions given by the council and for public festivities. Much later it was called the Hansesaal, because it was here that the so-called Cologne Confederation, at which the Hansa cities decided to make war on Denmark, took place in 1367. It was a rectangular room with a single nave, 29 metres long and 7.25 metres wide, covered by a wooden barrel-vaulted ceiling 9.70 metres high.[68] It was probably here that the communal meal of the councillors' wives took place on the occasion of the ceremonial entry to the city of Archbishop Friedrich of Saarwerden in June 1372; the expense was borne by the city of Cologne. To the festive tastes of the fifteenth century the hall was no longer sufficient; in 1437 the city planned the building of a special house for banquets and dances, which was completed between 1441 and 1452: the Gürzenich. Here the senate received the Emperor Frederick with his son Duke Maximilian in 1472. According to the *Koelhoffscher Chronik*, the emperor wished to see not only the city's canon but its beautiful women. Duke Maximilian had the first dance with a canoness from St Ursula's, a noble maiden from the house of Finstingen. Then the archbishop of Mainz and Trier saw to it 'that the women and girls took each other by the hand in pairs and danced up and down without men in front of the emperor.' The guildhouses were also places of conviviality.[69]

But there was another side to Cologne's everyday life and its

[67] Ibid., vol. 1, p. 10 (6 March 1327).
[68] P. Fuchs, *Das Rathaus zu Köln*, (1973), pp. 78ff.
[69] Cf. the list in H. Keussen, *Köln im Mittelalter. Topographie und Verfassung* (1918), p. 143*.

festivities. The lives of the many inhabitants of the city who belonged to the lower middle class or the upper stratum of the lower class were very different. In earlier times even the terraced houses of Cologne were not so close together; between them were open passages leading to outbuildings at the back, wells and courtyards, but serving primarily as conduits for rainwater and effluents from the houses. As a result of the increasing density of population they were gradually built over, being incorporated in the adjacent houses, or having small shopping booths or rented houses built on them. This can be shown to have begun in the twelfth century. It made firewalls and roof supports necessary. The rented houses, above all, were terraced without alleys. They stood with their eaves facing the street, 'so that they lacked garrets and gables, the true signs of independence and property of one's own' (Vogts). Such rows of dwellings are found particularly at farms, probably to accommodate the labourers. Sometimes they were united under a roof, like the 16 houses erected by Gottschalk and Gerhard Overstolz, between 1224 and 1233, on the site of the old Zederwald farmstead, which gave its name to the present-day Strasse Unter Sachsenhausen (Sachsen coming from *Sechzehn* – sixteen). In the fourteenth and fifteenth centuries not all the crafts journeymen belonged to the master's household; married journeymen were able to meet their own living costs. There were many single women, including a large number in straitened circumstances. For Cologne we must assume a surplus of women. As the city operated primarily with indirect taxes, the source material for an exact calculation of the population is poor.

A marginal group in Cologne society were the prostitutes.[70] As Graus shows, they first became a peripheral group in the late Middle Ages as a result of 'ghettoization' (confinement to certain streets) and 'stigmatization' (distinguishing marks). A precondition for this was their growing number. This process can be observed in Cologne. As early as the end of the thirteenth century a brothel existed in the Schwalbengasse near the Berlich, with the apt name 'domus Sconevrouwe' (house of beautiful women). This district, originally rather remote from the city, was again a main prostitutes'

[70]   Ibid., p. 135; Irsigler, 'Bettler, Dirnen und Henker im spätmittelalterlichen und frühneuzeitlichen Köln. Zur Analyse sozialer Randgruppen' (1980). On the general area cf. F. Graus, 'Randgruppen der städtischen Gesellschaft im Spätmittelalter' (1981).

quarter in the fifteenth century, but prostitution became established in all parts of the city. Sometimes the prostitutes lived near monasteries. In 1436, women of easy virtue lived in the Streitzeuggasse, where they were a hindrance to worship by the friars, who bought the house to gain some respite. Thus it was first by private arrangements that people tried to keep the harlots away from churches and convents. It was only in 1455 that the council began to make serious efforts to limit the 'nuisance' to two streets, having been content up to then with regulating the dress of harlots, the most important feature being a red headscarf, or with pronouncing that any 'common daughters who walk in the cathedral yard, the Haymarket or in the fields' should be handed over to the executioner. At that time the Berlich and the Altengrabengässchen became the main centre of prostitution. All the city's prostitutes had to give the executioner six Cologne pence per week, and the 'common daughters' of Rodenkirchen had to disburse a bottle of wine or every third penny of their income; the same applied to those of Mechteren, who were also under the executioner's supervision. The prostitutes newly arrived in the city had to pay the executioner 4 shillings as a kind of membership fee, and then 6 pence every week.[71] The control of prostitutes by the executioner is also found in Augsburg.

Near the harlots' quarter in the Altengrabengässchen was the foundlings' house. In the students' quarter, which formed the southern part of the Niederich district, the activities of the prostitutes had become so troublesome by 1484 that the council, urged on by the protestations of the three grammar schools situated there, prohibited the prostitutes from living in the Strasse Unter Sachsenhausen, the Komödienstrasse and the Marzellenstrasse. In the sixteenth century — again without decisive results — attempts were variously made to confine the prostitutes to a kind of barracks, to 'convert' them, and to achieve a certain social integration. The counterpart to the brothel, the Magdalenenhaus for reformed harlots, existed from about 1470 in the Convent of Bethlehem on the Eigelstein. The council tried to take action against pimps and procuresses, to eliminate at least one of the causes of prostitution.[72] Women caught procuring were to be

[71] W. Stein, *Akten zur Geschichte*, vol. 1, p. 768 (1435).
[72] Ibid., vol. 1, p. 693 (1437); vol. 2, p. 352 (mid-fifteenth century); Korsch, *Das materielle Strafrecht der Stadt Köln*, p. 83.

arrested, put in the stocks, branded and whipped from the town.
Innkeepers male and female, especially at the Marsportze, were
forbidden to allow burghers or their children, who had a dwelling
of their own in Cologne or were someone's lodger, to sleep at their
inns. Beer could be drawn only by brewers in open public houses.
It was particularly forbidden to the wholesalers who kept beer
taverns, because 'many sinful, shameful and inhuman things were
done by night and day' in these houses, and a 'wicked, loose, wild
and useless company of men and women was housed' in them.
The council tried to find work for the men and women, the rabble,
highwaymen and idlers who came to Cologne from other countries
or other parts of Germany; if they were not prepared to earn their
bread they were to be driven out of the town and, if they came
back, were to have their necks shackled and to be stripped and
whipped out of town.[73] In other words, these problems remained
unsolved.

Holy Cologne, the city was sometimes called. With good reason?
Many of the prostitutes bore the sobriquet of *Pfaffenhuren*, priests'
whores. Concubinage was certainly widespread among the clergy.
It often resembled marriage as in the case of Hermann Goch, i.e.
a long-lasting partnership which took care of the children and, if
possible, legitimized them.

In France,[74] the attempt of the pious Louis IX to drive the
harlots from every town and village was ineffective. Although, in
Paris, there had been a convent for reformed prostitutes since
1226, to which Louis paid a considerable annual allowance, it did
not by any means have room for all the repentant *filles de joie* of the
city. Here too it was only possible to restrict prostitutes to particular
areas. Such quarters, squares and streets, have been shown to
have existed in London, Venice, Bologna, Dijon, Amiens, etc. In
Paris these areas are very extensive, as is shown by Geremek's
map in his study on Parisian marginal groups. With probably
80,000 inhabitants at the beginning of the fourteenth century,
Paris was the largest city north of the Alps. Is prostitution here,
Geremek asks, a trade like any other? When, at the end of the
twelfth century, the Parisian *filles de joie* wished, like the other craft
corporations, to donate a stained-glass window for the cathedral
then being built, the bishop refused. The canon and theological

[73]   Stein, *Akten zur Geschichte*, vol. 2, pp. 353, 499.
[74]   B. Geremek, *Les marginaux parisiens aux XIVe et XVe siècles* (1976).

scholar Thomas Cobham took the view that as long as the women did not perform their work for the sake of lust, their earnings might well be used for good causes. At any rate, this trade was subject to the usual regulations governing crafts in Paris, which interestingly include a prohibition on night work; this is not so incomprehensible if one imagines all the dangers lurking in the barely lit streets of nocturnal Paris in those centuries. Geremek does not consider that a guild of harlots in Paris can be assumed to have existed, and believes a fellowship more probable. But despite elements of integration — despite a certain tolerance even on the part of the law — the world of prostitutes, pimps and procuresses existed on the margins of society.

From the twelfth century, encluses (women who had themselves locked in a cell next to a church) are known to have existed in Cologne. For the fourteenth and fifteenth centuries, a number of such hermitages, containing up to 11 women, can be identified. For example, in 1371 the convent of St Cecilia allowed a window to be made in the wall of the chapel of St Michael so that the occupants of the newly established hermitage could assist at mass and receive the sacraments. The last foundation of this kind was at the convent of Mariengarten; a hermitage for six nuns was founded in 1459. A barred window was made in the wall of the convent church, giving a view of the altar and communion.[75]

The number of Beguine convents in Cologne increased sharply in the late Middle Ages. In 1320 there were 89 beguinages in Cologne, more than in any other European city. In the fourteenth and fifteenth centuries their number grew rapidly, and between 1506 and 1634 there were five further foundations. In all 169 convents are recorded,[76] but not all of them existed simultaneously. The smallest, the cell on the Komödienstrasse, housed two Beguines, while the largest, Busse or Bethlehem on the Eigelstein, had room for 50. The average number of inmates was about 12. Some convents were open only to kinswomen of the founder, but most to all the women of Cologne. Some were well-equipped and allowed the Beguines to pursue their religious vocation without worrying about subsistence; many owned only the house in which the convent was situated. Its occupants had to work for their

[75] J. Asen, 'Die Klausen in Köln' (1926).
[76] Keussen, Köln im Mittelalter, pp. 150 ff; J. Asen, 'Die Beginen in Köln' (1927).

living. As a statistical comparison: there were 85 convents in Strasburg, 57 in Frankfurt, 55 in Hamburg, 28 in Mainz, 16 in Worms, 6 in Essen, 5 in Lübeck. Members of more than 40 patrician families of Cologne belonged to such convents. The free Beguine life gave way more and more under the pressure of the church's counter-measures, and in the fifteenth century the religious impulse was confined to the foundation of convents; everywhere women showed a willingness to accept rules. The economic activities of the Beguine convents were viewed with suspicion by the guilds, and restrictions were imposed on them. [77] The tending of graves or the visiting of the sick by Beguines was tolerated, but their weaving and embroidery gave offence. The silk-weavers saw them as cheap labour who might have fake silk foisted on them. Accordingly, a decree of the council of 1469 sought to prevent the working of silk in Beguine and other convents.

The council disapproved of the increase in the size and numbers of the convents. For this meant an unwelcome increase in property owned unproductively, and threatened a loss of taxation if the Beguines took advantage of all the privileges of the clerical estate. Conflicts over the privileges of the clergy were commonplace at the time. Finally, the council feared commercial competition from the poorly-endowed Beguine convents. In 1482 it forbade the convents of Struynden and zum Mummersloch to amalgamate and to fit a chapel with church windows. It ordered that the building be restored to its previous state,[78] and instructed the stonemasons and carpenters not to undertake any new building for Beghard or Beguine houses and convents.[79] In 1487 the senate appointed a commission to investigate the reform of the Beguine order. It soon presented a lengthy report[80] which recommended the amalgamation of small convents in order to recover houses for burgher use. The number of Beguines was to be reduced by letting many convents die out, that is, by allowing no new admissions: 'The 12 persons in the cells in the Smeirstrasse are to remain so and not to increase their number, for they are poor

[77] Stein, *Akten zur Geschichte*, vol. 2, p. 383 (1459): ban on domestic mills for clergy and Beguines; p. 575, no. 430 (1482) and pp. 659f, no. 498 (1499): ban on mills in the houses of burghers and Beguines.

[78] Ibid., no. 423, p. 571.

[79] Ibid., no. 457, p. 594.

[80] Ibid., no. 463, pp. 624f; no 507, pp. 687ff.

destitute sisters who beg their bread and care for the sick.' The poverty of many convents emerges clearly from the report: 'Item, there is an old person in the house next to the Haus zum Kessel; it is a dilapidated old house and the occupant should be placed in a hospital and the house used for other Beguines.' The resolution passed by the council on the basis of the report leaves 17 houses to the convents, making 48 available to the community. Annuities and *Ingedoms* (furniture) are allocated to the houses that remain. The council also wishes to know how the Beguines are to support themselves in future 'so that too much is not taken from the parish.' Rules are also to be established, for example ordering prayers for the founders. The reforms were discussed in Poppelsdorf by a deputation from the council and the archbishop or his chancellor. One Beguine convent is known to have been engaged in the education of girls. This was, however, a somewhat peculiar case. The convent concerned was the 'Zor Buyssen' on the Eigelstein. At the beginning of the 1470s the Cologne council had turned it into an institution for the rehabilitation of fallen women, but had to intervene as early as 1472 to quell a rising of the reformed sinners against the mother superior. In 1476 the convent was put under the spiritual guidance of the Augustinian hermits. It attracted many new members, having 63 inmates in 1486. The senate ordered that the number should be allowed to fall to 50 and that no children or girls from Cologne or elsewhere should be taken on to be educated, as was customary in other convents; the children and girls at present in the convent should be sent away within three days.[81] The council evidently did not have much confidence in the aptitude of these women as educators. The convents still did not solve all the problems of poor single women.

The schools of the Cologne *Damenstifter* are sure to have been reserved for the nobility, but the parish schools were open to burghers' daughters.[82] The Cologne trading magnate Slossgin sent his daughters, at the age of six or seven, to the parish schools of St Brigiden and Klein St Martin, where they stayed until they were 10 or 11. Then the elder was put to work in her father's business while the younger was to be apprenticed as a silk-maker, but both died young. Whether they were taught together with the boys

[81] Ibid., no. 452, pp. 590f.
[82] Oediger, *Vom Leben am Niederrhein*, p. 36, pp 389ff.

cannot be determined. Girls had no access to the university, the principal reason being that the members of the university were largely clerics, or had at least taken some orders. Of the 31 students who matriculated under one rector in Cologne, 30 were clerics or priests. We have already mentioned that it was not 'economic' to pay the enormous fees for a girl, although humanistic enthusiasm may sometimes have induced a father to turn his daughters into scholars. The *Koelhoffsche Chronik* reports that in the year 1489 a very learned youth of 18 from Groningen had come to Cologne; he had mastered every subject:

The words flowed from him like water without obstacles. He knew the Bible and was so proficient in the books of holy doctrine and the pagan poets that words came from his lips without any difficulty. He had several brothers and a sister who were all very well educated, with beautiful Latin, so that everyone who heard them speak could not have enough and never tired of listening to them. Their father is called Meister Johan Canter and is a doctor of the seven liberal arts, of medicine, the two laws, spiritual and secular, and the holy scripture. This venerable, famous and very learned man has a wife who is also very learned and has many sons and daughters to whom he taught Latin as soon as they could speak. So his children can speak Latin rather than German, and in his house no language other than Latin is used. And his maid is also so learned that she speaks good Latin. His daughter is called Ursula and is so learned in natural and divine arts and at the same time speaks such excellent Latin that she can answer all scholars in such a masterly way that nothing like it has been heard for many hundreds of years. And they cannot marvel enough that out of a female mouth such balanced and brave words come. This admirable and virtuous Ursula was taught from her earliest days like her brothers to speak Latin. And because of her great learning in all the arts she must be counted among the most learned women who have ever lived, of whom the city of Groningen and all Friesland can be proud. The daughter is still living with her dear parents in virgin purity.

This was an exception, of course, but a very revealing one. It shows us the enthusiasm that could value a non-vocational humanistic education as an end in itself, and share it with the whole household. A very modern spirit reigned in the house of this Groningen scholar, the house of Johannes Canter, his wife Abele, his sons Jacobus, Petrus, Andres, and 'the wonder of the world', Ursula.

If we called Cologne an exception, we did not mean that parallels could not be found, in one respect or another, for the position of women there. A recurrent feature is the intermarrying within the patriciate, the importance of advantageous marriages for social advancement. This is primarily but not only true of the large cities; it also applies to medium-sized towns such as Neuss.[83]

Neuss, in the late Middle Ages a town with about 5,000 inhabitants, had a definable upper class. One had to marry into it, as did Jakob Vormann, who exchanged vows with a patrician's daughter Agnes von Hege in 1314. The daughter from this marriage, Agnes, apparently an only child, first married Reinhard von Gohr, from a family of the rural nobility which had settled in Neuss; her second husband was Rutger von Uckelheim. Agnes was widowed for a second time in 1359 (at the latest), at the age of 43, and lived until at least 1389. She was commercially successful, buying bonds, land and houses in and around her native town, and like other members of the Neuss upper class she even owned a house in Cologne. Wisplinghoff calls her 'commercially the most active and successful woman in Neuss in the fourteenth and fifteenth centuries.' She was involved in the wine trade among others.

Bonn, situated to the south of Cologne, was no more than a middle-sized town in the late Middle Ages, smaller and economically less important than Neuss. While Neuss had considerable long-distance trading links, Bonn was the central market for a fairly limited area. The formation of guilds only began there towards the end of the fifteenth century. The minute-book of the shoemakers' guild, begun in 1483, shows clearly how the guild evolved from a pious confraternity.[84] Married couples belonged to the confraternity, whereas master shoemakers joined the guild. But any guild member could obtain master's rights for his son or his wife for relatively low fees. A wife who was made a *Meistersche* during her husband's lifetime could 'use the guild' as a widow, i.e. carry on her deceased husband's business. If this precaution had not been taken, the widow had, as the custom was, to 'win', i.e. acquire membership, but she was in any case allowed to sell 'from an open window' any finished goods and the leather in stock on

[83] E. Wisplinghoff, *Geschichte der Stadt Neuss*. (1975), esp. pp. 202ff and 221ff.
[84] E. Ennen, *Geschichte der Stadt Bonn*. (1962), pp. 129ff.

her husband's death. The guild's minute-book repeatedly contains entries to the effect that a master has made his son or wife a master or *Meistersche*. A widow could stand down from mastership in favour of an adolescent son. Apart from this widow's right — widespread in different forms — women did not have many opportunities to take part in the commercial life of Bonn in the Middle Ages. The lists[85] of persons assembled by Josef Dietz from fragmentary remnants refer only to women bakers, female shopkeepers and market traders, and washerwomen.

From these three examples a clear relation emerges between the level and diversity of the economic life of a town, and the opportunities women have to play an independent part in it.

How did patrician and commercially active women fare in the Flemish capital of **Ghent**? In the twelfth century Ghent was an important trading and exporting city.[86] Ghent cloth — thanks to the unsurpassed English wool it used, Flemish cloth was among the best available — was exported to Genoa before 1225, and was distributed from there throughout Italy, the Middle East and North Africa. Southern and western France and Spain were other markets for Flemish cloth. The Hansa merchants took it to northern Germany and the border regions on the Baltic; they also went to southern Germany and as far as Vienna and Hungary. Ghent's links with England and the Rhineland were very close. As their return freight the Ghent merchants brought Rhine wine; merchants from the countship of Flanders appear in the records of the Cologne customs about 1050. Cologne finally succeeded in blocking their passage up the Rhine; they had to buy their wine from Cologne merchants. Up to 1302 the city of Ghent was ruled by a patriciate structured on the same lines as that of Cologne, the *viri hereditarii*, rich families which we can trace for centuries in their economic activities, the incumbents of civic offices. They lived in the *Steenen*, fortified houses, and had extensive property and trading links. They bore the title *ser* (Sir) and, like the merchants of the Cologne *Richerzeche*, they married their daughters to patricians of

85   J. Dietz, 'Bonner Handwerker und Gewerbetreibende bis zur Mitte des 17. Jahrhunderts' (1961), pp. 274, 291, 294, 297.

86   H. Ammann, 'Die Anfänge des Aktivhandels und der Tucheinfuhr aus Nordwesteuropa nach dem Mittelmeergebiet' (1957); F. Blockmans, 'Twee patriziers: Een klassieke en een uitwijkeling' (1937); and, *Het Gentsche Stadspatriciaat tot omstreks 1302* (1938).

equal status or to nobles. The Braems family can be traced back as far as the twelfth century. About 1200 they were trading with England. Alexander ser Braemszoon — he died before August 1251 — and his wife Emma had eight children. Their daughter Katharina was married to the Ghent patrician Balduinus le Grutre, their daughter Avezoete to the knight Walter Vilain, a brother of the burgrave of Ghent, who was the official representative of the count. Elisabeth, daughter of the patrician Leo van Sloete, took Geeraard den Duivel, a son of the burgrave, as her first husband, and the knight Willem van Mortagne as her second. The patrician Katharina van de Putte married the knight Filips van Axel, even after the collapse of patrician rule on 5 June 1307. The dowry of this patrician's daughter amounted to about £2,000. From a very rich Ghent family came Ermentrudis uten Hove.[87] In 1204, with her sisters and, especially, with the support and advice of her brother Volker, a prebendary at the church of St Peter at Lille, she established the Hospital of the Virgin, which was moved to Bijloke in 1228. With continued support from the foundress's family it became the main hospital of the city. The beguinages of Ghent go back to the thirteenth century.

About 1300, with an area of 644 hectares within its walls, Ghent was larger than Bruges, Louvain and Brussels. The victory of the Flemish communities over the army of knights led by Philip the Fair of France at Kortrijk marked the fall of the francophile Ghent council and the end of patrician rule. In the fourteenth century trade became less important than craft manufacture in Ghent; Flemish cloth came under strong competition from cloth-producing areas. The labour market shrank. The city adopted protectionist measures, forbidding the import of foreign cloth, the rural manufacture of cloth within a radius of five miles and immigration, also restricting access to the position of master in textile guilds and finally making this position non-hereditary. The situation of women should be seen against this background. They were not admitted as master-craftswomen in any case, being confined to the role of family assistants, and working as spinners and dyers, although their involvement in blue-dyeing was opposed by the male journeymen. The married woman, Aleit van den Potijser, is

---

[87] C. Vleeschhouvers, 'Het beheer van het O.L. Vrouw-hospitaal te Gent en de stichting van de Cisterciënserinnenabdijen O.L. Vrouw' (1971).

shown to have been involved in social unrest about the middle of the century, a very rare case of a woman actively taking sides in a political dispute. These observation on Ghent show how much the relatively good situation of women in the crafts in Cologne and Paris owed to the silk industry.

Women from the Ghent middle classes worked as money-changers and money-lenders. Larger numbers of them are to be found in the innkeeping trade; one independent innkeeper in 1340/43 was Marie Rijm from an eminent Ghent family, widow of the Italian financier Conte Gualterotti. Alice van den Plassche was another independent tradeswoman, who managed the very profitable inn of the Three Kings, patronized primarily by German merchants. Drapery was often a second trade for both men and women. Wives worked in bakeries and breweries, continuing the business as widows. The daughters of these crafts-people received a certain degree of professional training through their work as helpers.[88]

Frankfurt, with its fair, attained the status of a large city in the late Middle Ages, with a population estimated at about 10,000 in 1520. The surplus of women calculated by Bücher has recently met with serious objections.[89] The late emancipation of the citizens of Frankfurt from imposed marriages has already been mentioned; in the thirteenth century the *homines nostri* of the king, the fiscal and palace personnel, became the citizens of Frankfurt.[90] The registers of citizens begin in 1311/12. In documents of the thirteenth century women already appear as citizens. In the fourteenth and fifteenth centuries — as in Cologne — new female citizens are entered in the register. Dilcher suggests they must be merchant women or craftsmen's widows who are practising a trade and running a household. Some resolutions of the council also indicate that women have civic rights. New citizens who marry a female citizen, or a citizen's widow or daughter, are admitted on favourable conditions. Dilcher writes:

---

[88] D. Nicholas, *The Domestic Life of a Medieval City: women, children and the family in 14th-century Ghent* (1985), pp. 11, 26ff.

[89] Wesoly began this tendency in his essay 'Der weibliche Bevölkerungsanteil'; however, it seems important to me to distinguish between findings for the medieval and for the early modern periods.

[90] Dilcher, 'Zum Bürgerbegriff im späteren Mittelalter. Versuch einer Typologie am Beispiel von Frankfurt am Main'.

But even the married woman clearly has a position in civic law over and above the one she receives through her husband. Women are mentioned beside their husbands as *concives* in documents, and one woman is investigated to find out 'whether she is a citizen through her kin and her husband ...' Citizenship therefore depends primarily on having a husband who has a household in Frankfurt, is an established resident and has a hearth. Yet the dependents, wives and children have full associate rights which continue independently after the citizen's death.

The Frankfurt fair attained its international importance in the fourteenth century. The city also had a variety of guild trades, which in the case of wool-weaving developed into an export industry. Bücher's studies on the population and social structures, pioneering in their day, have not yet been superseded, but need to be supplemented and tested by methods now available.[91] Unfortunately, the city archive suffered heavy losses in the Second World War.

For Frankfurt Bücher identified 65 professions in which women were involved; I quote:

The making of ribbons, braid, veils, buttons and tassels is entirely in women's hands. They are involved in tailoring and furriery, glove and hat making; they make wallets and purses, leather patches and stirrup straps. Their activity even extends to the light wood and metal industries: needles and buckles, rings and gold wire, brooms and brushes, mats and baskets, rosaries and wooden dishes are products of their hands. Confectionery seems to have been mainly their preserve; they are almost exclusively in charge of brewing and the production of candles and soap. They predominate in the highly specialized retail trades: vegetables, butter, chickens, eggs, herring, milk, cheese, flour, salt, oil, mustard, vinegar, feathers, yarn and seed are sold almost solely by them. Huckstering and second-hand goods trading, and even the highly developed trade in oats and hay are often in the hands of women. In Frankfurt's bathing rooms 30 or 40 bathmaids served; one could have oneself shaved by tender hands and in taverns one could always hear something played by female musicians – lute and cymbal players, pipers, fiddlers and bellringers. Women copyists and letter printers are found at least occasionally; a female painter is mentioned in 1346 and from 1484 Juttchen, the puppet-painter, is heard of frequently. Women are even used in the town services, not just as midwives and nurses, but as porters

[91]   Cf. Wesoly, 'Der Weibliche Bevölkerungsanteil'.

doorkeepers, lookouts, customs officers and cowherds. Of the 11 persons to whom the council entrusted the money-changing business in 1368, no fewer than six are women. We meet a woman as tenant of the toll-house for linen and another as supervisor and cashier at the city weighbridge. In the fourteenth century, secular shoolmistresses are no isolated phenomenon. Between 1389 and 1497 no fewer than 15 women doctors can be identified by name in Frankfurt, including three Jewish doctors and three eye specialists.[92]

Bücher also found that of 26 persons traceable as hucksters in the years 1424—31, 19 were women, mostly the wives of craftsmen. Frankfurt's rising prosperity is shown in the influx of religious orders;[93] the convent of St Maria Magdalena is founded in 1228, the Katharinenkloster in 1344, a Dominican convent in 1452; there were also 57 beguinages. The fifteenth century brings economic stagnation and a growing number of poor. In 1410 the proportion of those explicitly designated poor in relation to all taxpaxers was 13.7 per cent, but whereas only 7.8 per cent of men were poor, the figure was 33.6 per cent for women. Care of the poor was now largely the business of the council. In 1428 the council entrusted a large endowment to Johann Wiesebeder, a doctor from Idstein; it was later called the 'alms of St Nicholas' since the money was distributed at the Nicolaikirche. The payments were intended for citizens of good reputation who had 'secret cares' at home although they spent their days honourably; for the poor domestics whose wages were scarcely sufficient to keep them alive; for people incapable of working through age or sickness; for pious indigents 'burdened' with children whom they could not feed; for poor devout women in childbed or pregnancy; for poor, honourable and irreproachable daughters of citizens. Every year two girls who wished to marry were to be given 10 florins each for their dowries. The endowment made in 1502 by Elizabeth von Heringer was to be used among other things for the dowries of poor, honourable citizens' daughters, each receiving as much as 20 guilders. These dowry stipends were much sought

---

[92]   Bücher, *Die Frauenfrage im Mittelalter*, quot. in text pp. 21ff; and *Die Bevölkerung von Frankfurt a.M. im 14. und 15 Jahrhundert* (1886); and, 'Die soziale Gliederung der Frankfurter Bevölkerung im Mittelalter' (1887).

[93]   W. Moritz, *Die bürgerlichen Fürsorgeanstalten der Reichsstadt Frankfurt a.M. im späten Mittelalter* (1981).

after. It emerges from written applications to the council which have been preserved that marriage agreements, for example with a craftsman, were sometimes made on condition that the father succeeded in obtaining the money for a dowry. However, the senate first took care to check all the necessary qualifications. The family needed to be poor, the daughter pious, honourable and not yet promised. If the marriage had already been concluded or if the need was not proved, the application was rejected. Even the mediation of an influential man made little difference. If there were any doubts about the reputation of the suitor, the father was advised to look around for another. Sometimes an application foundered because all the funds for the current year had been used up. Couples who received the award not only had to be issued a formal receipt, but to promise that they would 'put it to good use, indulge in no luxuries, have no wedding feast, and not dissipate the money.' It was also expected that the spouses would remain citizens and residents of Frankfurt for a long time (Moritz, pp. 113f).

We have here touched for the first time on an important question: are women especially strongly represented among the lower classes in late-medieval urban society? It appears that this was the case. Maschke notes that, in Lübeck, the small hovels built along the side of a passageway or courtyard for the poor people, were occupied primarily by women, and that in Wismar the proportion of women living in such shacks was 24.8 per cent and in cellars 26.2 per cent, while they made up only 7.8 per cent of the house occupants.[94] He ascertains that the wages of maids were considerably lower than those of male servants, i.e. journeymen, since the latter had learned a trade. In two parishes in Basle in 1451, only 7 per cent of the male servants, but 61.7 per cent of the maidservants, received a weekly wage of 1s.2d, whereas 82.1 per cent of the male servants and only 13.8 per cent of the maids had a weekly wage of 2 shillings and more. Six out of 123 maids received a wage of 4 shillings and over and 51 of 57 male servants. The average annual wage for maidservants was 2 1/2—4 marks or 2—3 1/2 guilders, while for male servants it usually ranged from 5 marks 4 shillings (4 1/2 guilders) to 10 marks and 8 shillings (9 guilders). In Dresden in the same year (1452), the average wage

[94] Maschke, *Städte und Menschen*, pp. 332, 335.

of male servants (40 to 140 groschen) was twice that of maids (20 to 72 groschen).

Individual studies confirm these findings, for example, the analysis of the taxation lists of Trier for 1363/4.[95] **Trier** was an important medium-sized town in the late Middle Ages, the centre of a market area stretching from the middle Rhine between Andernach and Bingen to the east, to Metz, Arlon and St Vith to the west, with the Moselle and the Saar as the main transportation arteries.[96] Trier did not have a network of trading links or a highly developed export trade. The taxation list of 1363/4 is very detailed. The tax was levied on all property, movable and immovable, within and outside the town; taxable wealth included household furniture, gold, silver, inheritance, rent and fiefs. Payment was by a self-assessment which was subject to checks and had to be confirmed on oath. By Jutta Roth's calculation, the three lowest taxation classes accounted for more than half the taxpayers in the city centre, 56 per cent, and according to Annette Winter, 51 per cent of all taxpayers belonged to the lower classes; 12 per cent of the 56 per cent paid nothing owing to poverty. The middle taxation groups 4–6 embrace one-third of taxpayers, the top two classes making up 12 per cent. Winter establishes that of the 600 women on the taxation list, about 63 per cent belonged to the lower classes, and that in many streets the proportion of women from the lower classes exceeded that in the total population by 10–20 per cent. Where there were Beguine convents (only nine are mentioned in the tax lists) and in the weavers' quarters, between 70 and 100 per cent of the women were from the lower classes. Winter assigns 82 per cent of working women to this category, but stresses that not all maids belonged to it. Among linen-weavers, including veil-weavers, 36 per cent of men but only 9 per cent of women reached the average tax sum, and 54 per cent of the men and 90 per cent of the women belonged to the lower class. In the Trier textile trade there are hardly any women with the status of master-craftswoman.

Gerd Wunder has given a vivid account of the citizens of

---

[95]   A. Winter, 'Studien zur sozialen Situation der Frauen in der Stadt Trier nach der Steuerliste von 1364. Die Unterschicht' (1975); J. Roth, 'Die Steuerlisten von 1363/64 und 1374/75 als Quellen zur Sozialstruktur der Stadt Trier im Spätmittelalter' (1976).

[96]   R. Laufner, 'Der Handelsbereich des Trierer Marktes im Spätmittelalter' (1957), pp. 192ff, with map.

Schwäbish Hall,[97] another medium-sized town, but a rich one with its own rural territory. The town's economy was shaped by the salt spring, the basis of its prosperity and its extensive trade, by the Hohenstaufen currency (the heller) and by the territory it controlled as an imperial city, one of the largest in Franconia and Swabia after Nuremberg and Ulm and on a par with Rothenburg. As its upper class Schwäbisch Hall had an urban nobility whose families can be traced with certainty from the thirteenth century. Once Hohenstaufen vassals, they owned the old fortified houses in the city centre, with rich estates, mills, tenanted land and vineyards in the country, and they controlled most of the salt pans, when they were not in the hands of the clergy. The noble families dominated the council until 1512.

In his analysis of the names of the citizens of Hall, Wunder makes the interesting discovery that a better-known or more important family on the mother's side sometimes provides the surname. For example, Hermann Eisenmenger's daughter Lutret's name is used for years instead of that of his son-in-law, who is mentioned only once and not by name, and her son is the young Hans Eisenmenger, who bears the known and respected name of his mother instead of the clearly unfamiliar one of his father. Henslin Otterbach has a son-in-law called Peter Hefner, whose son is called Hans Otterbach, and so on. In Hall, the feminine form of a name ending in *-in* was expressed by the suffix *-hiltin*; Abelin, Negelin, Siferlin therefore have the counterparts Abelhiltin, Negelhiltin, Siferhiltin. The widow of the saltmaker Heinrich Siferlin was thus called Siferhiltin from 1396 on, and when her son Walter Siferlin died soon after 1425, from at least 1432 to 1456 a Siferhiltin again guided the family fortunes. Meanwhile, the original meaning of the ending *-hiltin* – to designate a female bearer of the name Siferlin – had been forgotten, so that widow Siferlin's son was called Heinrich Siferhilt, the ancestor of the large Seiferheld family.

The women of Hall had independent control of their wealth. Here too widows energetically administered the family estate, increasing it and putting it to public use. Among the owners of saltworks listed in 1317, there were 11 women and 39 men. In

[97]   G. Wunder in association with G. Lencker, *Die Bürgerschaft der Reichsstadt Hall von 1395–1600* (1956); G. Wunder, *Die Bürger von Hall. Sozialgeschichte einer Reichsstadt 1216–1802* (1980).

1577 the 20 richest citizens included 6 widows. It is true that the sources do not allow a comprehensive survey of all the activities in which women were involved until the early modern period. Nevertheless, the individual biographical sketches given by Wunder include two from the Middle Ages: 'Guta Veldner, the widow of the councillor Konrad Veltner, appears in documents from 1316 to 1345 and died before 1351.' She worked in the wine trade, owned saltworks, houses and fields, and was one of the richest citizens of the town. When a consortium of Hall citizens reorganized the bankrupt monastery of Komburg, she seems to have provided the major part of the capital. At any rate she retained valuable securities including the monastery library which the abbot had to hand over, and she refused to return it, probably because the loans had not yet been fully repaid. There was even a feud over this; finally emperor Lewis ordered the senate to compel widow Veldnerin and her children to return the Komburg property in exchange for payment. Guta Veldner resisted, knowing herself to be in the right; she was not an irreligious woman, as is shown by an endowment she made to the church shortly before her death. Sibilla Egen, born in Dinkelsbühl the daughter of the burgomaster Hans Egen, a politician involved in alliances between towns, married young Hans von Rinderbach in 1491; he died in 1500. In 1505 the rich young widow made an endowment for alms, and in 1509, with her brother Jeremias, a canon at Eischstätt, she made a donation to the sons of Hall who were studying. She later enlarged these endowments in sympathy with the Reformation, which her second husband supported. The Egen endowments were also intended to help unmarried girls, needy widows and young craftsmen, and to procure the help of the midwives for pregnant women in the country. Sibila Egen died, a benefactress of the city, at about 70.

Let us continue this far-flung survey with **Regensburg**. In its early stages Regensburg[98] resembles Cologne: a bishop's see within Roman walls as the main residence of the Bavarian dukes and as the site of a royal palace which was particularly used by the east Frankish rulers, it seems to surpass Cologne in its role as a leading political centre. In the early and high Middle Ages

---

[98] W. Gauer, 'Urbs, Arx, Metropolis und Civitas Regia. Untersuchungen zur Topographie der frühmittelalterlichen Stadt Regensburg' (1981).

Regensburg is the most important trading centre in the south-east, its influence extending far to the Russian east and the Danube region; from early on it had trading links with Venice. However, its further development did not keep pace with Cologne's, particularly in the growth of exports. All the same, at the end of the Middle Ages it still had the rank of a city, with just 10,000 inhabitants.

There are no women among the travelling merchants of Regensburg, but in the crafts and retail trades they are numerous.[99] They are found in fustian manufacture and in the spice trade; they are predominant in branches of commerce which deal in trifles, selling decorative materials for women: satin, velvet, the silk used for braid and veils, silver thread; and retailing vegetables, fruit, oatmeal, mash, oil and venison. Some of them develop an entrepreneurial spirit: 'Golden' Albrechtin, for example, controlled a large number of small retail booths which were partly her property and partly belonged to church institutions of the town, and two houses on the Watmarkt, in one of which she lived. Regensburg offers another, exceptionally well documented, case of female commercial activity within a husband's trading house, in the person of Margarete Runtinger.[100] The Runtingers' account book from 1368 to 1407 is one of the most comprehensive known ledgers from the Middle Ages, and is available in a well-annotated edition. In 1383 the Runtinger family was the fourth-largest tax-payer in Regensburg. The Runtingers probably came from outside the town and married into the Regensburg patriciate. Matthäus Runtinger, born in 1345, ran the trading house on his own after his father's death in 1389. In his first marriage he married Agnes Püterich, daughter of the richest burgher of Munich at the time; she died in 1337. He then married Margarete Grafenreuther from an old and influential Regensburg family, Matthäuss died in 1407, Margarete three years later. Matthäus was the city treasurer, and often represented Regensburg as an envoy; he was a *Hanssgrave*, an assessor on the senatorial court, a guradian of the hospice of St Catherine and the city's master builder — he had the streets of Ravensburg paved and laid out in large, pleasant squares. He

[99] F. Bastian, 'Das Manual des Regensburger Kaufhauses Runtinger und die mittelalterliche Frauenfrage' (1920).

[100] F. Bastian, *Das Runtingerbuch. Regensburg 1386–1407* (1935–44); W. Eikenberg, *Das Handelshaus der Runtinger zu Regensburg* (1976), incl. W. Boll, 'Zur Baugeschichte des Runtingerhauses in Regensburg'.

provided credit for the city and horsemen and footsoldiers for the tournaments and was a coiner and money changer. He lived in a patrician castle on the fish market — today No. 1, Keplerstrasse — that had been owned by his family since 1367 and which will concern us again. His many honorary offices and his travels in the service of the city made heavy demands, which gave rise to the important role played by Margarete.

The head of the house did not need to go on trading journeys. Buyers gave the wares to a carrier, who was sometimes accompanied by a servant of the house. The chief commodities were spices obtained through Venice, as well as silk cloth and thread and raw cotton, which were worked up in Regensburg and resold as finished products. Cloth was obtained from the Netherlands and western Germany, silver from Bohemia. The Runtingers' main reloading points were Venice, Prague, Vienna and the Brabant and Frankfurt fairs. From 1401 Runtinger ran a drapery shop; thus, despite a recession in cloth he could maintain his revenue by exploiting the whole profit between the original supplier and the retailer. The Runtingers also owned land; the grain supplied by their tenants was partly used up in their large household and partly passed on as a benefice to the tenants of their 11 vineyards, the rest being stored against bad harvests. They also ran a wine tavern. Their household included clerks (never more than three) servants, maids and minting personnel. The Runtingers invested in deals bringing a commission, and put money into bonds. In Regensburg they owned four houses, a part-share in the Augsburger Hof, two orchards, five tenanted farms outside the city and the eleven vineyards mentioned earlier. For ten years Matthäus Runtinger was the mortgagee on the fortress of Adelburg, which was assigned to him and his father in 1384, together with the toll-revenue for iron and salt on the Danube, by the duke of Bavaria against a security of 6,000 guilders.

Of the finest Brussels blue cloth bought in the Brabant in 1395, Margarete Runtinger received 19 ells (the Brabant ell was 69 cm) for a coat and another garment, and she also got the most expensive material of the whole consignment, a half-roll of scarlet material from Maastricht. Margarete was involved in the book-keeping of the trading house. When the assistant Hans Ernst joined the firm, her activity became more sporadic; but as Ernst needed support in his money-exchange calculations that Matthäus could not always provide, Margarete became more heavily involved in the exchange accounts. Her growing familiarity with this department later made it possible for her to perform all its calculations virtually without help for two and a half years. When old age made it difficult for Matthäus to write, he increasingly left the management of the books and the business to his wife. This case is revealing. The fact that it is an isolated example is certainly explained by the rarity of the account books that have been preserved from that time. We can assume that the wives of important merchants often performed such functions.

We also know the house in which Margarete lived and worked. The oldest part of the Runtingers' house consists of a squat tower almost square in section, at once living accommodation and a fortification of the Danube bank and the stone bridge at Regensburg. The first alterations and addition were made in 1260. The tower was extended by a narrow, four-storey structure opening on the courtyard side. The first floor was opened to form a loggia by large, slightly pointed arches above the strong, closed ground floor. These loggias were based on Italian models, but soon went out of fashion in the harsher northern climate. At the time the house was bought by the Runtingers there was a rectangular roof partly covering the courtyard on the southern side of the tower, but leaving enough room for two small courtyards. The entire ground floor had a vaulted roof. At the front of the house this floor served as sleeping space for servants and assistants in the business, and next to this was a room for simple business transactions and temporary storage. The rear part, adjoining the entrance, courtyard and well, was taken up by the kitchen and related offices. Next to the stove a staircase led to the storage cellar. The wine cellar was a vaulted room accessible from the courtyard; the raised position of this shallow vaulting is explained by the danger of Danube floods. The first floor was reserved for festivities, formal visits or the concluding of business deals. The second floor was the domain of the housewife, the daughters and the maids; it was here that family life took place. The rooms on the third and fourth storeys of the former tower were used for storage. It was not possible to store bulky commodities like iron or to accommodate horses and carts in the house; there was a separate warehouse. The house did not have its own chapel. It was furnished with expensive cupboards and chests.

We now turn to the Upper Rhine and finish our tour with **Strasbourg**. The strong economic postion of Alsace in the Middle

Ages was based primarily on viniculture. As far as manufacture was concerned, the output of its cloth industry gave Alsace a place in international trade, though without turning it into an industrial area comparable to the southern Netherlands. Strasbourg cloth is mentioned as a known product much later than cloth from the Maas region, Flanders or Cologne. About 1290 the father superior of the German Dominicans, Hermann von Minden, wrote to his counterpart in Provence, saying that he would have liked to send a good Strasbourg cloth to Provence as a gift, but thought that people there would be used to fine Flemish materials and would have little taste for the coarse, heavy German cloth. Although Strasbourg cloth was not of the best quality, it is to be found in Freiburg/Uechtland in the mid-fourteenth century, doubtless on its way to the fairs at Geneva, and in Lübeck and Regensburg.[101] Women are undoubtedly involved in this Freiburg export industry as owners of some of the craft shops; to what extent cannot be determined from the general texts that have been used so far. Wesoly[102] has recently criticized Gustav Schmoller's fundamental work[103] on the Strasbourg guild of clothmakers and weavers. The documents published by Schmoller include a council resolution of 1330 as the earliest source. It ordains that the women who make 'linen cloth' — e.g. tablecloths and towels — and silk cloth are not to 'serve' with the weavers, unlike those who work on wool cloth, serge, or tapestries, or who employ assistants. The Strasbourg cloth industry was divided between two guilds: weavers and wool-beaters. In the guild register of 1332 the wool-beaters hold fourth place and the weavers eighteenth (!) place among the 25 guilds. The weavers include many linen-weavers, and the wool-beaters the representatives of the supporting trades, e.g. the fullers. They formed the larger and wealthier group and became the actual wool-weavers' guild. It is traceable from 1381, and may earlier have called itself the clothmakers' guild. The more modest weavers' guild clearly endeavoured to bring women who were direct competitors, the wool-cloth weavers, into their guild, doubtless so that they could share the financial burdens. At present the

[101]   H. Ammann, 'Von der Wirtschaftsgeltung des Elsass im Mittelalter' (1955).

[102]   Wesoly, 'Der weibliche Bevölkerungsanteil', pp. 92ff.

[103]   G. Schmoller, *Die Strassburger Tucher- und Weberzunft. Urkunden und Darstellung* (1897).

full list of the many domestic industries still operating in Strasbourg at that time — linen-weaving and a small amount of silk-weaving, likely to have been mainly veils — is still a matter for discussion. The council's resolution applies to both the male and the female weavers, and is confirmed four years later. In the first register of the cloth-makers — before 1334 — 77 clothmakers including 7 fullers are listed, as well as 39 women — are they only widows and single women, as Ammann supposes? — who helped the craftsmen. In the fifteenth century the relationship between the weavers on one hand and the veil and linen-weavers on the other is resolved to the effect that the women have to contribute to the funds of the weavers' guild, although they do not need to perform military services and suchlike. They are, therefore, incorporated in the guild, though not quite as full members, I would suppose, as was the case with Strasbourg women generally, being excluded from the guild's governing body and playing no economic part in it. The female veil-weaver or linen-weaver who has one loom contributes 6 Strasbourg pence, the one who has two looms 1 shilling, and for three or more, 18 pence. Clearly some women have large workshops. Of the 'maidens' mentioned by name in the documents, Wesoly has identified two as members of old Strasbourg families. If *swester* preceded a name it may have indicated that the person was a Beguine; in Strasbourg as in Cologne the Beguines for a long time came from patrician or wealthy families.[104] But laywomen are also explicitly mentioned as weavers of veils and linen. As it was decided that members who have one loom pay the same dues as those who have two, three or more, small religious communities of women may have been incorporated. A resolution of 1484 explicitly mentions veil-weavers who work for wages or sell their products; they are to contribute a shilling a year. But if a woman wishes to weave half-cloth — this is now considered the most serious female competition — she may only have one loom; she pays 2 shillings a year. However, 'if a woman wants to do more, to produce master's work and keep more than one loom, she must pay an entrance fee of 30 shillings and must do full service but no night work. But a woman who has worked in this way up to now may work as prescribed and does not have to pay an entrance fee.' 'Thus the new rule has no retrospective force. Moreover, this passage contains clear evidence that there

---

[104] Schmitt, *Mort d'une hérésie.*

were independent master-crafts-women in the Strasbourg cloth industry. At the end of the fifteenth century, when there was strong competition in the cloth trade, access to master status for women is made considerably more difficult. Strasbourg's output of cloth was 1,800 to 2,000 bales a year at the end of the fifteenth century, so that it was not a major cloth-producing city. The resolution of 1484 presupposes that the master-crafts-woman keeps female apprentices. The apprenticeship agreement, however, is not to be concluded or registered before a court, unless a dispute has arisen. A somewhat later resolution, not precisely dated, attempts to impose a vigorous restriction: women, whether Beguines or lay people, are only to weave veils and not half-cloth or masterpieces, 'that is the main work from which the majority of weavers must live.' Now the contracts of female apprentices must be made before a court, 'so that they know that they are to be taught, otherwise they will learn how to make half-cloth, middle-cloth and masterpieces, and will not learn what it is necessary and fitting for them to do.' The attitude of the Strasbourg weavers' guild to working women and women's membership is entirely governed by the question of competition. Lacking political rights, the women can do little to help themselves when demand declines and they find themselves elbowed out.

How did women dress in this burgher world with its taste for enjoyment and luxury?[105] First, they wore a vest – as Arnegundis had done; it is the oldest and for a long time the only under-garment of women. As early as the eleventh and twelfth centuries vests began to be given a degree of luxury; knight's wives were fond of silk vests, and that of Arnedgundis was of fine linen. In the fourteenth century the vest was laced tightly to the upper body. In the early and high Middle Ages women and men wore a half-length linen shift under their long overgarment, held by a belt at the hips. Under the woman's dress, from the high Middle Ages on, an undergarment was worn that was made visible in various places. In the twelfth and thirteenth centuries it was particularly the long, tight sleeves and the ornamental border that showed beneath the overgarment. When, in the fourteenth century, the dress itself was made close-fitting with a loose, flowing skirt and a large décolleté, the undergarment was often omitted. But it had to

[105] L. C. Eisenbart, *Kleiderordnungen der deutschen Städte zwischen 1350 und 1700* (1962).

be worn with the *sorkot* or *Sukenie*. This was a woman's dress of French origin. (The name comes from *Sorkottim*, a long-sleeved ecclesiastical robe, and from *Suknie*, Polish woollen material.) In the thirteenth century there were two forms of this sleeveless dress, which was much worn about 1300 in Germany: one with very tight armholes, and another with large oval openings for the arms which reached to the hip and showed the tightly-laced undergarment. Later, the openings at neck and sleeves became so large that the *Sorkot* became a narrow tunic covering breast and back; it was also slit from the hem to knee-height. In this form the *Sorkot* was purely decorative. In the thirteenth century it was often worn long, trailing on the ground, with an undergarment and cloak; in the fourteenth, it was shortened so that the undergarment was visible up to the knee. Laws on clothing always mention undergarments in connection with a particular overgarment; they were not an item of underwear like our petticoat, but a part of the outer clothing; women simply wore one expensive garment over another.

The sumptuary laws on clothing of the fourteenth century did not take exception to the costliness of materials so much as to the fashion of tight lacing which – as we have seen – had even extended to the vest. From the end of the fifteenth century there are undergarments made of damask, satin, velvet, *Tobin* (double taffeta) or *Zendal* (a silk material in the thirteenth century, later a thin lining material), and ones which have fur borders, broad velvet trimmings, embroidery and quilted seams. The *Tappert* and the *Schaube*, a long mantle, primarily men's overgarments, were also worn by women. The *Tappert* was a close fitting, belted garment made with an ample use of cloth. Whereas men decorated its bottom edge with slashes, the woman's *Tappert* had wide, fur-lined hanging sleeves reaching to the ground; it was made of cloth, velvet and silk and held by a silver belt. The *Schaube* developed from the *Tappert* at the end of the fifteenth century. Women wore *Schauben* trimmed around the neck and down the front with borders of velvet, damask, satin and silk, edged with ermine, *Lassitz* (an expensive greyish-white fur) and minever, and lined with fur and *Schetter* (stiffened glossy linen). In the north-German sumptuary laws passed between 1340 and 1612, *Heuken* – sleeveless smocks worn as a woman's cloak, usually pulled over the head or fastened to the head by a cap or comb – were treated as a standard item of women's clothing. Wealthy women had several *Heuken*, and in

Hamburg even maids had everyday and Sunday versions. They were made of fabric, when they were called *Wandesheuken*. In Hamburg they were red, in Lübeck brightly coloured. In Göttingen about 1350 they were richly adorned with buckles and beads, braid and trimming and, in the fifteenth century, with fur lining. The typical thirteenth century cloak is the *Tesselmantel*, a semicircular cape held by a string fastened by two clasps (*Tassel*). The *Nuschenmantel* is cut tighter, and closed in front by a buckle (*Nusche*). The women's cloak has the same cut as the men's but is always worn with the clasp at the front. *Tassel-* and *Nuschenmantel* are also favoured by women in the fourteenth century, as is the hooded cloak, for practical reasons. The cloak, to which fashion sometimes added a train, is open at the front. In the time of scanty dress, when the décolleté grew ever larger, it was given a firm edge allowing it to be kept to the height of the neck opening, to which it was fixed with a brooch. In the fifteenth century the cloak's neckline rises again, and often ends with a small stand-up collar. According to the sumptuary laws the cloaks of the fourteenth century were made of velvet and silk or trimmed with silk and fur at the neck, along the bottom hem and along the front edges. The neck fastener was embroidered with silk loops. In Speyer women wore embroidered hoods on their cloaks.

The art of hairdressing was highly developed. The hair was anointed, treated with egg-white and twisted up into elaborate curls. It was exposed to sun and frost to attain the coveted blonde colour, and false hair was often used. Long plaits were worn, coiled up on the head, held in a net, or hanging down. The hair was often entwined with gold threads and strings of beads. The most important women's head-dress between 1225 and 1320 was the *Gebende* or wimple, which tightly framed the face and wreathed the head. It was usually of white linen and was made of a strip of cloth that was tied round the chin and an upright part that was placed on the head like a wreath. The *Gebende* was often combined with the *Schappel*. This was originally a wreath of fresh flowers, but was replaced by artificial flowers, embroidered bands, braid, peacock feathers, gold and silver. It was worn like a coronet, and was at first the prerogative of girls and youths, but from the mid-twelfth century it was also used by married women in conjunction with the *Gebende*. The most important head-dress of married women in the early and high Middle Ages was the veil. When the *Schappel* and *Gebende* were in vogue, a veil was often worn over them. From the fourteenth century the bonnet became popular; it evolved from the headscarf, which was pinned in intricate folds.

Who could afford all that? The poorer women benefited from the circumstance that in the Middle Ages people were not fond of either simplicity or thrift. The rich merchant's wife gave her cloak to her maid well before it was worn out. The second-hand clothes trade was very extensive and replaced the ready-to-wear ranges of the department stores of today. There was little ready-made clothing in the Middle Ages. The town councils tried to curb the obvious luxury of the upper class by restrictive laws — as we saw in the case of festivities in Cologne. Legislation on clothing began later in Germany than in Italy, Spain and France, in about the middle of the fourteenth century. It was a specifically urban affair. In the towns, above all, wealth had increased by leaps and bounds. Real administrative activities developed there while the kings and their representatives in Germany were still content to dispense justice and keep the peace themselves, though they too began to evolve a financial administration. It was only the local German rulers who exercised any extensive 'policing', and later issued their own regulations on clothing, as the towns had done earlier. These laws usually apply to all citizens, poor and rich. Some 'staggered' legislation made distinctions:

The earliest Göttingen law of 1342 allowed a *Hoyke*, a *Sorkot* and a skirt of good wool to be worn only by women whose husbands owned property valued at at least 90 marks. With wealth of more than 45 marks women can still wear all three garments, but only of lesser materials. And the poorest women have to do without a *Sorkot* entirely, and be content with skirt and cloak. (Eisenbart)

These laws do not express an endeavour to distinguish between 'estates' — this only happened towards the end of the fifteenth century. Two motives are uppermost in the councils' laws: the fight against exaggerated luxury and against immorality. They could prevent neither. The thinking behind the council resolutions was clear: a genuine concern that the pride and arrogance which manifest themselves in luxury might provoke divine wrath, endangering the earthly prosperity of the citizens and thus the common good, and a conservative temper that made 'ancient customs' its standard, as was understandable at a time of political unrest.

As early as the thirteenth century the moral concept of civic arrogance is clearly delineated in the sermons of Berthold of Regensburg. Berthold finds such pride not only among the rich who wish to display their wealth — although they seem to him particularly imperilled: 'And thereof speaks the good St Augustine: pride dwells in the man as the maggot in the apple' — but in the poor as well, who have no money for expensive clothes: 'And if they cannot afford fine clothes to show their arrogance, this woman pulls her belt higher, that one turns up the brim of her hat, another struts about while another speaks in an affected voice.' Most imperilled of all, he declares, are women. They are exposed to the temptations of pride beyond all measure, because in their piety, church-going, compassion and chastity they offer the Devil few other openings. But they pride themselves on their husbands, their beauty and their children. They show presumption even in church; they want to walk to the communion rail before everyone else. They are untiring in the discovery of new ornaments for themselves and are never satisfied with materials as God made them, red and green, yellow and blue, black and white, but want to make them as colourful and speckled as birds' feathers. (Eisenbart, p.90)

When the council of Speyer publishes its clothing laws in 1356, with the justification that it has noticed the 'great luxury and arrogance that are now abroad in the towns and the country, which is the first sin', it voices the same attitude as was expressed in the sermon. How well-stocked the wardrobe of a burgher's wife could be is shown by the legacy of a Nuremberg woman of the fifteenth century. It contained 4 cloaks of Arras and Malines cloth — i.e. Netherlandish material — 2 of them lined with silk, 6 skirts, 1 *Schaube*, 3 *Tapperte*, 3 undergarments, 6 white aprons and 1 black (probably worn for housework), 2 white dressing gowns, 5 under-vests, 2 chemises, 7 pairs of sleeves and 19 veils. The citizen of Regensburg, Diemut Hiltprand, née Neumburger, in her will of 26 June 1308, disposes of 1 green and brown cloak, 3 *Sukenien*, one of silk and a new scarlet one, 2 matching skirts, as well as 1 fur-trimmed skirt, 1 good fur skirt and 2 long dresses, one of them embroidered with beads. Among various pieces of jewellery she mentions 3 silver belts and 5 gold brooches. In women's clothing it was above all the low décolleté that aroused disapproval, and in it an eroticism of dress did indeed show itself to an extent unknown in the early and high Middle Ages. About 1375, the senate of Strasbourg decreed:

No woman, whoever she may be, may henceforth constrict her breasts, either with vests or with laced dresses or any other lacing-in. No woman may paint her face or wear false hair. Above all, her décolleté should not be so low that her breasts can be seen. The neckline should not be lower than the armpits, on pain of paying 5 marks. Nor shall any woman from the country, whoever she may be, wear a dress that costs more than 30 florins to a dance in this town. And if one of our citizens shelters overnight a woman from the country who wears an expensive dress, he also pays a fine of 5 marks, unless it be a noblewoman, to whom this order does not apply. Nor shall any woman wear a short coat or a boy's coat which is shorter than a quarter-ell above the knee, on pain of a fine. Longer coats may be worn.[106]

The council is not only concerned that female citizens should be modestly attired. It also prohibits the living together of couples who are not married, i.e. concubinage,[107] which was clearly no less frequent then than now. Within the jurisdiction of city and castle, it ordains in 1337, no one shall henceforth 'live in concubinage'. The people concerned should marry, and if they cannot because they are already married, they must separate in the following manner: the man and woman shall each take to himself or herself what they first brought into the concubinage and what he or she has inherited during its course. Anything that has been disposed of shall be replaced. What is left over − rent, revenues, property, cash, silver cutlery, furniture, wine, corn, etc. − shall be so divided that the man receives two-thirds and the woman one-third. Tha same division applies to the education and provision of children. If the two stay together despite this ruling, half of their property shall be confiscated by the city of Strasbourg.

In the towns we have considered so far, no major differences in the education of boys and girls have been observed in burgher circles. Many women, particularly merchants, could read, write, add up figures and keep their own or their husbands' accounts. But after about 1350 a development from which girls are excluded begins in the towns. In increasing numbers, the sons of burghers attend universities in far-off places, Italy and France, as well as newly-founded universities within the German empire, in Prague, Heidelberg, Cologne, Erfurt, Vienna, Leipzig, etc. The universities were outstripping monastic scholarship and education. They breached the traditional order of the estates − burghers' and even farmers' sons could study there. They raised a new social barrier

---

[106] Keutgen, *Urkunden zur städtischen Verfassungsgeschichte*, no. 355, pp. 455f.
[107] Ibid., no. 358, p. 457.

which has remained effective until today, between the educated person and the 'layman'. Just as the concept of the cleric has widened and shifted its meaning — most clearly in the English 'clerk' — referring not only to the clergy but to all who have studied, so the word 'lay' takes on a new meaning, being no longer a distinction from the cleric but from the scholar. At the same time the demand for academics, above all learned lawyers, was increasing. They were needed — especially in connection with the advancing adoption of Roman law — in the lay assessors' courts, the municipal councils and the gradually emerging colleges of government. But they also became notaries, procurators, licentiates, doctors. We have already mentioned one example of the enormous cost of university study, and pointed out that many members of universities were clerics — church livings often being the only way to pay university teachers — and we have indicated the loose morals of students. At that time parents could not even consider sending their daughters to a university. When the humanistic grammar schools emerged at the end of the fifteenth century, attendance by girls was similarly out of the question. Boys' and girls' education now went their separate ways. Thus began a development which has been fateful for women up to the twentieth century. Henceforth women were not only devoid of political rights, but in most cases they lacked the basic prerequisite for a political career. Wachendorf has noted that after 1500 female doctors largely disappear from the documents.[108]

CONDITIONS IN ITALY

What was the situation south of the Alps? The Renaissance begins in Italy after 1300. We use the illustrious concept here mainly to designate an epoch. Let us recall a criterion mentioned in the Introduction[109] — individualism. Burckhardt greeted it emphatically: 'man becomes a thinking individual and recognizes himself as such'.[110] The medievalist will counter this enthusiasm by saying that medieval man felt himself protected within a group — the guild, patrician society, a quarter of the town, the council; that

[108] Wachendorf *Die wirtschaftliche Stellung der Frau*, p. 28.
[109] Ibid., p. 28.
[110] J. Burckhardt, *Die Kultur der Renaissance in Italien* (1928), p. 123 (translated: *The Civilization of the Renaissance in Italy*, 1983).

the constraints exerted by the corporations were not only burden-some but beneficent, blunting rivalries, creating firm norms of behaviour, educating people to serve the common good — and that individualism brought with it much loneliness and coldness which many find hard to bear. Our present knowledge tells us that the Renaissance was not unChristian. However, its typical form of state, the *signoria*, was strongly secularized and marked by absolutism. Venice, however, remained a republic ruled by the nobility. The Great Council, which in 1512 had 1,651 members coming from about 200 families, was closed once and for all in 1510, i.e only members of these families could now be admitted. This is why the women of the Venetian aristocracy were objects of marriage politics to a particularly high degree.[111] Burckhardt again: 'Finally, to understand the higher conviviality of the Renaissance, one needs to know that men and women are made the same. One should not be misled by the subtle and sometimes malicious studies on the alleged inferiority of the fair sex, that are found again and again in the writers of dialogues, nor by a satire like Ariosto's third.'[112] When he then explains that the education of women was 'essentially the same as for men in the highest classes', Geiger points out in his addenda that there was no lack of voices demanding a different education for girls than for boys, and we have seen that women in the highest medieval classes were often better educated than men. Burckhardt emphasizes the active participation of women in Italian poetry, 'with *canzoni*, sonnets and improvizations which made a number of women famous after the Venetian Cassandra Fedele (late fifteenth century); Vittoria Colonna may be called immortal.' Women orators in Latin from the high aristocracy included Madonna Battista Montefeltro, by marriage Malatesta, who composed addresses to King Sigismondo and Pope Martin; Ippolita, the sister of Galeazzo Maria, who greeted Pius II at the congress of Mantua. Caterina Sforza, wife then widow of Girolamo Riario, had the reputation of a virago; she defended her husband's heir with all her strength, first against the party of his murderers and then against Cesare Borgia. She was defeated, but kept the title of 'prima donna d'Italiae'. But Burckhardt states, rightly: 'There was no question of a special,

[111] S. Chojnacki, 'Patrician women in early Renaissance Venice' (1974).
[112] Burckhardt, *Die Kultur der Renaissance in Italien*, pp. 368f.

conscious emancipation, because emancipation was taken for granted.'

We shall take the princely court of Ferrara as an example. Here the modern form of the *signoria* goes back to the thirteenth century. Although the town grew up as a reloading point for trade, the merchant class never had political importance in it. The appearance of the town speaks an unmistakable language even today: its dominant centre is the redoubtable citadel surrounded by moats. In Ferrara the d'Este family ruled practically as absolute monarchs. The most important female figures at this court[113] were Eleanor of Aragon[114] and Lucrezia Borgia. Ercole I d'Este married Eleanor in 1473, a highly educated and cultured woman who was able to manage the affairs of government during his absence. Of his two daughters, the younger, Beatrice, was married to Lodovico il Moro, the ruler of Milan, and Isabella to Francesco Gonzaga of Mantua; she is another of the outstanding intellectual women of the Renaissance, a friend of poets, a patroness of the arts and a zealous collector.[115] Very controversial even within the family was the plan to marry Ercole's son Alfonso to Lucrezia, the notorious pope's daughter, as his second wife.[116] Lucrezia, too, was better than her reputation. This conclusion has been reached by several Italians since 1866 in the light of an extensive study of the sources by Gregorovius, who published his still highly readable biography in 1874:

And if we judge her rightly, she was a woman who had been placed above the common run of her sex not by power but by the grace and charm of her nature. This young woman who has appeared to the Romantic fantasies of posterity like a Medea or an ever-smouldering torch of love, may never have felt a deep passion in reality. In the Roman phase of her life she was always dependent on the wills of others, since her fate was decided first by her father, then by her brother.

In his well-supported biography, which came out in 1932, Bellonci sees Lucrezia as less passive than this.

---

[113]   W. L. Gundersheimer, *Ferrara. The style of a Renaissance Despotism* (1973); F. Gregorovius, *Lucrezia Borgia* (1982); M. Bellonci, *Lucrezia Borgia* (1974).

[114]   L. Chiappini, *Eleanora d'Aragona, prima duchessa di Ferrara* (1956).

[115]   J. Lauts, *Isabella d'Este. Fürstin der Renaissance 1474–1539* (1952).

[116]   H. Diwald, *Anspruch auf Mündigkeit. Um 1400–1555* (*Propyläen Geschichte Europas*, vol. 1) (1975), pp. 88ff.

Lucrezia was born in 1480; her father was Cardinal Rodrigo Borgia, later Pope Alexander VI, her elder brother Cesare Borgia. She was a well-brought-up Roman girl, was as fluent in Spanish as in Italian, spoke French, had adequate Latin and some Greek. Her father, when a cardinal, betrothed her at 11 to a Spanish noble, but as pope he no longer found the match satisfactory, and in 1493 Giovanni, papal vicar of Pesaro, from the powerful house of Sforza, became her husband. Curiously, the heir to the prince of Ferrara, Alfonso d'Este, was also in Rome at the time, to commend his states to the pope. 'So, full of curiosity, he saw for the first time the beautiful child with the golden hair and the intelligent blue eyes' (Gregorovius). The duke of Ferrara, Ercole, sent her a pair of silver washing bowls with accesories as her wedding present. The wedding ceremony on 12 June sealed the political alliance between Pope Alexander and Ludovico il Moro, the regent of Milan, but the invasion by Charles VII of France in September 1494 changed the political landscape of Italy. Alexander's alliance with the Sforzas was no longer of any benefit, and he urged the annulment of Lucrezia's marriage, which allegedly had never been consummated. Lucrezia declared that she was willing to swear as much on her oath, and about that time ugly rumours about her were circulated. Sforza, deeply insulted and furious, was probably the source of the most serious charges, that she was guilty of multiple incest. It was now Alexander's plan to unite his children Cesare and Lucrezia with the royal house of Naples. Thus came about Lucrezia's second marriage, to the nephew of King Federigo of Naples, Alfonso, duke of Biselli. Alfonso was 17, a year younger than Lucrezia. The marriage produced her son Rodrigo. But this union too fell victim to politics. On 15 July 1500 Alfonso was wounded by assassins, and died on 18 August. The instigator was almost certainly Cesare, though strict proof is lacking. Hardly was Biselli out of the way than a new marriage was conceived, to Alfonso, the 24-year-old, childless and widowed, hereditary prince of Ferrara. The plan met strong resistance at the court in Ferrara; the negotiations dragged on. In this period Lucrezia even represented the pope once herself; during his absence she was empowered to open incoming post and take decisions in consultation with a cardinal. Ercole made heavy demands, the pope finally accepted them, and in September 1501 the marriage contract was signed. Apart from political concessions, the dowry was to be 300,000 ducats, excluding the bride's

expensive clothes, jewellery, silver utensils etc. Lucrezia'a entry to
Ferrara on 2 February 1502 was a magnificent spectacle. Seventy-
five bowmen on horseback, 80 trumpeters and 24 pipers headed
the procession, then came the nobility of Ferrara, then Don Alfonso
dressed in the French fashion, then the bride's cavalcade, and the
bride herself, on a white horse draped in scarlet, dressed in a
wide-sleeved *camorra* of black velvet with gold beading; she wore a
sbernia of gold brocade with ermine trimming, on her head a veil-
like net without a diadem, glittering with diamonds and gold, and
around her neck a large necklace of pearls and rubies. Her hair
hung freely to her shoulders. She rode beneath a purple canopy
borne by doctors of the university. A string of 26 mules carried the
bride's wardrobe and treasure, though other reports speak of 150
wagons and as many mules. At that time Lucrezia was of bewitch-
ing beauty: 'She is of medium height and delicate of figure; her
face is oval, her nose of fine profile, her hair bright gold, her eyes
blue. Her mouth is somewhat large, the teeth dazzling white, her
neck slender and white, dignified yet modest. Her whole being
radiates incessant gaiety.'

She was probably glad to leave behind her compromised Roman
past, at the side of a prince of calm and practical character whose
passion was the army, above all the new artillery. A new stage of
her life began at Ferrara. It was at that time a magnificent city,
adorned with many palaces, a centre of culture. By 1474 the
university, opened in 1391, had 75 professors. Ercole enlarged it
and introduced book-printing. Savonarola was a student at Ferrara;
since 1464 Niccolo Leoniceno of Vicenzo had shone there as a
physician, mathematician and philosopher; he was the pride of
Ferrara when Lucrezia arrived. She was celebrated above all by
the poets of Ferrara; by Titus and Ercole Strozzi, father and son,
by Antonio Tebaldeo, Celio Calcagnini, who dedicated a wedding
poem to her, Giraldi, Marcello Filosseno. The handsome, charming
and clever Bembo loved her. In 1503 Ariosto formed a closer link
to Ferrara, and in 1505 he began his poem *Orlando Furioso*. Ariosto, a
great poet, celebrated Lucrezia in the eighty-third stanza of his
epic, in the forty-second canto, where he set up her picture in the
temple in honour of women, borne by Antonio Tebaldeo and
Ercole Strozzi as her knightly witnesses. The inscription asserts
that her native Rome should prize her more for her beauty and
virtue than the Lucretia of Antiquity. In Ferrara, at any rate,

Lucrezia is regarded as a model of virtuous womanhood. On 9 April 1508 she finally bore her husband an heir to the throne. Life at the d'Este court was also marked by conspiracy and bloody crimes. Alfonso's brother Ferrante and his stepbrother Giulio rose against the duke in 1506 (justifiably in Giulio's case), were condemned to death and then reprieved, serving lifelong incarceration instead. On 6 June 508 Ercole Strozzi was murdered, aged only 27 and recently married to the highly-educated Barbara Torelli, who had previously had an unhappy marriage with Ercole Bentivoglio. The deed caused a great sensation: Ercole Strozzi was an accomplished poet, an ornament of the city, a friend of Bembo and Ariosto, a favourite of the duchess and, after the death of his father Titus, the head of Ferrara's 12 judges. He was given a sumptuous funeral, Celio Calcagnini holding the funeral oration – but the murder remained unexplained and unatoned. 'The confusion of opinions is everlasting' (Bellonci). Certainly, Lucrezia had nothing to do with the death. Bellonci suspects that it was committed by enemies of the Torelli, by Bentivoglio or Gian Galeazzo Sforza, in the certain knowledge that it would not be unwelcome to the house of Este.

Ferrara became embroiled in the wars that continued interminably in Italy. Pope Julius II wanted to seize Ferrara from the Este in alliance with Venice. Ferrara, closely allied to France, took part in the bloody war against Venice in the summer of 1512, in which Alfonso's artillery proved decisive at the Battle of Ravenna. During this war the famous Bayard, the legendary knight *sans peur et sans reproche*, made the acquaintance of Lucrezia. His biographer calls her the 'good duchess, a jewel of this world; she was beautiful and kind, gentle and charming to all.' On several occasions Lucrezia conducted the regency with great skill, for the first time in 1506. The year 1513, when the war over Ferrara came to an end, marks a certain turning-point in Lucrezia's life: from then on a tendency towards piety is noticeable. The court of Ferrara lost some of its brilliance through the war, and the Medici pope, Leo X, attracted the outstanding talent of Italy to Rome, including Tebaldeo and Bembo. But Ariosto remained the pride of Ferrara, and Lucrezia witnessed the height of his fame. He immortalized the house of Este.

The relationship between Lucrezia and her husband Alfonso was a good one. She bore him five sons and three daughters, but only three sons and one daughter survived her. On 14 June 1519 she gave birth to a stillborn child and foresaw her own end. On 22 June she wrote to Pope Leo:

And so great is the favour shown to me by our most gracious Creator that I now perceive the end of my life and in a few hours will be parted from it, after receiving all the holy sacraments of the church. And having reached this point, I remember as a Christian, although a sinner, to ask your Holiness graciously to consent to give me the support of the spiritual treasures, and to grant my soul the holy sacrament of benediction. Thus I beg you in humility and commend to your Holy Grace my husband and children.

She died in Alfonso's presence in the night of 24 June.

We shall leave the great women of the Renaissance to their fates and concern ourselves with something more commonplace, the structure of population and family in the city state of Florence in the fifteenth century. A source which is unique of its kind, the *catasto* or land register of Florence of 1427, makes it possible, with the aid of the electronic calculator, to describe this community demographically and anthropologically.[117] The *catasto* embraces the metropolis, the *contado* (country) and the *distretto*, i.e. the previously free city republics now incorporated into Florence, including Pisa (since 1405), Pistoia, Arezzo, Prato, Volterra, Cortona, Montepulcano, Colle and San Gimignano. It therefore allows us to compare conditions in the capital with those in medium and small towns and in the country. The *catasto* was compiled for taxation purposes, by an office specially formed to levy the tax. The basis of the levy is the household (*fuoco*). Herlihy has taken pains to identify all the sources of error that are built into the form and objectives of the *catasto*. In 1427 Florence, which had lost between 60.2 and 69 per cent of its population in epidemics between 1338 and 1426, had 38,000 inhabitants, Pisa 7,330, Pistoia 4,411, S. Gimignano 1,677. The observation often made that a high mortality rate heightens the desire to marry, with a resulting increase in the birth rate, is confirmed here: after

---

[117] D. Herlihy and C. Klapisch-Zuber, *Les Toscans et leurs familles*, (1978) (translated 1985). The study offers a careful analysis of the *cadastre* and uses other statistical sources, as well as the rich literature of the time: L. B. Alberti, *Antonio, Bernardino da Siena* etc.; D. Herlihy, 'Family and Property in Renaissance Florence' (1977).

the plague almost all women wanted to marry, and the patrician families strove for male heirs. Conscious population planning was generally effected through adapting the marrying age, but the city of Florence deviates from this in having a high marrying age among men. The age of marrying for women is generally about 16. Whereas in the country and the smaller towns the average age difference between husband and wife was six years, it was twice this figure in the capital. The proportion of single urban households was large. Many widows moved to the towns for the rest of their lives, increasing the number of non-working inhabitants. In Florence they accounted for a quarter of this group, and often more in the other towns. Women were hardly involved in urban economic life. The capital in female hands remained immobile.[118] In 1536, 15 per cent of heads of households in Florence were women; 72.8 per cent of these women did not state a profession, neither their own nor their husband's. This does not mean that in France — the city and its territory — there were no fully employed working women; there were some, but predominantly in jobs which were economically unimportant or even oppressed. Florentine wool and silk manufacture was organized on capitalist lines at a very early stage. Women worked within it, but only as dependent wage-earners. The female spinners and weavers were generally among the poorest workers in the city of Florence. In the Arte della Lana the full members were merchants, wool importers and cloth distributors; dyers, fullers and weavers were second-class members. Women were represented only as wage labourers. The women spinners lived mainly in the country; the weekly markets of the rural communities gave them an opportunity to take on work and deal with the merchants' agents. The agents paid for piece-work in cash. There were also male spinners, but not so many. The women weavers lived in the more confined conditions of the city, probably for technical reasons. They were dependent workers, usually lacking their own tools. The loom was often provided by the distributor and paid for by work; the money wage

---

[118] E. S. Riemer believes that we can observe in Siena in the thirteenth century the economic activities of women who had free control of their dowries, made money transactions and bought and sold property until they were restricted by legislation in the second half of the century; her study does not show whether women were able to sustain a profession or make profits by such activities, etc.: *Women in the Medieval City. Sources and uses of wealth by Sienese women in the 13th century* (1975).

was low. In the fourteenth century women predominate at the looms. In silk manufacture, too, women had been only dependent workers since the beginning of the fourteenth century.

Only in the guilds of physicians, bakers, oil traders and inn-keepers were women active as full master-craftswomen. They played a big part in the retailing of provisions. The Florentine guilds also recognized widows' rights.[119] The horizontal mobility of women was high. Marriage uprooted them. If the father of a family died, the family was often scattered; the widow might move to Florence, a daughter to a neighbouring village, a son to the neighbouring farmer.

At the time of the *catasto* there were 110 men to 100 women in Florence. In the age group between 15 and 20 in Tuscany the female element was preponderant; in the age group between 40 and 60 females slightly exceeded males. However, sources of error in the register cannot be ruled out. The girls did not by now attend the public schools to the extent that they did at the time of Giovanni Villani, in the early fourteenth century. They often enter a convent when very young (at seven), and many stay there until the age when they can commit themselves personally – at 9 or 10 – and take their vows – at 12–13. Among foundlings girls are in a majority. Families found it easier to leave their little girls at a hospice, to send them to a convent or to marry them below their station than to part with a boy. More children grow up within the households of the rich families, including illegitimate ones and adopted orphans. In the country the *mezzadri*, the tenant farmers, have the highest number of children under 14. More men than women remained unmarried. Through the age-difference with their husbands, women were often widowed early, and widowhood was often associated with loneliness and poverty. Girls' dowries were high. In 1425 the *Monte delle dotti*, a kind of dowry insurance for daughters, was established.

The household, the taxation unit, comprises on average 4.42 persons (264,210 persons in 50,770 households) in the whole of Tuscany in 1427. The size of households varies between town and country and depending on the profession and social rank of its head. In the towns the average number of persons per household

---

[119]   A. Doren, *Die Florentiner Wollentuchindustrie vom 14. bis zum 16. Jh.* (1901); and *Das Florentiner Zunftwesen vom 14. bis zum 16. Jh.* (1908); H. Lange, *Frauenerwerbsarbeit im mittelalterlichen Florenz (14. u. 15. Jh.)* (1924).

is only 3.91, and in Florence 3.30. Rich households have more
members than poor ones. Members of households are most often
related to each other on the male side. The family structure is
agnatic. In this epoch of declining population and high mortality,
members of more than two generations live in many households:
11.3 per cent in Florence, between 13 and 21 per cent in the six
cities, Pisa, Pistoia, etc., 20.2 per cent in the small towns. A
special phenomenon, though not a very widespread one, is the
'household of brothers' (*frérèche*), where married brothers' families
lived together. The largest family group identified by Herlihy was
that of Lorenzo di Jacopo, who lived within the jurisdiction of
Florence with his 3 brothers, a man of unknown degree of kinship,
his 3 married sons and 2 nephews, as well as 18 unmarried
nephews and children and 8 grandsons or grand-nephews; under
one roof, therefore, lived 10 married couples, a total of 47 people
spread over four generations, since the mother of the youngest
brother, the stepmother of the others, reached the age of 74.

The head of a household is normally a man in his fifties,
married, heading a household of 5–6 persons. Women become
heads of households at a greater age. The Florentine attains his
maximum wealth at the age of 55, then comes the provision for
the children. Widows are therefore poorer the older they are. In
the country women as heads of households are rare. The desire to
postpone the dividing up of the land causes families in the country
to stay together. The patriarchal family which unites one or more
married couples of the next generation under the regime of an
older man, makes up a third of all country households and a fifth
of all urban ones. Widows living on their own are a chiefly urban
phenomenon. They have the most chance to find a place within a
large household in rich families.

It is a special merit of the work of Herlihy and Klapisch that
they are not satisfied with a statistical analysis of the *catasto*, but
paint a vivid overall picture of Florentine society in that epoch,
using the abundant literature of the time. These descriptions, with
Brucker's collection of documents,[120] allow us to supplement the
quantitative account by a qualitative one. It was said from time to
time that it was better for a woman not to study; at most the
women of the nobility should be able to read, as they had to check

---

[120]   G. Brucker, *The Society of Renaissance Florence: a documentary study* (1971).

accounts, and so on, in their husbands' absence. In the fifteenth century great importance was attached to cultivated manners and education. A good education improved a girl's marriage prospects. The Strozzi women, for example, were regarded as very cultured. The Florentine Alessandra Scala had excellent Latin and Greek. Boys and girls were separated at the age of twelve, and children were to be kept in ignorance of sexual differences for as long as possible; boys and girls should not sleep in the same bed or see their parents naked. Parents should not exchange caresses before their children. The marriage partner for the girl should be found between her fifteenth and twentieth year. Young girls normally entered marriage as virgins, young men seldom. Boccaccio takes a rather dim view of women and marriage, but the attitude becomes more positive after 1350. Bernadin of Siena names four duties of a husband towards his wife: to instruct her, improve her, live with her and support her. Conversely the wife must serve the husband, obey him, encourage him. Each owes the other love, fidelity and respect.

A marriage began with the notarial marriage contract. The *instrumentum sponsalitii* was often concluded in or near a church. The bride's father or guardian — but never she herself — guaranteed that the bride wished to take the groom as her legitimate husband. The bridegroom, who often appeared with his father, promised to take the girl as his wife, to give her the wedding ring and take her to his house. At the same time the dowry was agreed. In the thirteenth century the *dos*, the dowry brought into the marriage by the bride, was usually paid before the wedding, and later — at least in practice — it was often paid by instalments. The bridegroom made a contribution on his side, the *donatio propter nuptias*. From the thirteenth century the *dos* increased while the *donatio* fell. A statute of 1325 resolved that in the whole state of Florence the *donatio* should be only half the *dos*, and should not exceed 50 pounds, or a quarter of the wealth of the husband. The wedding ceremony took place at the house of the bride's father or at the notary's, but seldom in or before a church. The notary presided, put the questions to the bridal pair and registered the marriage.[121] The father placed the daughter's hand in those of the husband, renouncing his guardianship, which now passed to the husband.

---

[121]   Cf. P. Leisching, 'Eheschliessung vor dem Notar im 13. Jahrhundert' (1977).

The husband put the ring on the bride's finger. Then a banquet took place, gifts were exchanged. Sometimes a bridal mass was celebrated and a priest's blessing given. The final act was the leading home of the bride, the wedding procession sometimes passing through a church, but often going straight to the house of the husband or the husband's father. The couple was ceremonially accompanied to the marriage bed. If we recall the weddings of the late Germanic, early Christian period, we recognize a high degree of coincidence in the outward sequence – betrothal – wedding – leading the bride home. The most important difference lies in the element of consent, in the couple's 'Yes' as the constitutive act. The position of the bride's father is still strong; he guarantees the dowry, which naturally gives him an indirect influence on his daughter's choice of husband. The church plays a modest part in the affair. The important role of the notary is a typical feature of Italian officialdom, with its educated body of notaries and the usual notarial witnessing of commercial transactions. The husband, so the literature of the time advises, should take the young woman by the hand and show her the whole house. The wife and mother is in charge of the house, the children and the servants. The men acquire, the women preserve – under the husband's supervision. The wife may not deny herself to her husband. In reality, her influence was great.

Bernardin describes the advantages of marriage for the husband. The mother of the family attends to corn, oil and pickling and protects everything from vermin. She weaves and cuts the linen, sometimes the woollen cloth also. She knows how to air clothes to drive away the moths, to do the washing when necessary. She mends the clothes from end to end, turns everything in the domestic community to advantage. Supported by her husband and the family, she tends the sick by day and night, and her husband's illness troubles her more than her own; it makes her lose her appetite and her sleep, she shares all his pain and suffering. She brings him peace and, wholly dedicated to God and his sacraments, she shows herself benevolent towards the poor and needy. She brings up children and keeps the family in the fear of God. What a contrast to the household of a bachelor: no fire to warm the dwelling, plates and dishes washed once a month, pots and saucepans licked clean by the dogs; the house is never swept, refuse is piled up in the kitchen, covered in spider's webs, crawling with flies which descend on heaps of offal. The tablecloth is never changed, the torn bedclothes serve for prowling dogs to lie on. The bachelor does not notice that his lamp has no oil, that mice, birds, maggots and rain spoil his corn. The wine barrel runs dry, mould and moths ruin his linen and his clothes. It matters not to him at what hour he comes home, at midnight, at cockcrow, at midday or at dusk – in short, he cannot manage his time. And when he falls ill, what woe! The poor avoid his door, the works of religion, the practice of virtue have so deserted his house that no one can say whether a Christian or a heathen lives in it. Such – both heightened – are the ideal and its antithesis.

To help us recognize what reality was actually like, there are the Florentine sources edited by Brucker.[122] Between 1393 and 1421 Gregorio Dati made the following three marriages: on 31 March 1393 he became engaged to Isabetta, called Betta, his second wife; on Easter Monday, 7 April, he gave her a ring and on 22 June he became her husband. The dowry was 900 gold guilders and income from a farm. On 26 June he received 800 gold guilders from the bank of Giacomino & Co.; he invested the money in the shop of Buonnaccorso Berardi and partners. At the same time he received the trousseau, estimated at 100 guilders (which he thought 30 guilders too much, but refrained from saying so out of politeness). On 2 October 1402 Betta died. On 8 May 1403 he was betrothed to Ginevra in the church of S. Maria sopra Porta. The dowry was 1,000 guilders, 700 in cash and 300 from a farm. They married on 20 May, but without a celebration owing to mourning for Gregorio's son. Ginevra was 21 and had a son from her first marriage. She died in 1411 after a long and painful childbirth. She received all the sacraments and a papal indulgence. On 28 January 1421 he came to an agreement with Niccolo d'Andrea dell Benino to take his niece Caterina as wife. They were engaged on 3 February. He met her relations in the church of S. Maria sopra Porta. Nicolo d'Andrea was the middleman. The dowry was 600 Florentine guilders. The notary was Ser Niccolo di SerVerdiano. They ate at the house of a relation, he gave her the ring, and on 30 March they entered his house without ceremony.

How marriages came about in high Florentine society is described in the diary of Bartolomeo Valori. On 15 July 1452 Niccolo di Piero Capponi paid him a visit and after much beating about the bush asked whether he wished to marry. He then told Bartolomeo

---

[122] Brucker, *The Society of Renaissance Florence.*

that Piero di Messer Andrea de Pazzi had two marriageable
daughters and would like to give him one of them. Bartolomeo
asked for two days to confer with his relations, who advised him
to accept. He then said that he would like the elder daughter,
since he knew her well, having been brought up with her until the
age of 12. As dowry Bartolomeo received 14,000 florins in municipal
bonds, valued at 2,000 florins. His wife Caterina died on 20
November 1476, leaving two boys and six girls. On 5 July 1476
Lorenzo de Medici desired to speak to him. Bartolomeo visited
him at once. Lorenzo told him that Averardo d'Alamanno Salviati
had been to see him and had told him that he had a daughter of
marriageable age whom he wished to give to Bortolomeo's son
Filippo, if Lorenzo would be the middleman. Bartolomeo expressed
his approval, but wanted to speak to his son first, which he did
the same evening. The son was in agreement; the next day
Bartolomeo asked Lorenzo to complete the transaction. Lorenzo
sent word to Averardo, and they agreed the terms. On 7 July
Lorenzo came to Bartolomeo's house and told him that Alessandra,
Averardo's daughter, and his son Filippo wished to marry with a
dowry of 2,000 florins. They sealed the agreement formally at the
palace of the Signoria, where Lorenzo himself announced details
of the contract. We are here moving in the highest circles in
Florence.

Let us juxtapose to this the will of a stonemason. Andrea di Feo
drew it up in 1380. First there are contributions to pious foundations and a bequest of land to a relation. As Cristofano di Piero,
Andrea's partner in the stonemasons' guild, has worked very well
with him, he wishes Cristofano to be his successor. If Cristofano
so wishes, five years after the testator's death he can buy the shop
where they ply their trade. The administrators of the estate will
divide the price. He leaves his wife Simona her dowry of 200
florins. He makes over the income from the house in which he
lives to his daughters Simona and Magdalena, both married,
when and for as long as they are widows. He leaves each daughter
10 lire. He names any legitimate sons born after making the will
as heirs, who will divide the rest of his property into equal parts.
If any daughters should be born to him after making the will, he
leaves 200 florins to each as a dowry, and food and clothing,
proportional to his wealth, until the day of their marriage. He
leaves his wife Simona the use of, and income from, his house in
Florence for as long as she remains a widow. If no children
survive him, he leaves Simona, for as long as she is a widow, 24

bushels of corn and 10 casks of wine per year. If she remarries, he leaves her only her dowry, her clothes and her bed. If no legitimate sons are born to him, he leaves his whole estate to the brothers of the Convent of S. Spirito, for which they are to hold masses for the dead. If these are neglected, the estate is to pass to the hospital of S. Maria Nuova.

In his will drawn up in 1348, Fetto Urbino provides for his large family — five daughters and eight sons. One of his sons has become a member of the Augustinian order. He would therefore like to be buried in the Augustinian habit by the Augustinians. He sets aside 100 florins for alms and masses for the dead, to be distributed by his wife Pia, his son Fra Ubertino and another priest. If the order wishes to send this son to the university, he shall receive 25 florins annually for four years to buy the books he needs. In the case of his wife Pia, his five daughters and his daughter-in-law, he makes the amount of their shares dependent on whether their dowries or the legacies made out to them stay within the family estate or not. Only if she remains a widow or becomes a tertiary, does his wife Pia receive 125 florins in addition to her dowry and the living costs for herself and a servant in his house. All daughters who are widowed may live in the paternal house. He leaves to each daughter a dowry of 400 florins if she marries, and 225 florins if she wishes to become a nun. As executors of the will and guardians of the children under 14 he appoints his wife and three of his sons, including Fra Ubertino.

Such is the everyday life of Florentine women. The wills show that a married woman belonged to two family communities and never exclusively to one family throughout her life, which is disadvantageous for her. It is very significant that in Siena the wife is absolutely excluded from rights of inheritance to the family tower, or the palace with a tower. The tower, the distinctive mark of the noble and rich families of the medieval Italian town — and still to be seen in S. Gimignano — is the symbol of the family; it could be inherited only in the male line.[123]

WOMEN IN POLITICS

The analysis of the land-register of Florence by Herlihy and Klapisch includes a note that girls sometimes had a room of their own in the parental home. This was true of Catherine of Siena, for

---

[123]   Riemer, *Women in the Medieval City*, p. 33.

example. We shall place this girl,[124] born in 1347 into a large family, living in modest but not impoverished circumstances in the *populo minuto* of Siena, at the beginning of our discussion of the role of women in political events in the late Middle Ages.

At the age of six Catherine is said to have had a vision; at 12 her parents wanted to marry her off, but she spent three years of her ascetic, meditative life in her parents' house and then became a tertiary of the Dominican order, the first virgin member of the Mantellettas, an association of widows. Their confessors and spiritual guides were Dominicans, and we owe the most important biographical information on Catherine to members of the convent of S. Domenico di Siena. She is thus deeply involved in the mystically tinged, religious women's movement. Spectacular conversions were attributed to her, and there gathered around her a small circle of deeply religious people who had a certain level of culture and education. Her political career began in the 1370s. A turning-point in her life was her meeting with Raimondo of Capua, and her relationship to Pope Gregory XI dates from 1374 at the latest. A new crusade, the return of the popes to Rome, and the reform of the church were her goals in church politics. But she entirely lacked the ability to make a sober evaluation of situations. Her relationships to politics was naive and sentimental. Her attempt to mediate between Pope Gregory XI and rebellious Florence during a stay at Avignon in the summer of 1376 was abortive. Although Raimondo of Capua believes she played a decisive part in Gregory's decision to return to Rome, other voices which concede only that she reinforced the pope's decision are likely to be more judicious. After the election of the antipope as Urban VI she took Urban's side in an intense burst of letter-writing which, however, is likely to have contributed to the schism rather than healing it. In 1378 she went to Rome, where she died on 29 April 1380. Pius II canonized her in 1461

Her literary works, critically edited by R. Fawtier and E. Dupré-Theseider[125] are copious: well over 300 letters, the liveliest record of her life and work, and her books, including the *Dialogue* which she dictated and which is likely to have been added to by others. Her 'teologia affetiva in alto grado' (thus Dupré-Theseider

---

[124]   E. Dupré-Theseider, 'Caterina da Siena' (1979); M. Denis-Boulet, *La carrière politique de Ste Catherine de Sienne* (1939).

[125]   Cf. the bibliographical information in E. Dupré-Theseider, and in the previous note.

in a detailed analysis) is strongly influenced by Dominican thinking. If we have reservations about the effectiveness of her political
activity, the fact remains that this young woman from the Sienese
lower-middle class corresponded with popes and princes, combined
ascetic religiosity with a passionate involvement in church politics
and possessed undoubted personal charisma.

In the highest levels of society north of the Alps, however, in
both the German empire and France, we must note a deterioration
in the position of women. The Golden Bull, the imperial law on
the election of the king and the rights of princes of 1356, clearly
expressed the fact that the ruler's wife was no longer the 'co-
empress', but was subordinate to the emperor. The Bull ordains
(ch. XXVI) that the empress and Roman queen, bearing the
signs of her dignity, shall proceed to the place where the sitting is
held behind the king or emperor of the Romans and after the king
of Bohemia (who was also an elector), who follows immediately
behind the emperor, at a fitting distance, accompanied by her
lords and attended by virgins. Chapter XXVIII ordains with
regard to the seating at banquets: the seat and table of the
empress or queen is placed at the side of the hall, so that her table
is set three feet below that of the emperor or king and as many
feet higher than the seats of the electors. This did not prevent
women in all empires and domains from proving themselves
regents of stature. But it was above all passively — as desirable
heiresses, as marriage-objects — that women contributed to processes of political concentration, and provided noble families with
opportunities to rise to often spectacular heights.

We shall pick out just a few examples. The Luxembourg–
Bohemia marriage was of European significance. In 1308 Heinrich
VII, count of Luxembourg, attained the rank of king of Germany.
He died as Emperor Henry VII, at Buonconvento near Siena in
1313. Of his two daughters, Maria married King Charles IV of
France and Beatrix married Charles II Robert, king of Hungary.
His son Johann was enfeoffed with the kingdom of Bohemia at the
age of 14, and married to Elizabeth of Przemysl, daughter of the
deceased King Wenzel II of Bohemia, who was some years his
senior. Johann's son became the German emperor, Charles IV,
and his grandsons Wenzel and Sigismund were successive rulers
of the German empire.

When Count Johann of Holland and Zealand, lord of Friesland,
died childless in 1299, his kinsman Johann of Hennegau claimed
the succession. His son William of Hennegau-Holland married

his daughter Margarete to the German emperor Lewis the Bavarian, his daughter Johanna to Wilhelm V, duke of Jülich and his daughter Philippine to King Edward III of England. He himself married a daughter of the duke of Brabant. The following list shows the important marriages in north-western Europe.

The Burgundy—Flanders wedding
19 June 1369   Philip the Bold of Burgundy
                        Margaret of Flanders

The Geldern—Wittelsbach wedding
19 September 1379 Wilhelm I of Geldern
                        Katharina, daughter
                        of Duke Albrecht of Bavaria, Regent of
                        Hennegau-Holland and Zealand

The Burgundy—Bavaria double wedding
12 April 1385   Jean, Duke of Burgundy
                        Margarete, daughter of Duke Albrecht of
                        Bavaria
12 April 1385   Wilhelm VI, Duke of Bavaria, Count of
                        Holland
                        Margarete, daughter of Philip the Bold,
                        Duke of Burgundy

The France—Wittelsbach wedding
13 July 1385   Charles VI, King of France (b. 1368)
                        Isabella, daughter of Duke Stefan of
                        Bavaria

The Burgundy—Luxembourg wedding
21 February 1402   Anton, son of Philip the Bold
                        Johanna, daughter of Walram of Luxem-
                        bourg, Count of St Paul
16 July 1409   Elizabeth of Görlitz, granddaughter of
                        Emperor Charles IV

The Geldern wedding
5 May 1405   Reinold, brother of Duke Wilhelm of Geldern
                        Maria, daughter of Count John of Har-
                        court

The Kleve—Burgundy wedding
12 July 1406   Adolf, Duke of Kleve
                        Marie, daughter of John of Burgundy

The Brabant (Burgundy)—Wittelsbach (Holland) wedding
10 April 1418   Johann IV, Duke of Brabant, son of Anton
                       Jakobäa, daughter of Wilhelm VI of
                       Bavaria, Count of Holland

The Lower Rhine becomes a prime example of territorial concentration through inheritance and marriage. In 1329, after the extinction of the Ravensberg line, Berg on the right bank of the Rhine passes to the younger Bergisch line ruling in Jülich; in Kleve a younger line of the house of Berg likewise comes to power in 1347 with Count von der Mark. In 1423 the branch of the von Berg family ruling in Jülich dies out. The Duchy of Jülich passed to Duke Adolf of Berg, and this Jülich—Berg union was definitive. Then, in 1510, came the great Düsseldorf wedding: the heiress of Jülich—Berg married the young Duke Johann of Kleve —Mark, who became ruler in 1521 and in 1524 also became duke of Jülich—Berg. However, this lower-Rhenish conglomerate of Jülich—Berg—Kleve—Mark did not coalesce into a single state structure. For Düsseldorf, the marriage meant its elevation to the status of residence and capital and a city of the German Renaissance. Even more important was the fact that Maximilian of Habsburg succeeded in winning the hand of the heiress Marie, daughter of Duke Charles the Bold of Burgundy (who was killed at the battle of Nancy in 1477), and in securing the major part of the inheritance. In the rise of the French dukes of Burgundy and the spread of their influence into the Netherlands, the main factor was the Flemish marriage of Philip the Bold of Burgundy to Margarete of Flanders in 1369. The Duchy of Burgundy was surrounded by an aura of courtly culture and late-chivalric splendour.

German history in the late Middle Ages offers no counterpart to the great female figures of the Ottonian period. But within the more modest framework of the individual principalities, women did distinguish themselves in this period. As feudal rulers they were able to hold their own against the great male politicians. We shall describe two examples in more detail.

In 1315 Loretta,[126] the young countess of Sponheim, moved into Burg Starkenburg on the middle Moselle. She came from the

---

[126] H. Disselnkötter, *Gräfin Loretta von Spanheim* [=Sponheim] *geborene von Salm* (1940).

house of Salm in the Vosges. Her father was Johann I, Count of
Salm since 1292, her mother a Frenchwoman, Johaneta of Joinville.
Loretta's husband, Heinrich of Sponheim, probably took part in
Henry VII's Italian campaign. When Loretta was finally married
by proxy in 1315, she was between 16 and 18 and the bridegroom
was 32. Loretta appears to have brought a handsome dowry with
her; she was supposed to bring 2,200 Metz pfennigs, for which her
father promised his son-in-law an annual payment of produce
from the demesne of Püttlingen west of Saargemünd. But neither
he nor his grandson Johann II of Salm was able to keep the
promise. The jointure assigned to Loretta, apart from a number of
villages, was the manor of Herrstein, where the young couple took
up residence and the children, three sons, came into the world.
The house was financially unsound and in 1319 the couple
abandoned Herrstein and moved to Burg Wolfstein on the Lauter
not far from Meisenheim. But Heinrich died in the autumn of
1323, leaving Loretta a widow with the children still minors. In
March of the following year her father-in-law also died. In
accordance with his last will and with the agreement of her kin,
Loretta took over the government, as guardian in her children's
name. Her economic situation was difficult, and a further worry
were the castles being built near her on the Hunsrück by the
powerful archbishop of Trier, Baldwin of Luxembourg, the brother
of King Henry VII. But first there was a feud with the notoriously
violent Count Friedrich, who thought the young widow would be
easy prey but was captured by three of the countess's soldiers,
brought back to her residence, the Starkenburg, and held there
until he capitulated to her demands. A far more dangerous foe
was Archbishop Baldwin. The main area of contention was some
ill-defined rights in the neighbourhood of Birkenfeld. Loretta
negotiated fruitlessly and then decided on an audacious course of
action. She had found out about a boat journey the prelate was to
make from Trier to Coblenz; it was to take place in May/June
1328 and would have to pass her territory. She laid an ambush for
the archbishop at the foot of the Starkenburg. Whether a number
of craft encircled his boat or whether, as a seventeenth-century
report has it, a chain stretched across the river was suddenly
drawn up out of the water to arrest the boat, at any rate it was
dragged to the shore, its occupants seized and all made to climb
the steep Starkenburg, the archbishop at their head. The travellers'
luggage was kept as booty by the countess's loyal retainers. Loretta's

sons, the eldest 12 years old, probably played their part. The distinguished prisoner was naturally well looked after, and attempts to rescue him by force were out of the question in view of the Starkenburg's impregnable position on top of a cliff. However, Loretta was subjected to church sanctions. Baldwin's nephew, the king of Bohemia and count of Luxembourg, intervened personally and probably persuaded Baldwin to give way. On 7 July a reconciliation was achieved and recorded in writing. It was not until the autumn of 1328 that Baldwin left the Starkenburg, in friendship with Loretta. But the valiant countess had been excommunicated by the church. Baldwin's relationship with the pope was strained at the time, and he was unable to give her the help he had promised. He did give her a letter of recommendation to Avignon, for she decided at short notice to travel there and present her case to the pope in person. Baldwin had presented her deed as a 'tiresome accident' in his letter of recommendation. Naturally, the countess and her main accomplices were condemned to do church penances, but John XXII received her personally and gave her a letter of safe conduct for her return journey:

As our beloved daugther in Christ, the noble Lady Loretta of Spaynheim, who has recently come to the Holy See on a matter weighing heavily on her conscience, is now turning her steps back towards Germany, she and her family [i.e her attendants] shall be allowed to pass unmolested and her people and baggage shall not in any way be damaged.

There were further acts of pardon. In 1331 her eldest son, who had come of age the previous year, married Mechtild, a daughter of Rudolf, a count palatine; Loretta retired to her own estates. She went to Burg Frauenberg on the Nahe where she continued to act as an energetic administrator until her death in the summer of 1346. In the last years of her life, when her health was failing, she endowed a number of religious foundations. Like her husband, she was buried in the monastery church at Himmerod.

Another woman called on as a widow to act as regent for under-age children was Anna of Nassau, duchess of Brunswick-Lüneburg.[127] She was born in 1440/1 the daughter of Count

---

[127] Otto von Boehn, 'Anna von Nassau, Herzogin von Braunschweig-Lüneburg' (1957).

Johann IV of Nassau-Dillenburg, Diez, Vianden and Breda and the countess of Loon-Heinsberg, and in 1467 married Duke Otto II, born in 1439, who had taken over the government of Lüneburg in 1464. The marriage contract stated that after the wedding Duke Otto would receive 14,000 Rhenish guilders; for his part he made over the Schloss Lüchow with all its furnishings to Anna as her *Leibgedinge* (marriage gift). The castle was mortgaged; in case the mortgage could not be redeemed, his wife was to receive Schloss Winsen on the Luhe as security. As her marriage gift she received the mansion and estate at Lüneburg and half the Elbe tolls at Hitzacker and Schnackenburg. Anna made a triumphal entry to Celle, which had been decked out for the occasion. In 1468 a son and future successor, Heinrich, was born, but a second son, Wilhelm, died young in 1480. By 1471 she was a widow and in 1473 the 71-year-old Count Philip of Katzenelnbogen made her a marriage proposal.

Philip had become one of the richest Rhenish lords through the revenue from Rhine tolls and rights of safe-conduct. In 1422, aged 20, he had married the 14-year-old Anna, daughter of Count Eberhard V of Württemberg and his wife Henriette of Mömpelgard in Darmstadt.[128] She brought her rich husband a large dowry; 32,000 guilders — earlier countesses of Katzenelnbogen had usually brought in 4,000 florins, and in one case 8,000 florins. The large dowry presupposed that the bridegroom was rich enough to match it with guarantees, jointure and marriage gift. When in 1458 Count Philip married his daughter Anna to Count Heinrich of Hessen, he gave her a dowry of 52,000 florins, and when his grand-daughter Ottilie married Count Christoph of Baden, her dowry was almost 80,000 florins. These were exceptionally large dowries, probably partly because the house of Katzenelnbogen was threatened with extinction and the dowries were disguised legacies; but the example of Anna of Württemberg's dowry was also a factor. Anna's bridal outfit of clothes, jewellery, furniture and carriages was also very expensive. Heavy silks embroidered with genuine gold thread were the material of her bridal gown, which had ermine lining and a velvet skirt trimmed with marten and sable fur. Green, red and black velvet dresses with bodice and sleeves studded with pearls; a skirt of white damask and a fur-lined silk mantle of green damask are listed,

[128] K. E. Demandt, 'Die letzten Katzenelnbogener Grafen und der Kampf um ihr Erbe' (1955).

and there are sure to have been matching caps and veils. The jewellery included three pearl coronets and four pearl necklaces, some of them with gold pendants. There were 20 pieces of silver tableware, and four gilded goblets. The bride had two palfreys and a bridal coach with six horses and cushions of gold cloth, shielded by a blue silk hanging with white tassels. But the marriage begun so brilliantly was unhappy. Anna's temperamental, passionate character made life difficult for her husband and their servants. She vainly tried to hold her husband with love-charms. In 1446 she confessed before a commission, of which her eldest son was a member, that she had enacted the following love charm: a nutshell containing a spider was taken into her mouth; if she kissed anyone with it in her mouth, he would be bound to love her unconditionally.[129] What is beginning to flicker here was to become the raging fire of witchcraft in the seventeenth century. On grounds of her confession of magic practices Count Philip banished her to her estate at Lichtenberg, and after the deaths of both her sons in 1453 and 1456 he had the marriage annulled by the pope. Anna went back to Württemberg, where she received an annuity of 1,000 florins from Count Philip and a large house with free maintenance from her brother Ulrich. She died there in solitude in 1471, aged 63. Count Philip was now free; he could think of a new marriage with the hope of legitimate heirs to Katzenelnbogen. The sole heiress of the countship at the time was his daughter Anna, married to Heinrich III, count of Hessen (Marburg). Philip's relationship to his daughter and his Hessian son-in-law continued to be cordial, and he saw the count as his heir. That he made a marriage agreement with Anna of Brunswick, née Nassau-Dillenburg, at the end of 1473 and married her at the end of January 1474, clearly resulted from pressure by the provincial diet, which did not want the countship to fall into the hands of a foreign lord. It so happened that Nassau-Dillenburg was already at odds with Hessen, whose prospects were seriously damaged by Philip's second marriage. The marriage agreement of Philip and Anna[130] determined, apart from the financial arrangements, that any sons should receive the countship of Katzenelnbogen and Diez; if Philip died before Anna, she was to appoint suitable

[129] K. E. Demandt, *Regesten der Grafen von Katzenelnbogen 1060—1468* (1954), vol. 2, pp. 1237f.
[130] Ibid., no. 5753, 30 November 1473, pp. 1603ff.

guardians for her sons and herself retire to her estate at Burgschwalbach. If there were only daughters, these were to inherit in equal parts with the countess of Hessen, Philip's daughter. In this case too, if Philip died before her, Anna was to retire to Burgschwalbach. For the rest, Count Philip was entitled to make assignments, exceeding those now stated, to his son-in-law Count Heinrich of Hessen, although these must not be to the detriment of Anna's jointure and bridal gift. For Hessen, the birth of a male heir would mean the end of his hopes of inheritance, while for Nassau, conversely, the failure to produce an heir would be disastrous for his own prospects, since this heir and the expected early death of the old count were likely to bring him the guardianship and regency of the land. Count Philip's marriage to the house of Nassau was bound to exacerbate the enmity already existing between Nassau and Hessen.

It is against this political background that we should see the trial over the real or alleged attempt to murder Duchess Anna by poisoning in the chapel of Schloss Rheinfels before the wedding.[131] In June 1474, before the official of the Cologne curia, Johann, the priest at Bornich and chaplain at Rheinfels, was accused by the bishops of Cologne, Trier, Mainz, Osnabrück, Liège, Cambrai and Speyer. The defendant confessed to the following: he had been bribed by a number of persons to poison Anna, daughter of Count Johann of Nassau, wife of Count Philip of Katzenelnbogen, for which service he and his sister had each been paid 1,000 florins. He committed the crime in the week after New Year 1474, in the chapel at Rheinfels, when he celebrated mass before Countess Anna. It was his custom to set up a chalice of wine on the altar for the countess, when she attended the mass, to consecrate it after the mass in honour of St John − it was not, therefore, the communion wine. Johann had put arsenic into the chalice and given it to the countess. As the poison had made the wine cloudy, she asked why the wine was discoloured and Johann had replied that perhaps birds or maggots had done it, or perhaps ginger had been cut in the chalice. After the countess had drunk she fell ill, but the doctor declared after a urine test that she had not been poisoned but had a fever. Asked who had induced him to do the deed, the priest of Bornich stated that it had been mainly Hans

[131] Ibid., no. 5785, pp. 1615ff; Demandt, *Die letzten Katzenelnbogener Grafen*, pp. 117ff.

von Dörnberg, the chief adviser to the count of Hessen. Shortly before Anna's wedding to Philip of Katzenelnbogen, von Dörnberg had met Johann in the inn 'Zum Rad' at St Goar, explained to him that count Philip was old and would soon die, and had urged him to poison Anna in exchange for gifts and fiefs in Hessen. The confession was extracted under torture. It was bound fatally to compromise the position of Hessen at the court of Katzenelnbogen. Under torture Johann of Bornich confessed to a series of other murders and attempted murders by poisoning, some of which confessions he withdrew during the trial, although he kept to the story of the attempt on Anna by Hans von Dörnberg. It was only just before his execution — following his expulsion from the priesthood he was condemned to death by burning by a secular court — that he withdrew the charge against Hans von Dörnberg. Demandt has pointed out a number of inconsistencies in the whole affair: the medical examination which discounted poisoning, the fact that the prosecution was not made by Count Philip as the husband, but by Anna's father, Johann of Nassau, and that the trial was held in Cologne, where two members of the cathedral chapter were counts of Nassau, although the accused belonged to the diocese of Trier — was not all this just a manoeuvre by Nassau designed to discredit the Hessian court?

Demandt believes that this whole process was set in motion because Count Johann IV of Nassau had learned through his daughter a few months after the wedding that children could not be expected from the marriage, so that Nassau's hopes of guardianship would not be fulfilled. Count Philip succeeded in reconciling the houses of Hessen and Nassau — the latter under Johann V — just as he was concerned to secure peace everywhere. His longserving chancellor, Thiele of Remagen, describes him with justice as an 'upright, true and stalwart' ruler. He was an able politician, had an excellent grasp of finance and was a careful governor of his lands. Philip died on 28 July 1479. His son-in-law, Heinrich of Hessen, took possession of the countship. On 3 August Countess Anna attested that her apanage and other dotal possessions had been guaranteed as her property by the count of Hessen, and that she in exchange renounced for all time the countship of Katzenelnbogen. In September 1478 she had written to Duke Ernst of Saxony to say that she had heard from her son's councillors that Ernst wished to take her son under his care; she was very happy about this and hoped her son would gain Ernst's approval, although he was still very young and heedless.

A new stage of Anna's life now began. At the end of 1479 she arrived at Lüneburg to take over the guardianship of her son with the councillors of the territory. She had an interest in administration and proved a frugal regent; she took care not to contract loans, wishing to avoid putting the ducal house into debt with towns or knights. Her motive in this was probably aristocratic pride and the desire to remain independent. She extended the castle at Celle and built the new toll-house opposite the town hall. She took care of the sick and the poor. Although she is supposed to have said once that 'a healthy woman should propagate the race', she stood up for a strict religious life in the monasteries and reformed a number of convents in 1842. She restored strict enclosure at Oldenstadt and Walsrode and took an interest in the Franciscan nuns and Beguines at Celle. She did not break off her ties with her old homeland, sending her kinsfolk in Nassau fresh and smoked salmon, eels, North Sea fish, salted sturgeon and plaice. Rüdesheim wine came back at Celle. When the chapel at Celle was consecrated in 1485 and she had invited the bishop of Hildesheim and the duke of Grubenhagen as her guests, she regaled them with old Rüdesheimer, olives, dates, almonds, figs, gingerbread and malmsey. In 1486 her son came of age and took over the government.

A peculiarity of Germany were the princess-abbesses. They were territorial rulers like any man. Many proved to be able administrators of their foundations who drew up registers of their property and visited German rulers to have their rights confirmed in writing. For their lands were small, surrounded and often oppressed by secular territories which were large and growing, since a male ruler could, as we have seen, enlarge his possessions by marriage and inheritance. They were often plagued by arrogant officials and refractory towns. They held court, as was fitting for a princess of the empire, and certified their position as ruler by minting gold and silver coins. There was internal dissension, and in the fifteenth century strong signs of secularization, within their domains − as was also the case, of course, in mediate convents.

In France, women, and finally even their descendants, were excluded from succeeding to the throne. This did not mean the complete elimination of female political influence from the royal court and the country as a whole; women could still act as regents. Paul Viollet[132] was the first to examine the historical situation which led to the exclusion of women from succession in 1316. In 1322 the exclusion was virtually taken for granted — 'The fact began to create the right.' A further consequence was that the woman excluded from succession could no longer be a bridge — *pont et planche* — for a male heir; that, as mentioned above, the woman's offspring were also excluded from the throne. This principle was upheld in 1328 against Edward III of England's claim to the French throne, when the resistance to foreign claims was clearly a factor. This case was only decided by the Hundred Years' War, and it was this war which led to the famous invocation of the *Lex Salica*. In it a misquotation was used. 'De terra vero salica nulla portio hereditatis mulieri veniat' became 'mulier vero in regno nullam habet portionem': 'The wife shall inherit no part of the Salian lands' becomes 'the wife shall have no share in government.' In his well-documented study, H. Scheidgen[133] discusses further arguments, such as those put forward by Giles of Rome in his *Mirror of Princes*: 'opportet autem talem dignitatem regiam magis transferre ad masculos quam ad foeminas quare masculus est foemina ratione praestantior, corde animosior; passionum minus insecutor' (royal dignity is better suited to men than to women, for men have superior understanding, are more stout-hearted and less emotional). The French myth of royalty, of the spiritual status of the king, the supra-personal conception of the French crown — all this supported the desired interpretation of the *Lex Salica*. 'But,' writes Viollet, 'it was not the pen of the lawyers but the sword of Joan of Arc and Charles the Victorious that fixed this article of our old constitution: the monarchy is passed by heredity from male to male, to the perpetual exclusion of women and their descendants'. The sword of Joan of Arc — what an irony of fate! However critically one may regard Joan's political and military achievements, for the French people the 'Maid of Orléans' is an inseparable part of their historical consciousness.

---

[132] P. Viollet, *Comment les femmes ont été exclues de la succession à la couronne* (1893).
[133] H. Scheidgen, *Die Französische Thronfolge (987–1500). Der Ausschluss der Frauen und das Salische Gesetz* (1976).

In this peasant girl from Domrémy — where she was born probably in 1412 — a visionary religious vocation combined with absolute devotion to the hereditary royal house and her desecrated homeland, to yield an infectious, irresistible force. France was ravaged both by the Anglo-French war and by civil war, since the duke of Burgundy was on the side of the English. The Anglo-French personal union under English leadership foundered on the Maid of Orléans.

When I was thirteen years old I heard a voice that came from God, which helped me to lead my life well. The first time I was very afraid. This voice came in summer at noon in the garden of my father. The voice was sent by God and when I had heard the voice three times I knew it was the voice of an angel. Before all things he [St Michael] told me I should be a good child and God would stand by me. And among other things he told me to hasten to the support of the king of France. And the angel told me of the great woe that is abroad in the kingdom of France[134]

The distress of France was indeed great. The wife of a high financial official who was to become one of Joan's followers describes the wretchedness, the shortage of money, the despair even of those loyal to the king: 'The town of Orléans was besieged by the English and there was no way to give it succour. Amid all this distress Joan appeared, and I firmly believe that she came from God and was sent to raise up the king and the people who had stayed loyal to him, for at that time there was no hope except in God.' The girl Joan now entered the battle dressed in armour like a commander — to lead, not to kill: 'I bore this flag when we attacked the enemy, and I avoided killing any human being. I have never killed anyone.' The proof of her mission was the relief of Orléans. On 29 April she marched into the besieged town. On 6 May she was 'the first to set the scaling ladder to the bastion at the bridge.' This bastion was the most important of those covering the fortifications of the bridgehead. On 8 May the English abandoned the siege that they had begun on 12 October 1428. Already the groups for and against Joan were beginning to form

---

[134] This and the subsequent quotations are from: Régine Pernoud, *Jeanne d'Arc. Zeugnisse und Selbstzeugnisse* (1965), the legends of her illegitimate birth are refuted on pp. 331ff, and of her not being burned on pp. 356f.; cf. H. Nette, *Jeanne d'Arc* (1977), pp. 116ff.

themselves in France. After the anointing of the king Joan obtained
tax freedom for the people of Greux and Domrémy, and in
December 1429 the king raised her to the nobility. On 23 May
1430 she was captured by the English, and she was burnt as a
heretic at Rouen on 30 May 1431, after a trial which was an
abominable travesty of justice to be blamed equally on the French
church authorities and the English army of occupation. Her canonization in this century belongs to modern, not medieval, history.

Joan was a laywoman, not a 'religious' woman. She lived in the
world and for the world. The liberation of France, the coronation
and anointing of the Dauphin from the house of Valois, were
political goals which she interpreted as 'willed by God'. Joan was
not influenced by the religious movement of women, nor did she
come from urban society, but from the country, from a region
which has kept its rural charm until today. Interestingly, the
formulary in the chancery of King Sigismund contains under
Joan's name a letter in Latin to the Hussites, which violently
attacks these heretics. It is signed by Joan's confessor and
announces that after driving out the English, Joan, being 'the
equal of all in human and divine strength', will come to exact
retribution. However this letter in Joan's name came into being, it
bears witness to her far-reaching influence, which even spread to
Sigismund and his court.[135]

Her fate took on a purely religious dimension during the trial,
when the simple country girl, despite her obedience to the church,
defended the decisions of her conscience vis-à-vis the church:
'I submit to God who sent me, to the Holy Virgin and to all the
saints in paradise. And in my opinion God and the church are one
and the same and one should not make difficulties out of this'
(Pernoud, p. 202). To the question: 'Do not your voices command
you to submit to the church which is fighting on earth, or to its
judgements?' Joan replies: 'I can give no other answer than what
my voices command me; they do not command me not to obey the
church, once God's will has been fulfilled' (Pernoud, p. 231).
How far she recanted — from understandable human weakness —
is in my view rather unimportant. In the end she died for holding

[135]   H. Thomas, 'Jeanne La Pucelle, das Basler Konzil und die "Kleinen" der
Reformatio Sigismundi' (1983, 1984). Note 19 in this work contains a good
survey of the literature.

fast to a decision of her conscience. Joan was not a heretic, nor had she practised magic as she was accused.

The question of heresy takes on renewed importance in the fifteenth century. Magic is now regarded as heresy. The fear of magic, the belief in witches had been strong and widespread among the Germanic tribes. Their law names magic as one of the grounds on which a husband may cast out his wife. The church at first fought against the belief in witchcraft. In the fifteenth century the fear of magic and witches increased again, an expression of general existential fear in an era of plague, long wars and political unrest. Pope Innocent VIII found himself impelled to order the inquisition of witches in 1484. The escalation of the persecution of witches belongs to the early modern period, the seventeenth century.

An institution of special character and significance was the Inquisition in Spain. On 19 October 1469 Isabella of Castile, the 18-year-old stepsister of the reigning monarch, Henry IV, and the 17-year-old Ferdinand of Aragon, Isabella's cousin and heir to the throne, and already king of Sicily, were married. After Henry's death in the night of 11 December 1474, Isabella proclaimed herself queen of Castile on 13 December. She met with resistance, especially from the Portuguese king, but he acquiesced in the Treaty of Alcadovas in 1479, which made Isabella's rule secure. In the same year Ferdinand became king of Aragon; from that time on there was a personal union between the two realms. In this union Castile was preponderant, if only for its size, which manifested itself in the increasing importance of the Castilian language. Moreover Catalonia, the most important of the lands of Aragon, was suffering an economic crisis. To begin with both realms preserved considerable autonomy. It is not always easy to distinguish Isabella's and Ferdinand's contributions to their common policy. What is certain is that Isabella was one of the outstanding rulers of the late Middle Ages. The Reconquest, recommenced in 1492, led to the conquest of the last bastion of Islam in Spain: the kingdom of Granada with the cities Granada, Malaga and Ronda became Spanish, and the original tolerance towards the Moorish population was not maintained. In politics, Isabella gave priority to religious questions. In 1478, at her request, the kings received a papal brief permitting them to set up a tribunal of the Inquisition and to summon the Inquisitors. Thereby the Inquisition became in Spain — uniquely in Europe — an instrument of the state. It meant the subordination of the church to the state on this important question, and increased state revenue. In 1491 the kings issued a decree expelling Jews who did not have themselves baptized, and in 1499 a decree expelling the Moors of Granada, which was extended to the Mohammedans of Castile and Leon. These measures were harsh, as well as unwise from an economic stand-point. For the religious history of Europe they were, as Diwald argues,[136] of decisive importance.

Isabella came to the throne of Castile at a moment when royal power was at a low ebb. Like her husband she understood the situation and took resolute steps to restore the financial basis of the throne and law and security in their territories. They fell back on the old institution of alliances (*hermandadas*, meaning literally brotherhoods), originally an urban institution. As early as 1476 Isabella brought into being a new alliance of all the Castilian estates, the 'Holy' *Hermandad*; it restored peace in the land. In the *Santa Hermandad* the nobles were excluded from the office of judge. In 1488 it was extended to Aragon, becoming one of the most powerful supports of the throne. The element of legal expertise was strengthened within the state. The state council was reorganized, becoming an institution which ensured continuity on the demise of the ruler. Isabella had a strong sense of justice, and her resulting severity towards the grandees was one of the foundations of the absolute monarchy of the Catholic kings in Spain.

A blemish on the administration of both rulers, but especially Isabella's, was a lack of insight into the causes of Castile's economic weakness. Spanish agriculture still suffers from the one-sided preference given to sheep-rearing at that time, the great migrant herds which crossed the country from the green plains of winter to the summer pastures in the mountains. Since the thirteenth century the Spanish sheep-owners had been organized in the *Mesta*. The wool of the Spanish merino sheep was the country's most important export. Isabella did not understand that the export of raw materials was paid for by expensive manufactured imports which lastingly hindered the development of a healthy infrastructure in the country. Isabella performed one other historical service: she gave Christopher Columbus the opportunity to make his first voyage of discovery when he was on the point of leaving Spain. The conquest and colonization were done from the first solely in

[136]   Diwald, *Anspruch auf Mündigkeit*, p. 281.

the name of the crown of Castile. Isabella sought to ensure that the native population was converted to Christianity and well treated. She also carried through internal reforms of the church with the help of her confessors. The foundations of Spain's position as a world power and of the important part it played in the church reforms of the sixteenth century were laid during the reign of Isabella and her husband.[137]

WOMEN IN THE COUNTRY

We have sketched some striking peculiarities of medieval agriculture, especially in Tuscany and Spain. Central Europe offers a very varied picture which was touched on in the Introduction. Regions with isolated farms and small hamlets contrast with regions where there are village settlements; the forms of settlements are as diverse as the kinds of houses. Moated castles with cultivated enclaves on the plains, fortified mansions in the villages beside large farms, and small farms and huts give an idea of the social differences among country dwellers. Here in central Europe, lords, knights, officials and village mayors also live in the country; the village includes a church with the priest's house and tithe barn, while in the regions of isolated farms there are small centres comprising houses grouped around the church. Somewhat more remotely situated in wooded valleys are the monasteries and convents. The peasant population is itself stratified; there are full peasants, cottagers, wealthy tenant farmers and poor rent-paying farmers, depending on the region in which we find ourselves. Manufacture is no longer exclusively confined to the towns; whole landscapes devoted to manufacture, particularly in the textiles sector, come into being in the rural areas of Westphalia and Lower Saxony and in southern Germany. Mining gains in importance, mills and foundries being a part of some landscapes. Agriculture is organized around the urban markets, with sheep-rearing, flax, woad and madder cultivation, hop-fields and vineyards wherever the grape has some chance of flourishing. The fallow land around the large cities is already used in summer to yield fodder for the horses of the town merchant. The farmer uses the town market to sell his surpluses. The big changes connected

---

[137] Tarzisio Pater De Azcona, *Isabel la Católica. Estudio crítico de sua vida y su reinado* (1964).

with the decline in population also bring crises with them: the towns make up for their losses in the plague at the expense of the country, attracting the scarce labour with high wages. Fields and even villages in the country fall into disuse. These changes and the great differences in the character of agriculture in the west, south and east probably changed the lives of women far less than the legal advantages and the economic opportunities they were offered in the towns. There were still obvious marital restrictions on peasant women in the country. In southern Germany, for example, the increasingly fragmented landowners could only make claims in the form of legal claims on the person; tax demands could only be based on the bodies of their subjects. Only where the feudal lord was also the judicial ruler could he exert his rights with confidence; with people who were subject to another judicial lord he was dependent on the goodwill of this lord. The position of the lord whose subjects were in another territory became particularly difficult. At the end of the Middle Ages the personal ties of subjects to their lords manifested themselves mainly in death duties and marriage restrictions, apart from the annual tribute of the Shrovetide hen. The territorial fragmentation limited the choice of marriage partners for bondsmen to an intolerable degree. The great religious corporations resisted the demands of the territorial lords, particularly by 'marriage communities'. Going beyond individual agreements on the exchange or allocation of children from marriages between the subjects of different lords, many feudal lords in the south Alemannian area tried to achieve a comprehensive solution. They made reciprocal agreements to abolish marriage restrictions for all their serfs.[138] The new legal institution was called *paritas, consortium in contrahendo matrimonium* or *concordia*, in German sources *genossame* (community). The further development of this institution was shaped by the great ecclesiastical landowners. Two kinds of community can be distinguished, the *ehegenossame* in the province of Zürich, which ended with the Reformation, and that in the 'twelve-and-a-half houses of God', the union of the cathedral chapter at Constance with the Benedictine monasteries and Augustinian foundations in the region of Lake Constance, which existed from the fourteenth century to 1786. There may be a connection between the termination of the

---

[138] W. Müller, *Entwicklung und Spätformen der Leibeigenschaft am Beispiel der Heiratsbeschränkungen. Die Ehegenosssame im alemannisch—schweizerischen Raum* (1974).

above kind of marriage community in the Zurich region and the fact that it was precisely here that the notorious but grossly exaggerated right of the 'first night' (*ius primae noctis*) is mentioned in two *Weistümer*, or custumals (collections of rural judicial sentences), of the sixteenth century. They are the only evidence of this right in the great collection of custumals made by Jakob Grimm. The documents concerned are from Hirslanden and Stadelhofen of 1538 and from Mur in Greifensee of 1543. In both cases the bridegroom is able to suspend the right by a money payment; and the right of the first night is not exercised by the landowner himself but by his official.[139] The bridegroom would have exposed himself to the scorn of the other villagers if he had not suspended the right. But is it not in fact the money, the duty, that is primarily at issue here, the manner of exacting it being merely a 'facetious exaggeration of the law', as Erler interprets it? This would fit the historical situation — the more and more contentious nature of such taxes — and the picturesque, colourful language of such custumals. Koebner's interpretation of 1911 does not seem adequate to the character of this kind of source material. He adduces three cases in which a single extramarital cohabitation by a wife did not entail dishonour: the husband can earn taxes with his wife's body by handing her over for the first night to the landlord's official; he can abrogate his marital rights for the sake of engendering an heir, as is stated by a number of south German custumals, though in terms which make a literal interpretation seem doubtful; and finally the husband can use his wife's body as a means of atonement: a custumal from Wilzhut near Salzburg ordains that a man who absents himself without excuse from the *Ding*, or village assembly, and is unable to pay the fine shall have his stove smashed, or if he has no stove the curator, official or clerk shall have the right to rape the offender's wife. It is hard to imagine that a married man who is obliged to attend the *Ding*, and so cannot be a vagrant, would not possess a stove. In all these

---

[139] J. Grimm, *Weistümer I*, p. 43 and IV, p. 321: 'and when the wedding is over the bridegroom shall let the bailiff lie with his wife the first night, or he shall redeem her with 5 shillings 4 denars' (Mur 1543); 'any member of the community coming from the estates belonging to the manor is obliged to let the bailiff sleep the first night with the wife he has just married; if he does not want to do so he must pay the bailiff 4 shillings 3 Zurich pfennigs if he will; the bridegroom has the choice' (1538 Hirslanden-Stadelhofen). Cf. A. Erler, 'Ius primae noctis' (1978), col. 498; Koebner, 'Die Eheauffassung des ausgehenden Mittelalters'.

cases Erler's interpretation seems more appropriate to the sources. At any rate, we are concerned with a peripheral phenomenon which, like so much hardship, affects men and women equally.

This south German feudalism thus prohibited freedom of movement and restricted the possibilities of marrying, but is not to be compared to the harsh treatment of the individual implied by eastern European serfdom, which only reached its full development in the early modern period. The death duty imposed on south German bondsmen meant a reduction in the inheritance of their children. The Upper Swabian landlords were suffering from a decline of income through money devaluation and the fall in grain prices. They tried to compensate for this by increasing taxes. The rise in duties was kept within limits, but began to make itself felt when the population began to increase again shortly before 1500 and more people had to find their livelihoods in farming. The splitting up of farms was subject to constraints, which was bad for the growing number of land-hungry people. Tensions arose within the village community; the number of day-labourers rose. Holders of fiefdoms, anxious for their position within the village, demanded control over common land, woods and fish ponds; they wanted to curb the disposal of common land to wage-labourers. The forestry protection policy introduced in the fifteenth century led to a prohibition on forest clearance, a restriction on the rights to use forests as pasture and to collect wood. The forestry policy was justifiable in itself but a disagreeable consequence was the devastation of fields by wild boar and deer, and by hunting. Farmers were accustomed to use streams, rivers and lakes for fishing. From the second half of the fifteenth century the use of water was also controlled, not only fishing but the watering of cattle and the irrigation of meadows being restricted.

The beginnings of rationalization and bureaucratization now called into question much that had previously given a certain human warmth to the relationship between the bondsman and his lord, for example, the considerate treatment of pregnant women and women who had just given birth.[140] A pregnant woman had been allowed to cut grapes in the manorial vineyard, her husband to catch a fish for her in the lord's pond. In times of war the manorial farmstead at Hillesheim in the Eifel opened its gates and

---

[140]   H. Fehr, *Die Rechtsstellung der Frau und der Kinder in den Weistümern* (1912); B. Markgraf, *Das moselländische Volk in seinen Weistümern* (1907).

admitted her until the danger was past. There was a custumal
which instructed the baker to knead the pregnant woman's dough,
and to provide her with a chair and a cushion while she waited.
In a forest in which no one could fish or hunt without the lord's
permission, the pregnant woman who felt a craving for venison
could have game caught until the craving was stilled. Wine could
not be tapped until the jurors had tested and 'opened' it; the only
exception was when the lord or a woman in childbirth wished to
drink it. When all hands were required for a task, the husband of
a woman who was lying-in after giving birth was allowed to stop
work so that he could be home at night. The lying-in woman was
exempted from duties: the master's messenger would cut off the
head of the Shrovetide chicken — as a symbol of obligation — but
he had to throw the hen back into the woman's house. The law
provided a warm room for a woman in childbed: her husband had
the right to a cart of wood if she bore him a daughter and two
carts if she bore him a son. Widows, too, were shown consideration:
a Prüm custumal ordered that a widow could pay the *Kurmede* —
normally a tribute in cattle — with a three-legged stool, which in
the picturesque language of such custumals meant that she need
pay nothing at all. The magistrate who lodged with a peasant had
to take off his sword and spurs before the door, so that he did not
startle the peasant's wife. Interference with these customs by the
lords particularly incensed the peasants — fostering the mood of
unrest which led to the peasant risings of the fifteenth century in
south Germany.

Women had to appear at the landowners' courts, where they
could also represent their husband if the latter were prevented
from attending by genuine need. But they had no voting right in
the community. They were allowed to make statements about
their marriage gift and about rape, and in many cases they could
also give legal testimony. It is noticeable that the custumals were
little concerned with the belief in witchcraft. The widow exercised
maternal rights; the mother had the right to approve a marriage
as well as the father. But peasant laws did not include constraints
on marriage. Boys and girls could represent their parents in community service; the work of boys was preferred to that of girls.

The local custumals, that give us a more personal view of
medieval life than documents, are lacking in the region east of the
Elbe. Franz tells us of a report from a source which, she says, is
unique and therefore unsuitable as a basis for generalization, on a

peasant family in the Werder district of Danzig.[141] The family's progenitor, Jacob Lubbe from Grosslichtenau, whose daughter bore the Rhenish name Ursula, was born in 1400. At 20 he made a pilgrimage on foot to Santiago de Compostela in Spain. Throughout his life he ate only bread and water on Fridays and on three feast-days of the Virgin each year he made a pilgrimage to Marienburg. On Sundays three beggars always shared his table, at Christmas he fitted out three poor people, a man, a woman and a schoolboy, with a new suit of clothes. His farm was called a refuge for monks and priests. After his return from Spain he planned to become a townsman, like the other peasants who sold their land and moved, but he stayed behind out of a simple love of the land and married a farmer's daughter. After his son had attended the village school, he sent him to school at Danzig and had him learn the trade of a merchant with a kinsman, whose partner he later became. The farm was inherited by his daughter Ursula, the first woman in the family who could read and write. She had really wanted to go into a convent, but her family married her young to a rich farmer, to whom she bore three children. She kept to her pious mode of life; seven poor people sat in turn at her table each day, each Friday she fasted and went barefoot. With her husband and sons she made a pilgrimage to Gnesen.

Accounts of the living standards of the peasants are contradictory. Reports of peasant extravagance can be countered by statements like that of Johannes Boemus (about 1500): 'The situation of the peasants is rather harsh and pitiable. Their huts are made of wood and clay, rise little higher than the ground and are covered in straw. Meagre bread, gruel and boiled vegetables are their food, water and whey their drink. A linen coat, a pair of boots, a brown hat is their dress.'[142] Johannes Boemus speaks earlier of the exquisite meals of the nobles and the moderate life of the burghers. He gives a generalizing picture of the estates: we know that not all burghers lived 'moderately'. Wiegelmann calculates an enormously high consumption of meat for the sixteenth century. The feast-day meals of peasants also consisted

[141] G. Franz, *Geschichte des deutschen Bauernstandes vom frühen Mittelalter bis zum 19. Jahrhundert* (1970), p. 116.
[142] Abel, *Geschichte der deutschen Landwirtschaft*; G. Wiegelmann, *Alltags- und Festspeisen. Wandel und gegenwärtige Stellung* (1967) pp. 28ff.

primarily of meat. On weekdays soups and vegetables pre-dominated. Wiegelmann reproduces the following list of the food that was offered on normal days at the farm of the priory at Indersdorf, Upper Bavaria, taken from a record of 1493. The list applies both to male workers and to the cook and female workers.

From St George's Day to Michaelmas [24 April–29 September] the servants and maids and all who work at the farm are given a water soup with pork fat, called a *Rabl*. Then at midday it might be a barley loaf, cabbage and some milk. If fruit, peas and millet are available it is for the steward to distribute them if the people have been good-tempered and hard-working. At night a milk soup, called *Gräman*, cabbage and milk as usual.

The winter diet differed little. In the mornings there was additional stewed fruit, buttermilk instead of milk at midday, but only a milk soup in the evening. A separate section on meat meals indicates that meat consumption was rising in Lower Bavaria at that time:

The above is given every week from Easter to Whitsun on three days – Sunday, Tuesday and Thursday, each day four pounds of pork cooked with the cabbage, making 12 pounds of meat in a week, which was not usual earlier, only on feastdays. From Christmas to Shrovetide 12 pounds of meat are cooked with the meat each week as above described.

The publican Erasmus at Erbach in the Odenwald drew up the following bill of fare for his servants in 1493:

all hired day-labourers and all bondsmen shall usually, like the servants and maids, be given meat twice daily and something with it and half a jug of wine, excepting on feast-days, when they shall have fish or other nutritious food. And all those who have worked during the week shall be generously treated on Sundays and feast-days after mass and the sermon. They shall have sufficient bread and meat and half a jug of wine. On high feast-days there will also be plentiful roasts. They shall be given a good loaf of bread to take home and as much meat as two can eat in one meal.

An instruction by the archbishop of Mainz, Berthold of Henneberg (1484–1504) for his estates at Rheingau reads: 'Each day-worker, whether he works in the field or elsewhere, receives soup with bread in the morning, a strong soup, good meat and vegetables and half a jug of wine for lunch, and meat and bread or a strong

soup in the evening.[143] The detailed menus which Count Joachim
of Oettingen (d. 1520) had written down for his household, both
for his servants and his own table, make possible a comparison
between the rural estates; the keepers, agricultural servants, hunt-
boys, workers and bonded peasants were given: 'In the morning,
soup or a mash of corn or legumes, milk for the workers, soup for
the rest. At midday, soup and meat, cabbage, a spiced broth or
preserved meat, a mash or milk... At night soup and meat,
turnips and meat or preserved meat, a mash or milk.' On days of
fasting and abstinence there was no meat but pastries and mashes.
There was also to be variety in the preparation, sometimes sweet,
sometimes sour, turnips either split, diced or chopped small with
a cheese sauce, peas and lentils either whole or mashed, etc. The
count expected eight courses on his table at midday, as against
four for the workers, and six courses in the evening — three for the
workers. The simple foods are the same for master and servants;
what the master gets in addition are the many varieties of meat —
venison, fowl, offal — and the special forms of preparation: pickled
sirloin, roast pork, brawn, sausage. The rice pudding of the
master's dessert — as rice was imported — was unattainable for
the peasants. The number of courses went down with social class,
councillors and young ladies receiving six courses at midday,
priests, nobles and stable-keepers five. The sharpest division therefore came immediately above the servants, peasants and workers.
Fish is lacking on the servants' table on fast-days. Wiegelmann
identifies[144] the following regional difference: in Bavaria and
Franconia there is a preponderance of mashes and soups, while in
the fertile landscape of parts of middle Germany much bread is
eaten. The food given to the servants and maids by the master
must have been similar to that in the peasants' houses.

The gap between the living standards of peasants and knights
varied. Lords who had a small territory suitable only for agriculture, and in a fairly infertile region, did not live much better than
their peasants, quite unlike the landlords who owned mines or
foundries, or were successfully involved in trade, or made profits
in the service of a prince.[145] The burgher's house was generally

---

[143]   Abel, *Geschichte der deutschen Landwirtschaft*, p. 125.
[144]   Wiegelmann, *Alltags- und Festspeisen*, pp. 32ff.
[145]   Cf. F. Irsigler, 'Die Wirtschaftsführung der Burggrafen von Drachenfels
im Spätmittelalter' (1982).

better furnished than the peasant's, with glass windows, stoves, four-poster beds, and perhaps even a small library. A list of the furniture in the castles of Gerolstein and Kasselburg of 1381[146] mentions for Gerolstein 15 beds,, a considerable number of pillows, sheets and blankets of all kinds, 25 towels and 25 table cloths, 3 hand-bowls, 2 washing vats, 3 pots and a pan. The equipment at Kasselburg was much more modest, particularly as regards linen; there were only 4 beds, 2 hand-bowls, 3 bowls and a pot. The Drachenfels household accounts of 1395−8, analysed recently by Irsigler,[147] give a good impression of living conditions at the time. They confirm the high consumption of meat and fish. The lords of Drachenfels had three to six oxen bought each year at the Cologne ox-market; the fish came from their own ponds and streams, while salt water fish, particularly herring and bloaters bought by the barrel came from the Cologne fish warehouse. The expenditure for spices was less than that of the Cologne upper-middle class merchant Hermann Goch. However, Adelheid, the wife of Count Godaert, would not forgo expensive spices. When she appeared unexpectedly at Burg Drachenfels or stayed there in childbed, the spices were quickly bought from a shopkeeper in Königswinter, where they were much more expensive than in Cologne. Honey was the main sweetener used at Drachenfels, not the expensive cane sugar used by the rich burghers. But fine salt was used in the kitchen, bought by the loaf and sack in Cologne, like the beer wort for the castle brewery; wine came from their own vines. The consumption of shoes was high, although even the members of the Count's family wore wooden clogs indoors. Textiles came from Cologne. Tailors were employed at Cologne, but also at Königswinter and Godesberg. The servants clothes were made at the castle in the winter months, when there was less work. Wool from their own sheep was also used. The countess sometimes took embroidery with her to their house at Sieglar, where heated rooms were reserved for her. The importance of female work is well documented in the accounts: from the countess, who was heavily involved in running the finances, particularly during her husband's absence, to the stewardess and the maids and paid female workers in the fields; the women's wages were lower than

---

[146] J. Joester, *Urkundenbuch der Abtei Steinfeld*, (1976), no. 340, 1 January 1381, p. 278.

[147] Irsigler, 'Die Wirtschaftsführung der Burggrafen von Drachenfels'.

the men's. Irsigler has also described the luxuriously furnished household of Konrad of Weinsberg (approx. 1370−1448), again using exact and colourful documentation.[148] His wife was assisted by several 'maidens' and maids, and from time to time she recuperated from her household duties by taking the waters at Wildbad in the Black Forest. The numerical proportion of male to female servants varies greatly; at the courts of English nobles there was an absolute preponderance of male staff. The surviving cookery books from the fourteenth and fifteenth centuries are written by men who belonged to royal, ecclesiastical or princely households.[149]

But even the everyday drudgery of the peasant woman was interrupted by family celebrations, weddings, baptisms, funerals − or a pilgrimage. Then the men and women of whole parishes would travel across the country with relics, crosses and flags, 'on the pretext of prayer and divine service' but in reality, as Archbishop Walram of Cologne thunders,[150] to get drunk, which often ended in bloody strife. The secular authorities also felt constrained to take action against over-indulgence at country fairs and family festivities. But every possible kind of excess was laid at the door of clerics, burghers and even nuns − this was typical of the time, not of a particular class.

We have already pointed out more than once that the number of children and the size of the nuclear family in the late Middle Ages should not be overestimated. This is also confirmed in the case of the unfree rural population by Patault's study of rural conditions in the south Champagne.[151] She arrives at a figure of 2.5 to 3.1 children per family in the fourteenth century. She believes this to be a general tendency, not confined to the fifteenth century. From 1460 on there is an increase in the birthrate: the

---

[148]   F. Irsigler, 'Konrad von Weinsberg (etwa 1370−1448). Adeliger − Diplomat − Kaufmann' (1982).
[149]   M. Girouard, *Life in the English Country House: a social and architectural history* (1978). I am indebted for this information to my colleague K. U. Jäschke; J. M. van Winter, 'Kochen und Essen im Mittelalter' (1986), pp. 94ff.
[150]   Joester, *Urkundenbuch der Abtei Steinfeld*, no. 267, 10 July 1340, p. 206.
[151]   A.-M. Patault, *Hommes et femmes de corps en Champagne méridionale à la fin du Moyen-Age* (1978). The works by P. Laslett, '*Family life and illicit love in earlier generations*' (1977), and J. L. Flandrin, *Familien. Soziologie-ökonomie-Sexualität* (Transl. *Families in Former Times, Kinship, Household and Sexuality*, 1979), contain statistics for the early-modern period only.

average number of children rises to between 3.3 and 4. Grain production rises in the same period.

A countess of Foix has already crossed our path, a heretic in the early thirteenth century. In the mountainous south of the countship of Foix, the bishop of the diocese of Pamiers, Jacques Fournier, later to be Pope Benedict XII, held an inquisition in 1318–25. Its records have been used by the French scholar Le Roy Ladurie to give a picture of the village of Montaillou.[152] In the 98 cases judged by Jacques Fournier, 114 defendants were involved; most of them were convicted of Albigensian heresy. Of these, 94 were brought before the court, mostly simple people, craftsmen, shopkeepers and, above all, peasants and their wives; 48 of the accused were women. At the time of the trial Montaillou had barely 250 inhabitants. The village was situated on a plateau surrounded by pasture and forest, with the castle on a hill, peasants' houses in terraces on the slope and the parish church below the village. The comte de Foix was also the *seigneur*, the landlord, of Montaillou; his warrants were enforced by the *châtelain* and the *bayle*. The *ostal* or house, the *domus*, was the basic unit of which the village was composed. The *dominus domus* is still in full possession of his domestic power. 'My son Raymond,' Alazaïs Azéma testified, 'was in the habit of taking food to the *perfecti* in a sack and did not ask my permission, since he was master of the house.' Pons Rives of Montaillou is portrayed as a true domestic tyrant. Despite this patriarchal family structure a woman who owned her own *ostal* had a certain influence and could claim the title 'Madame'. In Montaillou there was no statutory inheritance, but testamentary freedom did exist, in line with Occitanian and Roman legal ideas. The power of the master of the house prevented the fragmentation of the *domus*, but put the children disregarded by a will in a difficult position. If they left the house, they could take only their dowry or their lawful share of the inheritance. The dowry was regarded as the wife's personal property; it remained the property of the widow. The necessity of giving the daughters a dowry was seen as a threat to the survival of the *domus*; this favoured concubinage, which frequently occurred. The household of the *domus* embraced more than just a nuclear family; it included other family members, servants and maids, and even an

---

[152] E. Le Roy Ladurie, *Montaillou, Cathars and Catholics in a French Village, 1294–1324* (1984). Quotations from 1978 ed.

unmarried lodger in the better-off houses. The extended family
consisting of several generations living under one roof was rare,
and the *frérèche*, a community of siblings, is recorded in neighbouring villages, but not often. The *domus* were often interrelated;
memories went back as many as four generations, but the ancestors
were further away than cousins, uncles and aunts in Montaillou
and the surrounding country. Relationships were created by the
fact of being neighbours, by friendships and enmities. There was
also a dominant peasant *domus* and a stratification of wealth within
the village.

The itinerant shepherds had a special place in the social structure.[153] There were such shepherds in eight families in the village;
they had no houses and founded no families. They lived in their
cabanes. The zone of the *cabanes* — the area of pasture used by the
migrant shepherds — stretched as far as Andalusia. While the
traditional division of labour between the sexes held good in the
domus — the men working in the fields, the women in the house —
in the *cabane* there was work only for adult men.

Monogamy was the central social institution in the village.
Even the prophet and Catharist *perfectus* defended it.

But when a man is attached to one woman, she helps him to maintain a
good *ostel*. As for incest with women of one's own blood or related
through marriage, that is a shameful act, and I in no way advise believers
to indulge in it ... so you two want to get married? If you mutually
desire one another, all right. Promise you will be faithful to one another,
and serve one another in times of health or sickness. Embrace one
another. I now declare you united in marriage. Well there you are! No
need to go to church! (Le Roy Ladurie, p. 179)

A marriage was brought about by the actions of many relatives or
other qualified match-makers. 'Her wedding was the great event
in the life of a peasant woman of Montaillou. The bridal dress was
kept carefully until her death' (Le Roy Ladurie). The circle of
marriage partners was narrow. A thesis directed by Ladurie has
established that of 63 women only seven married outside the
village, and only one from another village married into Montaillou.
Eighty per cent of those born in Montaillou married within their
native parish. This endogamy is bound up with attachment to the

153   M. T. Kaiser-Guyot, *Le berger en France aux XIVe et XVe siècles* (1974).

sect: Catharists wanted a consort who shared their faith. These narrow boundaries of the *connubium* intensify the problem of inter-marriage. Love marriages also occurred — at least for the men, the girls married young, at 15 to 18, and had little time for 'love'. As wives they sought to win their husbands' affections, usually by love-spells. The men did not generally marry before the age of 25. 'The situation of the young bride in Montaillou and its environs about 1300 was not an enviable one,' Le Roy Ladurie notes, quoting a series of reported cases as evidence of chastisement within marriage and reproducing derogatory comments on women. He also tells of energetic widows who acted as heads of households when there were no male successors.

'It was the custom to give these women the honorary title 'Na', for 'domina', and the name of their father or deceased husband with the feminine suffix 'a'. Old Na Roqua in Montaillou was one of the mothers of the Catharist community and adviser to the heads of member families. Na Carminagua was also an influential woman and the mistress of a *domus*. Na Ferriola in Mérens owned a house and a herd of goats tended by goatherds she had appointed for this purpose. She too was a heretic.

Some women lived in their sons' households.

An exception to the normal division of labour was occasional work done by women in the wine and cheese trades, or as inn-keepers. The household sphere exacted hard work from women, but their duties also earned them influence and respect. The mother was always a respected figure. Peasant society also had a strict concept of honour. A woman's *verguenza* — her reserve, her care for her good reputation — could not be restored once it had been lost. Only in one case did a husband cast off his wife — because she was not a heretic.

The relationship between parents and children was loving and heartfelt. A mother who left her house and children to join the heretics could hardly tear herself away from the baby in the cradle; again and again she ran back to kiss the infant. The observations made by Ariès on the undeveloped nature of filial love in the Middle Ages[154] should not, therefore, be generalized or overestimated. The large number of children born in one marriage, and the deaths of so many babies and infants, had the natural result that the individual child did not receive as much parental

[154]   P. Ariès, *Geschichte der Kindheit* (1975).

love as today. But even then the deaths of small children affected
their parents deeply.

The respect shown to women increased with their age. The lack
of church registers precludes statistical information on mortality.
On each death fixed ceremonies were to be performed, for which
the women of the *domus* of the deceased were primarily responsible.

Death in Montaillou was, of course, attended by certain prescribed
social activities. These mainly concerned the women, and were organized
in terms of the *domus* system. They entailed ritual laments on the part of
daughters and daughters-in-law when their mother or mother-in-law
was dead or dying or even merely in danger. The Mediterranean *lamentu*
is much older than Catharism, or even Christianity. But in Montaillou it
was structured by the *domus*, and so did not include the women of the
village as a whole. (Le Roy Ladurie, p. 223)

The *perfecti* tried to abolish this practice completely. The women
kept watch at the bedside of the dying; it was their task to lay out
the corpse.

Convivial relations between women transcended the boundaries
of social rank within the rural parishes. The mistress of the manor
had to have to do with the village women if she was not to be
completely isolated. And the maids played an important part in
the community's system of communications. The mill was a meeting place where news was exchanged, women usually bringing the
corn for grinding. The women adopted a fairly passive stance
towards Catharist agitation. The relationships between the men of
the village were more extensive, and politically more significant,
than the social intercourse of the women.

Conclusion
Constants and Variables, and
Continuity in Change

In the history of women in the Middle Ages there are
constants and changes — and there is permanence within the
changes. The most powerful constant: woman as the rich heiress,
woman as bearer of successors and heirs. This is true for monarchs
and peasants, nobles and burghers. The higher the rank, the more
important this 'function', the value of which, for the fertile and the
pregnant woman, is calculated in money terms in the *weregeld*-
regulations of the Frankish *leges*. The survival of the dynasty
depends on her. If her husband is absent for long periods, if he
dies young and leaves behind a son who is not of age, this function
becomes a task, whether it be the regency in a monarchy or
principality, the administration of the property, investments and
capital of a trading house, or the continuation of a craft workshop.
Women for the most part showed themselves equal to these tasks.
Agnes of Poitou, who was unsuccessful as guardian of her under-
age son, later Henry IV, seems almost the sole exception. Women
had male advisers, but they also had clear goals of their own.
These almost always had a conserving, balancing effect. In the
German empire, up to the twelfth century, they had the right of
consortium imperii, co-imperial rank, even while their husband was
alive. This proved useful in their later role as regent. Otto II's
widow, Theophanu of Byzantium, guided the destiny of the empire
for seven years, and when she signs charters in Ravenna as
'Theophanius imperator', she expresses a self-confidence which
concedes nothing to that of a modern female head of state. These
women rulers of the imperial age were often more educated than
their husbands; some of them came from different cultures and
acted as cultural mediators, giving an important stimulus to poetry
and court customs, like Matilda, the second wife of Henry the

267

Lion, or Beatrix, the wife of Barbarossa. The book is seen as an attribute of these women, as in pictures of Beatrix of Tuscia, of Eleanor of Poitou. True, we cannot credit any medieval female ruler with an epoch-making achievement — but nor can we to many men.

In the medieval town women were allowed no political role. While they may have shared their husbands' civic rights they did not rise to a position of political responsibility — indeed they do not seem to have aspired to one. This had grave consequences in view of the growing importance of towns and the middle class. Nor do we find them among the court jurors of a feudal territory, the high officials or the assemblies of estates. Therefore, the number of women who could prove their capacity in a political or administrative role was very small, and was normally limited to the ruling houses and the high nobility. That the empress was subordinated to the emperor after the Golden Bull of 1356, and that women and their descendants were excluded from succession to the throne of France in the fourteenth century, did not prevent women later distinguishing themselves as regents. History continually offers surprises: a simple peasant girl rescues the French ruler's crown and throne and prevents an impending union between England and France. But Joan of Arc's charismatic aura was something apart from sober political reality.

'I have never killed,' said Joan of Arc. This creed too is a constant, which threatens to be abandoned only in our day. Not even the Germanic women at the time of Tacitus normally took part in battle; they stayed inside the wagon barricade and only entered the fight in dire emergency. We recall that centuries later the Langobard king Liutprand ordered that women who banded together to perform violent acts should be shaved and whipped, and threatened that all women who took violence upon themselves in future could be wounded and killed with impunity. The Merovingian queen Brunichilde did not succeed in holding her army together in the final struggle against Chlotar II, and while proud abbesses like Sophie of Gandersheim mustered a fighting force, they did not themselves fight. The medieval mannner of fighting on horseback was itself beyond the physical strength of women. To withstand a clash of lances in full armour demanded an incomparably greater exertion than the operation of modern automatic weapons. But it also went against custom, manners and feeling for women to act violently, as is seen clearly in Liutprand's reaction. Her lack of fighting qualities was a handicap to a women in her political efforts. She could not lead a military force like a king, a duke, a count — although this did not prevent her from functioning politically as regent. She could not offer military help as a knight to a feudal lord, nor take her place in the urban militia to defend the town and her freedom. The 80 women who, according to a chronicle, defended the towers of Amiens at the beginning of the twelfth century, are an exception. In general, a woman who had civic rights and guild membership had to make her military contribution through a representative. A different view to mine is taken by a Swiss historian, who has justified the exclusion of women from the franchise in the Swiss Confederation — recently abolished in some cantons — on the grounds that women do not perform military service. Anyone who could not bear arms to defend herself or her dependents was in need of protection and therefore, in the old Germanic view, not completely free. We do not need to reiterate here the consequences for woman that resulted from the view — how, according to the *leges*, they were subject to male tutelage and legally incompetent. By Germanic law they were the object of a contractual marriage and passed from the guardianship of their father to that of their husband.

On the other hand, the strict provisions of the *leges* ensuring the protection not only of a woman's life, but of her honour and modesty, prove that the lack of legal competency did not prevent an honourable woman or an innocent girl from enjoying high respect. In the course of the Middle Ages there were significant improvements in the legal position of women; their scope for activity outside marriage increased, a wide range of professional opportunities opened. Two institutions were responsible for this: the church and the town.

Church law made the consent of the partners the only condition of a valid marriage. We saw how this law gradually became accepted. It prevented imposed marriages in theory and in law; it gave the unfree rural population the power to marry, if not complete freedom in the choice of partner. Marriage develops into a partnership of the spouses — though it still includes guardianship by the husband. As late as the fifteenth century the Cologne woman declares to the marriage-maker that she will take this man as her 'guardian and companion'. The patriarchal family structure is therefore another constant. It was moderated by a degree of commercial independence for the housewife, by fundamental changes in the law of matrimonial property and in the law on inheritance for wives and daughters. Also curbed was the husband's right to chastise, which had originally included the right to kill his wife. Killing is no longer allowed by church or secular law — but secular law is lenient on the husband who kills an adultress. The husband continues to be encouraged to 'educate' his wife, and to be permitted to punish her. The punishment merely must not exceed the proper marital measure (*ultra modum maritale*)! The widow — and some improvements in women's legal status begin with widows — acquires parental power in relation to her underage children.

The importance attaching to heiresses can hardly be imagined from the modern standpoint. In a marriage two families combine, increasing their power and influence. It is with this end in view that marriages are made, partners chosen; the partners' feelings have to take a back seat. I remind the reader of Judith of England —Flanders, Matilda of Tuscia. 'Tu felix Austria, nube' ('You have triumphed by marriage, not war') applied not only to the Habsburgs. In the emergence of the new Burgundian empire, whose heiress Marie married the Habsburg Maximilian, advantageous marriages — the Burgundian—Flemish wedding of 1369, the Burgundian—Bavarian double wedding of 1385, the Burgundy—Luxembourg wedding of 1402 — played an important part. The Lower Rhine was a prime example of territorial union through marriage in the late Middle Ages. This importance of political marriages is, of course, a feature of monarchic rule. But even with the urban patriciate, marriage was often the only means of gaining entry to the closed circle of influential people. The widow of a guild master-craftsman was often not free in her decision to re-marry. The feudal lord imposed compulsory marriages. How does Henry VI proceed in his contract with the captive Richard the Lionheart? 'The king shall give in marriage his niece, the daughter of the earl of England, to the son of the duke of Austria within seven months of his release. He will convey her to the border of the empire, if she is wanted. If she is not wanted, the king incurs no penalty.' Here the woman was truly no more than an object. We meet the same attitude in the Renaissance, which may have encouraged women to develop their own personalities but continued to marry them as in the Middle Ages; consider the marriages of

Lucrezia Borgia. A constant peculiarity of the fate of women (which is detectable even today) is the fact that a married woman belongs to two families and is never linked to a single family throughout her life. The parents have to give away their daughter, and they also have to provide her dowry. The daughter leaves the house where she was born and enters a strange house. Is she welcome to everyone there? Was she as much loved as the sons in her parental house? I do not believe that daughters were not also loved. But less was invested in them, less education, for example. This has remained so up to our time.

For women of all social strata the gender-specific division of labour which assigns household work to the woman has also survived to this day. For the peasant wife and women in the urban craftsman's household this meant lifelong drudgery, particularly as housework then included many tasks now performed by machines or dealt with by outside tradesmen, for example, home slaughtering and brewing. This division of labour also applied to the women of the nobility, but they had their maidservants. On a statistical average, households were not so large in earlier times as we often imagine. The birthrate was high in the early and high Middle Ages, but many children died as babies or infants. In the towns we reckon average households to have comprised four or five people. In the early period women married from their thirteenth year; in the late Middle Ages the age is somewhat higher.

There are also significant constants in the image which public opinion had of women at that time, of the characteristics that were either peculiar to a woman or attributed to her — good and bad. On this point we can only give indications, since we have not taken account of the contemporary literature, poetry and artistic representation of women. They tend to be regarded as quarrelsome. It may be that the woman's role in the household, where she could decide and arrange things on her own, made her less accustomed to collective activity than men, who depended on friendly or collegial collaboration in politics and war, in the councils of the lords and of the towns. We recall the conflict in the convent at Poitiers, the complaints in the reports of episcopal commissions on conditions in convents in the late Middle Ages. 'Ve illi domui, in qua uxor litigiosa propio viro dominatur' (woe to the house in which a quarrelsome wife dominates her own husband), sighs Caesarius of Heisterbach and goes on to tell an anecdote about a pugnacious and 'pert' woman of Cologne. By no means was the medieval wife a compliant tender of the hearth. Consider Adela of the house of Wichmann, who vigorously fought for her share of the estate. Many women took pleasure in ownership and power, and most also delighted in jewellery, fine clothes and expensive furs. Woman had a caring disposition. The saintly Abbess Adelheid played a maternal role in the convent. Woman could become man's indispensable companion, as Gisela did for as hard a man as Conrad II. 'Sanctum aliquid providumque': magical powers were attributed to women. Their piety was emotional; they had a native capacity for mystical vision; this is true of a woman as learned and intellectually lucid as Hildegard of Bingen as it is of the naive Catherine of Siena. It was a dangerous gift: the charismatic leadership of the Maid of Orléans led the king to his coronation at Rheims and Joan to the pyre at Rouen.

If we wish to summarize more briefly the changes that took place in the Middle Ages in women's daily lives, in their scope for individual thought and action, we must again proceed chronologically.

Most alien to us are the early Middle Ages. The savagery of the Merovingian kings and lords, hardly restrained by a Christianity adopted only in externals, a savagery which did not spare women and also emanated from them — this we find frightening. The religious requirement of strict monogamy and the indissolubility of the marriage bond is — to judge by what happened in the ruling house — scarcely heeded; and the same is true of the Carolingian period. The contrasts between high and low were extraordinarily sharp. Let us call to mind the Merovingian queen Arnegunde in her sumptuous clothes, her precious jewellery. Such women enjoyed all the comforts then possible and had a large number of servants (although their lives also had their ups and downs). Then let us consider the unhappy slave couple of whom Gregory of Tours tells, who wanted to belong to each other in love and were buried alive by a cruel master. A spectacular case, to be sure — but one which illustrates what was generally true, that slaves at the Germanic manors could not have legitimate marriages until the eighth century. This affected women and men alike. For this unfree section of the population, as we saw, the Carolingian period brought a change: the removal of slaves from the manor, permission to live as families, the settlement on a small plot given by the lord. They become peasants, bound to the land. Slave purchase then disappears increasingly from central Europe. It survives in the Mediterranean area, though not on a very large scale, as we showed for Genoa. The enormous gap between the style of life enjoyed by the rulers and by the mass of unfree people persists everywhere.

The position of women living on their own was always difficult. In their legislation the Langobard kings showed a sympathetic attitude towards widows, unmarried women living in their fathers' houses, and aunts. But it was obviously necessary for them to do so. They protected feminine modesty, but also told of widows given to loose living, whom they condemned, ordering that such women should be dispatched to convents. Extreme moral purity was demanded of women — men being treated more leniently. Again and again in the tenth and eleventh-centuries and later, unmarried women who were legally free handed themselves over to a convent as tribute-payers, losing their free status to gain the protection of an ecclesiastical lord. This also happened in the case of free males but, it appears, not nearly as often.

Convents existed from the second half of the fourth century. They offered shelter and opportunites for charitable action, education and intellectual and literary work. Many women paid little heed to the price of unmarried status, either because they had seen more than enough of marriage and entered as widows, or because they had been handed over to the convent as children and grew into the spiritual life as a matter of course. In its whole style of life — food and drink, servants, banquets with guests — life in the convent or *Stift* was not so very different to that in the royal palace or the castle. These convents and foundations were endowed by the king or the high nobility and reserved for daughters of the high nobility. The sharp division between a narrow ruling stratum and a broad lower one ran through the church as well.

But at the end of the eleventh, and in the twelfth and thirteenth centuries, one sees a major change: urban communities are created as a new stratum between the nobility and the unfree peasants. This period is characterized by an intense and successful striving for freedom and peace, and for a better legal system.

The church strives to free itself from the tutelage of lay power. In Matilda of Tuscia we encountered a women who played a part in the great conflict between Henry IV and Pope Gregory VII. A broad reform movement springs up, seeking to renew the church radically, to lead an apostolic life, to imitate the poverty of Christ. Women of all estates and groups, from the high noblewoman to the harlot, are swept up by the poverty movement. The wives of the knightly vassals who rise to become the lesser nobility, the daughters of urban patricians, and impoverished widows all struggle passionately to be able to lead a life dedicated to Christ, whether in the convent or in a free community. Women also demand the right to become lay preachers. The otherwise conservative Hildegard of Bingen (who upheld the privileges of the nobility in the convent) went on several preaching journeys. Only in very recent times have a number of Catholic bishops restored this right to suitably trained women. We described the poverty movement as walking a knife-edge between renewal of the church and heresy. It remains to be noted that although, in their first enthusiasm, the new orders — Premonstratensians, Cistercians, Dominicans and Franciscans, as well as the Catharists — welcomed women's desire to take part in the mass and spiritual care, they distanced themselves from the women's movement as soon as they became more institutionalized. The popes saw to it that women did not go without the necessary pastoral care from the orders. The number of convents increased sharply; life in these institutions was often one of extreme simplicity, indeed of penury. Quite new forms of the religious life emerge, in the family or in free communities not bound by the rules of an order, as Beguines. 'Beguine' was originally a name for a heretic, and the Beguines were again and again suspected of heresy. Women also made a major contribution to mysticism, Beguine mysticism in particular being distinguished by its literary achievements in the vernacular. The variety of the spiritual life for women thus steadily increased, and around the abbey, the *Stift*, the convent, formed a large group of people: converses, lay sisters, paid servants, women who acquired through gifts the right to receive material sustenance and spiritual care from the nuns and their superiors. It is against the background of this many-sided and intense women's religious movement that we can understand such figures as Elizabeth of Thuringia.

We noted a striking contrast in the degree of commitment shown by women in the high Middle Ages. They clearly took little interest in the burghers' struggles for freedom. In general, although they play their part in the political sphere when they are needed, in the absence or incapacity of their husbands or on behalf of an underage son, and are often notably successful, they do not as a

rule seek out these roles. By contrast, they are passionately con
cerned about the religious movement, although they are excluded
from the clergy no less than from the municipal councils. Here
they show initiative, oppose their whole family, negotiate with
popes, spare themselves no pains, taking the apostolic life of
poverty and abasement entirely seriously. There must have been
deep-seated reasons for this. Women clearly live on a more
emotional level than men and have a strong religious need, stronger
than their political interest. At least, this is true of many women.
And it does not mean — we have given examples enough — that
women are unable to perform well in the spheres of politics and
administration. The differences we have alluded to are not polar
antitheses between men and women, but diverging tendencies.

In the same period as the poverty movement, chivalry and the
court culture emerge. Women play their part here too, helping to
civilize rude warriors; and devotion to a lady, the courtly *Minne*, is
a feature of chivalry, becoming a new mode of life among the
upper class. 'L'amour, cette invention du XII. siècle,' Régine
Pernoud entitles one of the chapters of her book *La femme aux temps
des cathédrales*. She apostrophizes the *Traité de l'amour* of André le
Chapelain and women like Eleanor of Aquitaine, her daughter
Marie of Champagne and others from the French cultural sphere.
To be sure, the courts of love of that time, the refined forms of
amorous behaviour, were new, but love between man and woman
has always existed; we think of Baldwin and Judith, Otto and
Irmgard, whom no power could separate.

It was only a small group of women who could take part in
these erotic games and pleasures. And the new styles of living of
the Italian Renaissance fully benefited only a narrow stratum of
women at the tip of the social pyramid.

In the late Middle Ages the *élan* of the women's religious movement is dissipated. The breadth attained by the religious life led
to a shallowness; the idea of being provided for often lay behind
the decision to enter a convent or beguinage. In poorly endowed
convents the Beguines had to live by the work of their hands,
which allowed little scope for spiritual progress. The level of
education at the convents declined. Worldliness and abuses grew
rampant, even in the reformist orders. It was only in the *devotio
moderna* of the fifteenth century that a reform movement grew up
that seems like a calm afterglow of the great impulses of the
twelfth and thirteenth centuries. In this age visited by epidemics,

torn by economic structural changes and the resultant crises, and by political unrest, the dominant urges are materialistic — even in the religious life — lust for life, fear of death, laxity of morals. This is seen in the eroticization of dress, and in the increase in concubinage, prostitution, witchraft, magic practices, love-spells, etc. Public opinion is now more lenient towards women, while adultery by the husband can sometimes have unpleasant consequences. Agnete Willeken was mocked, but her conduct was accepted. The age of marriage shifts somewhat; for women it is now 15–18, sometimes higher.

In the late Middle Ages, society is still divided into estates, but distinction can now be won by achievements as well as birth — even earlier, the lack of noble birth did not prevent individuals or whole groups from rising in society. The tripartite division into nobility, burghers and peasantry generally softened the differences between estates. A society had come into being in the towns which was particularly dominated by the principle of achievement and very mixed in terms of its members' origins, the losses in the plague being partly made up by immigration. It had assimilated many members who had risen from the lower orders, and showed sharp differences of wealth and social prestige. The large cities already exhibited the first signs of that anonymity of relationships which has become a feature, though a sometimes exaggerated one, of the modern city. A. von Brandt has characterized the Lübeck society of the fourteenth century as 'an open, achievement-orientated society with horizontal and vertical mobility.' This is true of many towns which lacked a closed patriciate. The social differences are expressed not only in terms of wealth, but in the dress and jewellery of women, in access to festivities and dances, in the whole attitude to life. In the urban upper class outright luxury prevails, in houses and furniture, in a refined palate and general taste. The municipal councils find themselves obliged to legislate against luxury, partly to curb shameful and sinful extravagance and partly to consolidate class boundaries.

There is a large underclass of poor widows and of maidservants whose wages are always lower than those of their male counterparts, particularly crafts journeymen. The latter had a professional training, formed associations and articulated their demands. Maids continued to live in their employers' houses and evolved no solidarity, their low wages being improved — to a very variable degree — by the personal favour of their masters. Women are often demonstrably over-represented in the lower classes. Prostitutes form a marginal group. The church institutions were not always able to provide sufficient care for needy women or to integrate marginal groups — to convert them, as it was then called.

The sources, on which the historian always finally depends, now flow more freely, but this does not prevent many questions from remaining unanswered — for example, the important question of the numerical relationship between men and women in towns. Earlier, a surplus of women was assumed to exist in medieval towns; more recent research has given grounds to doubt this assumption, as least in some cases. Since scholarship cannot indulge in generalizations, the investigation must proceed town by town — but for some towns almost all the evidence needed for a calculation is lacking. Schuler, who has convincingly demonstrated a surplus of men in Freiburg/Breisgau, draws on a source previously somewhat neglected, the *Register des Gemeinen Pfennigs* of 1496—9. More can be done here. Because of the sources available to us, large cities are in the foreground of our study, and it was probably only they which offered women significant new opportunities to work. Here, a number of general conclusions are possible. In some medieval towns not only unmarried women, girls and widows engage in professional work, but a considerable number of married women, particularly the well-to-do wives of merchants and town councillors. The question arises whether these women take on independent commercial work for the same reasons as many professional married women today: to achieve a higher standard of living, or to finance their husband's careers, which in the Middle Ages meant an honorary political career in the council or senate. Professional work was made easier for women in the late-medieval town by the fact that crafts were organized in such a way, even in the manufacture of exports, that there was as yet no division between the home and the workplace. The workshop of the independent craftswoman was in her house, as was the counting-house of the housewife—merchant. Employment opportunities for women were particularly good in towns which produced goods for export in particular crafts and therefore needed large numbers of workers. Here the women favoured the silk industry, probably because of their special aptitude for working with such a delicate material. This has been documented in the case of London, Paris, Zürich, Strasbourg (veils) and Cologne. In Cologne, where we can base our comments on the ecomonic situation of women on the modern, reliable and very informative study by Margret Wensky, the processing of silk is exclusively done by women. For this branch of manufacture there are two women's guilds, the silk-makers and the silk-spinners. The guilds of yarn-makers and gold-spinners were also purely women's guilds. This has been discussed in detail in the text. Another branch of trade favoured by women is the selling of trifles and 'fripperies', documented for Regensburg and Frankfurt. Women also worked independently and successfully as merchants. As we know, everything has two sides. For example, a married woman's dowry in Lübeck could not be used as security for her husband's debts; admittedly, she could only incur trifling debts (2½ denars) herself. By contrast, a merchant woman, although able to incur unlimited debts, was also liable for them and exposed to bankruptcy; her own wealth was her security. Her collaboration in her husband's business could also take on considerable dimensions. In the great Regensburg trading house of the Runtingers, Margarete Runtinger kept the books and managed the money-changing over a long period. This enabled her husband to fill his many honorary offices.

Cologne is probably the best-researched and most impressive example of professional work by women in the Middle Ages. The preconditions for the role of women there were, firstly, the constitution of the free imperial city, which always included female citizens in its basic rights, and secondly, the development of a broad range of export industries which were not organized on such strongly capitalist lines as the wool and silk industries of Florence. An interesting division of labour grew up between working spouses. The husbands of silk-makers were often importers of raw silk or were responsible for selling the goods, whereas in the smiths' guild the women took over the commercial side of the business. Such craftsman—merchant combinations were prevalent in silk and yarn production up to about the end of the fifteenth century, when there was 'a process of concentration which led to the domination of the market by a small group of distributors' (Irsigler). In this respect the situation in the Florentine textile trade was somewhat different. Here the distributors achieved dominance much earlier, and employees of the capitalist organizations hired women as cheap labour at the rural markets as well as in the city. The female spinners involved in the production of Florentine wool cloth were predominantly country women working at home. Women were very numerous in the textile industry as a whole in Florence, but at the lower economic levels, often simply as waged labour.

The school education of women merchants was clearly enough to enable them to deal with the written tasks involved in a commercial enterprise. However, from the fifteenth century a discrepancy began to emerge between the level of education available to boys and girls. The burghers' sons now attend the universities which have spread throughout central Europe. Women do so only in romantic special cases. This gave rise to a development in the late Middle Ages which became a serious handicap to women in professional life. For the 'scholars' conquered one new position after another. They forced their way into the municipal councils and on to the feudal collegial boards. Doctors, notaries, licentiates and procurators had studied at university. That women were continually forced into subordinate positions was primarily due to their lack of academic training. They were nurses but not doctors, teachers but not at the rising humanistic grammar schools; they were not officials in leading positions and they were not judges. In the crafts it was other factors, the reduced scope for earning, the rise of new forms of production, which led to the guilds closing their doors to women; this was already seen very markedly in the sixteenth century. (For the same reasons women have been still more disadvantaged in professional life in the modern period, up to about 1918, than in the late Middle Ages.) As women did not attend universities, they were largely excluded from intellectual developments. In the early Middle Ages upper-class women were often better educated than their husbands; that was now ended. The phenomenon was general throughout Europe. In Florence, too, school education for boys and girls went separate ways after the fourteenth century. The Renaissnce did produce highly educated women, but they are exceptions. Why is this so? Less money was invested in the education of a daughter than of a son. The daughter had to be provided with a dowry in any case, either for marriage or for the convent. And the cost of study was enormously high, as we have demonstrated. There were no clerical livings for girls at the universities. In addition, a caring father was reluctant to expose his daughter to the often unbridled ways of students. The primarily economic reasons for the beginning of this development are reinforced by others: separate male and female schools with very different educational goals emerge. The landlords

who now have an interest in promoting education want to produce a new generation of officials, not to provide girls with a non-
utilitarian education. In the house of the learned councillor, the
role of women is to put on a cultural show: to play music and
speak French. They cannot support their husbands or fathers in
their professional work.

The peasant husband was entitled to one cart of wood if his
wife bore a daughter and two if she bore a son. There was no
rational reason for this preferential treatment of the son; it was
simply custom. This regulation was part of the welfare measures
laid down for pregnant and lying-in women in the peasant
custumals of the late Middle Ages; they also gave the relation
between the bondsman and his master a certain human warmth.
The erosion of such benefits in the course of bureaucratization
and rationalization made bad blood − the late Middle Ages in
western Europe are full of peasant unrest, the reasons for which
are naturally diverse and vary between regions. There were still
marriage restrictions for the unfree rural population. Through the
great fragmentation of property and rights in the southern
Alemannian region conditions became unbearable there. Many
masters therefore made reciprocal agreements with their bondsmen
concerning the marriage restrictions. This shows us how slowly
improvements for the unfree population permeated the peasant
sector. The discrepancy between the legal situation and the scope
for advancement and independence of the middle-class woman in
the town and the peasant woman in the country was very wide.
The division of labour between husband and wife in the peasant
economy had stayed the same. Peasant households are larger than
those in towns, particularly where there are communities of
brothers: (frérèches) in southern France and Italy. We have figures
for Tuscany in 1427: the average household in the whole of
Tuscany comprised 4.42 persons; in the towns the figure was 3.91
and in the metropolis, Florence, only 3.8. The largest family
group identified at that time was that of Lorenzi do Jacopo, who
lived within the jurisdiction of Florence with his three brothers, a
man of unknown degree of kinship, his three married sons and
two nephews, as well as 18 unmarried nephews and children; or
eight grandchildren or grand-nephews. Thus 10 married couples,
and 47 people, lived under one roof; they were spread over four
generations, as the mother of the youngest brother, the stepmother of
the others, lived to the age of 74. So widely can reality diverge
from the statistical average.

The bills of fare for agricultural workers and servants that we reproduced showed that even the rural population shared in the growing prosperity. The consumption of meat increased generally, the feast-day meals of the peasants consisting largely of meat — fish was masters' fare. In everyday meals soups and vegetable dishes were predominant. Soups and mashes were prevalent in Bavaria and Franconia, but in the fertile landscape of parts of middle Germany bread was already eaten on quite a large scale.

The style of life of the knights was very varied, some living little better than peasants while others, e.g. Conrad of Weinsberg, could afford a princely standard of luxury which his wife shared, making trips to health spas into the bargain.

I hope I have made it clear how widely conditions differed with time and place. We still need a wealth of individual studies to arrive at a typology that embraces the whole of Europe. An overview which pays insufficient attention to regional differences will always be erroneous. From our present standpoint two peculiarities of the Middle Ages are especially prominent: there was a degree of freedom for unmarried women and widows, but it existed only within a commitment to religion and the church; they alone offered a secure and fulfilled existence with plentiful opportunities for education and effective action. The choice between a life in the world or in the convent ceased to arise when children were placed in a monastery or convent by their parents; girls probably found it easier to adapt to the monastic life. Of course, there were also individuals like Chrodechilde who were totally out of place in a convent. In the pioneering period in the twelfth and thirteenth centuries women clamoured to enter convents simply for the sake of imitating Christ. In the late Middle Ages the idea of being cared for was the main motive of those entering the much enlarged religious communities, and women often did so simply to escape from marriage. There were many women living on their own in the Middle Ages: widows, maidservants. Some widows were well-to-do or rich, but even for them it was not always easy. In the midst of entries in her 'Gift Book', in which she listed the silver dishes and spoons, the brass candlesticks, baby clothes, etc., that she gave to relatives and friends, the Nuremberg patrician's wife Walburg Kuncz Kressin the Elder writes: '1430 Saturday on St Agnes's Day, my dear husband Conrad Kress died, God rest his soul. And left me Barbara, Aennlein, Keterlein (Katharina) Walpurglein and Cecily, my five daughters, and Fritz, Sebald, Hieronymus, Kaspar, my four sons. May God let me raise them all in love to praise Him, amen.' Life was still more difficult for the poor widows who had to support themselves and their children. Maidservants earned little, but many lived in prosperous houses and did not suffer need. But those women who found no work, who owned no annuities, were not members of a pious sisterhood and had no place at a hospice in old age, took their place among the honourable poor or joined marginal groups such as prostitutes.

What we also find disturbing is the presence of noble privilege even in the church, and the enormous inequality created by the estates system and social differences. It was most glaring in the early Middle Ages. The first amelioration came in the Carolingian period, with the conversion of slaves into bondsmen. A much more profound and widespread change was brought about by the emergence of the urban economy and the burgher class as a new legal estate with many beneficial implications for women. The fully developed town offered women important opportunities for professional activity, but no share in political power. This was reserved for a small stratum of regents and noblewomen. The situation of peasant women improved far less.

What remained unknown in the Middle Ages was the idea of a purely personal freedom. Even the burgher did not fight for his own liberty, but for that of his community against the town ruler or against government by a few patrician families. Women strove for the right to live outside marriage in a religious community. Men and women alike sought their freedom anchored within a group.

Sources and Bibliography

SOURCES

Altmann, W. and Bernheim, E., *Ausgewählte Urkunden zur Erläuterung der Verfassungsgeschichte Deutschlands im Mittelalter*, Berlin, 1904[5], 1920.

Bastian, F., *Das Runtingerbuch 1383–1407 und verwandtes Material zum Regensburger südostdeutschen Handel und Münzwesen*, 3 vols (Deutsche Handelsakten des Mittelalters und der Neuzeit 6–8), Regensburg, 1935–44.

Beyerle, F. (ed.), *Gesetze der Burgunden*, (Germanenrechte 10) Weimar, 1936.

Beyerle, F. (ed.), *Die Gesetze der Langobarden*, Weimar, 1947.

Bodemann, E. (arr.), *Die älteren Zunfturkunden der Stadt Lüneburg*, (Quellen und Darstellungen zur Geschichte Niedersachsens 1), Hanover, 1883.

Brucker, G., *The society of Renaissance Florence, A documentary study*, New York, 1971.

Buchner, R. (ed.), *Gregor von Tours, Zehn Bücher Geschichten*, 2 vols (Freiherr vom Stein-Gedächtnisausgabe 2–3), Darmstadt, 1967.

Die Nürnberger Bürgerbücher. Part 1: *Die Pergamentenen Neubürgerlisten 1312–1448*. With an introduction to the medieval sources on the population and social history of Nuremberg, (Quellen zur Geschichte und Kultur der Stadt Nürnberg 9, 1) Nuremberg, 1974.

Die Chroniken der deutschen Städte vom 14, bis ins 16. Jarhundert, Leipzig, 1862–1931.

Demandt, K. E., *Regesten der Grafen von Katzenelnbogen 1060–1486*, 4 vols (Veröffentlichungen der Historischen Kommission für Nassau 11), Wiesbaden, 1953–7.

Diestelkamp, B., 'Quellensammlung zur Frühgeschichte der deutschen Stadt (bis 1250)', in: C. van de Kieft and J. F. Niedermeyer (eds), *Elenchus fontium hist. urb.*, Leiden, 1967.

Doll, A. (ed.), *Traditiones Wizenburgenses. Die Urkunden des Klosters Weissenburg 661–864*, Darmstadt, 1979.

Eckhardt, K. A., *Die Gesetze des Karolingerreiches*, (Germanenrechte 2) Weimar, 1934.

Eckhardt, K. A., *Die Gesetze des Merowingerreiches*, (Germanenrechte 1) Weimar, 1935.

Eckhardt, K. A., *Lex Salica*, 100 Titel/Text. Weimar, 1953.

Eckhardt, K. A., *Pactus Legis Salicae. 1*, Einführung und 81 Titel/Text, Göttingen, 1954; *11*, 65 Titel/Text, Göttingen, 1955–6.

Eckhardt, K. A., *Lex Ribvaria*, Hanover, 1966.

Ennen, L. and Eckertz, G. (eds), *Quellen zur Geschichte der Stadt Köln*, 6 vols, Cologne, 1860ff.

Frau und spätmittelalterlicher Alltag, (Veröffentl. des Instituts für mittelalterliche Realienkunde Osterreichs 9) Vienna 1986.

Fritz, W. D. (arr.), *Die Goldene Bulle Kaiser Karls IV, vom Jahre 1356*, Edited by the Deutsche Akademie d. Wissenschaften zu Berlin, Weimar, 1972.

Fritz, W. D. (ed.), *Lampert von Hersfeld, Annalen*, (Freiherr vom Stein-Gedächtnisausgabe 13) Darmstadt, 1973.

Grégoire, P. *Das 'Yolanda'–Epos*, Brother Hermann's poem in the original text, with a metrical translation and a historical and literary introduction, Luxembourg, 1979. See the critique by H. Beckers in *Annalen d. Historischen Vereins f. d. Niederrhein* 184, 1981.

Gregory of Tours – see under Buchner.

Grimm, J., *Weisthümer*, Göttingen, 1840ff.

Gysseling, M. and Koch, A. C. F. (eds), *Diplomata Belgica ante annum millesimum centesimum scripta*, Tongeren, 1950.

Hilka, A. *Die Wundergeschichten des Caesarius von Heisterbach*, (Publikationen der Gesellschaft für rheinische Geschichtskunde 43) Bonn, 1933–7.

Joester, I. *Urkundenbuch der Abtei Steinfeld*, (Publikationen der Gesellschaft für rheinische Geschichtskunde 60), Cologne, Bonn, 1976.

Kallfelz, H., *Lebensbeschreibungen einiger Bischöfe des 10.–12. Jarhunderts*, (Freiherr vom Stein-Gedächtnisausgabe 22) Darmstadt, 1973.

Ketsch, P., *Frauen im Mittelalter, vol. 1: Frauenarbeit im Mittelalter, Quellen und Materialen; vol. 2: Frauenbild und Frauenrechte in Kirche und Gesellschaft. Quellen und Materialen*, ed. A. Kuhn, (Geschichtsdidaktik, Studien Materialen 14, 19) Düsseldorf, 1983–4.

Keutgen, F., *Urkunden zur städtischen Verfassungsgeschichte*, Berlin, 1899.

van de Kieft, C. and Niermeyer, J. F. (eds), *Elenchus fontium historiae urbanae quem edendum curaverunt* ... Leiden, 1967. See also Diestelkamp, and Martens.

Kollnig, K. *Elsässische Weistümer, Untersuchungen über bäuerliche Volksüberlieferung am Oberrhein*, (Schriften des wissenschaftlichen Instituts der Elsass–Lothringer im Reich N. F. 26) Frankfurt, 1941.

v. Kress, G. 'Das Schenkbuch einer Nürnberger Patriciersfrau von 1416–1438', in *Anzeiger f. Kunde der deutschen Vorzeit N. F.* 23, 1876.

Kuske, B., *Quellen zur Geschichte des Kölner Handels und Verkhers im Mittelalter*, 4 vols (Publikationen der Gesellschaft für rheinische Geschichtskunde 33), Bonn, 1917–34.

Lautemann, W., *Mittelalter*, (Geschichte in Quellen 2) Munich, 1970.

Lespinasse, R. and Bonnardot, F. (eds), *Etienne Boileau, Le livre des métiers. Les métiers et corporations de la ville de Paris*, Paris, 1877.

v. Loesch, H., *Die Kölner Zunfturkunden nebst anderen Gewerbeurkunden bis zum Jahre 1500*, 2 vols (Publikationen der Gesellschaft für rheinische Geschichtskunde 22), reprinted Düsseldorf, 1984.

Martens, M., 'Receuil des textes d'histoire urbaine belge des origines au milieu du XIIIᵉ siècle', in C. van de Kieft and J. F. Niermeyer (eds), *Elenchus fontium hist. urb.*, Leiden, 1967.

Meissner, R. (ed.), *Stadtrecht des Königs Magnus Hakonarson für Bergen, Bruchstücke des Birkinselrechts* ... (Germanenrechte N. F. Nordgerm. Recht 3) Weimar, 1950.

Menzel, O. (ed.), *Das Leben der Liutbirg, Eine Quelle zur Geschichte der Sachsen in karolingischer Zeit*, (Deutsches Mittelalter 3) Leipzig, 1937.

Meuthen, E., *Aachener Urkunden 1101–1250*, (Publikationen der Gesellschaft für rheinische Geschichtskunde 58) Bonn, 1972.

Möncke, G., *Quellen zur Wirtschafts- und Sozialgeschichte mittel- und oberdeutscher Städte im Spätmittelalter*, (Freiherr vom Stein-Gedächtnisausgabe 37) Darmstadt, 1982.

Monumenta Germaniae historica, Diplomata Karolinorum. 1ff. Hanover, 1906ff. (Cited as *MGDD Karolinorum*)

Monumenta Germaniae historica, Diplomata regum Germaniae ex stirpe Karolinorum. 1ff. Berlin, 1956ff. (Cited as *MGDD ex stirpe Karolinorum*)

Monumenta Germaniae historica, Diplomata regum et imperatorum Germaniae. 1ff. Hanover, 1879ff. (Cited as *MGDD*)

Monumenta Germaniae historica, Epistolae, 3ff. *Epistolae Merovingici et Carolini aevi*, Berlin, 1892–1919. (Cited as *MG Epp.*)

Monumenta Germaniae historica, Legum sectio IV, Constitutiones et acta publica imperatorum et regum. 1ff. Hanover, 1893ff. (Cited as *MG Const.*)

Monumenta Germaniae historica, Scriptores. 1ff. Hanover, 1826ff. (Cited as *MGSS*)

Monumenta Germaniae historica, Scriptores rerum Merovingicarum, 1ff. Hanover, 1951. (Cited as *MGSS rer. Merov.*)

Much, R., *Die Germania des Tacitus*, Heidelberg; ³1967.

Mummenhof, W. (arr.), *Regesten der Reichsstadt Aachen*, vol 1, *1251–1300*, (Publikationen der Gesellschaft für rheinische Geschichtskunde 47) Bonn, 1961.

Rau, R. (ed.), *Briefe des Bonifatius. Willibalds Leben des Bonifatius* (Freiherr vom Stein-Gedächtnisausgabe Vol. ivb) Darmstadt, 1968.

Rau, R. (ed.), *Quellen zur karolingischen Reichsgeschichte*, 3 parts, (Freiherr vom Stein-Gedächtnisausgabe 5–7) Darmstadt, 1955–60.

Die Regesten der Erzbischöfe von Köln im Mittelalter. Bonn, 1901ff: vol. 1, *313–1099*, arr. F. W. Oediger (1954–61); vol. 2, *1100–1206*, arr. R. Knipping (1901); vol. 3, *1205–1304*, arr. R. Knipping (1909); vol. 4, *1304–1332*, arr. W. Kisky (1915); vol. 5, *1332–1349*, arr. W. Janssen (1973); vol. 6, *1349–1362*, arr. W. Janssen (1977); vol. 7, *1362–1370*, arr. W. Janssen (1982); vol. 8, *1370–1381*, arr. N. Andernach (1981);

vol. 9, *1381—1390*, arr. N. Andernach (1983). (Publ. d. Ges f. rh. Gesch. 21).

Riché, P. (ed.), *Dhuoda, Manuel pour mon fils* (Liber manualis), Paris, 1975.

Schmale, F.-J. (ed.), *Bischof Otto von Freising und Rahewin. Die Taten Friedrichs, oder richtiger: Cronica*, (Freiherr vom Stein-Gedächtnisausgabe 17) Darmstadt, 1965.

Statuto dell' Arte della Lana di Firenze (1317—1319), (Fonti e studi sulle corporazioni artigiani del medio evo, Fonti 1) Florence, 1939.

Stein, W., *Akten zur Geschichte der Verfassung und Verwaltung der Stadt Köln im 14. und 15. Jahrhundert*, (Publ. d. Ges. f. rh. Gesch. 10) vol. 1, Bonn, 1893; vol. 2, Bonn, 1895.

Stoob, H. (ed.), *Helmold von Bosau, Slawenchronik*, (Freiherr vom Stein-Gedächtnisausgabe 19) Berlin, 1963.

Tenckhoff, F. (ed.), *Vita Meinwerci Episcopi Patherbrunnensis*, (*MGSS rer. Germ. in usum scholarum*) Hanover, 1921.

Wartmann, H. (arr.), *Urkundenbuch der Abtei St. Gallen*, Zürich, 1863.

Weinrich, L., *Quellen zur deutschen Verfassungs-, Wirtshafts- und Sozialgeschichte bis 1250*, (Freiherr vom Stein-Gedächtnisausgabe 32) Darmstadt, 1977).

Das Buch Weinsberg. Kölner Denkwürdigkeiten aus dem 16. Jahrhundert, vols 1—2, arr. K. Höhlbaum, Leipzig, 1886—7; vols 3—4, arr. F. Lau, Bonn, 1897—8; *Kulturhistorischer Ergänzungsbd. 5*, arr. J. Stein, Bonn, 1926.

Widemann, J. *Die Traditionen des Hochstifts Regensburg und des Klosters St. Emmeram*, (Quellen und Erörterungen zur bayerischen Geschichte N.F. 8) Munich, 1943.

Zeumer, K., *Quellensammlung zur Geschichte der Deutschen Reichsverfassung in Mittelalter und Neuzeit*, Leipzig, 1904.

BIBLIOGRAPHICAL

Kaminsky, H. H., 'Die Frau in Recht und Gesellschaft des Mittelalters', in: A. Kuhn and G. Schneider (eds), *Frauen in der Geschichte*, vol. 1, Düsseldorf, 1979.

LITERATURE

Abel, W. *Geschichte der deutschen Landwirtschaft vom frühen Mittelalter bis zum 19. Jahrhundert*, (Deutsche Agrargeschichte 2) Stuttgart, [3]1978.

Accarie, M., 'Féminisme et antiféminisme dans le Jeu d' Adam', in: *Le Moyen Age, 87*, 1981.

Aders, G., *Das Testamentsrecht der Stadt Köln im Mittelalter*, (Veröffentlichungen des Kölnischen Geschichtsvereins 8) Cologne, 1932.

Affeldt, W. and Kuhn, A., *Frauen in der Geschichte 7. Interdisziplinäre Studien zur Geschichte der Frauen im Frühmittelalter. Methoden — Probleme — Ergebnisse*, (Geschichtsdidaktik 39) Düsseldorf, 1986.

Aus dem Alltag der Mittelalterlichen Stadt, (Hefte des Focke-Museums 62) Bremen, 1982.

Ammann, H., 'Bevölkerung von Stadt und Landschaft Basel am Ausgang des Mittelalters', in: *Basler Zeitschrift f. Geschichte u. Altertumskunde*, 49, 1950.

Ammann, H., 'Von der Wirtschaftsgeltung des Elsass im Mittelalter', in: *Alemannisches Jahrbuch*, 3, 1955.

Ammann, H., 'Die Anfänge des Aktivhandels und der Tucheinfuhr aus Nordwesteuropa nach dem Mittelmeergebiet', in: *Studi in onore di Armando Sapori*, Milan, 1957.

Andreas, W., *Deutschland vor der Reformation. Eine Zeitwende*, Stuttgart, Berlin, 1932, [2]1934, [3]1959.

Angenendt, A., 'Die irische Peregrinatio und ihre Auswirkungen auf dem Kontinent' in: H. Löwe (ed.), *Die Iren und Europa im früheren Mittelalter*, 2 vols, (Veröffentlichungen d. Europa-Zentrums Tübingen, Kulturwissenschaftliche Reihe) vol. 2, Stuttgart, 1982.

Appuhn, H. and Wittstock, J., 'Mittelalterliche Hausmöbel in Norddeutschland', in: *Aus dem Alltag der mittelalterlichen Stadt*, (Hefte des Focke-Museums 62) Bremen, 1982.

Ariès, P., *Centuries of Childhood*, London, 1986 (Paris, 1920; Munich, 1975).

Asen, J., 'Die Klausen in Köln', in: *Annalen d. Historischen Vereins f. d. Neiderrhein*, 110, 1926.

Asen, J., 'Die Beginen in Köln', in: *Annalen d. Historischen Vereins f. d. Niederrhein*, 111, 1927.

Augustinus Aurelius — works edited by A. Kunzelmann and U. Zumkeller. Vol. 3, *Schriften gegen die Pelagianer: Ehe u. Begierlichkeit; gegen zwei pelagianische Briefe*, S. Kopp, D. Morrick and G. Zumkeller (eds), Würzburg, 1977.

de Azcona, T., *La elección y reforma del episcopado espanõl en tiempo de los Reyes Católicos*, Madrid, 1960.

de Azcona, T., *Isabel la Católica. Estudio critico de su vida y su reinado*, Madrid, 1964.

Baker, D. (ed.), *Medieval Women*. Dedicated and presented to Prof. Rosalind Hill, on the occasion of her seventieth birthday. Oxford, 1978.

Baldinger, K., 'Der freie Bauer im Alt- und Mittelfranzösischen', in: *Frühmittelalterliche Studien*, 13, 1979.

Barchewitz, J., *Beiträge zur Wirtschaftstätigkeit der Frau. Untersuchungen von der vorgeschichtlichen Zeit bis in das Hochmittelalter auf dem Bodem des Karolingerreiches*, Diss. phil., Breslau, 1937.

Bastian, F., 'Das Manual des Regensburger Kaufhauses Runtinger und die mittelalterliche Frauenfrage', in: *Jahrbuch f. Nationalökonomie u. Statistik*, 115 (3. Folge 60), 1920.

Bauch, A., *Quellen zur Geschichte der Diözese Eichstätt*, vol. 2 (Eichstätter Studien N. F. 12), Regensburg, 1979.

Baur, V., *Kleiderordnungen in Bayern vom 14. bis zum 19 Jahrhundert*, (Miscellanea Bavarica Monacensia 62) Munich, 1975.

Bellonci, M., *Lucrezia Borgia*, (Scrittori italiani e stranieri) Milan, 1974.

Bellù, A., 'Margarete von Wittelsbach', in: *Zeitschrift f. bayerische Landesgeschichte*, 44, 1981.

Bernards, M., *Speculum Virginum. Geistigkeit und Seelenleben der Frau im Hochmittelalter*, (Forschungen zur Volkskunde 36−38) Cologne, Graz, 1955, ²1982.

Bernards, M., 'Zur Seelsorge in den Frauenklöstern des Hochmittelalters', in: *Revue bénédictine*, 66, 1956.

Bernhart, J., 'Hildegard von Bingen', in: *Archiv f. Kulturgeschichte*, 20, 1930.

Beumann, H. (ed.), *Karl der Grosse. Lebenswerk und Nachleben* (ed. W. Braunfels), vol. 1, *Persönlichkeit und Geschichte*, Düsseldorf, 1965.

Binding, G., 'Spätkarolingisch−ottonische Pfalzen und Burgen am Niederrhein', in: *Château Gaillard*, 5. Caen, 1972.

Bischoff, B., 'Die Kölner Nonnenhandschriften und das Scriptorium von Chelles', in: *Mittelalterliche Studien. Ausgewählte Aufsätze zur Schriftkunde und Literaturgeschichte*, vol. 1, Stuttgart, 1966.

Blessing, E. 'Frauenklöster nach der Regel Benedikts in Baden-Würtemberg (735−1981)', in: *Zeitschrift f. württembergische Landesgeschichte*, 41, 1982.

Blockmans, F., 'Twee Patriciërs: Een klassieke in een uitwijkeling', in: *Revue belge de philologie et d' histoire*, 16, 1937.

Blockmans, F., *Het Gentsche Stadspatriciaat tot omstreks 1302*. Antwerp, 1938.

Boehm, L., 'Das Haus Wittelsbach in den Niederlanden', in: *Zeitschrift f. bayerische Landesgeschichte*, 44, 1981.

v. Boehn, O., 'Anna von Nassau, Herzogin von Braunschweig-Lüneburg. Ein Fürstenleben am Vorabend der Reformation', in: *Niedersächsisches Jahrbuch f. Landesgeschichte*, 29, 1957.

Bohne, G., 'Zur Stellung der Frau im Prozess- und Strafrecht der italienischen Statuten', in: *Gedenkschrift f. L. Mitteis*, (Leipziger Rechtswissenschaftliche Studien 11) Leipzig, 1926.

Boll, W., 'Zur Baugeschichte des Runtingerhauses in Regensburg', in: W. Eikenberg, *Das Handelshaus der Runtinger zu Regensburg. Ein Spiegel süddeutschen Rechts-, Handels- und Wirtschaftslebens im ausgehenden 14. Jahrhundert*, (Veröffentlichungen d. Max-Planck-Instituts f. Geschichte 43) Göttingen, 1976.

Bonds, W. N., 'Genoese noblewomen and gold thread manufacturing', in: *Medievalia et Humanistica*, 17, 1966.

Borger, H. and Zehnder, F. G., *Köln. Die Stadt als Kunstwerk*, Cologne, 1982.

Borst, A., *Die Katharer*, (Schriften d. Monumenta Germaniae historica

12) Stuttgart, 1953.

Borst, A. (ed.), *Mönchtum, Episkopat und Adel zur Gründungszeit des Klosters Reichenau*, (Vorträge und Forschungen, ed. Konstanzer Arbeitskreis f. mittelalterliche Geschichte 20) Sigmaringen, 1974.

Borst, A. (ed.), *Das Rittertum im Mittelalter* (Wege der Forschung 349) Darmstadt, 1976.

Bosl, K., *Die Sozialstruktur der mittelalterlichen Residenz- und Fernhandelsstadt Regensburg*, (Bayerische Akademie der Wissenschaften, Phil.-Hist. Klasse, Abhandlungen N. F. 63) Munich, 1966. Also in: *Untersuchungen zur gesellschaftlichen Struktur der mittelalterlichen Städte in Europa*, (Vorträge und Forschungen, ed. Konstanzer Arbeitskreis f. mittelalterliche Geschichte 11) Konstanz, Stuttgart, 1966, Sigmaringen ²1974.

Bovet, S., *Die Stellung der Frau im deutschen und im langobardischen Lehnsrecht*, Diss. iur. Basle, 1927. Abstract in: *Jahrbuch d. Basler Juristenfakultät*, 5−7, 1926−8.

v. Brandt, '*Die gesellschaftliche Struktur des spätmittelalterlichen Lübeck*', in: *Untersuchungen zur gesellschaftlichen Struktur der mittelalterlichen Städte in Europa*, Vorträge und Forschungen, ed. Konstanzer Arbeitskreis f. mittelalterliche Geschichte 11) Konstanz, Stuttgart, 1966, Sigmaringen, ²1974.

v. Brandt, A., 'Lübeck und die Lübecker vor 600 Jahren', in: *Zeitschrift d. Vereins f. Lübeckische Geschichte u. Altertumskunde*, 58, 1978.

Braudel, F., *Civilization and Capitalism*, 15th−18th Century, 3 vols, London, 1981−4. (Paris, 1979)

Braunfels, W. (ed.), *Karl der Grosse. Lebenswerk und Nachleben*, 5 vols, Düsseldorf, 1965−8.

Bruder, R. *Die germanische Frau im Lichte der Runeninschriften und der antiken Historiographie*, (Quellen u. Forschungen zur Sprach- u. Kulturgeschichte der germanischen Völker N. F. 57) Berlin, New York, 1974.

Brück, A. P. (ed.), *Hildegard von Bingen 1179−1979*, (Quellen und Abhandlungen zur mittelrheinischen Kirchengeschichte 33) Mainz, 1979.

Brück, J., *Die Grundzüge des in der Stadt Köln bis zur Einführung des französischen Rechts geltenden Ehelichen Güterrechts*, Diss. iur., Bonn, 1900.

Brucker, G. A., *Florenz, Stadtstaat − Kulturzentrum − Wirtschaftsmacht*, Munich, 1984.

Brühl, C., *Palatium und Civitas. Studien zur Profantopographie spätantiker Civitates vom 3. bis zum 13. Jahrhundert* vol. 1, *Gallien*, Cologne, Vienna, 1975.

Bruns, F., *Die Lübecker Bergenfahrer und ihre Chronistik*, (Hansische Geschichtsquellen N. F. 2) Berlin, 1900.

Buchda, G., 'Untertanenpflicht, Frauenschwurgebärde und ein paar ältere Rechtswörter in einem Meusebacher Gerichtsbuch', in: *Zeitschrift der Savigny-Stiftung f. Rechtsgeschichte*, Germ., sect. 57, 1937.

Buchner, R., *Die Rechtsquellen*, (Supplement to: Wattenbach-Levison, Deutschlands Geschichtsquellen im Mittelalter. Vorzeit und Karolinger) Weimar, 1953.

Bücher, K., *Die Frauenfrage im Mittelalter*. Tübingen 1882, [2]1910.

Bücher, K., *Die Bevölkerung von Frankfurt am Main im 14. und 15. Jahrhundert*, (Sozialstatistische Studien 1) Tübingen, 1886.

Bücher, K., 'Die soziale Gliederung der Frankfurter Bevölkerung im Mittelalter', in: *Berichte d. Freien Deutschen Hochstifts*, new series, 3, 1887.

Bücher, K., *Die Berufe der Stadt Frankfurt am Main im Mittelalter*, (Abhandlungen d. Sächsichen Akademie d. Wissenschaften, Phil.-Hist. Klasse 30, 3) Leipzig, 1914

Büttner, H., 'Zur Stadtentwicklung von Worms im Früh- und Hochmittelalter', in: *Aus Geschichte und Landeskunde. Forschungen und Darstellungen*. Festgabe F. Steinbach, Bonn, 1960.

Burckhardt, J., *The Civilization of the Renaissance in Italy*, Topsfield, 1983.

Carlsson, L., *"Jag giver dig min dotter"*, (Skrifter utgivna av Inst. f. rättshist. forskning, Serie I, Rättshist. Bibliotek 8) vol. 1, Stockholm, 1965.

Carpentier, E. and Glenisson, J., 'Bilans et méthodes: La démographie française au 14ᵉ siecle', in: *Annales*, 17, 1972.

Charles, J. L., *La ville de Saint-Trond au Moyen-Age*, (Bibliothèque de la Faculté de Philosophie et Lettres de l'Université de Liège 173) Paris, 1965.

Chaunu, P., *Die verhütete Zukunft*, Stuttgart, 1981.

Chiappini, L., *Eleanora d' Aragona, prima duchessa di Ferrara*, Rovigo, 1956.

Chojnacki, S. J., 'Patrician women in early Renaissance Venice', in: *Studies in the Renaissance*, 21, 1974.

Cipolla, C. M. and Borchardt, K., *Bevölkerungsgeschichte Europas. Mittelalter bis Neuzeit*. Munich, 1971.

Claude, D., 'Die Handwerker nach den erzählenden und urkundlichen Quellen der Merowingerzeit', in: *Das Handwerk in vor- und frühgeschichtlicher Zeit*, part 1. Göttingen, 1981.

Coleman, E. R., 'Medieval marriage characteristics: a neglected factor in the history of medieval serfdom', in: *Journal of interdisciplinary History*, 2, 2, 1971.

Conrad, H., *Deutsche Rechtsgeschichte, vol.* 1, Karlsruhe, [2]1962.

Corsten, S., 'Die Grafen von Jülich unter den Ottonen und Saliern', in: *Bibliothek, Buch, Geschichte*. (Sonderveröffentlichungen d. Deutschen Bibliothek 5) Frankfurt, 1977.

David, M., 'Le mariage dans la société féodale', in: *Annales*, 36, 1981.

Decker-Hauff, H., 'Das Staufische Haus', in: *Die Zeit der Staufer, Katalog der Ausstellung*, vol. 3, Stuttgart, 1977.

Deeters, W., 'Zur Heiratsurkunde der Kaiserin Theophanu', in: *Braunschweigisches Jahrbuch*, 54, 1973.

Degler-Spengler, B., 'Zisterzienserorden und Frauenklöster. Anmerkung zur Forschungsproblematik', in: *Die Zisterzienser*. Supplement, ed. K. Elm and P. Joerissen, (Schriften d. Rheinischen Museumsamtes 18) Cologne, 1982.

Deissner, K., *Zum Guter- und Erbrecht im ältesten Schleswiger Stadrecht*. Diss.

iur. Kiel, 1966.

Delumeau, J., *La peur en Occident (14ᵉ−18ᵉ siècles). Une cité assiégée*. Paris, 1978.

Demandt, K. E., 'Die letzten Katzenelnbogener Grafen und der Kampf um ihr Erbe', in: *Nassauische Annalen*, 66, 1955.

Demelius, H., *Eheliches Güterrecht im spätmittelalterlichen Wien*, (Osterreichische Akademie der Wissenschaften, Phil.-Hist. Klasse, Sitzungsberichte 265, 4) Vienna, 1970.

Denis-Boulet, M., *La carrière politique de Sainte Catherine de Sienne. Etude historique*. Paris, 1939.

Dhondt, J., 'Sept femmes et un trio de rois', in: *Contributions à l'histoire économique et sociale*, 3 1964−5.

Diestelkamp, B. (ed.), *Beitrage z. hochmittelalterl. Städtewesen*. (Städteforschung. Veröffentl. d. Inst. F. Vergl. Städtegesch. i. Münster, Reihe A, 11) Cologne, Vienna, 1982.

Dietz, J., 'Bonner Handwerker und Gewerbetreibende bis zur Mitte des 17. Jahrhunderts', in: *Bonner Geschichtsblätter*, 15, 1961.

Dilcher, G., 'Zum Bürgerbegriff im späteren Mittelalter. Versuch einer Typologie am Beispiel von Frankfurt am Main', in: J. Fleckenstein and K. Stackmann (eds), *Uber Bürger, Stadt und städtische Literatur im Spätmittelalter*. (Abhandlungen d. Akademie der Wissenschaften in Göttingen, Phil.-Hist. Klasse. Dritte Folge Nr. 121), Göttingen, 1980.

Dilcher, G., 'Ehescheidung und Säkularisation', in: L. Lombardi Vallauri and G. Dilcher (eds), *Christentum, Säkularisation und modernes Recht*. Baden-Baden, Milan, 1981.

Dillard, H., *Daughters of the Reconquest: women in Castilian town society, 1100−1300*. Cambridge, 1984.

Dinzelbacher, P., 'Die Offenbarungen der hl. Elisabeth von Schönau: Bildwelt, Erlebisse u. Zeittypisches', in: *Studien und Mitt. zur Geschichte des Benediktiner-Ordens*, 97, 1984.

Dinzelbacher, P. and Bauer, D. R. (eds), *Frauenmystik im Mittelalter*. Ostfildern, Stuttgart, 1985.

Dirlmeier, U., *Untersuchungen zu Einkommensverhältnissen und Lebenshaltungskosten in oberdeutschen Städten des Spätmittelalters (Mitte 14. bis Anfang 16. Jahrhundert)*, (Abhandlungen d. Heidelberger Akademie der Wisenschaften, Phil.-Hist. Klasse, Jahrgang 1978, 1) Heidelberg, 1978.

Dirlmeier, U., 'Die kommunalpolitischen Zuständigkeiten und Leistungen süddeutscher Städte im Spätmittelalter', in: J. Sydow (ed.), *Städtische Versorgung und Entsorgung im Wandel der Geschichte. 18. Arbeitsgagung in Villingen*, 1979, (Stadt in der Geschichte, Veröffentlichungen des Südwestdeutschen Arbeitskreises für Stadgeschichtsforschung, vol. 8) Sigmaringen, 1981.

Dirlmeier, U., 'Zum Problem von Versorgung und Verbrauch privater Haushalte im Spätmittelalter', in: A. Haverkamp (ed.), *Haus und Familie in der spätmittelalterlichen Stadt*. Cologne, Vienna, 1984.

Disselnkötter, H., *Gräfin Loretta von Spanheim [= Sponheim] geborene von Salm*, (Rheinisches Archiv 37) Bonn, 1940.

Diwald, H., *Propyläen Geschichte Europas. Anspruch auf Mündigkeit. Um 1400–1555*, (Propyläen Geschichte Europas 1) Frankfurt, Berlin, Vienna, 1975.

Dörrenhaus, F., *Wo der Norden dem Suden begegnet: Südtirol. Ein geographischer Vergleich*, Bozen, 1959.

Dörrenhaus, F., *Urbanität und gentile Lebensform*, (Erdkundliches Wissen 25) Wiesbaden, 1971.

Doppelfeld, O., 'Das fränkische Frauengrab unter dem Chor des Kölner Domes', in *Germania*, 38, 1960.

Doppelfeld, O., 'Koln von der Spätantike bis zur Karolingerzeit', in: *Vor- und Frühformen der europäischen Stadt im Mittelalter*, vol. 1, (Abhandlungen der Akademie der Wissenschaften in Göttingen, Phil.-Hist. Klasse 3, 83) Gottingen, 1973.

Doren, A., *Die Florentiner Wollentuchindustrie vom 14. bis zum 16. Jahrhundert*, Stuttgart, 1901.

Doren, A., *Das Florentiner Zunftwesen vom 14. bis zum 16. Jahrhundert*, Stuttgart, Berlin, 1908.

Duby, G., *La société aux 11e et 12e siècles dans la région mâconnaise*, (Bibliothèque générale de l'Ecole pratique des Hautes Etudes) Paris, 1953.

Duby, G., *L'économie rurale et la vie des campagnes dans l'Occident médiéval (France, Angleterre, Empire, 9e–15e s.). Essai de synthèse et perspective de recherches*, (Collection historique) 2 vols, Paris, 1962.

Duby, G., *The Knight, the Lady and the Priest: the making of modern marriage in medieval France*, London, 1985. (Paris, 1981).

Dübeck, I., *Købekoner og konkurrence: studier over mydighets- og herhvervsrettens udvikling med stadigt henblik på kvinders historiske retstilling*, (Skrifter fra det retsvidenskabelige Institut ved Kobenhavns Universitet 29) Copenhagen, 1978.

Düffel, J., 'Gräffin Adela von Hamaland und ihr Kampf um das Stift Hochelten', in: *Gedenkbuch für J. Duffel*, Emmerich, 1978.

Dupré-Theseider, E., 'Caterina da Siena', in: *Dizionario Biografico degli Italiani*, Rome, 1979.

Ebel, W., *Forschungen zur Geschichte des lübischen Rechts*, (Veröffentlichungen zur Geschichte der Hansestadt Lübeck 14) Lübeck, 1950.

Ebel. W., 'Das Soester Recht. Wesen, Herkunft und Bedeutung', in *Soester Zeitschrift*, 72, 1959.

Ebel, W., 'Uber das "ungezweite Gut" im Sachsenspiegel, Landrecht I, 31', in: *Zeitschrift der Savigny-Stiftung f. Rechtsgeschichte, Germ. Abteilung*, 92, 1975.

Ebel, W., 'Uber die rechtsschöpferische Leistung des mittelalterlichen deutschen Bürgertums', in: *Untersuchungen zur gesellschaftlichen Struktur der mittelalterlichen Städte in Europa*, (Vortrage und Forschungen, ed. Konstanzer Arbeitskreis f. mittelalterliche Geschichte 11) Constance, Stuttgart, 1966, Sigmaringen,[2] 1974.

Ehbrecht, W. (ed.), *Städtische Führungsgruppen und Gemeinde in der werdenden Neuzeit*, (Städteforschung, Veröffentlichungen des Instituts f. vergleichende Städtegeschichte, Reihe, A., 9) Cologne, Vienna, 1980.

Ehbrecht, W. (ed.), see under Schuler, P. J., *Die Bevölkerungsstruktur* ...

Eikenberg, W., *Das Handelshaus der Runtinger zu Regensburg. Ein Spiegel süddeutschen Rechts-, Handels- und Wirtschaftslebens im ausgehenden 14. Jahrhundert*, (Veröffentlichungen d. Max-Planck-Instituts f. Geschichte 43) Göttingen 1976.

Eisenbart, L. C., *Kleiderordnungen der deutschen Städte zwischen 1350 und 1700*, (Göttinger Bausteine zur Geschichtswissenschaft 32) Göttingen, 1962.

Elm, K., (ed.), *Ordensstudien*, vol. 1: (Beiträge zur Geschichte der Konversen im Mittelalter', (Berliner Historische Studien 2) Berlin, 1980.

Elm, K. (ed.), *Ordensstudien*, vol. 2: 'Stellung und Wirksamkeit der Bettelorden in der städtischen Gesellschaft', (Berliner Historische Studien 3) Berlin, 1981.

Elm, K., 'Die Stellung der Frau in Ordenswesen, Semireligiosentum und Häresie zur Zeit der hl. Elisabeth', in: *Sankt Elisabeth. Fürstin, Dienerin, Heilige*, Sigmaringen, 1981.

Elm, K., 'Die Stellung der Zisterzienserordens in der Geschichte des Ordenslebens', in: *Die Zisterzienser. Ordensleben zwischen Ideal und Wirklichkeit*, (Schriften des Rheinischen Museumsamtes 10) Bonn, 1980.

Elm, K. and Manselli, R., 'Beg(h)inen', in: *Lexikon des Mittelalters*, vol. 1, Munich, Zürich, 1980.

Elze, R., 'Uber die Sklaverei im christlichen Teil des Mittelmeerraumes (12.–15. Jahrhundert)', in: H. Mommsen and W. Schulze (eds), *Vom Elend der Handarbeit. Probleme historicher Unterschichtenforschung*, (Geschichte und Gesellschaft. Bochumer Historische Studien 24) Stuttgart, 1981.

Ennen, E., *Geschichte der Stadt Bonn*, part 2, Bonn 1962.

Ennen, E., 'Das Gewerbe auf dem europäischen zisalpinen Kontinent vom 6. bis 11. Jahrhundert in verfassungsgeschichtlicher Sicht', in: *Early Medieval Studies* 8, 1975.

Ennen, E., 'Kölner Wirtschaft im Früh- und Hochmittelalter', in: H. Kellenbenz (ed.), *Zwei Jahrtausende Kölner Wirtschaft*, vol. 1, Cologne, 1975.

Ennen, E., 'Die Grundherrschaft St. Maximin und die Bauern von Wasserbillig', in: E. Ennen, *Gesammelte Abhandlungen zum europäischen Stadtwesen und zur rheinischen Geschichte*, Bonn, 1977.

Ennen, E., 'Zur Typologie des Stadt-Land-Verhältnisses im Mittelalter', in: E. Ennen, *Gesammelte Abhandlungen zum europäischen Stadtewesen und zur rheinischen Geschichte*, Bonn, 1977.

Ennen, E., 'Zur Städtepolitik der Eleonore von Aquitanien', in: *Civitatum Communitas. Festschrift H. Stoob zum 65. Geburtstag*, part 1, Cologne–Vienna, 1984.

Ennen, E., 'Die Frau in der Landwirtschaft vom Mittelalter bis zur frühen Neuzeit', in: H. Pohl and W. Treue (eds), *Dir Frau in der deutschen Wirtschaft*, (Zeitschrift für Unternehmensgeschichte, Beiheft 35) Wiesbaden, 1985.

Ennen, E., *Die europäische Stadt des Mittelalters*, Göttingen, [4]1987.

Ennen, E. and Janssen, W., *Deutsche Agrargeschichte vom Neolithikum bis zur*

Schwelle der Industriezeit, (Wissenschaftliche Paperbacks 12) Wiesbaden, 1979.

Enright, M. G., 'Charles the Bald and Aethelfwulf of Wessex: the alliance of 856 and strategies of royal succession', in: *Journal of Medieval History*, 5, 1979.

Erdmann, W., 'Die Entwicklung des Lübecker Bürgerhauses im 13. und 14. Jahrhundert unter dem Einfluss von Profanarchitektur des Ostseeraumes', in: *Die Heimat, Zeitschrift f. Natur- u. Landeskunde von Schleswig-Holstein und Hamburg*, 89, 1982.

Erdmann, W., 'Entwicklungstendenzen des Lübecker Hausbaus 1100 bis um 1340 − eine Ideenskizze', in: *Lübecker Schriften zur Archäologie und Kulturgeschichte* 7, 1983.

Erdmann, W., 'Zum staufischen Saalgeschossbau Kleine Burgstrasse 22 zu Lübeck, dem sogenannten "Cranenkonvent"', in: *Zeitschrift f. Lübeckische Geschichte u. Altertumskunde* 63, 1983.

Erler, A., 'Ius primae noctis', in: *Handwörterbuch zur deutschen Rechtgeschichte*, vol. 2, Berlin, 1978.

Ewig. E., 'Das Privileg des Bischofs Berthefrid von Amiens für Corbie von 664 und die Klosterpolitik der Königin Balthild', in: *Francia*, 1, 1973.

Ewig, E., 'Studien zur merowingischen Dynastie', in: *Frühmittalterlicher Studien*, 8, 1974.

Ewig, E., 'Das merowingische Frankenreich (561−687)' in: T. Scheider (ed.) *Handbuch der europäischen Geschichte*, vol. 1, Stuttgart, 1976.

Falk, A., 'Hausgeräte aus Holz', in: *Aus dem Alltag einer mittelalterlichen Stadt*, (Hefte des Focke-Museums 62) Bremen, 1982.

Farmer, D. H., *The Oxford Dictionary of Saints*, Oxford, 1978.

Feger, O., 'Herzogin Hadwig von Schwaben in Dichtung und Wirklichkeit', in: *Hohentwiel. Bilder aus der Geschichte des Berges*, Constance, ²1957.

Fehr, H., *Die Rechtsstellung der Frau und der Kinder in den Weistümern*, Jena, 1912.

Fehring, G. P. 'Der Beitrag der Archäologie zum "Leben in der Stadt des späten Mittelalters"', in: *Das Leben in der Stadt des Spätmittelalters*, (Veröffentlichungen des Instituts f. mittelalterliche Realienkunde Osterreichs 2) Vienna, 1977, ²1981.

Fehring, G. P., 'Zur archäologischen Erforschung topographischer, wirtschaftlicher und sozialier Strukturen der Hansestadt Lübeck', in: *Berichte z. dt. Landeskunde*, 54, 1980.

Fehring, G. P., 'Alt-Lübeck und Lübeck. Zur Topographie und Besiedlung zweier Seehandelszentren im Wandel vom 12. zum 13. Jahrhundert', in: *Die Heimat, Zeitschrift f. Natur- und Landeskunde von Schleswig-Holstein und Hambrug*, 89, 1982.

La Femme, vol. 2, (Receuils de la Société Jean Bodin 12). Brussels, 1962.

'La femme dans les civilisations des 10ᵉ−13ᵉ siècles'. Actes du colloque tenu à Poitiers les 23−25 septembre 1976', in: *Cahiers de civilisation médiévale* 20, 1977.

Flandrin, J.-L., *Families in Former Times, Kinship, Household and Sexuality*, Cambridge, 1979, (Vienna, 1978).

Fleckenstein, J., 'Friedrich Barbarossa und das Rittertum. Zur Bedeutung der grossen Mainzer Hoftage von 1184 und 1188', in: *Festschrift für H. Heimpel*, 3 vols, (Veröffentlichungen d. Max-Planck-Instituts f. Geschichte 36, 1–111) Gottingen, 1971–2, vol. 2, 1972. Also in: A. Borst (ed.), *Das Rittertum im Mittelalter*, (Wege der Forschung 349) Darmstadt, 1976.

Fleckenstein, J., *Grundlagen und Beginn der deutschen Geschichte*, (Deutsche Geschichte, ed. J. Leuschner, 1) Göttingen, 1974.

Fleckenstein, J., see under Dilcher.

Fleckenstein, J. (ed.), *Das ritterlicher Turnier im Mittelalter. Beiträge zu einer vergleichenden Formen- und Verhaltensgeschichte des Rittertums*, (Veröffentlichungen des Max-Planck-Institus für Geschichte 80) Göttingen, 1985.

Flossman, U., 'Die Gleichberechtigung der Geschlechter in der Privatrechtsgeschichte', in: *Rechtsgeschichte und Rechtsdogmatik*. Festschrift H. Eichler zum 70. Geburtstag, (Linzer Universitätsschriften. Festsschriften 1) Vienna, 1977.

Flossman, U. and Lehner, O. (eds), *Frau – Recht – Gesellschaft. Seminar zur Frauenrechtsgeschichte* (Sozialwissenschaftliche Materialien 11) Linz ²1986.

France-Lanord, A. and Fleury, M., 'Das Grab der Arnegundis in Saint-Denis', in: *Germania*, 40, 1962.

Franz, G., *Geschichte des deutschen Bauernstandes vom frühen Mittelalter bis zum 19. Jahrhundert*, (Deutsche Agrargeschichte 4) Stuttgart, 1970.

Fuchs, P. (ed.), *Das Rathaus zu Köln*, Cologne, 1973.

Führkötter, A., 'Hildegard von Bingen (1089–1179)', in: *Rheinische Lebensbilder*, 10, Cologne, 1985.

Ganshof, F. L., 'Le statut de la femme dans la monarchie franque', in: *La Femme*, vol. 2, (Recueils de la Société Jean Bodin 12) Brussels, 1962.

Ganshof, F.L., *Qu'est-ce que la féodalite?* Brussels, ⁴1969.

Gaudemet, J., 'Les lèges du droit romain en matière matrimoniale', in: *Il Matrimonio nella società altomedievale*, vol. 1, (Settimane di studio del Centro italiano di studi sull'alto medioevo 24) Spoleto, 1977.

Gaudemet, J., 'Le célibat ecclésiastique. Le droit et la pratique du 11ᵉ au 13ᵉ siècle, in: *Zeitschrift der Savigny-Stiftung f. Rechtsgeschichte, Kan.*, sect. 68.

Gauer, W., 'Urbs, Arx, Metropolis und Civitas Regia. Untersuchungen zur Topographie der frühmittelalterlichen Stadt Regensburg', in: *Verhandlungen d. Hist. Vereins f. Oberpfalz und Regensburg*, 121, 1981.

Gauwerky, U., *Frauenleben in der Karolingerzeit. Ein Beitrag zur Kulturgeschichte*, Diss. phil., Göttingen, 1951. (typescript)

Geremek, B., *Margins of Society in Late Medieval Paris*, Cambridge, 1987 (Paris, 1976).

Giesen, D., *Grundlagen und Entwicklung des englischen Eherechts in der Neuzeit bis zum Beginn des* 19. *Jahrhunderts. Vor dem Hintergrund der englischen Geschichte, Rechts- und Kirchengeschichte,* (Schriften zum deutschen und europäischen Zivil-, Handels- u. Prozessrecht 74) Bielefeld, 1973.

Gieysztor, H., 'La femme dans les civilisations des 10ᵉ−13ᵉ siècles. La femme in Europe orientale', in: *Cahiers de civilisation médiévale* 20, 1977.

Gieysztor, H., 'Le tradizioni locali e le influenze ecclesiastiche nel matrimonio in Polonia nei secoli 10−13', in: *Il Matrimonio nella societa altomedievale,* vol. 1. (Settimane di studio del Centro italiano di studi sull'alto medioevo 24) Spoleto, 1977.

Girouard, M., *Life in the English Country House. A social and architectural history.* New Haven, London, 1978.

Glass, D. V. and Eversley, D. E. C., *Population in History,* London, 1965.

Goetting, H., *Das Bistum Hildeshein.* vol. 1: *Das reichsunmittelbare Kanonissenstift Gandersheim.* (Germania Sacra N. F. 7,1 (Berlin, New York, 1973.

Goetting, H. and Kuhn, H., 'Die Sog. Heiratsurkunde der Kaiserin Theophanu (DO II,21), ihre Untersuchung und Konservierung', in: *Archivalische Zeitschrift,* 64, 1968.

Goetz, H. W., 'Unterschichten im Gesellschaftsbild karolingischer Geschichtsschreiber und Hagiographen', in: H. Mommsen and W. Schulze (eds), *Vom Elend der Handarbeit,* (Geschichte und Gesellschaft. Bochumer Historische Studien 24) Stuttgart, 1981.

Goez, W., *Gestalten des Hochmittelalters. Personengeschichtliche Essays im allgemeinhistorischen Kontext,* Darmstadt, 1983.

Gössmann, E., 'Das Menschenbild der Hildegard von Bingen und Elizabeth von Schönau vor dem Hintergrund der frühscholastischen Anthropologie', in: P. Dinzelbacher and D. R. Bauer (eds), *Frauenmystik im Mittelalter,* Ostfildern, 1985.

Gräfe, R., *Das Eherecht in den Coutumiers des* 13. *Jahrhunderts. Eine rechtsvergleichende Darstellung des französischen Ehepersonen- und Ehegüterrechts im Mittelalter,* (Göttinger Studien zur Rechtsgeschichte 6) Göttingen, Zürich, Frankfurt, 1972.

Graus, F., 'Ketzerbewegungen und soziale Unruhen im 14. Jahrhundert', in: *Zeitschrift f. Historische Forschung,* 1, 1974.

Graus, F., 'Randgruppen der städtischen Gesellschaft im Spätmittelalter', in: *Zeitschrift f. Historische Forschung,* 8, 1981.

Gregorovius, F., *Lucrezia Borgia* (1874), Vienna, Leipzig, 1939, Munich, 1982.

Grimal, P. (ed.) *Histoire mondiale de la Femme,* vol. 2: *L'Occident des Celtes à la Renaissance,* Paris, 1966.

Grimm, P., 'Zwei bemerkenswerte Gebäude in der Pfalz Tilleda. Eine zweite Tuchmacherei', in: *Prähistorische Zeitschrift,* 41, 1963.

Grundmann, H., 'Die geschichtlichen Grundlagen der deutschen Mystik', in: *Deutsche Vierteljahresschrift f. Literatur u. Geistessgeschichte,* 12, 1934.

Grundmann, H., 'Die Frauen und die Literatur im Mittelalter', in *Archiv f. Kulturgeschichte,* 26, 1936.

Grundmann, H., *Religiöse Bewegungen im Mittelalter.* Supplement: *Neue*

Beiträge zur Geschichte der religiösen Bewegungen im Mittelalter, Darmstadt, [3]1970.

Gudian, G., *Ingelheimer Recht im 15. Jahrhundert*, (Untersuchungen zur deutschen Staats- und Rechtsgeschichte N. F. 10) Aalen, 1968.

Gundersheimer, W. L., *Ferrara. The Style of a Renaissance Despotism*, Princeton, 1973.

Haas, A. M., 'Mechtild von Hackeborn. Eine Form zisterziensischer Frauenfrömmigkeit', in: *Die Zisterzienser, Ergänzungsbd.*, (Schriften d. Rheinischen Museumsamtes 18) Cologne, 1982.

Haass, R., *Devotio moderna in der Stadt Köln im 15. und 16. Jahrhundert*, (Veröffentlichungen d. Kölnischen Geschichtsvereins 25) Cologne, 1960.

Haedeke, H. U., 'Eisen, Zinn, Bronze', in: *Herbst des Mittelalters. Spätgotik in Köln und am Niederrhein*, (Ausstellungskatalog Kunsthalle Köln 1970) Cologne, [2]1970.

Handler-Lachmann, B., 'Die Berufstätigkeit der Frau in den deutschen Städten des Spätmittelalters und der beginnenden Neuzeit', in: *Hessisches Jahrbuch für Landesgeschichte*, 30, 1980.

Haff, K., 'Die Kaufmannschaften nach dem hamburgischen Privatrecht', in: *Beiträge zum Wirtschaftsrecht*. (Arbeiten zum Handels-, Gewerbe- und Landwirtschaftsrecht 62) I, Festgabe E. Heymann zum 60 Geburtstag, Marburg, 1931.

Hagemann, H. R., 'Basler Stadtrecht im Spätmittelalter', in: *Zeitschrift d. Savigny-Stiftung f. Rechtsgeschichte, Germ.*, sect. 78, 1961.

Hartwig, J., 'Die Frauenfrage im mittelalterlichen Lübeck', in: *Hansische Geschichtsblätter* 14, 1908.

Hasse, M., 'Neues Hausgerät, neue Hauser, neue Kleider. Eine Betrachtung der städtischen Kultur im 13. und 14. Jahrhundert, sowie ein Katalog der metallenen Hausgeräte', in: *Zeitschrift f. Archäologie des Mittelalters* 7, 1979.

Haverkamp, A., Zur Sklaverei in Genoa während des 12. Jahrhunderts', in: *Geschichte in der Gesellschaft. Festschrift K. Bosl*, Stuttgart, 1974.

Haverkamp, A. (ed.), *Zur Geschichte der Juden im Deutschland des Mittelalters und der frühen Neuzeit*, (Monographien zur Geschichte des Mittelalters 24) Stuttgart, 1981.

Haverkamp, A. (ed.), *Haus und Familie in der spätmittelalterlichen Stadt*, (Städteforschung. Veröffentlichungen des Instituts f. vergleichende Städtegeschichte in Münster A, 18) Cologne, Vienna, 1984.

Haverkamp, A., 'Tenxwind von Andernach und Hildegard von Bingen. Zwei "Weltanschauungen" in der Mitte des 12. Jahrhunderts', in: *Institutionen, Kultur und Gesellschaft im Mittelalter. Festschrift fur J. Fleckenstein zu seinem 65. Geburtstag*. Sigmaringen, 1984.

Heers, J., *Le clan familial au Moyen-Age. Étude sur les structures politiques et sociales des milieux urbains*, Paris, 1974.

Heimpel, H., *Das Gewerbe der Stadt Regensburg im Mittelalter, (Beihefte zur Vierteljahrsschrift f. Sozial- u. Wirtschaftgeschichte* 9) Stuttgart, 1926.

Heimpel, H., 'Auf neuen Wegen der Wirtschaftsgeschichte', in:

Vergangenheit und Gegenwart, 32, 1933.

Heimpel, H., 'Seide aus Regensburg', in: *Mitteilungen d. Instituts f. Osterreichische Geschichtsforschung*, 62, 1954.

Heinzelmann, M., 'Beobachtungen zur Bevölkerungsstruktur einiger grundherrschaftlicher Siedlungen im Karoling. Bayern', in: *Frühmittelalterliche Studien*, 11, 1977, 12, 1978.

Hellmann, S., 'Die Heiraten der Karolinger', in: *Festgabe K. Th. von Heigel zur Vollendung seines 60. Lebensjahres*, Munich, 1903.

Herborn, W., *Die politische Führungsschicht der Stadt Köln im Spätmittelalter*, (Rheinisches Archiv 100) Bonn 1977.

Herborn, W., 'Die Familie von Schwelm/von Weinsberg. Entwicklungsstufen einer bauderlichen Familie im Grossstädtischen Milieu an der Schwelle zur Neuzeit', in: *Beiträge zur Heimatkunde der Stadt Schwelm und ihrer Umgebung* N.F., 3, 1982.

Herlihy, D., 'The agrarian revolution in southern France and Italy', in: *Speculum*, 33, 1958.

Herlihy, D., 'Land, family and women in Continental Europe, 701–1200', in: *Traditio*, 18, 1962.

Herlihy, D., 'Family and property in Renaissance Florence', in Miskimin, H. A., Herlihy, D., Udowitsch, A. L., *The Medieval City*, New Haven, London, 1977.

Herlihy, D. and Klapisch-Zuber, C., *Tuscans and their Families: a Study of the Florentine Catasto of 1427*, New Haven 1985 (Paris, 1978).

Hermann, B., (ed.), *Mensch und Umwelt im Mittelalter*, Stuttgart, 1986.

Herzog, H. U., *Beiträge zur Geschichte des eherechtlichen Güterrechts der Stadt Zürich. Mit 3 unveröffentlichten Urkunden aus dem 14. bis ins 18. Jahrhundert*, (Zürcher Beiträge zur Rechtswissenschaft N.F. 92) Aarau, 1942.

Hess, L., *Die deutschen Frauenberufe des Mittelalters*, (Beiträge zur Volkstumsforschung 6) Munich, 1940.

Hess, U., 'Oratrix humilis. Die Frau als Briefpartnerin von Humanisten, am Beispiel der Caritas Pirckheimer', in: F. J. Worstbrock (ed.), *Der Brief im Zeitalter der Renaissance*, (Mitteilungen der Kommission f. Humanismusforschung 9) Weinheim, 1983.

Hess, W., 'Rechnung Legen auf Linien. Rechenbrett und Zahltisch in der Verwaltungspraxis in Spätmittelalter und Neuzeit', in: E. Maschke and J. Sydow (eds), *Städtisches Haushalts- und Rechnungswesen*, (Stadt in der Geschichte, Veröffentlichungen d. Südwestdeutschen Arbeitskreises f. Stadtgeschichtsforschung 2) Sigmaringen, 1977.

Higounet, A., 'La femme du Moyen-Age en France dans la vie politique, économique et sociale', in: P. Grimal (ed.), *Histoire mondiale de la Femme*, vol. 2, Paris, 1966.

Hlawitschka, E., 'Zur landschaftlichen Herkunft der Karolinger', in: *Rheinische Vierteljahrsblätter*, 27, 1962.

Hlawitschka, E., 'Die Vohfahren Karls des Grossen', in: W. Braunfels (ed.), *Karl der Grosse. Lebenswerk und Nachleben*, vol. 1: *Persönlichkeit und Geschichte*, ed. H. Beaumann, Düsseldorf, 1965.

Hlawitschka, E., 'Zu den klösterlichen Anfängen in St. Maria im Kapitol in Köln', in: *Rheinische Vierteljahrsblätter*, 31, 1966—7.

Hlawitschka, E., 'Zum Werden der Unteilbarkeit des mittelalterlichen Deutschen Reiches', *Jahrbuch d. Universität*, Düsseldorf, 1969—70.

Hlawitschka, E., 'Beiträge und Berichte zur Bleitafelinschrift aus dem Grab der Kaiserin Gisela', in: *Historisches Jahrbuch* 97—8, 1978.

Hlawitschka, E., 'Beobachtungen und Überlegungen zur Konventsstärke im Nonnenkloster Remiremont während des 7—9. Jahrhunderts', in: *Secundum regulam vivere. Festschrift für P. N. Backmund O. Praem*, Windberg, 1978.

Hlawitschka, E., 'Studien zur Genealogie und Geschichte der Merowinger und der frühen Karolinger', in: *Rheinische Vierteljahrsblätter*, 43, 1979.

Hlawitschka, E., 'Die Widonen im Dukat von Spoleto', in: *Quellen und Forschungen aus italienischen Archiven und Bibliotheken*, 63, 1983.

Hollingworth, T. A., 'A demographic study of the British ducal families', in: D. V. Glass and D. E. C. Eversley, *Population in History*, London, 1965.

Höppner, M., *Die Frauenarbeit in Paris im Mittelalter*, Diss. Göttingen 1922 (typescript).

Hörger, K., 'Die reichsrechtliche Stellung der Fürstäbissinnen', in: *Archiv. f. Urkundenforschung*, 9, 1926.

Huizinga, J., *The Waning of the Middle Ages*, London, 1955 (Stuttgart, 1953).

Hundsbichler, H., 'Stadtbegriff Stadtbild und Stadtleben des 15. Jahrhunderts nach ausländischen Berichterstattern über Österreich', in: *Das Leben in der Stadt des Spätmittelalters*, (Veröff. d. Inst. f. mittel. Realienkunde Österreichs 2) Vienna, 1977, [2]1981.

Irsigler, F., *Untersuchungen zur Geschichte des frühfränkischen Adels*, (Rheinisches Archiv 70) Bonn, 1969, mentioned in postscript, 1981.

Irsigler, F., 'Divites und pauperes in der Vita Meinwerci', in: *Vierteljahrsschrift f. Sozial- u. Wirtschaftsgeschichte*, 57, 1970.

Irsigler, F., 'Ein grossbürgerlicher Kölner Haushalt am Ende des 14. Jahrhunderts', in: E. Ennen and G. Wiegelmann (eds), *Festschrift M. Zender. Studien zu Volkskultur, Sprache und Landesgeschichte*, vol. 2, Bonn, 1972.

Irsigler, F., 'Kölner Wirtschaft im Spätmittelalter', in: H. Kellenbenz (ed), *Zwei Jahrtausende Kölner Wirtschaft*, 2 vols, vol. 1, Cologne, 1975.

Irsigler, F., 'Peter Rinck (Gest. 8 Februar 1501)', in: *Rheinische Lebensbilder*, 6, Cologne, 1975.

Irsigler, F., *Die wirtschaftliche Stellung der Stadt Köln im 14. und 15. Jahrhundert. Strukturanalyse einer spätmittelalterlichen Exportgewerbe- und Fernandelsstadt*, (Beihefte zur Vierteljahrsschrift f. Sozial- u. Wirtschaftsgeschichte 65) Wiesbaden, 1979.

Irsigler, F., 'Bettler, Dirnen und Henker im spätmittelalterlichen und frühneuzeitlichen Köln. Zur Analyse sozialer Randgruppen', in: *Geschichte in Köln. Studentische Zeitschrift am historischen Seminar*, 7, 1980.

Irsigler, F., 'Hermann von Goch (†7.5. 1398)', in: *Rheinische Lebensbilder*, 8, Cologne, 1980.

Irsigler, F., 'Die Wirtschaftsführung der Burggrafen von Drachenfels im Spätmittelalter', in: *Bonner Geschichtsblätter*, 34, 1982.

Irsigler, F., 'Konrad von Weinsberg (etwa 1370—1448). Adeliger — Diplomat — Kaufmann', in: *Württembergisch Franken*, 66, 1982.

Irsigler, F. and Lassotta, A., *Bettler und Gaukler, Dirnen und Henker. Randgruppen und Aussenseiter in Köln 1300—1600*, (Aus der Kölner Städtegeschichte) Cologne, 1984.

Jaacks, G., 'Städtische Kleidung im Mittelalter', in: *Aus dem Alltag der mittelalterlichen Stadt*, (Hefte des Focker-Museums 62) Bremen, 1982.

Jahn, R., *Essener Geschichte*, Essen, 1952, ²1957.

Jannsen, W., 'Essen und Trinken im frühen und hohen Mittelalter aus archäologischer Sicht', in: *Liber Castellorum, 40 variaties op het thema kasteel*, Zutphen, 1981.

Jannsen, W., see under Ennen.

Jenks, S., 'Frauensiegel in den Würzburger Urkunden des 14. Jahrhunderts', in: *Zeitschrift f. bayerische Landesgeschichte* 45, 1982.

Jordan, K., *Heinrich der Löwe*, Munich, 1979.

Kaiser-Guyot, M.T., *Le berger en France aux 14ᶜ et 15ᵉ siècles*, Paris, 1974.

Kalsbach, A., *Die altkirchliche Einrichtung der Diakonissen bis zu ihrem Erlöschen*, (Römische Quartalschrift f. christliche Altertumskunde u. Kirchengeschichte, Supplement 22) Freiburg, 1926.

Keller, H., 'Der Übergang zur Kommune. Zur Entwicklung der italienischen Stadtverfassung im 11. Jahrhundert', in: B. Diestelkamp (ed.), *Beiträge zum hochmittelalterlichen Städtewesen*, (Städteforschung, Veröffentlichungen d. Instituts f. vergleichende Städtegeschichte in Münster, Reihe A, 11) Cologne, Vienna, 1982.

Kelly, A., *Eleanor of Aquitaine and the Four Kings*, Cambridge, Mass., 1973 (Munich, 1953).

Kentenich, G., *Aus dem Leben einer Trierer Patrizierin. Ein Beitrag zur Kunst- und Wirtschafsgeschichte der Stadt Trier im 15. Jahrhundert*, Trier, 1909.

Ketsch, P., see under Quellen.

Keussen, H., *Köln im Mittelalter. Topographie und Verfassung*, (Rev. Sonderabdruck aus der 2. Preisschrift der v. Mevissen-Stiftung) Bonn, 1918.

Kieckhefer, R., *European Witch Trials: their foundations in popular and learned culture 1300—1500*, London, 1976.

Klapisch-Zuber, C., see under Herlihy.

Klose, O., *Die Familienverhältnisse auf Island vor der Bekehrung zum Christentum auf Grund der Ilendingasogur, (Nordische Studien* 10) Braunschweig, Berlin, Hamburg, 1929.

Köbler, G., 'Das Familienrecht in der spätmittelalterlichen Stadt', in: A. Haverkamp (ed.), *Haus und Familie in der spätmittelalterlichen Stadt*, (Städteforschung. Veröffentlichungen d. Instituts f. vergleichende Städtegeschichte in Münster A, 18) Cologne, Vienna, 1984.

Koch, G., *Frauenfrage and Ketzertum im Mittelalter*, Forschungen zur mittelalterlichen Geschichte 9) Berlin, 1962.

Koebner, R., 'Die Eheauffassung des ausgehenden deutschen Mittelalters', in: *Archiv f. Kulturgeschichte*, 9, 1911.

Kohl, W., 'Inventar eines Kölner Hauses aus dem Jahre 1519', in: *Jahrbuch des Kölner Geschichtsvereins*, 31/32, 1957.

Köhler, E., 'Observations historiques et sociologiques sur la poésie des troubadours', in: *Cahiers de civilisation médiévale*, 7, 1964.

Köhler, E. 'Die Rolle des niederen Rittertums bei der Entstehung der Troubadourlyrik', in: A. Borst (ed.), *Das Rittertum im Mittelalter*, (Wege der Forschung 349) Darmstadt, 1976.

Konecny, S., *Die Frauen des karolingischen Königshauses. Die politische Bedeutung der Ehe und die Stellung der Frau in der fränkischen Herrscherfamilie vom 7. bis zum 10. Jahrhundert*, (Dissertationen d. Universität Wien 132) Vienna, 1976.

Köpf, U., 'Bernhard von Clairvaux in der Frauenmystik', in: P. Dinzelbacher and D.R. Bauer (eds), *Frauenmystik im Mittelalter*, Ostfildern, 1985.

Kopp, S., see Aurelius Augustinus.

Korsch, H.P., *Das materielle Strafrecht der Stadt Köln. Vom Ausgang des Mittelalters bis in die Neuzeit*, (Veröffentlichungen des Kölnischen Geschichtsvereins 20) Cologne, 1958.

Koschaker, P., 'Die Eheformen der Indogermanen', in: *Deutsche Landesreferate zum 2. Internationalen Kongress fur Rechtsvergleichung im Haag*, (Zeitschrift f. ausländisches u. internationales Privatrecht, Jahrgang 11, Sonderheft) Berlin, 1937.

Köstler, R., *Die väterliche Ehebewilligung. Eine Kirchenrechtliche Untersuchung auf rechtsvergleichender Grundlage*, (Kirchenrechtliche Abhandlungen 51) Stuttgart, 1908, Amsterdam, 1965.

Köstler R., 'Raub-, Kauf- und Friedelehe bei den Germanen', in: *Zeitschrift der Savigny-Stiftung f. Rechtsgeschichte, Germ.*, 63, 1943.

Kossert, K., *Aleydis Raiscop. Die Humanistin von Nonnenwerth*, (Gocher Shcriften 6) Goch, 1985.

Kottje, R., 'Ehe und Eheverständnis in den vorgratianischen Bussbüchern', in: W. van Hoecke and A. Welkenhuysen (eds), *Love and Marriage in the Twelfth Century*, Lörren, 1981.

Kottje, R., 'Claustra sine armario? Zum Unterschied von Kloster und Stift im Mittelalter', in: *Consuetudines monasticae. Eine Festgabe f. Kassius Hallinger aus Anlass seines 70 Geburtstages*, (Studia Anselmiana 85) Rome, 1982.

Kottje, R., 'Eine wenig beachtete Quelle zur Sozialgeschichte: Die frühmittelalterlichen Bussbücher. Probleme ihrer Erforschung', in: *Vierteljahresschrift für Sozial- und Wirtschaftsgeschichte*, 73, 1986.

Krabbel, G., *Caritas Pirckheimer. Ein Lebensbild aus der Zeit der Reformation*, (Vereinsschriften der Gesellschaft zur Herausgabe des Corpus Catholicum 7) Münster, 1940.

Krebs, P.-P., *Die Stellung der Handwerkerswitwe in der Zunft vom Spätmittelalter bis zum achtzehnten Jahrhundert. Diss. iur. Regensburg, 1974*, Regensburg, 1974.

Kroeschell, K., *Deutsche Rechtsgeschichte*, 2 vols, (rororo Studium 8–9) Hamburg, 1972–3.

Kroeschell, K., 'Söhne und Töchter im germanischen Erbrecht', in: G. Landwehr (ed.), *Studien zu den germanischen Volksrechten. Gedächtnisschrift f. W. Ebel*, (Rechts-historische Reihe 1) Frankfurt, 1982.

Kuchenbuch, L., *Bäuerliche Gesellschaft und Klosterherrschaft im 9. Jahrhundert Studien zur Sozialstruktur der Familia der Abtei Prüm*, (Beihefte zur Vierteljahrsschrift f. Sozial- u. Wirtschaftsgeschichte 66) Wiesbaden, 1978.

Kuhn, A., see under Affeldt and Ketsch.

Kuhn, H., see under Goetting.

Kuhn-Rehfus, M., 'Zisterzienserinnen in Deutschland', in: K. Elm (ed.), *Die Zisterzienser. Ordensleben zwischen Ideal und Wirklichkeit*, (Schriften des Rheinischen Museumsamtes 10) Bonn, 1980.

Kuhn-Rehfus, M., 'Die soziale Zusammensetzung der Konvente in den oberschwäbischen Frauenzisterzen', in: *Zeitschrift f. württemberg. Landesgeschichte* 41, 1982.

Kupper, J.-L., 'Une "conventio" inédite entre l'évêque de Liège Théoduin et le comte Albert II de Namur (1056–64)', in: *Bulletin de la Commission royale d'Histoire*, 145, 1979.

Kuske, B., 'Die Frau im mittelalterlichen deutschen Wirtschaftsleben', in: *Zeitschrift f. handelswissenschaftliche Forschung*, new series 11, 1959.

Landwehr, G. (ed.), *Studien zu den germanischen Volksrechten*, Frankfurt, Bern, 1981.

Lane, F. C., 'Family partnerships and joint ventures in the Venetian Republic', in: *Venice and History*, Baltimore, 1966.

Lange, H., *Frauenerwerbsarbeit im mittelalterlichen Florenz (14. u. 15. Jh.)* Diss. iur. Göttingen, 1924 (typescript).

Laslett, P., *Family life and illicit love in earlier generations. Essays in historical sociology*, Cambridge, 1977.

Laufner, R., Der Handelsbereich des Trierer Marktes im Spätmittelalter', in: *Rheinische Vierteljahrsblätter*, 22, 1957.

Laufner, R., 'Die "Elenden-Bruderschaft" zu Trier im 15. und 16. Jahrhundert. Ein Beitrag zur Sozialgeschichte der untersten Unterschichten im ausgehenden Mittelalter und der frühen Neuzeit', in: *Jahrbuch für westdeutsche Landesgeschichte* 4, 1978.

Lauts, J., *Isabella d'Este. Fürstin der Renaissance 1474–1539*, Hamburg, 1952.

Das Leben in der Stadt des Spätmittelalters, (Veröffentlichungen des Instituts für mittelalterliche Realienkunde Österreichs 2) Vienna 1977, ²1981.

Leclercq, J., 'Neue Perspektiven in der monastischen Theologie: Das Weibliche und die eheliche Liebe', in: *Renovatio et Reformatio. Wider das bild vom "finsteren" Mittelalter. Festschrift für L. Hödl zum 60. Geburtstag*,

Münster, 1985.

Legner, A. (ed.), *Ornamenta ecclesiae. Kunst und Künstler der Romanik. Katalog der Ausstellung*, Cologne, 1985.

Leineweber, A., *Die rechtliche Beziehung des nichtehelichen Kindes zu seinem Erzeuger in der Geschichte des Privatrechts*, (Beiträge zur Neueren Privatrechtsgeschichte 7) Königstein/Ts., 1978.

Leisching, P., 'Eheschliessung vor dem Notar im 13. Jahrhundert' in: *Zeitschrift der Savigny-Stiftung f. Rechtsgeschichte, Kanon.* section 63, 1977.

Lenckner, E., see under Wunder.

Le Roy Ladurie, E., *Montaillou, Cathars and Catholics in a French Village*, London, 1984 (Paris, 1975).

Levison, W., *England and the Continent in the Eighth Century*, Oxford, 1946.

Levison, W. and Lowe, H. (eds), *Deutschlands Geschichtsquellen im Mittelalter. Vorzeit und Karolinger*, part 2, Weimar, 1953.

Leyser, K. J., *Rule and Conflict in an Early Medieval Society. Ottonian Saxony*, London 1979.

Löhr, G. M. 'Das Necrologium des Dominikanerinnenklosters St. Gertrud in Köln', in: *Annalen d. Historischen Vereins f. d. Niederrhein*, 110, 1927.

Löwe, H., *Die Iren und Europa im Früheren Mittelalter*, 2, vols, (Veröffentlichungen des Europa Zentrums Tübingen, Kulturwissenschaftliche Reihe) Stuttgart, 1982.

Loose, H. D., 'Erwerbstätigkeit der Frau im Spiegel Lübecker und Hamburger Testamente des 14. Jahrhunderts', in: *Zeitschrift d. Vereins f. Lübeckische Geschichte u. Altertumskunde*, 60, 1980.

Lorenzen-Schmidt, K. J. 'Zur Stellung der Frauen in der frühneuzeitlichen Städtegesellschaft Schleswigs und Holsteins', in: *Archiv für Kulturgeschichte*, 61, 1979.

Manns, P. (ed.), *Die Heiligen: Alle Biographien zum Regionalkalender für das deutsche Sprachgebiet*, Mainz, 1975.

Manselli, R., see under Elm.

Markgraf, B., *Das moselländische Volk in seinen Weistümern*, (Geschichtliche Untersuchungen 4) Gotha, 1907.

Maschke, E., *Die Familie in der deutschen Stadt des späten Mittelalters*, (Sitzungsberichte d. Heidelberger Akademie d. Wissenschaften, Phil.-Hist. Kl. Jg. 1980, 4 Abh.) Heidelberg, 1980.

Maschke, E., *Städte und Menschen. Beiträge zur Geschichte der Stadt, der Wirtschaft und Gesellschaft 1959–77*, (Beihefte zur Vierteljahrsschrift f. Sozial- und Wirtschaftsgeschichte 68) Wiesbaden, 1980.

Il Matrimonio nella società altomedievale, 2 vols, (Settimane di studio del centro italiano di studi sull'alto medioevo 24) Spoleto, 1977.

Matheus, M., *Trier am Ende des Mittelalters. Studien zur Sozial-, Wirtschafts- und Verfassungsgeschichte der Stadt Trier vom 14. bis 16. Jahrhundert*, (Trierer Historische Forschungen 5) Trier, 1984.

May, G., 'Zu der Frage der Weihefähigkeit der Frau', in: *Zeitschrift der Savigny-Stiftung f. Rechtsgeschichte, Kanon*, sect. 60, 1974.

Melicher, T., *Die germanischen Formen der Eheschliessung im westgotisch-*

spanischen Recht, Vienna, 1940.

Mertens, V., see under Ruh.

Metzger, T. and M., *Jüdisches Leben im Mittelalter nach illuminierten hebräischen Handschriften vom 13. bis ins 16. Jahrhundert*, (German edition) Würzburg, 1983.

Meuthen, E., *Das 15. Jahrhundert*, (Oldenbourg-Grundriss der Geschichte 9) Munich, Vienna, 1980.

Meyer, H., 'Friedelehe und Mutterrecht', in: *Zeitschrift der Savigny-Stiftung f. Rechtsgeschichte, Germ.*, sect. 47, 1927.

Meyer, H., 'Ehe und Eheauffassung der Germanen', in: *Festschrift E. Heymann zum 70. Geburtstag*, vol. 1: *Rechtsgeschichte*, Weimar, 1940.

Mikat, P., *Religionsrechtliche Schriften. Abhandlungen zum Staatskirchenrecht und Eherecht*, (Staatskirchenrechtliche Abhandlungen 5) 2 vols, Berlin, 1974.

Mikat, P., *Dotierte Ehe — rechte Ehe. Zur Entwicklung des Eheschliessungsrechts in fränkischer Zeit*, (Rheinisch-Westfälische Akademie d. Wissenschaften, Geisteswissenschaften: Vorträge G. 227) Opladen, 1978.

Mitteins, H., *Lehnrecht und Staatsgewalt*, Weimar, 1933.

Mitterauer, M., 'Familie und Arbeitsorganisation in städtischen Gesellschaften des späten Mittelalters und der frühen Neuzeit', in: A. Haverkamp (ed.), *Haus und Familie in der spätmittelalterlichen Stadt*, (Städteforschung. Veröffentlichungen des Instituts f. Vergleichende Städtegeschichte in Münster A, 18) Cologne, Vienna, 1984.

Mitterauer, M. and Sieder, R., *The European Family: patriarchy to partnership from the Middle Ages to the present*, Oxford, 1982 (Munich, 1977).

Mohr, W., 'Boso von Vienne und die Nachfolgefrage nach dem Tode Karls des Kahlen und Ludwigs des Stammlers', in: *Archivum Latinitatis Medii Aevi*, 26, 1956.

Molitor, E., 'Zur Entwicklung der Munt', in: *Zeitschrift der Savigny-Stiftung f. Rechtsgeschichte, Germ.*, sect. 64, 1944.

Mollat, M., 'La notion de pauvreté au Moyen Age: position des problèmes', in *Revue d'histoire de l'Eglise de France*, 52, 1966.

Mollat, M., *The Poor in the Middle Ages: an essay in social history*, New Haven, 1986 (Paris, 1978).

Mollat, M. and Wolff, P., *Ongles bleus. Jacques et Ciompi. Les révolutions populaires en Europe aux 14ᵉ et 15ᵉ siècles*, Paris, 1967.

Mommsen, H., see under Elze, also under Goetz.

Mor, C. G., 'Consors regni: La Regina nel diritto pubblico italiano dei secoli IX—X', in: *Archivio giuridico*, 6, 1948.

Mordek, H., 'Ehescheidung und Wiederheirat in der Frühkirche', in: *Revue de droit canonique*, 28, 1978.

Morewedge, R. T. (ed.), *The Role of Women in the Middle Ages*, (Papers of the Sixth Annual Conference of the Center for Medieval and Early Renaissance Studies 1972) Albany, 1975.

Moritz, W., *Die bürgerlichen Fürsorgeanstalten der Reichsstadt Frankfurt am Main im späten Mittelalter*, (Studien zur Frankfurter Geschichte 14) Frankfurt, 1981.

Morrick, D., see under Aurelius Augustinus.

Moser, O., 'Zum Aufkommen der "Stusse" im Bürgerhaus des Spätmittelalters', in: *Das Leben in der Stadt des Spätmittelalters*, (Veröffentlichungen des Instituts f. mittelalterliche Realienkunde Osterreichs 2) Vienna, 1977, ²1981.

Mühlberger, J., *Lebensweg und Schicksale der staufischen Frauen*, Esslingen, ²1977.

Müller, W., *Entwicklung und Spätformen der Leibeigenschaft am Beispiel der Heiratsbeschränkungen. Die Ehegenossame im alemannisch—schweizereischen Raum*, (Vorträge und Forschungen, ed. Konstanzer Arbeitskreis f. mittelalterliche Geschichte, Sonderband) Sigmaringen, 1974.

Müller-Lindenlauf, G. H., *Germanische und spätrömisch-christliche Eheauffassung in fränkischen Volksrechten und Kapitularien*. Diss. iur., Freiburg, 1969.

Mummenhoff, E., 'Frauenarbeit und Arbeitsvermittlung', in: *Vierteljahrsschrift fur Sozial- und Wirtschaftsgeschichte*, 19, 1926.

Munier, C., 'Le témoignage d'Origène en matière de remariage après séparation', in: *Revue de droit canonique*, 28, 1978 (L'exception à la norme dans le domaine du mariage).

Nehlsen, H., *Sklavenrecht zwischen Antike und Mittelalter. Germanisches und Römisches Recht in den germanischen Rechtsaufzeichnungen*, Göttingen, 1972.

Nelson, J. L., 'Queens as Jezebels: the careers of Brunhild and Balthild in Merovingian history', *in D. Baker (ed.)*, *Medieval Women*, Oxford, 1978.

Nette, H., *Jeanne d'Arc in Selbstzeugnissen und Bildokumenten*, Reinbek/Hamburg, 1977.

Neumann, E. G. *Rheinisches Beginen- und Begardenwesen*, (Mainzer Abhandlungen zur mittleren u. neueren Geschichte 4) Meisenheim am Glan, 1960.

Nicholas, D., *The Domestic Life of a Medieval City: women, children and the family in fourteenth century Ghent*, Lincoln, London, 1985.

Nonn, U., 'Erminethrud — eine vornehme neustrische Dame um 700', in: *Historisches Jahrbuch*, 102, 1982.

Noonan, J. T., *Contraception: A history of its treatment by the Catholic theologians and canonists*, Harvard Univ. Press, 1986 (Paris, 1969).

Nübel, O., *Mittelalterliche Beginen- und Sozialsiedlungen in den Niederlanden. Ein Beitrag zur Vorgeschichte der Fuggerei*, (Studien zur Fuggergeschichte 23) Tübingen, 1970.

Oediger, W. F., *Das Bistum Köln von den Anfängen bis zum Ende des 12. Jahrhunderts*, Cologne, 1972.

Oediger, W. F., *Vom Leben am Niederrhein*, Düsseldorf, 1973.

Oexle, G. O., 'Die funktionale Dreiteilung der "Gesellschaft" bei Adalbero von Laon', in: *Frühmitterlalterliche Studien*, 12, 1978.

Ohnesorge, W., 'Das Mitkaisertum in der abendländischen Geschichte des früheren Mittelalters', in *Zeitschrift der Savigny-Stiftung f. Rechtsgeschichte*, *Germ.*, sect. 67, 1950.

Ohnesorge, W., 'Die Heirat Kaiser Ottos II. mit der Byzantinerin

Theophanu (972)', in: *Brauschweigisches Jahrbuch*, 54, 1973.

Opitz, C., 'Mutterschaft und Mütterlichkeit im 13. Jahrhundert', in: *Schweizerische Historikerinnentagung*, Beiträge 3, Zürich, 1986.

Painter, S., 'Die Ideen des Rittertums', in: A. Borst (ed.), *Das Rittertum im Mittelalter*, Darmstadt, 1976.

Pappe, H., *Methodische Strömungen in der eherechtsgeschichtlichen Forschung (bis zur Epoche der germanischen Christianisierung). Ein literargeschichtlicher Beitrag*, Würzburg, 1934.

Parisse, M., *Les nonnes au Moyen Age*, Le Puy, 1983.

Patault, A.-M., *Hommes et femmes de Corps en Champagne méridionale à la fin du Moyen Age*. (Annales de l'Est, Mémoire no. 58), Saint-Nicholas-de-Port, 1978.

Patze, H., 'Adel und Stifterchronik. Frühformen territorialer Geschichts-schreibung im hochmittelalterlichen Reich', in: *Blätter f. dt. Landesgesch.* 100, 1964 and 101, 1965.

Patze, H., 'Die Wittelsbacher in der mittelalterlichen Politik Europas', in: *Zeitschrift f. bayerische Landesgeschichte* 44, 1981.

Pauli, L., *Infirmitas sexus* − [*Die rechtliche Lage der Frau im Lichte der strafrechtlichen Vorschriften der Statutengesetzgebung italienischer Städte*], Warsaw, Krakow, 1975 (With summary in French).

Pauly, F., 'Anfänge und Bedeutung der Chorherrenreform von Springiersbach', in: *Rheinische Vierteljahrsblätter*, 26, 1961.

Payer, P. J., 'Early medieval regulations concerning marital sexual re-lations', in: *Journal of Medieval History*, 6, 1980.

Pernoud, R., *Jeanne d'Arc. Zeugnisse und Selbstzeugnisse*, Freiburg, Basle, Vienna, 1965.

Pernoud, R., *Eleonore von Aquitanien*, Düsseldorf, Cologne, 1966.

Pernoud, R., *La Reine Blanche*, Paris, 1972.

Pernoud, R., *La femme au temps des cathédrales*, Paris, 1980.

Perst, O., 'Die Kaisertochter Sophie, Abtissin von Gandersheim und Essen (975−1039)', in: *Braunschweigisches Jahrbuch*, 38, 1957.

Peters, G., 'Norddeutsches Beginen- und Begardenwesen im Mittelalter', in: *Niedersächs. Jahrbuch f. Landesgeschichte* 41−42, 1969−70.

v. Petrikovits, H., *Der diachorische Aspekt der Kontinuität von der Spätantike zum frühen Mittelalter*, (Nachrichten d. Akademie d. Wissenschaften in Göttingen, Phil.-Hist. Klasse, Jg. 1982, no. 5) Göttingen, 1982.

Pfaff, V., 'Das kirchliche Eherecht am Ende des 12. Jahrhunderts', in: *Zeitschrift d. Savigny-Stiftung f. Rechtsgeschichte, Kanon*, sect. 63, 1977.

Pohl, H. and Treue, E. (eds), *Die Frau in der deutschen Wirtschaft*, (Zeitschrift für Unternehmensgeschichte, Beiheft 35) Wiesbaden, 1985.

Portmann, M. L., *Die Darstellung der Frau in der Geschichtsschreibung des frühen Mittelalters*, (Basler Beiträge zur Geschichtswissenschaft 69) Basle, Stuttgart, 1958.

Postan, M. M., see under Power.

Power, E., *Medieval Women*, ed. M. M. Postan, Cambridge, 1975.

Prieur, J., *Das Kölner Dominikanerinnenkloster St. Gertrud am Neumarkt*,

(Kölner Schriften zur Geschichte und Kultur 3) Cologne, 1983.

Prinz, F., *Frühes Mönchtum im Frankenreich. Kultur und Gesellschaft in Gallien, den Rheinlanden und Bayern am Beispiel der monastischen Entwicklung (4. bis 8. Jahrhundert)* Munich, Vienna, 1965.

Prinz, F., *Askese und Kultur. Vor- und frühbenediktinisches Mönchtum an der Wiege Europas*, Munich, 1980.

Prinz, F., *Grundlagen und Anfänge. Deutschland bis 1056*, (Die Neue Deutsche Geschichte 1) Munich, 1985.

Raming, I., *Der Ausschluss der Frau vom priesterlichen Amt. Gottgewollte Tradition oder Diskriminierung? Eine rechtshistorisch-dogmatische Untersuchung der Grundlagen von Kanon 968 § 1 des Codex iuris canonici*, Cologne, Vienna, 1973.

Ranieri, F. (ed.), *Rechtsgeschichte und quantitative Geschichte*, (Ius commune, Sonderheft 7). Frankfurt, 1977.

v. Ranke, E., 'Der Interessenkreis des deutschen Bürgers im 16. Jahrhundert', in: *Vierteljahrsschrift f. Sozial- u. Wirtschaftsgeschichte*, 20, 1928.

Rapp, F., 'Die Mendikanten und die Strassburger Gesellschaft am Ende des Mittelalters', in: K. Elm, *Ordensstudien*, vol. 2, see under Elm.

Rassow, P., *Der Prinzgemahl. Ein Pactum Matrimoniale aus dem Jahr 1188*, (Quellen und Studien zur Verfassungsgeschichte des Deutschen Reiches in Mittelalter und Neuzeit 8, 1) Weimar, 1950.

Razi, Z., *Life, Marriage and Death in a Medieval Parish. Economy, society and demography in Halesowen 1270–1400*, Cambridge, 1980.

Rehm, G., *Die Schwestern vom gemeinsamen Leben im nordwestlichen Deutschland*, (Berliner historische Studien 11, Ordensstudien 5) Berlin, 1985.

Reincke, H., *Agneta Willeken. Ein Lebensbild aus Wullenwevers Tagen*, (Pfingstblätter des Hansischen Geschichtsvereins 19) Lübeck, 1928.

Reincke, H., 'Bevölkerungsprobleme der Hansestädte', in: *Hansische Geschichtsblätter*, 70, 1951.

Richardson, H. G., 'The letters and charters of Eleanor of Aquitaine', in: *English Historical Review*, 74, 1959.

Riché, P., 'Les bibliothèques de trois aristocrates laïcs carolingiens', in: *Le Moyen Age* 69, 1963.

Riché, P., *Les écoles et l'enseignement dans l'Occident chrétien de la fin du 5ᵉ siècle au milieu du 11ᵉ siècle*, Paris, 1979.

Riché, P., *Daily Life in the World of Charlemagne*, Philadelphia, 1988 (Stuttgart, 1981).

Riemer, P., *Women in the Medieval City. Sources and uses of wealth by Sienese women in the 13th century*, Diss. phil., New York University, 1975.

Ritzer, K., *Formen, Riten und religiöses Brauchtum der Eheschliessung in den christlichen Kirchen des ersten Jahrtausends*, Münster, 1962.

Rorig, F., *Hansische Beiträge zur deutschen Wirtschaftsgeschichte*, Breslau, 1928.

Roth, J., 'Die Steuerlisten von 1363/64 und 1374/75 als Quellen zur Sozialstruktur der Stadt Trier im Spätmittelalter', in: *Kurtrierisches Jahrbuch*, 16, 1976.

Ruh, K., 'Beginenmystik. Hadewich, Mechtild von Magdeburg, Marguerite Porète', in: *Zeitschrift für deutsches Altertum und deutsche Literatur*, 106, 1977.

Ruh, K., *Vorbemerkungen zu einer neuen Geschichte der abendländischen Mystik im Mittelalter*, (Sitzungsberichte der Bayerischen Akademie der Wissenschaften, Phil.-Hist. Klasse Jhg. 1982, 7) Munich, 1982.

Ruh, K., *Kleine Schriften 2. Scholastik und Mystik im Spätmittelalter*, ed. V. Mertens, (Kleinere Schriften 3. Literatur- u. Geistesgeschichte 8) Berlin, New York, 1984.

Ruh, K., '"Le miroir des simples ames" der Marguerite Porète', in: *Kleine Schriften 2. Scholastik und Mystik im Spätmittelalter*, (Kleinere Schriften 3. Literatur- und Geistesgeschichte 8) Berlin, New York, 1984.

Ruh, K. (ed.), *Abendländische Mystik im Mittelalter*, (Symposion Kloster Engelberg 1984) Stuttgart, 1986.

Salmen, W., 'Vom Musizieren in der spätmittelalterlichen Stadt', in: *Das Leben in der Stadt des Spätmittelalters*, (Veröffentlichungen d. Instituts f. mittelalterliche Realienkunde Osterreichs 2) Vienna, 1977, ²1981.

Sankt Elisabeth. Furstin — Dienerin — Heilige. Aufsätze. Dokumentation. Katalog. Ausstellung zum 750. Todestag der hl. Elisabeth, Marburg, Landgrafenschloss und Elisabethkirche, 19. November-6. Januar, 1982, Sigmaringen, 1981.

Schabinger, K. F. M., *Freiherr v. Schowingen, Das St. Gallische Freilehen*. Ein Beitrag zur Geschichte des deutschen Grundeigentums, Diss. iur., Heidelberg, 1938.

Schäfer, K. H., *Die Kanonissenstifter im deutschen Mittelalter. Ihre Entwicklung und innere Einrichtung im Zusammenhang mit dem altchristlichen Sanktimonialentum*, (Kirchenrechtliche Abhandlungen 43—44) Stuttgart, 1907.

Scheibelreiter, G., 'Königstöchter im Kloster. Radegund (†587) und der Nonnenaufstand von Poitiers (589)', in: *Mitteilungen des Instituts für österreichische Geschichtsforschung*, 87, 1979.

Scheidgen, H., *Die Französische Thronfolge (987—1500). Der Ausschluss der Frauen und das Salische Gesetz.*, Diss. phil. Bonn, 1976, Stuttgart, 1976.

Schieffer, R., 'Ludwig "Der Fromme". Zur Entstehung eines karolingischen Herrscherbeinamens', in: *Frühmittelalterliche Studien*, 16, 1982.

Schieffer, T., *Winfried-Bonifatius und die christliche Grundlegung Europas*, Freiburg, 1954.

Schieffer, T., 'Eheschliessung und Ehescheidung im Hause der karolingischen Kaiser und Könige', in: *Theologisch-praktische Quartalschrift*, 116, 1968.

Schieffer, T., 'Das karolingische Ostreich (751—843)', in: *Handbuch der europäischen Geschichte*, ed. T. Schieder, vol. 1: *Europa im Wandel von der Antike zum Mittelalter*, Stuttgart, 1976.

Schimmelpfennig, B., 'Zölibat und Lage der "Priestersöhne" vom 11—14. Jahrhundert', in: *Historische Zeitschrift*, 227, 1978.

Schmelzeisen, G. K., *Die Rechtsstullung der Frau in der deutschen Stadtwirt-*

schaft, (Arbeiten zur deutschen Rechts- u. Verfassungsgeschichte 10) Stuttgart, 1935.

Schmid, K., 'Heirat, Familienfolge, Geschichtsbewusstsein', in: *Il matrimonio nella società altomedievale*, (Settimane di studio del centro italiano di studi sull'alto medioevo 24) vol. 1, Spoleto, 1977.

Schmid, K., 'Die Erschliessung neuer Quellen zur mittelalterlichen Geschichte', in: *Frühmittelalterliche Studien*, 15, 1981.

Schmidt, M., 'Elemente der Schau bei Mechtild von Magdeburg und Mechtild von Hackeborn. Zur Bedeutung der geistlichen Sinne', in: P. Dinzelbacher and D. R. Bauer (eds), *Frauenmystik im Mittelalter*, Ostfildern, 1985.

Schmidt, M. and Bauer, D. (eds), *Eine Höhe, über die nichts geht. Spezielle Glaubenserfahrung in der Frauenmystik?* (Mystik in Geschichte und Gegenwart section 1, vol. 4) Stuttgart, 1986.

Schmitt, E., *Le mariage chrétien dan l'oeuvre de Saint Augustin. Une théologie baptismale de la vie conjugale*, Paris. 1983.

Schmitt, J. C., *Mort d'une hérésie. L'Eglise et les clercs face aux béguines et aux béghards du Rhin supérieur du 14ᵉ au 15ᵉ siècle*, (Civilisations et Sociétés 56) Paris, The Hague, New York, 1978.

Schmitz, G., *Die Berufstätigkeit der Frau in der Reichsstadt Nürnberg bis zum Ende des 16. Jahrhunderts*, Diss. phil., Erlangen, 1950 (typescript).

Schmoller, G., *Die Strassburger Tucher- und Weberzunft. Urkunden und Darstellung*, Strasbourg, 1897.

Schmülling, G., *Das Strafrecht der Stadt Köln bis zum 16. Jahrhundert*, Diss. iur., Münster, 1937, Bottrop, 1937.

Schneider, R., 'Katharina von Siena als Mystikerin', in: P. Dinzelbacher and D. R. Bauer (eds), *Frauenmystik im Mittelalter*, Ostfildern, 1985.

Schneider, T. (ed.), *Handbuch der europäischen Geschichte, vol.* 1, Stuttgart, 1976.

Scholten, R., *Die Stadt Kleve. Beiträge zur Geschichte derselben aus archivalischen Quellen*, Kleve, 1879.

Schormann, G., *Hexenprozesse in Deutschland*, (Kleine Vandenhoeck-Reihe 1470) Göttingen, 1981.

Schott, C., 'Der Stand der Leges-Forschung', in: *Frühmittelalterliche Studien*, 13, 1979.

Schramm, P. E., 'Der hl. Bonifaz als Mensch', in: *Archiv f. mittelrhein. Kirchengeschichte*, 20, 1968.

Schreiner, K., 'Adel oder Oberschicht. Bemerkungen zur sozialen Schichtung der fränkischen Gesellschaft im 6. Jahrhundert', in: *Vierteljahrsschrift f. Sozial- u. Wirtschaftsgeschichte*, 68, 1981.

Schröder, R., *Geschichte des ehelichen Güterrechts in Deutschland*, part 1: *Die Zeit der Volksrechte*, 2 vols, Stettin, Danzig, Elbing, 1863, 1868; part 2: *Das Mittelalter*, 2 vols. Stettin, Danzig, Elbing, 1871, 1874.

Schubart-Fikentscher, G., *Das Eherecht im Brünner Schöffenbuch*, Diss. iur. Berlin, 1933, Stuttgart, 1935.

Schubart-Fikentscher, G., 'Eine Ehescheidung im 14. Jahrhundert', in:

Die Frau, March 1936.

Schubart-Fikentscher, G., 'Römisches Recht im Brünner Schöffenbuch', in: *Zeitschrift d. Savigny-Stiftung f. Rechtsgechichte, Germ.* sect. 65, 1947.

Schuler, P. J. 'Die Erhebungslisten des Gemeinen Pfennigs von 1496–1499. Eine demographische, wirtschafts- und sozialgeschichtliche Untersuchung', in: F. Irsigler (ed.), *Quantitative Methoden in der Wirtschafts- und Sozialgeschichte der Vorneuzeit*, (Historisch-sozialwissenschaftliche Forschungen 4) Stuttgart, 1978.

Schuler, P. J., 'Die Bevölkerungsstruktur der Stadt Freiberg im Breisgau im Spätmittelalter. Möglichkeiten und Grenzen einer quantitativen Quellenanalyse', in: W. Ehbrecht (ed.), *Voraussetzungen und Methoden geschichtlicher Städteforschung*, (Städteforschung, Veröffentlichungen des Instituts für vergleichende Städtegeschichte in Münster, Reihe A, 7) Cologne, Vienna, 1979.

Schulte, A., *Der hohe Adel im Leben des mittelalterlichen Köln*, (Sitzungsberichte d. Bayerischen Akademie der Wissenschafte, Phil.-Hist. Klasse, 8) Munich, 1919.

Schultze, A., *Zum altnordischen Eherecht*, (Berichte über die Verhandlungen d. Sächsischen Akademie der Wissenschaften, Phil.-Hist. Klasse 91, 1), Leipzig, 1939.

Schultze, A., *Das Eherecht in den älteren angelsächsischen Königsgesetzen*, (Berichte über die Verhandlungen d. Sächsischen Akademie der Wissenschaften, Phil.-Hist. Klasse 93, 5), Leipzig, 1941.

Schultze, A., Review of: Th. Melicher, 'Die germanischen Formen . . .', in: *Zeitschrift d. Savigny-Stiftung f. Rechtsgeschichte, Germ.* sect. 63, 1943.

Schulz, K., 'Zensualität und Stadtentwicklung im 11/12. Jahrhundert', in: B. Diestelkamp (ed.), *Beiträge zum hochmittelalterlichen Städtewesen*, (Städteforschung, Veröffentlichungen des Instituts für vergleichende Städtegeschichte in Münster, Reihe A, 11) Cologne, Vienna, 1982.

Schulze, W. see under Elze, also Goetz.

Schuster, D., *Die Stellung der Frau in der Zunftverfassung*, (Quellenhefte zum Frauenleben in der Geschichte 7) Berlin, 1927.

Schütze-Pflugk, M. *Herrscher- und Märtyrerauffassung bei Hrotsvit von Gandersheim*, (Frankfurter historische Abhandlungen 1) Wiesbaden, 1972.

Schwind, F., 'Beobachtungen zur inneren Struktur des Dorfes in karolingischer Zeit', in: *Das Dorf der Eisenzeit und des frühen Mittelalters*, (Abhandlungen der Akademie der Wissenschaften in Göttingen, Phil.-Hist. Klasse 3. F. 101) Göttingen, 1977.

Sestan, E., 'Die Anfänge der städtischen Signorien: Ein erschöpfend behandeltes europäisches Problem?' in: *Altständisches Bürgertum*, ed. H. Stoob, vol. 1, (Wege der Forschung 352) Darmstadt, 1978.

Shahar, S., *The Fourth Estate: a history of women in the Middle Ages*, London/New York, 1984.

Sieder, R., see under Mitterauer.

Skalweit, S., *Der Beginn der Neuzeit. Epochengrenze und Epochenbegriff*, (Erträge der Forschung 178) Darmstadt, 1982.

Smith, R. M., 'Hypothèses sur la nuptialité en Angleterre aux 13ᵉ et *14ᵉ* siècles, in: *Annales*, 38, 1983.

Société Jean Bodin — see under *La Femme*.

Sproemberg, H., *Beiträge zur belgische-niederländischen Geschichte*, Berlin, 1959.

Stachnik, R. and Triller, A. (eds), *Dorothea von Montau. Eine preussische Heilige des 14. Jahrhunderts, Münster*, 1976.

Stackmann, K., see under Dilcher.

Stasiewski, B., 'Der historische Wert der ältesten nicht urkundlichen Quelle zum Leben der hl. Hedwig und zur Gründung der Zisterzienserinnenabtei Trebnitz aus der Feder des Caesarius von Heisterbach', in: *Beiträge zur schlesischen Kirchengeschichte. Gedenkschrift für K. Engelbert*, (Forschungen u. Quellen zur Kirchen- u. Kulturgeschichte Ostdeutschlands 6) Cologne, Vienna, 1969.

Stein, F. M., *The Religious Women of Cologne, 1200–1320* Diss., Phil. Yale Univ. 1977, Xerox Univ. Microfilms, Ann Arbor Michigan 48/06.

Steinbach, F., 'Das Frankenreich', in: *Handbuch der deutschen Geschichte*, new ed. by L. Just, vol. 1, sect. 2, Konstanz, 1979.

Steinbach, H., *Jeanne d'Arc. Wirklichkeit und Legende*, (Persönlichkeit und Geschichte 78) Göttingen, 1973.

Stephan, H. G., 'Die mittelalterliche Keramik in Norddeutschland (1200– 1500)', in: *Aus dem Alltag einer mittelalterl. Stadt*, (Hefte des Focke-Museums 62) Bremen, 1982.

Steuer, H. (ed.), *Zur Lebensweise in der Stadt um 1200. Ergebnisse der Mittelalterarchäologie*, (Zs. f. Archäologie des Mittelalters Beiheft 4). Cologne, 1986.

Strätz, H. W., *Der Verlobungskuss und seine Folgen, rechtsgeschichtlich besehen*, (Konstanzer Universitätsreden 112) Konstanz, 1979.

Straub, T., 'Isabeau de Bavière, Legende et Wirklichkeit', in: *Zeitschrift f. bayerische Landesgeschichte*, 44, 1981.

Stroheker, K. F., *Germanentum und Spätantike*, Zürich, Stuttgart, 1965.

Struve, T., 'Zwei Briefe der Kaiserin Agnes', in: *Historisches Jahrbuch*, 104, 1984.

Struve, T., 'Die Romreise der Kaiserin Agnes', in: *Historisches Jahrbuch*, 105, 1985.

Sydow, J., see under Dirlmeier.

Theuerkauf, G., 'Burchard von Worms und die Rechtskunde seiner Zeit' in: *Frühmittelalterliche Studien*, 2, 1968.

Thomas, H., *Deutsche Geschichte des Spätmittelalters*, Stuttgart, 1983.

Thomas, H., 'Jeanne la Pucelle, das Basler Konzil und die "Kleinen" der Reformatio Sigismundi', in: *Francia*, 11, 1983, 1984.

Thomas, H., 'Zur Datierung, zum Verfasser und zur Interpretation des Moritz von Craûn, in: *Zeitschrift für deutsche Philologie*, 103, 1984.

Thompson, R., 'Women in Stuart England and America. A comparative study', in: *Journal of American Studies*, Spring 1978.

Till, R., 'Die berufstätige Frau im mittelalterlichen Wien', in: *Wiener Geschichtsblätter*, 25, 1970.

Tillmann, *Zum Eheprozess Philipp II. Augusts von Frankreich*, (Bonner Historische Forschungen 3) Bonn, 1954.

Timbal, P. C. and Turlan, J. M., 'Justice läique et lien matrimonial en France au Moyen Age', in: *Revue de droit canonique*, 30, 1980.

Toepfer, M., 'Die Konversen der Zisterzienserinnen von Himmelspforten bei Würzburg. Von der Gründung des Klosters bis zum Ende des 14. Jahrhunderts', in: K. Elm (ed.), *Ordensstudien I. Beiträge zur Geschichte der Konversen im Mittelalter*, (Berliner Historische Studien 2) Berlin, 1980.

Torsy, J., *Lexikon der deutschen Heiligen*, Cologne, 1959.

Toubert, P., 'La théorie du mariage chez les moralistes carolingiens', in: *Il matrimonio nella società altomedievale*, (Settimane di studio del centro italiano di studi sull'alto medioevo 24) vol. 1, Spoleto, 1977.

Treue, W., see under Pohl.

Triller, A., see under Stachnik.

Uhlirz, M., *Die Jahrbücher des Deutschen Reiches unter Otto II. und Otto III.* Vol. 2: *Otto III. 983–1002*, Berlin, 1954.

Uhlirz, M., 'Die rechtliche Stellung der Kaiserinwitwe Adelheid im Deutschen und im Italischen Reich', in: *Zeitschrift d. Savigny-Stiftung f. Rechtsgeschichte, Germ.*, sect. 74, 1957.

Untersuchungen zu Kloster und Stift, (Veröffentlichungen des Max-Planck-Instituts für Geschichte 68, Studien zur Germania Sacra 14) Göttingen, 1980.

Ulbrich, C., *Leibherrschaft am Oberrhein im Spätmittelalter*, (Veröffentlichungen des Max-Planck-Instituts für Geschichte 58) Göttingen, 1979.

v. Uslar, R., *Die Germanen vom 1. bis 4. Jahrundert nach Christus*, (Handbuch der europäischen Wirtschafts- und Sozialgeschichte, ed. H. Kellenbenz, Teilveröffentlichung) Stuttgart, 1980.

Vaccari, P., *Il matrimonio germanico*, (Pubblicazioni della R. Università di Pavia 52) Pavia, 1935.

Vercauteren, F., *Etude sur les civitates de la Belgique seconde*, (Académie Royale de Belgique, Classe des lettres et des sciences morales et politiques, Mémoires, Série 2, 33) Brussels, 1934.

Verdon, J., 'La femme vers le milieu du 9ᵉ siècle d'après le polyptique de l'abbaye de Saint-Rémi de Reims', in: *Mémoires de la Société d'agriculture, commerce, sciences et arts du département de la Marne*, 91, 1976.

Verhulst, A., *Die Frühgeschichte der Stadt Gent*, (Studia Historica Gandensia 174) Ghent, 1972.

Verhulst, A., 'La diversité du régime domanial entre Loire et Rhin à l'époque carolingienne. Bilan de quinze années de recherches', in: W. Janssen and D. Lohrmann (eds), *Villa–Curtis–Grangia*, (Beihefte der Francia 11) Munich, 1983.

Verlinden, C., 'Le "mariage" des esclaves', in: *Il matrimonio nella società altomedievale*, (Settimane di studio del centro italiano di studi sull'alto medioevo 24) vol. 2, Spoleto, 1977.

Vilfan, S., 'Le tradizioni locali e le influenze ecclesiastiche nel matrimonio in Slovenia e nelle reioni vicine', in: *Il matrimonio nella società altomedievale*, (Settimane di studio del centro italiano di studi sull'alto medioevo 24) vol. 1, Spoleto, 1977.

Viollet, P., *Comment les femmes ont été exclues de la succession à la couronne*, (Extrait des Mémoires de l'Académie des Inscriptions et Belles-Lettres 34, part 2) Paris, 1893.

Vleeschouvers, C., 'Het beheer van het O.L. Vrouw-hospitaal te Gent en de stichting van de Cisterciënserinnenabdijen O.L. Vrouw-ten-bos (1215) in Bijloke (1228) door uten Hove's', in: *Annales de la Société belge d'histoire des hôpiteaux*, 9, 1971.

Vogelsang, T., *Die Frau als Herrscherin im hohen Mittelalter. Studien zur "consors regni"-Formel*, Göttingen, Frankfurt, Berlin, 1954.

Vogt, H. J., 'Zur Spiritualität des frühen irischen Mönchtums', in: H. Löwe (ed.), *Die Iren und Europa im früheren Mittelalter*, 2 vols (Veröffent-lichungen d. Europa-Zentrums Tübingen, Kulturwissenschaftliche Reihe), vol. 1, Stuttgart, 1982.

Vogts, H., *Das Kölner Wohnhaus bis zur Mitte des 19. Jahrhunderts*, 2 vols (Rheinischer Verein für Denkmalpflege und Heimatschutz, Jahrbuch 1964−65), Neuss, [2]1966.

Wachendorf, H., *Die wirtschaftliche Stellung der Frau in den deutschen Städten des späteren Mittelalters*, Diss. phil., Hamburg, 1934.

Weber, M., *Ehefrau und Mutter in der Rechtsentwicklung*, Tübingen, 1907

Wehrli-Johns, M., *Geschichte des Zürcher Predigerkonvents (1230−1524). Mendikantentum zwischen Kirche, Adel und Stadt*, Zürich, 1980.

Wehrli-Johns, M., 'Aktion und Kontemplation in der Mystik. Uber Maria und Martha', in: *Lerne Leiden. Leidensbewältigung in der Mystik*, (Herrenalber Texte 67) Karlsruhe, 1985.

Weidemann, M., *Kulturgeschichte der Merowingerzeit nach den Werken Gregors von Tours*, (Römisch-Germanisches Zentralmuseum, Monographien 3, 1) Mainz, 1982.

Weigand, R., 'Zur mittelalterlichen kirchlichen Ehegerichtsbarkeit. Rechtsvergleichende Untersuchung', in: *Zeitschrift d. Savigny-Stiftung f. Rechtsgesch., Kanon*, Sect. 67, 1981.

Weiss, H., *Lebenshaltung und Vermögensbildung des "mittleren" Bürgertums. Studien zur Sozial- und Wirtschaftsgeschichte der Reichsstadt Nürnberg zwischen 1400−1600*, (Zeitschrift f. bayerische Landesgeschichte, Beiheft 14) Munich, 1980.

Wemple, S. F., *Women in Frankish Society: Marriage and the Cloister, 500 to 900*, Philadelphia, 1981.

Wensky, M., '*Die Stellung der Frau in der stadtkölnischen Wirtschaft im Spätmittelalter*, (Quellen und Darstellungen zur Hansischen Geschichte N.F. 26) Cologne, Vienna, 1980.

Wensky, M., 'Die Stellung der Frau in Familie, Haushalt und Wirtschaftsbetrieb im spätmittelalterlichen und frühneuzeitlichen Köln', in: A. Haverkamp (ed.), *Haus und Familie in der spätmittelalterlichen Stadt*, (Städteforschung, Veröffentlichungen des Instituts f. vergleichende Städtegeschichte in Münster A, 18) Cologne, Vienna, 1984.

Wentersdorf, K. P., 'The clandestine marriage of the Fair Maid of Kent', in: *Journal of Medieval History*, 5, 1979.

Wesoly, K., 'Der weibliche Bevölkerungsanteil in spätmittelalterlichen und frühneuzeitlichen Städten und die Betätigung von Frauen im zünftigen Handwerk (insbesondere an Mittel- und Oberrhein)', in: *Zeitschrift für die Geschichte des Oberrheins* 128, new series 89, 1980.

White, L. jr, *Medieval Technology and Social Change*, Oxford, 1962.

Wiedenau, A., 'Form, Funktion und Bedeutung romanischer Wohnhäuser in Köln und im Rheinland', in: *Wallraf-Richartz-Jahrbuch*, 51, 1980.

Wiegelmann, G., *Alltags- und Festspeisen. Wandel und gegenwärtige Stellung*, (Atlas der deutschen Volkskunde N.F., Beiheft 1) Marburg, 1967.

Winter, A., 'Studien zur sozialen Situation der Frauen in der Stadt Trier nach der Steuerliste von 1364. Die Unterschicht', in: *Kurtrierisches Jahrbuch*, 15, 1975.

van Winter, J. M., *Van Soeter Cokene. Recepten uit de romeinse en mitteleeuwse keuken*, Bussum, 1971.

van Winter, J. M., 'Die Hamaländer Grafen, Angehörige der Reichsaristokratie im 10. Jahrhundert', in: *Rheinische Vierteljahrsblätter*, 44, 1980.

van Winter, J. M., 'Ernährung im spätmittelalterlichen Hanseraum', in: *Aus dem Alltag der mittelalterlichen Stadt*, (Hefte des Focke-Museums 62) Bremen, 1982.

van Winter, J. M., 'Kochen und essen im Mittelalter', in: B. Hermann (ed.), *Mensch und Umwelt im Mittelalter*, Stuttgart, 1986.

van Winterfeld, L., *Handel, Kapital und Patriziat in Köln bis 1400*, (Pfingstblätter des Hansischen Geschichtsvereins 16) Lübeck, 1925.

van Winterfeld, L., 'Die stadtrechtlichen Verflechtungen in Westfalen', in: *Der Raum Westfalen*, vol. 2, part 1, ed. H. Aubin and F. Petri, Münster, 1955.

Wirtz (*née* Henningsen), A., 'Die Geschichte des Hamalandes', in: *Annalen d. historischen Vereins f. d. Niederrhein*, 173, 1971.

Wisplinghoff, E., *Geschichte der Stadt Neuss. Von den mittelalterlichen Anfängen bis zum Jahre 1974*, Neuss, 1975.

Wittstock, J., see under Appuhn.

Wohlhaupter, E., 'Das Privatrecht der Fueros de Aragón', in: *Zeitschrift der Savigny-Stiftung f. Rechtsgeschichte, Germ.*, sect. 62, 1942.

Wolff, H. J., 'Zur Stellung der Frau im klassischen römischen Dotalrecht', in: *Zeitschrift der Savigny-Stiftung f. Rechtsgeschichte, Roman.*, sect. 53, 1933.

Wolff, P., 'Famille et mariage en Toulousain aux 14e et 15e siècles', in: *Regards sur le Midi médiéval*, Toulouse, 1978.

Wolff, P., see under Mollat.

Wollasch, J., 'Eine adelige Familie des frühen Mittelalters', in: *Archiv. f.*

Kulturgeschichte, 39, 1957.

Wollasch, J., 'Das Grabkloster der Kaiserin Adelheid in Selz am Rhein', in: *Frühmittelalterliche Studien*, 2, 1968.

Wood, C. T., 'Queens, Queans and Kingship: An Enquiry into Theories of Royal Legitimacy in Late Medieval England and France', in: W. Jordan (ed.), *Order and Innovation in the Middle Ages. Essays in honour of J. R. Stranger*, Princeton, 1976.

Führer, K., 'Zum altschwedischen Eherecht', in: *Zeitschrift d. Savigny-Stiftung f. Rechtsgeschichte, Germ.*, sect. 74, 1957.

Würdinger, H., 'Einwirkungen des Christentums auf das angelsächsische Recht', in: *Zeitschrift d. Savigny-Stiftung f. Rechtsgeschichte, Germ.*, sect. 55, 1935.

Wunder, G., *Die Bürger von Hall. Sozialgeschichte einer Reichsstadt 1216–1802*, (Forschungen aus Württembergisch Franken 16) Sigmaringen, 1980.

Wunder, G., 'Gisela von Schwaben, Gemahlin Kaiser Konrads II., gest. 1043', in: *Lebensbilder aus Schwaben und Franken*, vol. 14, Stuttgart, 1980.

Wunder, G., 'Sibilla Egen. Wohltäterin der Reichsstadt Hall, um 1470–1538', in: *Lebensbilder aus Schwaben und Franken*, vol. 15, Stutgart, 1983.

Wunder, G. and Lenckner, G., *Die Bürgerschaft der Reichsstadt Hall von 1395–1600*, (Württembergisch Geschichtsquellen 25) Stuttgart, Cologne, 1956.

Zender, M., *Räume und Schichten mittelalterlicher Heiligenverehrung in ihrer Bedeutung für die Volkskunde*, Cologne, ²1973.

Ziegler, J. G., *Die Ehelehre der Pönitentialsummen von 1200–1350. Eine Untersuchung zur Geschichte der Moral- und Pastoraltheologie*, (Studien zur Geschichte der katholischen Moraltheologie 4) Regensburg, 1956.

Zimmerman, H., *Das dunkle Jahrhundert. Ein historisches Porträt*, Vienna, Cologne, 1971.

Zimmerman, H., *Der Canossagang von 1077. Wirkungen und Wirklichkeit*, (Akademie der Wissenschaften und der Literatur Mainz, Abhandlungen der geistes- u. sozialwissenschaftlichen Klasse, Jahrgang 1975, no. 5) Mainz, 1975.

Die Zisterzienser. Ordensleben zwischen Ideal und Wirklichkeit, eds K. Elm, P Joerissen and H. J. Roth (Schriften des Rheinischen Museumsantes 18), Cologne, 1982.

Zöllner, E., *Die Geschichte der Franken bis zur Mitte des 6. Jahrhunderts*, Munich, 1970.

Zumkeller, A., see under Aurelius Augustinus.

Index